F 3031.5 .

Thornton, Richard C.

The Falklands sting

DATE DUE

The
Falklands
Sting

The Falklands Sting

Reagan, Thatcher, and Argentina's Bomb

Richard C. Thornton

Brassey's
Washington • London

Brassey's Editorial Offices: Brassey's Order Department:
22883 Quicksilver Drive   P.O. Box 960
Dulles, Virginia 20166   Herndon, Virginia 20172

Brassey's books are available at special discounts for bulk purchases for sales promotions, premiums, fund-raising, or educational use.

Library of Congress Cataloging-in-Publication Data

Thornton, Richard C.
    The Falklands sting : Reagan, Thatcher, and Argentina's bomb / Richard C. Thornton.
        p.   cm.
    Includes bibliographical references and index.
    ISBN 1-57488-155-8
    1. Falkland Islands War, 1982—Diplomatic history. 2. United States—Foreign relations—Great Britain. 3. Great Britain—Foreign relations—United States. 4. Argentina—Foreign relations—Great Britain. 5. Great Britain—Foreign relations—Argentina.
6. Argentina—Foreign relations—United States. 7. United States—Foreign relations—Argentina. 8. Argentina—Military policy.
I. Title.
F3031.5.T49   1998
997'.11—dc21   97-41127
                                                         CIP

First Edition
Typeset by Page Graphics, Inc.
10 9 8 7 6 5 4 3 2 1

Printed in the United States of America

*To my wife Joanne and my two sons, Douglas and James,
whose encouragement and support made this work a labor of love.*

"Ignorance of remote causes disposeth men to attribute all events to the causes immediate and instrumental; for these are all the causes they perceive."

Hobbs, *Leviathan*, chapter 11

Contents

Acknowledgments

I would like to express my gratitude to Professor James Millar, director of the Institute for European, Russian, and Eurasian Studies, The George Washington University, for his continuing support of my work. Special thanks go to Dr. James Perry, Louise Perry, Lajos Szaszdi, and Alan Capps, whose assistance in acquiring needed sources strewn across three continents made this book possible and whose willingness to offer critical comment and analysis helped make it what it is. I'm also indebted to Carol Clark and Kathleen Graham, who judiciously edited the manuscript, and to Elizabeth Fraser, who constructed the map. Finally, I would like to express my appreciation to those students, faculty, and administration of The George Washington University's Elliott School of International Affairs who contributed in one way or another to the final product.

...

Introduction

The war over the Falkland Islands was a significant event, whose far-reaching effects have hardly been recognized.* Best understood are the military events, which have been the overwhelming focus of more than one hundred and fifty books and articles devoted to the subject. Argentine forces seized the islands, located 400 miles off the southern tip of Argentina, on April 2, 1982. Great Britain immediately responded, deploying a task force of one hundred and thirteen ships and twenty-eight thousand men eight thousand miles from home. After a brief but intense struggle, on June 14, British forces triumphed, reestablishing British authority. A clean-cut, if not simple, instance of aggression defeated; end of story.

Least understood have been the origins of the conflict, its strategic implications, and the domestic political dynamics in each of the nations involved. Overwhelmingly, and quite naturally, the conflict has been analyzed from the perspective of the victor—Great Britain. To a much lesser extent has the conflict been analyzed from the Argentine viewpoint. There is yet a third perspective, however, which offers a more inclusive explanation of events— the perspective of American foreign policy.

In examining the origins of the conflict from the strategic perspective of the incoming Reagan administration, two-long term concerns—nuclear

---

*Argentines refer to the islands as the Malvinas. Both terms will be employed depending on the context.

nonproliferation and civilian rule—as well as President Reagan's decision to reintroduce a policy of containment, combined to focus U.S. interest in the Falkland Islands. A solution to these concerns would intersect in the Falkland Islands dispute between Britain and Argentina. The issues of nuclear nonproliferation and promotion of civilian rule, of course, were long-term, national goals transcending any particular American administration, while the issue of reintroducing containment was an objective specific to the new Reagan administration as it sought to recover from the unsuccessful policy of détente during the seventies.

Historically, the origins of the Falkland Islands War lay in competing and unresolved claims to sovereignty that began in 1833, when Britain took control of the islands. Britain's claim rested on early settlement and continuous possession of the islands since then by English-speaking people of British stock. Argentina formally disputed the British claim on the grounds that Spain had transferred its colonial possessions to Argentina before that date; it consistently referred to the islands as the Malvinas. Indeed, the quest for the Malvinas became an integral part of the Argentine national psyche.

British power decided the question of possession, but not of sovereignty. The Falkland Islands became part of Britain's global network of outposts, along with Gibraltar, Hong Kong, Singapore, Aden, Simonstown, and Free-mantle—to use Lord Curzon's phrase, the "tollgates and barbicans of empire," which enabled Britain to control passage on the high seas. The Falkland Islands outpost controlled passage around Cape Horn, but its value diminished when the Panama Canal offered another even shorter route from Pacific to Atlantic.

Waning British power combined with waxing Argentine power reopened the possibility of regaining control of the Falklands/Malvinas for Buenos Aires. The deep origins of the Falkland Islands War lay in the gradual shift of the relative military balance between Argentina and Great Britain, punctuated by the Argentine junta's secret decision in the spring of 1978 to acquire a nuclear weapons capability.[1] Although the junta had been brutally successful in eradicating the domestic threat during the two years since achieving power, its foreign policy had been a complete failure.[2] The junta had failed to resolve any of the three main foreign policy problems facing Argentina: the struggle with Brazil for Latin hegemony, the conflict with Chile over the Beagle Channel Islands, and the dispute with Great Britain over the Malvinas.

In 1975, Brazil, Argentina's neighbor and rival, had embarked upon a major public program to develop nuclear power (as well as a secret one to produce nuclear weapons). The public nuclear power program, combined with Brazil's rapid evolution as a military power, would catapult Brasilia into the hegemonic position in South America. With regard to the dispute with Chile, Buenos Aires had agreed to submit the dispute over three islands in the Beagle Channel to arbitration—and had lost. Chilean control of Picton, Lennox, and Nueva would confer advantages in the South Atlantic and strengthen Chile's claim against Argentina in Antarctica. Finally, the almost century-and-a-half-long dispute with Great Britain had taken a turn for the worse by early 1978, making it plain that London would not willingly relinquish sovereignty.[3]

In an attempt to break out of the foreign policy stalemate in which it found itself, the junta decided secretly in the spring of 1978 to acquire its own nuclear weapons. An expansion of Argentina's public nuclear power program was the cover for the secret weapons program, just as it was in Brazil. There was also a missile program, Condor I, disguised as a meteorological rocket. By 1982, Argentina's first ballistic missile was already being tested.[4] Expected operational capability was the 1983–84 time frame, but one American intelligence group—Defense Intelligence Agency—estimated that Argentina could have an initial operational capability as early as the end of 1982.[5]

The decision to acquire a nuclear weapons capability was an extension of the junta's original decision to make Argentina a formidable military power. A nuclear weapons capability, however small, combined with the more formidable conventional military power Argentina was already rapidly acquiring, would greatly strengthen the nation. The junta would then be able to conduct its foreign policy from a position of strength, if not dominance, and to resolve favorably its foreign policy problems. Until then, however, it would be necessary to buy time.

Toward the Malvinas, the period between 1978 and 1982 indicated two clear trends, both of which were in Argentina's favor—quite aside from the implications contained in the secret nuclear weapons program. First was the obvious increase in Argentine conventional military power, particularly air and naval capability. The junta spent $16.7 billion on weapons' acquisition from foreign suppliers, including Great Britain, during this period.[6] Second was the change in the character of British military power, particularly with regard to the power balance in the South Atlantic. Since 1967, Britain had been deliberately constricting its imperial position. Especially since the 1974 defense review, London had been reshaping its force structure to reinforce NATO Europe and publicly reduce its presence in the South Atlantic.

Regular "out of area" naval deployments were being curtailed worldwide. In the South Atlantic, plans were being made to close the British Antarctic Survey (BAS) station on the island of South Georgia. Early 1982 would mark the final work period for London's sole naval presence in the South Atlantic— the Antarctic support ship, HMS *Endurance*. If existing trends continued, it would not be long before Britain would have little choice but to negotiate a transfer of sovereignty over the Falkland Islands to Argentina. Indeed, throughout the seventies, successive British governments had indicated a willingness to discuss sovereignty, until the election of Margaret Thatcher.[7]

The Videla-Viola Strategy Toward the Malvinas

Initially, upon seizing power in 1976, the junta under Jorge Videla adopted the gradualistic strategy toward the Malvinas of working from the outside in—that is, establishing "scientific" stations on the outlying islands claimed by Britain as the "Dependencies," working in toward the Malvinas.[8] Argentine marines had set up a small station on South Thule in the South Sandwich group in October 1976. South Thule was also the easternmost point of Argentina's Antarctic claim. The junta's objective appears to have been to displace Britain gradually from the entire South Atlantic as well as the Antarctic. In the case of South Thule, British intelligence learned of the maneuver, but London did nothing. (See map on page 133.)

The following October 1977, Buenos Aires planned to reinforce its position on the station. This time, British intelligence learned of the junta's intention, and London moved to preclude it. The Callaghan government deployed a nuclear submarine to the South Atlantic and quietly informed the junta that it had done so.[9] The result was that the junta called off the plan to reinforce South Thule, but learned a valuable lesson. Any future attempt to establish a "scientific" station would have to be well disguised and occur rapidly to forestall any preemptive response from Britain.

Thus, in spring 1978, as part of the set of decisions made then, the junta decided to take another step in its outside-in approach to the Malvinas. The next target was South Georgia, and this time the plan involved establishing a purely commercial cover first that would be transformed later into an Argentine state presence after Britain had withdrawn. (The military operation that would convert the commercial presence into an Argentine one was called "Operation Alpha.") Thus, a Constantine Davidoff, who may or may not have been a witting accomplice to this scheme, approached Salvesens Corp. of Edinburgh, owner of two defunct whaling stations on the island, to negotiate an option contract to salvage the stations for scrap metal.

The circumstances surrounding Davidoff's request were unusual. Salvesens owned only two of four defunct whaling stations on the island, at Leith and Stromness on Stromness Bay.[10] The other two were owned by Albion Star Inc., an Argentine firm that had gone bankrupt and was attempting to sell off its holdings. Albion Star had a whaling station at Husvik on Stromness Bay and at Grytviken on Cumberland East Bay, near King Edward Point where the British Antarctic Survey (BAS) was located. To the Foreign Office, Davidoff's interest in obtaining a salvage contract from Salvesens, while ignoring the more easily available Albion Star's stations, raised eyebrows.

In autumn 1979, the newly installed Thatcher government not only gave Salvesens permission to extend Davidoff a salvage contract, but also sweetened the deal by authorizing the company to acquire Albion Star's holdings for itself and to include the Husvik station as part of the Davidoff contract.[11] In other words, if, as British intelligence suspected, the Argentines were preparing to establish a presence on South Georgia, their activities would be localized at Leith Harbor, for that is the way the Thatcher government structured Davidoff's contract. King Edward Point and Grytviken, approximately twenty miles away at Cumberland East Bay, would remain entirely under British control. Davidoff's scrap metal venture on South Georgia would lay dormant for two years before being activated, however, at which time it would function quite differently than originally planned.

Thatcher's Political Problems

Thatcher entered office in May 1979 with grand plans to transform the structure of the British state by dismantling the welfare system and strengthening the market economy through emphasizing supply-side principles and policies. She was also committed to an anti-Soviet stance in foreign policy, anticipating by a few months the beginning of President Jimmy Carter's own departure from the détente strategy he had so assiduously pursued since entering office. Thus, she obstructed full British collaboration with the European Union and sought to strengthen the "special relationship" of Atlantic partnership with the United States. Her domestic policies, however, had been singularly unsuccessful by the end of 1980.

By December 1980, Thatcher was being described as "the most unpopular prime minister since polls began."[12] Under relentless attack from adversaries within and outside her administration, Thatcher, many thought, would soon be replaced by a moderate, who would proceed to reverse her policies. Thatcher referred disparagingly to the moderates in the Conservative Party as "wets." As Cosgrave observes, "it seemed that the Thatcher experiment was crumbling to disaster."[13] The fundamental split in the Conservative Party, therefore, was between the "Thatcherites" who pressed for an increasingly privatized, free market economy at home and the special relationship with the United States and the "wets" who sought a "U-turn" on the economy and Britain's full involvement in the European Union. In December 1980, just as President-elect Ronald Reagan was beginning to formulate policy for a new administration, Margaret Thatcher was at her low point.

American Strategy Under Reagan

Reagan's overall strategy called for the resurrection of anti-Soviet containment and the reconstruction of American military strength and geopolitical position, both of which had atrophied alarmingly during the previous seven years of détente. Containment required a strong partnership with Britain, which would enable defense of the continent. This was as true in 1980 as it was in 1940. Therefore, of the many foreign policy problems associated with resurrecting containment that confronted the incoming Reagan administration, one of the most important was that of strengthening the special relationship with Great Britain. Specifically, this meant ensuring that the political position of Margaret Thatcher remained strong.

In addition, perceiving a Soviet threat to the oil fields of Southwest Asia, Reagan had decided to build a three-ocean, 600-ship navy to permit deployment of additional naval power to the Persian Gulf region. It would, of course, take several years to increase ship numbers to required levels, so ways were sought to achieve the desired goals more quickly. Several ships were taken out of mothballs, upgraded, and brought into service, and Britain (and Japan) were asked to increase their naval contributions in the Atlantic and Pacific. It was believed that such steps would enable the United States to divert ships to the Persian Gulf without attenuating overall defense. During 1981, however, Japan and, especially, Britain were moving in the opposite direction.

Thatcher herself was committed to the containment strategy and strong defense, but was hampered severely by resistance among the "wet" members of her government. The removal of Thatcher and her replacement by one of her adversaries would sharply undercut the containment strategy that President Reagan was attempting to rebuild. For that reason alone, it was essential to strengthen her position. There existed, in strategic terms, to say nothing of their mutual personal and ideological affinity, a clear coincidence of interest between Margaret Thatcher and Ronald Reagan. The question was how to maintain and strengthen it?

The second problem facing the incoming Reagan administration was the growing danger represented by Argentina's imminent emergence as a nuclear weapons state. It was the failure to resolve that problem bilaterally that led to what I have termed the "Falklands Sting"—the scheme to overthrow the junta by leading it into disastrous conflict with Britain over the Falkland Islands. Military defeat would discredit the junta and see its replacement by civilian political leaders already demanding a return to civilian rule. At the very least, a return to civilian rule would set back the timetable for Argentina's nuclear weapons program, if not lead to its abrogation. (In the event, it led to its abrogation.)[14] Moreover, a British military victory would strengthen Prime Minister Thatcher and ensure her reelection.

It was not long after the junta had decided to acquire a nuclear weapons capability, during the latter half of the Carter administration, that American, and perhaps British, intelligence discovered it. President Carter began an abrupt but quiet turn toward Argentina in an attempt to improve relations.[15] It was President Reagan, however, who embraced the junta with open arms. Reagan's election coincided with the appointment of Gen. Roberto Viola as president of the junta, succeeding Jorge Videla. Reagan invited Viola to Washington in March 1981, according him all of the trappings of a head of state, rather unusual treatment for a military dictator whose regime had only recently been excoriated by the United States.[16]

Reagan's purpose was to establish a friendly cooperative relationship with Argentina, which would quietly attempt to influence the junta to desist in its plan to acquire a nuclear weapons capability. Despite promises to remove all impediments to trade and cooperation, however, including restrictions on weapons supply, and promises to assist Argentina in its public nuclear power program, Viola declined, insisting that Argentina would continue to pursue an independent path between the two superpowers.[17]

Rebuffed, the Reagan administration then immediately began to court Viola's opponent within the junta, Gen. Leopoldo Fortunato Galtieri, with the evident objective of promoting a more cooperative leader. Beginning in spring 1981, the Reagan administration lavished attention on Galtieri, sending a stream of high-level visitors to Buenos Aires.[18] Galtieri was also invited to the United States for two lengthy visits during which he met with the highest ranking members of the Reagan administration—including Vice President George Bush. Galtieri was taken on excursions to Hollywood and Disneyland and flattered as Argentina's "General Patton," to whom he bore a vague physical resemblance. (There was no other similarity.)

Reagan administration officials pressed offers for an alliance in return for Argentine cooperation in the Sinai Peacekeeping Force, for the Contras, and other projects.[19] To one degree or another, Washington led Galtieri to assume that the United States would also assist in Argentina's quest for the Malvinas. At any rate, that is clearly what Galtieri believed. Galtieri quickly became identified as "Washington's man," which perhaps explains his increasingly active opposition to President Viola in matters of policy—specifically regarding relations with the United States and over the issue of the Malvinas. Galtieri publicly advocated an alliance with the United States and the direct seizure of the Malvinas from Great Britain—policies that were in direct opposition to Viola's policy of independence toward the superpowers and gradualism toward the Malvinas.

Galtieri Changes Argentine Strategy

When Viola suffered a heart attack in early November, Galtieri moved to replace him, which Viola bitterly resented.[20] Unable to prevent Galtieri's rise to power, Viola and his supporters set in motion a plan that they hoped would discredit his leadership and lead to Galtieri's eclipse.[21] In late November, while still in power, Viola resurrected the plan to use a commercial enterprise to establish an Argentine presence on South Georgia—the Davidoff salvaging operation.[22] He set it in motion with an ominous twist, however. Instead of employing the salvage operation as a commercial cover for a later military penetration, Viola hoped to use it to provoke an incident with Great Britain, thereby forestalling any move by Galtieri to seize the Falkland Islands.

All involved understood that a provocative incident on South Georgia would prevent any move to seize the Malvinas because the British, being forewarned, would simply reinforce the islands or send another nuclear submarine. Either response would preclude an invasion. The Malvinas could only be taken in a preemptive move, which prior action on South Georgia would negate. In late November, Viola could not have known when Galtieri would attempt to seize the Malvinas, but he had to set his own plan in motion before being ousted—a foregone conclusion by then. In short, Viola activated a political time bomb that would not detonate until months after he had left the political scene. His intent, it must be emphasized, was to trigger a crisis with London that would discredit and destroy the Galtieri regime, not to provoke a war.

Once in power, the new president, strongly supported by the naval member of the junta, Adm. Jorge Anaya, immediately authorized the initial planning for the direct seizure of the Malvinas. What is abundantly clear from the record is that two separate operations were under way from the time Galtieri assumed power. One, initiated by Viola, to create an incident on South Georgia and the other, by Galtieri, to achieve a quick seizure of the Malvinas. Separate personnel were involved in each plan, operating from different Argentine bases. (Ushuaia, Argentina's southernmost port, was the base for the South Georgia provocation.) The irony is that, upon coming to power, Galtieri discovered the Davidoff-Alpha scheme and canceled it. Nonetheless, the South Georgia scheme was executed.[23]

Ultimately, although several different dates were leaked, Galtieri's planners had decided to seize the Malvinas on May 20, five days before Argentine National Day, but less than a month before the onset of winter in the South Atlantic. The ferocity of the South Atlantic winter made extended naval operations impossible. The original plan was for a heliborne assault on Stanley, taking the capital by surprise. Thus, there would not be sufficient time for Britain to respond to the Argentine move—even by sending a submarine as it had in 1977. During the winter hiatus, the junta hoped to negotiate a transfer of sovereignty with American assistance.

A Hobson's Choice for Buenos Aires

Viola's provocation occurred in mid-March, however, two months before the planned seizure of the Malvinas, which enabled Thatcher to transform a minor provocation of scrap metal workers on South Georgia into a crisis of the Argentine regime.[24] Crucial to understanding subsequent events is an appreciation of the proficiency of British (and American) intelligence in breaking Argentine codes, which resulted in advance knowledge of virtually every planned Argentine move. There was, of course, no secret about the political infighting between the Viola and Galtieri factions, which filled the press.[25]

In short, Thatcher turned an internal Argentine factional struggle to her own (and America's) advantage. The objective was not simply to strengthen Thatcher's political position, which by early 1982 was a fait accompli, although that was an important part of the scheme. London deliberately escalated the South Georgia scrap workers incident into a crisis of the regime to precipitate the overthrow of the junta and its replacement by a civilian leadership. Only civilian rule offered the prospect for diverting Argentina from the junta's decision to acquire nuclear weapons. Nonproliferation was the American agenda.

London issued an ultimatum to Argentina, demanding that Buenos Aires immediately remove the "workmen" from South Georgia, or Britain would do it for them.[26] Galtieri—faced with the choice of crumbling in the face of the British ultimatum, or fighting—chose not only to fight for South Georgia, but also to seize the moment to invade the Malvinas. He had been maneuvered into a lose-lose situation. If he backed down in the face of a British ultimatum, he would be discredited and removed, which, undoubtedly, had been Viola's intention and expectation. If he chose to fight, however, he understood he would probably be defeated because London now had sufficient time before winter to deploy forces to recover the islands.

Galtieri and the junta hesitated to make the decision to fight. The timing was off; the South Georgia crisis had occurred too soon; Argentina was unprepared for war. Orders placed for military equipment had not yet been filled. At this moment, on March 26, Britain gave the junta the final nudge, putting out disinformation that the nuclear-powered submarine HMS *Superb* was being sent to the South Atlantic for what appeared to be a replay of London's response of 1977.[27]

Galtieri realized that the British response to the South Georgia incident would be, at the very least, to deploy another submarine to the South Atlantic and probably reinforce the Falkland Islands. Thus, he knew that the window of opportunity for seizing the Malvinas was closing fast and would be closed as soon as the nuclear submarine arrived. In fact, after the conflict, Admiral Anaya said exactly that. "When this nuclear-powered submarine arrived on the scene, it would not be possible to execute the surface operations that would be required to place Argentine troops ashore at Port Stanley. The window of opportunity was limited by the steaming time it would take HMS *Superb* to get from Gibraltar to the vicinity of the Falklands."[28] That evening, the junta made the decision to invade the Falkland Islands.

Immediately before the invasion of the Falkland Islands, on March 31, the Latin America Current Intelligence Group of British intelligence assessed the South Georgia incident. Its conclusion echoes the conclusion of the author:

> The landing on South Georgia had *not* been contrived by the Argentine Government, but that the Junta was taking full advantage of the incident to speed up negotiations on the transfer of sovereignty. Despite Sr. Davidoff's close contacts with some senior Argentine naval officers, the unauthorized landing was *not* considered to be part of the navy's plans. There was *no* central coordination of Argentine policy and the Junta's intentions were *not* known.[29]

The crisis on South Georgia in March 1982 was, therefore, not a planned, preliminary step toward the seizure of the Falkland Islands, although that was obviously the result. The South Georgian crisis was intended to achieve the opposite reaction from Galtieri. It was Margaret Thatcher who took advantage of the Argentine internal factional struggle and maneuvered Galtieri into a lose-lose position. The Argentine leader's decision to seize the Falkland Islands sooner than planned gave Thatcher just enough time to take action to recover them.

Once Argentine forces seized the islands, the American role became decisive in two ways, but not in the manner Galtieri anticipated. First, through its mediation, Washington delayed the junta's recognition of the true position of the United States in the dispute, thus isolating the junta and precluding any opportunity to make alternative support arrangements. Second, in secretly providing Great Britain with timely and sufficient matériel, intelligence, and weaponry from the outset, the United States aided British victory and en-sured Argentine defeat. The United States sought not only the military defeat of Argentina, but the removal of the junta as a prelude to larger objectives, the fundamental purpose of the "Falklands Sting."

Thatcher also maneuvered skillfully within her own government to win approval for a military response. In fact, fundamental strategic differences within both the British and American leaderships permeate this history. In Great Britain, Thatcher and her "wet" foreign secretary, Francis Pym, dis-agreed on most policy issues, particularly on containment. In the United States, President Reagan was opposed by his secretary of state, Alexander Haig. Haig's preference was for the pursuit of détente with the Soviet Union, "hard-headed détente," but détente, nonetheless. Their strategic differences found direct expression in policy preferences for the resolution of the Falklands crisis.

During the Falklands drama, Haig, as mediator, and Francis Pym, each pursued an outcome that would have led to the transfer of sovereignty over the Falkland Islands to Argentina and left the junta in power. Not only would such a negotiated settlement have strengthened Haig vis-à-vis Reagan, it would have precipitated Thatcher's fall from power and her replacement by Francis Pym. Pym, predisposed toward the strategy of détente, would have been in position to reinforce Haig's strategic preferences over those of the president.

Instead, both Haig and Pym were overruled and lost power. British mili-tary victory served the interests of both Thatcher and Reagan. Thatcher was assured of reelection and, subsequently, would literally transfigure the Brit-ish economy, making it one of the most productive in Europe. Thatcher's victory would reinforce Reagan's. Britain, the linchpin of containment, would be held firmly in place. In addition, long-term American objectives would also be fulfilled in the Western Hemisphere.

Argentine defeat and the subsequent overthrow of the junta was a water-shed event in Argentine and Latin American history. Under the demo-cratically elected Alfonsín government that followed the junta's downfall, Argentina followed a historic change of course from the junta's policy to

build Argentina into a major military power to the path of peaceful development, reducing its military power and abrogating plans to acquire nuclear
weapons. In fact, Argentina and Brazil would agree to abandon policies to
acquire nuclear weapons, leaving the region nuclear-free, as of this writing.
Argentina's return to civilian rule and abandonment of nuclear weapons
must be considered major successes of American foreign policy.

The
Falklands
Sting

PART I

... The Setup ...

CHAPTER 1

Argentina Militarizes
Under the Junta

By the mid-1970s, Argentina was on the verge of all-out civil war, as Isabela Perón's government battled to suppress a large-scale Communist-led, urban terrorist and rural guerrilla insurgency. (Isabela, Juan Perón's third wife, had succeeded her husband upon his death in 1974.) The militant left wing of the Peronist party, the Montoneros; the Marxist-Leninist Revolutionary Workers' Party (Partido Revolucionario de los Trabajadores), with its People's Revolutionary Army, the ERP (Ejercito Revolucionario del Pueblo); the Socialist Workers Party; and the Revolutionary Communist Party, sought to overthrow the Peronist regime. They fielded approximately thirty thousand active fighters, with an estimated two hundred seventy-five thousand passive supporters providing money, information, weapons, and refuge.[1]

Increasing violence brought Argentine daily life to a virtual standstill. Perón's government had been unable to contend with the insurgency, and law and order had collapsed. By the spring of 1976, guerrilla attacks and terrorism had produced counterattacks and counterterrorism. The growing civil strife brought Argentina to the verge of anarchy, as bombings and kidnapping became a daily occurrence. Political anarchy translated into economic anarchy; capital fled the country, and inflation soared to nearly 1,000 percent. The economic condition of Argentina shifted from "chronic moderate inflation to chronic high inflation."[2]

During this time of expanding crisis, an ailing Isabela Perón gradually lost her grip on the presidency. In early 1976, she had temporarily delegated

3

power to the head of the Argentine senate, Italo Ludo, for "reasons of health" (it was rumored that her personal doctor was slowly poisoning her).[3] Meanwhile, as had occurred twenty-three times during the previous forty-six years, Argentina's generals were again preparing to intervene in the nation's politics.

The Junta Takes Power

On March 24, 1976, General of the Army Jorge Rafael Videla abducted Isabela Perón, placed her under house arrest, and assumed control of the government, forming the Process of National Reorganization. The coup had been quick, quiet, bloodless, and, at the time, welcomed by many for its promise to restore order. The Proceso, as it was known, was headed by a president, Videla, a three-man military junta including representatives from the army, navy, and air force, and an eight-man cabinet. The junta professed its intention to remain in power until it had rid the nation of its insurrectionaries, dismantled the Peronist state it replaced, restructured the political and economic systems, and restored Argentina to what was believed to be its rightful place in the world.[4]

In seizing power, Videla and the junta assumed as their mandate the continued suppression of the revolutionaries, which they undertook with renewed and excessive zeal. By December 1975, under Isabela Perón, the military had succeeded in obliterating the core of the Montoneros' strength in Tucumán province northwest of Buenos Aires. The junta now focused its efforts on eradicating subversives in the cities, but with a dual purpose. The war in the cities was designed not only to eradicate the urban guerrillas, but also to undermine the support for the Peronist state, which the junta was determined to dismantle and restructure.[5]

Intensifying the reign of state terror against subversives, Gen. Alfredo St. Jean, the hard-line governor of Buenos Aires province, announced the junta's brutal intentions when he declared, "First we will kill the subversives; then their collaborators; then their sympathizers; then those who are indifferent; and finally, the timid."[6]

Each service arm of the armed forces conducted its own campaign of repression, which, because it was deliberately "arbitrary, uncoordinated, and indiscriminate," intensified its powers of intimidation.[7] "Suspects" were taken from the street, whisked away to secret interrogation and torture centers, and never heard from again. No records were kept, and those who disappeared became untraceable. In what was known as the "dirty war," death squads expunged over thirteen thousand people, according to official estimates, although human rights activists claim more than thirty thousand "vanished."[8] Less than a war (there were few battles), it was a massive police action characterized by "kidnappings, torture, and assassinations."[9]

The Desaparecidos (the disappeared) as they were known, in many cases were not guerrillas, but part of the Peronist labor opposition the junta had also vowed to crush. A January 1978 report on the desaparecidos, for example, estimated that 37 percent of those arrested were "second-level or shop floor union leaders," while fewer than 20 percent were guerrillas.[10] The drive to break the unions, the core of the Peronist state, occurred simultaneously with, and was related to, the initial economic recovery, and the plan to change the structure of the economic system.

Under the direction of economics minister José Martínez de Hoz, the only civilian technocrat the junta entrusted with a ministerial position, the government pursued a tight monetary and fiscal regime, whose immediate objective was to bring down inflation, reduce the public sector deficit, and attract foreign investment.[11] In the short run, high interest rates, abolition of capital controls, lowering of tariffs, lifting of restrictions on profit repatriation, and the dismissal of pending court cases against several large multinational corporations, did attract foreign capital, reduce inflation, and the deficit, as the peso appreciated in value.[12]

A major effort was undertaken to strengthen agriculture. Resources were shifted from relatively inefficient small and medium-sized industries, which went out of business, into the agricultural sector, which responded with a bumper harvest in 1976–77. Grain and meat exports increased substantially, helping to turn a $1 billion balance of payments deficit into a $650 million surplus. The public sector deficit dropped from 12 percent of GDP to 6.5 percent, and inflation fell.

Abroad, Martínez de Hoz was hailed as the "wizard of Hoz" for what was considered to be a remarkable achievement. In two years, he had brought the country back from the brink of economic collapse. Through exchange-rate manipulation, he had greatly reduced inflationary expectations—although the inflation rate never dipped much below 100 percent. Nevertheless, he had accomplished the initial objective of promoting recovery, reducing unemployment, attracting foreign investment, eliminating inefficient industry, redeveloping the export sector, and forcing reliance upon market forces.[13]

Martínez de Hoz's stringent policies, while economically orthodox, also served the purpose of facilitating the extension of military control over Argentine society by undermining the Peronist state structure. In the name of free-market economics, he intensified state intervention in the economy. In the name of economic efficiency, he banned union activity and strikes, curtailed welfare subsidies and public services, and raised prices for food and imported goods. The result was a rapid suppression of consumption and wages, which not only served the economic purposes of Martínez de Hoz, but also the political purposes of the junta.[14] Martínez de Hoz's usefulness to the junta was directly proportional to his willingness to tailor his economic goals to their political aims. When his policies intruded into the junta's domain, he was removed.

By spring 1978, although the economy was recovering well, it was beginning to lose momentum. One of Martínez de Hoz's main objectives had been to privatize as much of the state-controlled portion of the economy as possible. Although initially he had been led to believe that he would be permitted to undertake this part of his program, when he attempted to do so, the junta balked. The military bluntly refused to permit privatization of major sectors of the economy, particularly its own industrial complex, the DGFM (Dirección General de Fabricaciones Militares). DGFM was "the most powerful economic group in the country," controlling all or substantial parts of twenty-two corporations, representing 2.5 percent of Argentina's GNP, roughly $2.2 billion.[15]

In addition to meddling in the economy, the junta immediately extended its control over every other important sector of society. Political parties were banned, censorship introduced, and extraordinary powers vested in military security organs. Military officers were placed in charge of union organizations, where they eliminated militant opposition at all levels. Military officers "guided" judicial procedure, which removed effective legal redress against arbitrary action.[16] Military administrators took charge of industries and thereby controlled production. Generals and admirals assumed places on the management boards of the major media organizations, which enabled them to determine broad editorial policies. The junta created a "Pastoral Commission" to establish "consultation" with the church, which was brought into effective compliance with its objectives.

Within two years of seizing power, the junta had gained control of Argentine society and brutally suppressed all dissent on the pretext of combating the insurgency. By spring 1978, the internal war had been won, although actual military operations would continue to intensify through the following year. The junta under Videla had accomplished most of its domestic agenda and had assumed the power to address foreign policy concerns. By spring 1978, however, the junta faced a self-created dilemma.

The junta's very success had eroded its rationale for continued rule. The internal threat had been subdued and economic vitality restored. Those who had been silenced or acquiesced in the junta's rule on national security grounds—the political parties, unions, church, intellectuals, industrialists—now began to raise their voices demanding an early return to civilian rule. The military leadership was not ready to permit an early return to civilian rule, but disagreed on precisely how to proceed. The issue of how soon, or whether, to return to civilian rule was disputed within the junta, which still believed there was much work left to be done. Indeed, Argentina was entering a period of its greatest military power, both in absolute and relative terms, and the junta was determined to be able to exercise it in an effort to resolve intractable foreign policy problems.

While the "dirty war" had attracted most of the attention, the junta had quietly embarked upon a major program of weapons acquisitions, setting aside "special funds" for this purpose. Military control of Argentine industry, which had been extended after the takeover, helped to conceal the extent of the buildup (and explained the military's refusal to permit privatization). Budget numbers were "cooked," showing a better economic performance than was actually occurring, with only moderate defense spending.[17] In fact, however, between 1976 and 1982, Argentina spent over $16.7 billion on arms imports, amounting to two-thirds of its total foreign debt.[18] Most ominous, the junta was on the verge of deciding to embark upon a very ambitious, but highly secret, nuclear missile program.[19]

Throughout the spring of 1978, having accomplished the domestic objectives of quelling the rebellion and promoting economic recovery, the top Argentine leadership engaged in a heated debate over whether or not to begin a transition to civilian rule, as well as over future strategy. There was an apparent consensus that the military should remain in power indefinitely. Videla, however, took a conciliatory position in favor of eventual political liberalization, based upon economic recovery—a gradual transition to civilian rule in the near, but unspecified, future.[20]

Videla was opposed by his vice president, Adm. Emilio Massera, who also vehemently objected to the economic policies of Martínez de Hoz. Extremely ambitious, Massera posed as an advocate of return to civilian rule, but was actually an extreme hard-liner who hoped to perpetuate the dictatorship— and his own rise to the presidency within it. He sought the support of the Peronist Party's right wing, with which he had developed contacts from his days as naval minister under Isabela Perón, including his involvement in a business partnership with a Peronist union leader.[21]

Massera attempted to establish a kind of military populism based upon defense against the foreign threat. He advocated war with Chile over Santiago's refusal to cede control over three islands in the Beagle Channel, which Argentina claimed, and demanded an invasion of the Falkland Islands because of Great Britain's refusal to transfer sovereignty. In both cases, he sought to inflame nationalist sentiment. His scheme was to perpetuate a national security crisis as a pretext to "penetrate, mobilize, and coopt popular institutions." A related motive apparently was his desire to prod Videla into making bad decisions in order to discredit him.[22] His ultimate objective, as Rock notes, was to "don the mantle of Perón and establish a popular dictatorship—Bonapartism in a raw form."[23]

There was yet a third group of military hard-liners violently and openly opposed to a return to civilian rule. Led by Gen. Crestino Nicolaides, and including generals Carlos Suarez Mason and Luciano Menéndez, among others, this group sought to justify perpetuation of military rule based on the continuing domestic threat. They insisted on a sweeping repression, an all-out war on the "Left" and all of its organizations, particularly the Peronist Party and its union affiliates.[24] Clearly, Admiral Massera and the army hard-liners were diametrically opposed.

After lengthy deliberation, triggered by Massera's "formal" proposal to seize the Falkland Islands, the junta reached a series of crucial decisions. First, Videla would be permitted to remain as president until March 1981, but would be required to retire from his post as head of the army, August 1, 1978.[25] Gen. Roberto Viola, Videla's close ally, would succeed him as army commander, effectively ensuring the ascendancy of the army over the navy within the junta (and, within the army, for the time being, of the infantry over the cavalry). Admiral Massera's proposal to seize the Falkland Islands was rejected.[26]

In return for the support of the hard-liners against Massera, Videla agreed to an intensification of the domestic repression through the following year, suggesting a combination of the Videla-Viola faction with the army hard-liners against the navy. From this point, Massera's power and influence within the junta began to wane, until his retirement in the fall of 1979. His retirement from active duty did not signal the end of either his political ambitions or activity, however. Retirement simply removed any constraints on his pursuit of an understanding, or "concertacion," with the right wing of the Peronist Party, which Raul Alfonsín would later denounce as a "military-syndicalist pact."[27] Nor, apparently, did this "inveterate conspirator" cease his plotting against the junta.[28] He was not alone.

The junta also reached crucial decisions on the issues of strategy and foreign policy. By spring 1978, in foreign affairs, the junta had stumbled badly, heading into a strategic cul de sac. Brazil had embarked upon a nuclear program that would enable Rio to leapfrog into preeminence in Latin America. Chile, through arbitration, had won its dispute with Argentina over three islands in the Beagle Channel (Picton, Lennox, and Nueva), and the conflict with Great Britain over the Falkland Islands and Dependencies (South Georgia and the South Sandwich Islands) was at an impasse. Furthermore, the struggles with Chile and Great Britain involved the larger issues of control over the South Atlantic and substantial parts of Antarctica. Argentina was stymied on all of these issues, with no obvious means of recovery.

The Failure of Argentine Foreign Policy

The problem with Brazil was long-standing, but had taken a decisive turn in 1975 when West Germany had agreed to provide Brasilia with a complete nuclear fuel cycle. The contract involved the construction of as many as eight light water nuclear reactors, with the first scheduled to come on-line in 1982, and the remaining reactors annually thereafter. The contract included technology for prospecting, mining, and processing of uranium ore, production and enrichment of uranium compounds, manufacture of fuel elements, and reprocessing of irradiated fuels. Protestations notwithstanding, the program clearly indicated that Brazil sought to become Latin America's first "self-sufficient nuclear state with a nuclear weapons capability."[29]

Brazil possessed a larger and more technologically advanced military industrial base than Argentina and was rapidly augmenting it. By the mid-seventies, Brazil was already manufacturing much of its own conventional weaponry, including light tanks and jet aircraft, which it was also exporting. In addition, it was either importing advanced technology directly, for example, through the purchase of submarines from West Germany and Great Britain, fighter jets from France and Italy, and antiaircraft guns from Sweden, or indirectly through coproduction and development arrangements with these and other advanced countries.[30]

In the spring of 1978, the question facing the junta was how to respond to Brazil. Clearly, Argentina was already behind its larger neighbor. To do nothing would mean that Argentina would fall further, and perhaps permanently, behind, and Brazil would surge into an undisputed position of South American hegemony. Argentina would fall to second rank in relation to its larger neighbor. The strategic debate of the spring of 1978, therefore, necessarily addressed the issue of Brazil.

Also addressed in the debate were the related issues of the Beagle Channel and the Falkland Islands. From Argentina's standpoint, these were not equally important strategically, but the Beagle Channel issue required an immediate response. Argentina and Chile had signed a Treaty of Arbitration in 1902 binding them to a peaceful dispute-resolution system. In 1972 the two countries entered into a ten-year agreement to arbitrate conflicting claims over Picton, Lennox, and Nueva, and accepted Britain as arbiter. London appointed a five-member international court to adjudicate the claims. Five years later, in February 1977, the court awarded the islands to Chile.

In January 1978, the Argentine government rejected the court's ruling on the grounds that "errors, omissions and abuses . . . seriously damage Argentine rights and interests."[31] As the junta deliberated on Argentine strategy through the spring, the question regarding Chile was: How to respond to the adverse ruling on the islands? The Beagle Channel issue was important but paled in significance to that of the Falkland Islands. Indeed, favorable resolution of the Falkland Islands issue would effectively nullify the significance of the Beagle Channel issue, but the reverse was not true. Control of the Falklands would provide Buenos Aires with an unobstructed base from which to dominate the South Atlantic and Cape Horn. A Falklands base would negate Chile's stranglehold over Argentina's southernmost naval base in the Beagle Channel at Ushuaia whose eastern outlet was dominated by the three disputed islands. The Chilean naval base at Punta Arenas dominated the Pacific side. Nevertheless, Argentina could not permit Chilean control of the three islands for it would give Santiago a major entrée into Atlantic waters at Argentina's expense.

That geographical position combined with application of the 200-mile economic zone would effectively enable Chile to encompass a substantial part of the waters of the South Atlantic. There was the further disagreement regarding the dividing line between the Pacific and the Atlantic Oceans. Argentina, following a 1919 ruling, argued that the Cape Horn meridian divided the two oceans, while Chile argued on geographic grounds that the submerged Antillean loop bounded by the South Georgia, South Sandwich, and South Orkney Island groups constituted "the true delimitation of the Atlantic and Pacific Oceans."[32]

The respective arguments strengthened each country's claims against the other in the Antarctic, where they not only overlapped against each other, but also with Great Britain's claims. For the moment, the Antarctic Treaty (conceived by the United States in 1958, signed by twelve participating nations on December 1, 1959, and in effect from June 23, 1961) enhanced peaceful scientific cooperation while maintaining the status quo, holding conflicting claims in abeyance.[33] But the treaty would be open to amendment after June 23, 1991, thirty years after coming into effect. At that time, any party to the agreement could withdraw citing grounds of fundamental changes in conditions.

The focus of the junta's strategic debate in the spring of 1978, however, was the dispute with Great Britain over the Falkland Islands and Dependencies, which had reached a dead end. The dispute originated nearly one hundred and fifty years before in January 1833 when British forces landed and occupied the islands. Since then, successive Argentine governments had attempted to regain the islands from British control. At one point, in 1940, Great Britain apparently was prepared to propose a transfer of sovereignty with leaseback, but World War II interrupted the process.[34] In 1942, Britain garrisoned the islands against possible attack by Germany or Argentina.

Following WWII, the venue shifted to the United Nations, where in December 1960, UN Resolution 1514 called generally for an end to colonialism in all its forms. Five years later, this led to passage of UN Resolution 2065, inviting Argentina and Great Britain to "proceed without delay with negotiations . . . with a view to finding a peaceful solution to the problem, bearing in mind . . . the interests of the populations of the Falkland Islands (Malvinas)."[35]

Great Britain objected to identification of the Falklands dispute as a "colonial" problem, but agreed to enter into negotiations based on UNR 2065. The resolution also specifically referred to the "interests" of the Falkland Islanders, not their "wishes," which excluded them as a party to the negotiations. To allay islander fears of a "sellout," however, Britain referred not only to the "wishes" of the islanders, but to their "paramount wishes," specifically including them as a party to the dispute. Contributing to the British attitude at this time was the concurrent declaration of independence from the crown by Ian Smith of Rhodesia.

Six years later, the negotiations produced a shift in British policy, contained in the Communications Agreement of 1971. The shift, which entailed no prejudice to either side's position on sovereignty, was an attempt to promote a change in the political attitudes of the islanders through their increased contact, economic cooperation, and interaction with Argentina.[36] A ten-year time frame was envisaged, although not mentioned in the agreement. According to Lord Chalfont, foreign office minister of state at the time: "If, at the end of ten years, nothing had been resolved, then it was time to get together and ask why."[37] In the Communications Agreement, Argentina agreed to provide weekly air and sea service to the Falkland Islands, improve postal, telephone, telegraph, and customs services, provide health, education, and agricultural assistance, and fuel oil at subsidized prices.

These were not economically profitable ventures because the islands were in economic decline. Indeed, for many years, the economic pattern had been "depressingly consistent." Absentee owners exploited the indigenous wool industry, taking profits without making long-term investment for future growth and diversification.[38] Population had also dwindled from a peak of almost twenty-four hundred in 1931 to just over nineteen hundred in 1978. (There would only be 1,813 at the time of the war.) In the fall of 1971, on the grounds of "declining profits from the wool trade," steamer service between Port Stanley and Montevideo, Uruguay, was discontinued.[39] London promised to initiate ferry service to the Argentine mainland, but never did so.[40]

As part of the effort to reshape islander opinion, Great Britain reduced its connection to the islands. In less than two years, the Falklands Islands Company, largest of several British land-owning companies in the islands and owner of nearly one-half of the utilizable land, was sold twice. In 1972, it was acquired by a subsidiary of the Slater-Walker Securities empire, Dundee, Perth and London Southern Ships Stores Limited.[41] A few months later, in 1973, the DP&L group was absorbed by yet another financial conglomerate, Charringtons Industrial Holdings Limited. Sold twice in less than two years, the FIC "had become just one more name in a portfolio of shareholdings . . ."[42] (In 1977, FIC would be taken over by yet a third holding company, the Coalite Group, which further eroded the connection between shareholders and islanders.)

Argentine leaders, carefully observing the financial journey of the FIC, made substantial investments in Falklands infrastructure, improving the airstrip at Port Stanley to accommodate larger (but not long-range) aircraft, constructing an unloading pier, and a fuel-oil storage facility. After an initial period of good will, however, it became clear that islander opposition to any alteration in status would doom the "economic interchange" approach. In frustration, Argentina returned to the United Nations in late 1973, obtaining another favorable resolution, UNR 3160, "calling on both parties to accelerate negotiations toward a solution of the sovereignty issue."[43]

This momentarily produced movement. In early 1974, the British government "broached" the subject of condominium, but, "in the face of the Islanders' continuing refusal to participate, it was decided that there would be no purpose in proceeding without them, and the Argentine Government was so informed in August 1974."[44] Relations soured immediately thereafter, particularly when Argentine authorities also learned that Great Britain was attempting to grant offshore oil exploration concessions in Falklands waters.

In mid-1975, Buenos Aires made several attempts to merge the British economic approach with its own on sovereignty. Argentina initially sought through a London intermediary to "buy the Falklands Islands Company outright" from Charrington's, but was turned down.[45] Buenos Aires then proposed to link joint development of economic resources with "simultaneous leaseback for a period of years, as a means of settling the dispute."[46] The Argentine government also proposed that it should "occupy the uninhabited islands of South Georgia and the South Sandwich Islands, and that the occupation should be accepted without condemnation by the British Government."[47]

These proposals led nowhere at the time. Within sixteen months, however, when the junta took power, Buenos Aires would actually adopt this very approach of occupying the outlying islands, to which Britain would seemingly acquiesce—at least initially. In 1975, however, concerns in Buenos Aires heightened when London, proceeding unilaterally with its economic approach, announced that it would conduct an economic and social survey of the islands. Although Argentina declared the British proposal "unwelcome," London proceeded with the survey in early 1976 under Lord Shackleton (son of the famous Antarctic explorer buried on the island of South Georgia). The result simply exacerbated tensions.

Manifesting its displeasure, the Argentine government decried the unilateral British "survey" and demanded the recall of Ambassador Derek Ashe from Buenos Aires, until London was prepared to negotiate on the issue of sovereignty. In February, the Argentine destroyer *Almirante Storni* fired shots across the bow of the RRS *Shackleton* research vessel in an effort to assert sovereignty over the Falklands and surrounding waters and to exert pressure on the British government to negotiate.[48]

The "Outside-In" Approach to the Falklands/Malvinas

A month later, in March 1976, the junta unseated Isabela Peron and, assuming power, embarked upon the very strategy of occupying the Dependencies that the Peron regime had proposed the previous year. Choosing the island farthest from the Falklands, which also marked "the eastern extreme of the zone on continental Antarctica claimed by Argentina," the junta secretly authorized the establishment of a "scientific research station" on South Thule, an uninhabited island of the South Sandwich group.[49] Fifty military personnel landed in November and quickly set up a station like the dozen or so research facilities, huts really, that Argentina had placed throughout its Antarctic claim area.[50]

A helicopter from the British antarctic patrol ship, HMS *Endurance*, discovered the presence of the station in late December. Generally believed to have been a chance event, it was anything but. British intelligence had broken Argentine codes and "for many years" was well-informed about Argentine plans.[51] That view of Britain's intelligence capability vis-à-vis Argentina was subsequently confirmed by the former deputy head of MI6, George Kennedy Young. Speaking of the later conflict over the Falkland Islands, Young observed: "We had a very good assessment of the situation before it happened. . . . Even our embassy was getting reports of the Argentineans' plans. But Carrington played the information down."[52]

Indeed, British intelligence knew the Argentine plan for South Thule in detail, as the Franks report discloses, including the junta's planned riposte to an expected strong British reaction. Thus, if Britain had acted to remove the "research station" on South Thule, Argentine forces were prepared to seize, "as a reprisal," the British Antarctic Station on South Georgia.[53] British intelligence also knew of Argentine contingency plans, should the crisis escalate, for an invasion of the Falkland Islands and a diplomatic initiative to the United Nations. In fact, Buenos Aires did undertake an initiative in the United Nations in December, gaining passage of Resolution 31/49 by a vote of 102 to 1, with 32 abstentions. Only Great Britain voted against. The resolution expressed "gratitude" to Argentina for its attempt to "facilitate the process of decolonization" and requested the governments of Argentina and Great Britain to "expedite the negotiations" on the Falklands.[54]

In the event, however, London confounded the junta by taking no action at all beyond quietly calling in the chargé d'affaires on January 5, 1977, and requesting an "explanation" of the Argentine presence on South Thule. In fact, not only did the British government take no action, it kept the existence of the establishment of an Argentine research station on South Thule a secret from the British public until May 1978. The Argentine government followed suit.[56] Instead, London announced an interest in resolving the Falklands issue. On February 2, Foreign Office Secretary Anthony Crossland declared that:

> The time has come to consider both with the Islanders and the Argentine Government whether a climate exists for discussing the broad issues which bear on the future of the Falkland Islands, and the possibilities of co-operation between Britain and Argentina in the region of the South West Atlantic.[57]

After discussions with the Falkland Islanders and Argentine officials, the British government announced on April 26, 1977, that negotiations would commence in July concerning

> ... future political relations, including sovereignty, with regard
> to the Falkland Islands, South Georgia and South Sandwich Is-
> lands, and economic cooperation with regard to the said terri-
> tories. . . . Negotiations will be directed to the working out of a
> peaceful solution to the existing dispute on sovereignty between
> the two states and the establishment of a framework for Anglo-
> Argentine economic co-operation.[58]

A clearer statement regarding the British government's readiness to arrange a transfer of sovereignty is difficult to imagine, but the actual transfer
of sovereignty was not its intention. During the first round of talks in Rome
during July, the British position became clear. The British government's
"strategy was to retain sovereignty for as long as possible, if necessary making concessions in respect of the Dependencies and the maritime resources
of the area."[59] This strategy recognized that "ultimately only some form of
leaseback arrangement was likely to satisfy Argentina." The government
also advanced the idea that the issue of sovereignty for the Dependencies
"might be looked at separately" from the issue of sovereignty for the
Falkland Islands.

No agreement on the sovereignty question was reached during the July
talks, but Britain raised the issue of scientific cooperation, that is, "the establishment of scientific research stations by Argentina in the dependencies."[60] Agreement on scientific cooperation would, of course, effectively
legitimize after the fact the Argentine maneuver in South Thule. Meanwhile,
however, negotiations were purely a "holding operation" to buy time. Ironically, both Britain and Argentina were moving on a parallel course, as Argentina nibbled at the Dependencies, working from the outside in toward
the Falklands, and Britain made concessions in the Dependencies, attempting to delay Argentina's advance to the Falklands for as long as possible.

This play for time could not continue indefinitely, particularly considering
the two countries' public agreement to negotiate on sovereignty, and British
intelligence soon noted the "hardening" of the Argentine attitude before the
talks resumed.[61] During September and October, Argentine ships arrested
seven Soviet and two Bulgarian fishing vessels in Falkland waters, firing on
one of the Bulgarian ships and wounding one of its crew. The Argentine navy
was ordered to mount "a similar riposte to intrusions by any other flag

carrier"—a statement that the Argentine naval attaché in London, Admiral Jorge Anaya, drew to the attention of the British Foreign Office.[62]

British intelligence learned that, at winter's end, the Argentines were planning to land another naval party on South Thule in mid-October, an apparent replay of the previous year's landing. In its October 11 assessment, the Joint Intelligence Committee believed that the junta was prepared to resolve the issue peacefully, as long as the British government negotiated seriously. If there were no progress, then Buenos Aires would take more forceful action, possibly establishing a presence on one of the other Dependencies, such as South Georgia, coming to the support of a "private adventurist operation" in the Falklands, or attacking British shipping. An outright invasion of the Falklands was considered unlikely.[63]

Under these circumstances, the Callaghan government devised a subtle, but threatening, response to what it knew privately to be an increasingly aggressive Argentine attitude. It was decided to deploy a nuclear-powered submarine to the "immediate vicinity" of the Falklands and two frigates one thousand miles to the north. Rules of engagement were decided in the event of confrontation. The presence of the powerful submarine, if known to the Argentines, would make a landing on the islands very risky. Although the Franks report asserts that Cabinet papers "clearly show that it was agreed that the force should remain covert" and that "we have found no evidence that the Argentine Government ever came to know of its existence," this was an evasion.

Key British and Argentine officials, in high office at the time, have said that the British government conveyed the fact of the deployment of the submarine to the Argentine government.[64] Dennis Healey, Chancellor of the Exchequer in 1977, revealed in his memoir that Prime Minister Callaghan, in sending the nuclear-powered submarine to the Falklands, "allowed the Argentine Government to discover this through secret channels. This deterrent was sufficient. There was no invasion."[65] Callaghan himself admitted that "he had told the head of MI6, Sir Maurice Oldfield, of the committee's action but did not know whether this information was passed on."[66] But, of course, he expected it to be.

Adm. Jorge Anaya, naval member of the Galtieri junta during the war in the Falklands, declared in an interview after the conflict that "he knew about the presence of the Royal Navy submarine in the vicinity of the Falklands in the 1970s."[67] He knew, it may be added, because Anaya, as naval attaché to London in late 1977,[68] was himself in all probability one of the "secret channels" Callaghan employed to allow the Argentine government to "discover" the submarine's presence.[69]

Because the very purpose of the submarine, as the Franks report notes, was "to buttress the government's negotiating position by deploying a force of sufficient strength, available if necessary, to convince the Argentines that military action by them would meet resistance," to have kept it a secret from the Argentine leadership would have served no purpose.[70] For the government to acknowledge that it had deployed a nuclear submarine, however, would only have escalated the level of the conflict, which was not in London's interest. Thus, the government's denial is fully understandable—as a diplomatic nicety, even if not precisely factual.

In fact, as before, the British government was employing a carrot and stick approach in a continuing play for time. Deployment of the nuclear-powered submarine was the "stick," and a renewed willingness to discuss sovereignty was the "carrot." As soon as Argentina agreed to resume talks, however, London changed the game to bait and switch. In December, Britain agreed with an earlier Argentine suggestion to set up two working groups—on sovereignty and on economic cooperation. After a recess, the two working groups held their first meeting in February 1978. Having offered as bait a discussion on sovereignty, London now switched to propose "an arrangement to provide for British and Argentine scientific activities in the Dependencies."[71] This would simply have retroactively legitimized what the Argentines already had—that is, a presence on South Thule. Of course, the Argentines declined.

Britain's "bait and switch" tactic was probably the last straw that precipitated the junta's strategic review in spring 1978. The February working groups' unproductive discussion convinced the Argentine leadership that Britain had no intention of negotiating seriously on sovereignty. Nor could the junta marshal sufficient force to counter the subtle and invisible British submarine threat. Thus, when London's stall on sovereignty became apparent to them, they broke off the talks by raising an extraneous argument. Because the Falkland Islands and Dependencies did not generate a continental shelf, they said, "shelf rights therefore belonged to Argentina and were outside the scope of negotiations."[72] There would be no further formal negotiations until the end of the year—nearly nine months. Meanwhile, the Argentine junta made momentous decisions.

To ensure freedom of maneuver, Buenos Aires proceeded through the year to extricate itself from any potentially entangling relationships with Great Britain. The primary example was Argentina's decision to switch a billion dollar naval ship contract from Great Britain to West Germany. Hugh Carless, head of the Latin American desk, mistakenly thought that the Germans had "filched this very important contract . . . from under the nose of Vospers," but, of course, that was not the reason for the Argentine switch.[73] As Carless noted, the contract would have taken ten to fifteen years to execute. "We would have been locked into a major industrial relationship with Argentina. Both parties would have found it very difficult to withdraw."

1978: Strategic Choices

By early spring 1978, Argentina had been backed into a corner on all three foreign fronts of importance to the junta—Brazil, Chile, and Great Britain. With the possible exception of Chile, in all of the power relationships, Buenos Aires was left with no way forward. This, then, was the context for the junta's strategic debate, which resulted in a momentous set of decisions that ultimately led Argentina to war with Great Britain over the Falkland Islands.

The fundamental question confronting the junta involved determining its response to the triple deadlock. After lengthy deliberation, the junta secretly decided to acquire a nuclear missile capability and employ it, politically, to emerge from the looming strategic dead end facing them. A nuclear weapons capability would establish Argentina as a Latin American power that would equal, if not eclipse, Brazil. When combined with its growing conventional weapons strength, a militarily resurgent Argentina would also be able to resolve what had been, until then, intractable foreign policy problems with Chile and Great Britain.

Argentina had been ahead of Brazil in nuclear technology until 1975, operating the only commercial heavy water reactor in Latin America. Brazil's nuclear decision threatened to catapult Brasilia into preeminence in that field. Now, the junta publicized the decision to construct five additional nuclear power reactors. The first, a joint venture with Canada, was a reprocessing plant at Ezeiza, near the capitol, which was scheduled to begin operating in the summer of 1982.[74] The Ezeiza project alone triggered fears that such a "facility would provide Buenos Aires with direct access to weapons-usable plutonium by the early 1980s."[75] Contracts had also been let to West German and Swiss firms for two others for completion by the mid-eighties. (West Germany had built Argentina's first reactor.)

Kept secret was the decision to construct a uranium enrichment plant at Pilcaniyeu, deep inland a thousand miles to the south.[76] (The existence of the Pilcaniyeu facility was not made public until 1983 following the end of military rule.) The secret enrichment plant would, of course, greatly accelerate the publicly estimated timetable. Finally, Argentina sought to acquire enriched weapons-grade uranium from the Soviet Union, China, and South Africa, which would further accelerate their timetable. (In mid-1982, American intelligence estimated that it would take Argentina anywhere from six months to three years to "build a bomb.")[77]

While the navy managed the entire nuclear reactor program, the air force was placed in charge of a complementary program to develop a "nuclear-capable ballistic missile." Named Condor I, it was publicly designated as a single-staged "weather" rocket, but "had the potential to serve as a short-range tactical missile."[78] Thus, in early 1978, the junta had made the momentous decision to acquire a nuclear weapons capability based on ballistic missiles. It also decided to conceal this effort under civilian nuclear power and meteorological programs.

The fundamental decision to acquire by stealth a nuclear weapons capability meant that the junta was planning eventually to present the world with a fait accompli. Although this would not give Argentina a decisive advantage over Brazil, which was acquiring its own capability, it would match it. It would certainly confer an advantage over Chile on the Beagle Channel question. And a nuclear weapons capability would permit Argentina to deal with Great Britain over the Falkland Islands dispute from a position of equality, if not strength.

The nuclear decision estimated a usable capability sometime in the early eighties, possibly as early as 1983. It meant that each of the foreign policy problems—with Brazil, Chile, and Great Britain—would have to be carefully managed to reach a favorable resolution-point when Argentine military power was also peaking. This necessarily dictated a policy of buying time over the next few years, at the very least, to prevent an adverse outcome, but also to remain engaged on the issues and well positioned for the optimum moment.

Of course, a policy of buying time did not necessarily dictate passivity. Indeed, there was more than one way to buy time, and the junta adopted a varied approach. Vis-à-vis Brazil, Buenos Aires adopted a publicly subordinate position, minimizing any competition with its larger neighbor. Toward Chile, however, the decision was to exacerbate the crisis over the Beagle Channel, prolonging it until the arbitration treaty expired in 1982, placing Argentina in a more powerful military position to exert pressure for a favorable outcome. Concerning Great Britain, the decision was to take the next step in the indirect approach in the Dependencies, initiated when the junta took power, gradually building a position of strength both diplomatically and militarily.

In its relations with Brazil, the specific manifestation of the new subordinate approach was the decision to accept a compliant position in a dispute over the allocation of resources of the upper River Plate Basin where Brazil had constructed a large hydroelectric project on the Paraná River involving Paraguay.[79] The junta parlayed this decision into an improvement in political relations, including the first visit by a Brazilian president to Argentina in 1979, publicly downplaying any suggestion of competing for hegemony in the region. This was followed, during 1980, by agreements on cooperation in the nuclear field and political consultation.[80]

Notwithstanding, Argentina's competition with Brazil had secretly entered into a new, nuclear, stage from the spring of 1978. The long-term outlook was for the stabilization of relations based on a mutual possession of nuclear weapons, but the first to acquire a nuclear weapons capability would enjoy a brief window of opportunity and maneuverability. Furthermore, Argentine entry into the "nuclear club" would give Buenos Aires an undeniable edge in dealing with its larger neighbor.

Vis-à-vis Chile, the junta's decision was to create a war scare and move to the brink of conflict before backing away. From spring 1978, the junta adopted the policy of intensifying the conflict with Chile throughout the year, evidently determined to await the expiration of the arbitration treaty and resolve the issue through military pressure at the point when Buenos Aires would be far more powerful. The war scare would also divert attention from the main thrust of Argentine strategy toward the Malvinas.

In that context, Argentina attempted to build a "kind of triple alliance" with Bolivia and Peru against Chile in the event of any clash arising from the

Beagle dispute.[81] Indeed, in October, Argentina and Bolivia issued a joint communiqué ratifying their solidarity.[82] Displaying its power and resolve, the junta sailed a naval task force headed by the aircraft carrier, the *25 de Mayo* (formerly the WWII era HMS *Venerable*), to Tierra del Fuego in November, forcing the withdrawal of the less capable Chilean navy, while the army deployed along their common border.

The army proceeded to expel some of the numerous Chileans living in Patagonia, Argentina's southernmost province, and the junta demanded that Chile hand over control of three of eight tiny islands in what is called the Cape Horn group—islands that were traditionally Chilean.[83] Coffins were ostentatiously shipped south for the return of war dead and military operations planned only to be canceled at the last moment.[84] Only the intervention of Pope John Paul II in December averted all-out conflict, or so it was believed.

Finally, a decision was reached concerning the Malvinas. Despite the tough British response during the latter part of the previous year, the actual trend in the military balance between Great Britain and Argentina was highly favorable to Argentina. Great Britain, since 1967, had been gradually withdrawing from its remaining outposts of empire, while reshaping and reducing the size of its fleet. The 1974 Defence Review had outlined a "phased rundown of overseas commitments outside NATO," including the only naval vessel in the South Atlantic, the HMS *Endurance*.[85] *Endurance*, however, was permitted to remain for another tour after the events of late 1977 noted above.

Argentina, however, had begun a major conventional military buildup. That, along with the clandestine nuclear weapons program, promised to give Argentina a superior position in the South Atlantic and effectively eclipse the British position in the Antarctic, the Falklands, and Dependencies. The crossover point lay in the near, but calculable, future. Under these circumstances, there would be no repeat of the South Thule operation, in which a slowly evolving overt challenge had given Great Britain time to respond with superior power. Any future action involving Great Britain would have to occur under the cover of plausible deniability and emerge as a fait accompli.

Commercial "Cover" for South Georgia

The military trends clearly counseled patience for Argentina, until the balance was in its favor. However, at least superficially, the trends should have counseled the opposite for Great Britain, but it also opted to play for time. In the British government's defense, however, there was no immediate urgency. It would be some time, perhaps several years, before the power balance between Great Britain and Argentina would shift dangerously in favor of Buenos Aires. So London played for time—and was carefully vigilant. It may be confidently assumed that British intelligence, capable of reading Argentina's secret plans, would note every Argentine step and every order placed for additional weaponry; subject each move to sharpest scrutiny; and calculate every possible impact on Argentine leaders—even while publicly conveying the very opposite impression of benign neglect.

The junta, however, continuing with the indirect "nibbling" approach, set about carefully planning to establish an eventual Argentine presence on the next target—South Georgia. In keeping with the precept derived from the abortive attempt to land on South Thule in late 1977, future actions against Great Britain would have to be deniable and preemptive. The junta authorized as the initial step a purely commercial operation that could eventually be transformed rapidly into an Argentine state presence at the appropriate time. This was the genesis of the plan initiated by Constantine Davidoff to dismantle defunct whaling stations on South Georgia. The related plan to establish a military detachment on South Georgia under its cover was called "Operation Alpha."

In mid-1978, Davidoff, an Argentine of Greek extraction, approached Christian Salvesens Company of Edinburgh, Scotland, with a business proposition.[86] Salvesens was an old English firm engaged in the shipping and whaling industry since its founding in 1846. Between 1909 and 1963, Salvesens operated two large whaling stations at Leith and Stromness on Stromness Bay, South Georgia. The whaling operation had been closed down in 1965 and the stations left to rust and deteriorate in the harsh weather of the frigid South Atlantic. The only active presence on the island was the British Antarctic Survey (BAS), a scientific research station.

Sight unseen, Davidoff proposed to purchase an option contract from Salvesens to salvage the two stations for their scrap metal value to "dispose of . . . as best he might, and at his own risk."[87] Although a potential windfall for Salvesens, as the old whaling stations were of no use, Davidoff's offer did not seem quite right for at least two reasons. First, Davidoff had never been to South Georgia and could not have known the value of the scrap metal contained in the old whaling stations. That alone suggested he was not acting independently, but on behalf of some third party with knowledge of the economic potential of the whaling stations.

Second, there were actually four old unused whaling stations on South Georgia—the two at Leith and Stromness controlled by Salvesens, and two others at Husvik and Grytviken, controlled by an Argentine firm, the Albion Star Company. Albion Star had gone under and the "liquidator of the company was seeking a buyer for these leases."[88] Presumably, they could be acquired at a reasonable price. The commercially obvious question was: Assuming there was sufficient scrap metal to make the venture profitable, why ask Salvesens? Why did Davidoff not acquire the leases from Albion Star, which, from a purely commercial point of view, seemed to be an ideal opportunity?

The politically obvious answer was that obtaining leases from Salvesens would, at one stroke, substitute a legitimate Argentine for a British presence. And once the British Antarctic Survey left, which was widely anticipated as part of continuing expenditure cuts, the only presence on South Georgia— even though purely commercial—would be Argentine. Once established, with BAS gone, the scrap metal operation could easily be transformed into an Argentine military or "scientific" base. Objectively, therefore, although Davidoff undoubtedly expected to profit from the venture, which explains his involvement, British authorities had to draw the obvious conclusion that he was either a witting or unwitting pawn of the Argentine government.

Salvesens, however, recognized an opportunity to preempt any future commercial competition on South Georgia—although one must be skeptical about the assumption that the whaling industry would ever be revived. In any case, Salvesens planned to acquire the Albion Star Company's leases with Davidoff's money and preclude any potential Argentine commercial presence. After pondering Davidoff's offer for a few months, in 1979, as Margaret Thatcher took office, the director of Salvesens contacted the Foreign Office and the Falkland Islands governor, James Parker, to see if there were any objections. "Parker liked the idea that Salvesens should replace the Argentine presence as represented by the Albion Star Company, but was unenthusiastic about the deal with Davidoff."[89] The Foreign Office overruled him.

The question remained concerning both Davidoff's identity and the interests he represented. In the literature of the history of the South Atlantic war, considering that the incident on South Georgia was the trigger and that

Davidoff constructed the trigger, very little is known of this enigmatic figure, although all accounts exonerate him from culpability. Perkins, for example, described Davidoff as a person who was

> known for many years around the ports of Latin America as a businessman, never outstandingly successful but always keeping an eye open for the main chance. That he, an Argentine, should have been able to insert himself into the scenario, with the full knowledge and initial approval of the British authorities, was to prove in time to be a particularly unfortunate coincidence.[90]

Burns also saw him as "a young Argentine entrepreneur of Greek extraction, with an eye for a good deal, however bizarre."[91] Freedman and Gamba-Stonehouse saw him as "a free-wheeling entrepreneur."[92] The Franks report portrayed him simply as a "scrap metal merchant from Buenos Aires."[93] Charlton echoed this view.[94] Only the *Sunday Times* report, which was also the earliest account, offered a different glimpse, noting that:

> Davidoff . . . was well known in London. It was considered possible, though by no means definite, that he was being used by the Argentine government to spark an incident. But that in itself was not seen as particularly threatening. Indeed, it positively confirmed the original judgment: that the junta would begin to apply a series of pin pricks. A provocative landing on South Georgia was just the kind of thing that had been predicted.[95]

Thus it was with some understanding of the risks that the Foreign Office not only cleared the way for Salvesens to enter into an options contract with Davidoff, it sweetened the deal by making it far more profitable, at least on paper, than the one he had initially proposed. First, the Foreign Office granted "formal approval" for Salvesens to acquire the Albion Star leases at Husvik and Grytviken, giving them control of all four of the remaining whaling stations on South Georgia.[96]

Then, the Foreign Office authorized Salvesens to offer Davidoff an option contract to dismantle the stations at Leith, Stromness, and Husvik (in other words, one more than he had originally bargained for), which were all located at Stromness Bay, for the nominal sum of approximately $175,000 (£115,000).[97] The station at Grytviken was excluded from the deal, presumably because it was located twenty miles away at Cumberland East Bay and adjacent to the British Antarctic Survey station at King Edward Point. If there were to be a "pin prick" at South Georgia, it would be at Stromness Bay.

Davidoff signed a contract with Salvesens in September 1979 for a three-year option to dismantle the whaling stations. With no funds of his own, he searched for financing for the expedition. The project would take two years or more, which meant sustaining a workforce on the island, providing supplies, equipment, and transportation for the scrap metal back to Argentina. It seems that the Banco Juncal and an unidentified wealthy lawyer from Buenos Aires agreed to finance the enterprise. In 1980, upon forming the company Georgia del Sur, S.A., Davidoff exercised his option. He now had access to South Georgia until March 1983, after which time whatever was left would revert to Salvesens.[98]

The expected profit seemed large, although, once again, Davidoff himself had never been to South Georgia to assess the worth of the scrap metal contained in the old whaling stations. Presumably, his partners knew of the profit-making potential, estimating the value of the scrap metal at current prices to be eleven million dollars, minus expenses of approximately five million, for a tidy profit of nearly six million dollars. Of course, much hinged on scrap steel prices. Fortunately for Davidoff, the world recession, which hit shortly after he signed the contract with Salvesens, drove scrap steel prices up to their highest level in history (with the exception of the world recession year of 1974), and they remained there through 1980 and 1981. The price plunged in 1982 back to the level of 1977.

Scrap metal: average annual price per long ton[99]

Year	In dollars
1977	64.06
1978	77.14
1979	98.97
1980	92.89
1981	93.33
1982	63.73

U.S. Bureau of Mines, *Metal Prices in the United States Through 1991* (Washington: GPO, 1991), 80.

Throughout the period 1979–1981, Davidoff maintained contact with the British embassy in Buenos Aires where the staff was aware of his intentions. Evidently, he was also talking with officers of the Argentine navy among whom he had numerous friends and acquaintances.[100] There had been no progress in his enterprise, however, which was quite surprising given the rapid increase in the price of scrap metal. Davidoff had sought to hire workers from the Falkland Islands, but was turned away by Governor Parker, and London had turned down a request for transportation aboard HMS *Endurance*.[101]

The scrap metal venture on South Georgia would lie dormant until 1981, when all of the conditions impinging on the issue of the Falkland Islands changed both domestically and internationally. Indeed, the thesis argued here is that, when elements of the Argentine navy "activated" Davidoff's South Georgia scrap metal commercial scheme in late 1981, it was to discredit the new Galtieri regime and to forestall seizure of the Falkland Islands, which the junta was planning for May 1982. Such are the vagaries of human interaction, however, that it had precisely the opposite effect regarding the Falklands and resulted in the total collapse of junta rule in Argentina. But more about that later.

Meanwhile, in 1979 and 1980, there was subtle activity over the Falkland Islands. The Coalite Group, a large holding company, had acquired Charrington Industrial Holdings, Limited, in 1977, and, therefore, the Falkland Islands Company (FIC). From this point, "no islanders [were] represented either as shareholders or directors of the company controlling FIC."[102] Nor did this condition change in 1979, when Coalite agreed to the sale of ninety thousand acres of FIC landholdings to local ownership. Six plots of fifteen thousand acres each were sold to "Kelper" families, marginally strengthening private ownership on the island.[103] The FIC still owned 46 percent of the usable land.

In 1980, as attempted earlier in 1975, Argentina sought to negotiate the purchase of the FIC through a London intermediary. "A leading entrepreneur, a well-known figure in the city of London" approached the chairman of the board of Coalite, Mr. Ted Needham. When Needham learned that the prospective buyer was actually representing Argentine interests, he "terminated the conversation."[104] Looking ahead a bit, it was, perhaps, to disguise the absentee ownership structure of the FIC that on February 26, 1982, just before the war, an Extraordinary Meeting of the Coalite board of directors decided that "FIC would no longer be registered as a public limited company."[105] In addition, it must be added that it was no longer required to disclose its financial data.

Because the basis of the Thatcher government's subsequent decision to defend the Falkland Islands was principally to protect the islanders' right of self-determination, closing the books on the FIC made it quite difficult to examine this fundamental proposition. Clearly, if it could be demonstrated that the islanders were little more than tenant farmers, living in a "company town," with little pride of ownership in the land they worked and with no voice in the affairs of the FIC, let alone in governing the islands, the case for British action would be difficult to justify.

CHAPTER 2

Reagan and Thatcher:
A Strategic Convergence

American military power, particularly naval power, had atrophied dramatically during the years of détente. During the seventies, the carrier force had dwindled from 25 to 13, major surface combatants from 267 to 189, and attack submarines from 105 to 80.[1] This force was judged barely sufficient for a one-and-a-half ocean mission.[2] The incoming Reagan administration sought not only to restore the navy to its traditional Atlantic and Pacific roles, but also to expand it to a three-ocean navy, including the Indian Ocean. This involved expanding overall strength to 600 ships, including the addition of two carrier task force groups. Each carrier battle group consisted of missile-armed surface combatants and submarines.

Soviet naval power, however, had increased substantially during the interim, rapidly becoming a blue-water force.[3] Soviet naval power was approaching the point where it would be possible to deny American reinforcement of Europe, or the Pacific, should war come. In addition, the Soviet strengthening of Cuban military capabilities in the Caribbean further concerned American planners, who feared that in time of war substantial naval resources would be drawn off from Atlantic and Pacific tasks to ensure safe passage through Caribbean waters.

Of immediate concern was the continuing Iran-Iraq war, which offered Moscow opportunities for gaining leverage over Persian Gulf petroleum flows as well as subsequent political influence over Eurasian politics that would result. The Carter administration had created the Rapid Deployment Force to respond to a Southwest Asian contingency following the outbreak of the conflict, but had not allocated more than token resources to it. Indeed, by the time Reagan took office, overall force capabilities not only had deteriorated in an absolute sense, they had also withered relative to the increased threat.[4]

Although the Reagan administration had decided to increase the size of the navy to six hundred ships, naval expansion was a lengthy process, and the need for reinforcement was immediate. To compensate for immediate and short-term needs, the administration proposed to reactivate WWII moth-balled ships, such as the aircraft carrier *Oriskany* and battleships *New Jersey* and *Iowa*, and pressed its allies for greater contributions to the common defense. In particular, in the context of a more assertive posture toward the Soviet threat, termed the Maritime Strategy,[5] the Reagan administration sought greater naval contributions from Great Britain, Japan, and West Germany.[6]

Increased allied contributions to Atlantic and Pacific tasks would permit the United States to reallocate resources to meet the pressing need of a permanent Indian Ocean–Persian Gulf presence, establishing a three-ocean navy. As Secretary Weinberger noted in congressional testimony in September 1981, "the free world is better off with respect to likely threats in Europe and Northeast Asia...than we are with respect to Southwest Asia."[7] Thus, he continued, the United States was making several logical changes in its force planning.

First, "substantial portions of U.S. ground and air forces were reallocated from their previous Europe-reinforcing role to the Rapid Deployment Force which was oriented entirely toward Southwest Asia." Second, in-theater base facility improvements and equipment prepositioning were underway to accompany "augmented" strategic air and sea lift forces. And, finally, the increase in naval power would "enable the United States to threaten the Soviets with the prospects of a wider war if they began to get the upper hand there." The larger navy would ultimately "enable the United States to maintain naval deployments in European and East Asian waters and in the Southwest Asian region."[8]

The American strategic shift caught the allies moving in the opposite direction. This was particularly the case with Great Britain, which, under Prime Minister Margaret Thatcher, was not only in the midst of a severe economic downturn, but was also experiencing a leadership struggle over Great Britain's strategic orientation between Atlanticists and Continentalists. The Atlanticists under Thatcher sought to strengthen the traditional Anglo-American partnership at the expense of Europe, while the Continentalists sought the reverse. Within the government, the strategic argument centered on, but was not limited to, the differences between the prime minister and the Foreign Office. By the time that Ronald Reagan had entered office, both the economic and the strategic developments in Britain were of almost two years' duration and had reached critical levels.

The Reagan leadership quite naturally sought the resolution of both issues in ways that would strengthen Prime Minister Thatcher, who, perhaps alone among European allies, was supportive of the turn in American strategy. During late 1980, however, the prospects were not promising. Indeed, it appeared that Margaret Thatcher herself might not survive the economic crisis and that the "Continentalists" would prevail in the strategic argument. Within eighteen months, however, the situation would be reversed. Margaret Thatcher would engineer a turnaround in the British economy, defeat her political opponents, and solidify the Atlanticist strategic orientation with the United States. The reason for Thatcher's victory was largely attributable to the conflict over the Falkland Islands—a conflict both before and during which the United States played a significant role, both directly and indirectly.

Indeed, it would be accurate to state that Reagan and Thatcher reached a fateful coincidence of interests over policy toward Argentina, which led to the Falkland Islands War. The policies themselves were opposite—the United States sought to improve relations with Argentina, while Great Britain backpedaled on the issue of sovereignty over the Falkland Islands. Both policies, however, had the desired effect of accelerating the Argentine junta's plans to recapture the islands, creating a crisis from which Thatcher and Reagan would benefit most dramatically. Argentine defeat in war would eventually lead to the collapse of the military junta, the emergence of civilian rule, and abolition of the hitherto secret Argentine nuclear weapons program.

Thatcher's Crises

Upon entering office in May 1979, Margaret Thatcher considered her primary tasks were to dismantle Britain's welfare state structure and to revitalize the economy to propel the nation toward higher growth and prosperity.[9] The means through which she proposed to accomplish this task were different from former methods and proved controversial even within her own cabinet. Presaging many of Ronald Reagan's programs, Thatcher proposed nothing less than a restructuring of the British economic system—moving away from welfare statism toward a more firmly rooted, market-oriented economy. The fundamental key to promoting economic growth and higher productivity was the creation of economic conditions that would spur private initiative. The means to this end were believed to be a supply-side approach involving a reduction of the inflation rate and a shift of greater income back into the hands of the taxpayers.

Her initial policy proposal involved lowering the tax rate, reducing the money supply, cutting government spending, and raising interest rates.[10] The top marginal tax rate was reduced from 83 percent to 60 percent, and the basic rate from 33 to 30 percent. These cuts were to be financed by an increase in indirect taxes (the Value Added Tax, or the VAT) from 8 percent to 15 percent and an overall cut in government spending of 2.25 percent. Inflation would be controlled by a gradual reduction in the money supply, from an 8 to 12 percent range to a 7 to 11 percent range, and a 2 percent rise in interest rates. Controls over pay, prices, dividends, and the exchange rate were either ended or significantly ameliorated.[11]

Applied through 1979 and 1980, the results were disheartening. Inflation and unemployment continued to rise, seemingly unaffected by government policy. The reason was primarily because the arrival of the Thatcher government coincided with the onset of the second global oil crisis, which sparked a severe world recession, exacerbating inflation. The inflation was "unexpectedly deep," exerting a greater-than-expected impact on the economy.[12] The global recession was not the only reason for poor results, however. There were domestic reasons, as well.

By early 1980, it was also clear that Thatcher's economic policy was ineffective because of internal resistance to it. For example, the Bank of England—the central bank—had not reduced the money supply as planned. On the contrary, the money supply target was exceeded, and inflation had risen to more than 20 percent. Nor had there been any actual reduction in government spending. Cuts were made from the baseline budget—that is, from future projected spending. Thus, although there were cuts from projected spending, there were no reductions in actual spending, and tax cuts had failed to produce the desired response.

Ultimately, not only had economic conditions not improved, they had deteriorated, and the structure of the economy remained unchanged.[13] The promised turnaround had failed to materialize, and there seemed to be little apparent prospect for one. Furthermore, social conditions had deteriorated, punctuated by strikes and riots in many cities throughout the realm. By autumn 1980, as Cosgrave notes, "it seemed that the Thatcher experiment was crumbling to disaster."[14] Indeed, as the prime minister herself observed in her memoir, "The Party was worried, and so was I. Our strategy was the right one, but the price of putting it into effect was proving so high, and there was such limited understanding of what we were trying to do, that we had great electoral difficulties."[15]

Pressure grew from "wets" in the cabinet for the prime minister to change strategy. Francis Pym, Ian Gilmour, Mark Carlisle, and Christopher Soames were not inclined to persevere in an austere policy and urged her to execute a "U-turn," increase government spending, and reflate the economy as the previous Conservative prime minister, Ted Heath, had done in 1974.[16] Many, indeed, felt that the "wets" had prevailed—until Thatcher spoke out on the matter. In an address to the Conservative Party conference on October 10, 1980, she insisted that there would be no "U-turn." Britain would stay the course.

> To those waiting with bated breath for that favourite media catch-phrase, the 'U-turn', I have only one thing to say. 'You turn if you want to. The lady's not for turning.' I say that not only to you, but to our friends overseas—and also to those who are not our friends.[17]

The message, she said, "was directed as much to my colleagues in the Government as it was to politicians of other parties." Thatcher held firm, arguing that, while there were alternatives to what she proposed, "There Is No Alternative." Indeed, the acronym TINA became a powerful rhetorical weapon in the arsenal of arguments that swirled over Thatcher's policies.[18] Nevertheless, for a "worried" and beleaguered Margaret Thatcher, faced with "great electoral difficulties," the end of 1980 was a grim period. Her domestic policies had not produced expected results, and opposition to her was rising within the party, the government, and the nation. As Thatcher acknowledged: "Our credibility was at stake."[19]

Initial Foreign Policy Problems

On the foreign policy front, the situation was not much better. During the period of détente in the seventies, Great Britain had gradually moved toward closer relations with continental Europe and away from the special relationship with the United States. This was partly the inevitable corollary to Washington's effort of attempting to strengthen relations with Moscow and of withdrawing from forward positions in Eurasia. It was also partly a function of the longer-evolving, gradual constriction of Britain's imperial role.

Upon entering office in May 1979, Margaret Thatcher had sought to reverse the continental strategy and reestablish strong Atlantic ties, based on an anti-Soviet stance, which was initially encouraged by Carter's own halting turn away from détente that summer. The continental constituency within the Conservative Party, including several within the cabinet around Foreign Secretary Lord Peter Carrington, remained a powerful force, however, and strongly, yet subtly, exerted pressure in the opposite direction to that proposed by the prime minister.

Thus, the central strategic argument within the cabinet was the question of Britain's geopolitical orientation. Should London continue movement toward full collaboration with the European community or strengthen the Atlantic relationship with the United States? In this argument, Margaret Thatcher, in the minority in her own cabinet, found herself opposed by the Foreign Office, her foreign secretary, Peter Carrington, and several of the "wets," who argued in favor of closer cooperation with the community.[20]

Three additional issues formed the early battleground—negotiations over independence for Rhodesia/Zimbabwe; defense policy; and the Falklands. Overall, Thatcher's view prevailed on these issues, although there were compromises. Thatcher would block movement toward the European community; accept, but turn to her own advantage, the Foreign Office position of a more inclusive settlement for Rhodesia; compromise on defense policy by reluctantly accepting cuts; and stall on the issue of the Falkland Islands. It quickly became apparent that the prime minister knew where she wanted to go in foreign affairs and was determined to get there, despite formidable opposition.

Thatcher's main objective was to halt further movement toward integration into the European community. The means she chose was the issue of the size of the British contribution to the EEC budget, which represented less than

1 percent of total government spending. From the fall of 1979, Thatcher turned what the Foreign Office saw as a "regrettable problem which could be dealt with through goodwill on all sides...[into] a matter of fundamental difference."[21] Serving notice of her concern during a speech in Luxembourg on October 18, she declared, "I must be absolutely clear about this. Britain cannot accept the present situation on the Budget. It is demonstrably unjust. It is politically indefensible: I cannot play Sister Bountiful to the Community, while my own electorate are being asked to forego improvements."[22]

At the Dublin summit of the European powers in November, Thatcher reiterated that the British overpayment to the EEC of one billion pounds was excessive and must be returned. Believing either that Thatcher could not sustain this position or that a deal could be struck, the European leaders, principally Giscard d'Estaing and Helmut Schmidt, offered a package deal. In return for a "rebate" of an undisclosed amount, Britain would agree to sell North Sea oil below OPEC's current price, agree to include more of the UK's waters in the common fisheries agreement, and join the European Monetary System.[23]

Thatcher was incredulous at what was "a derisory offer."[24] In return for additional British concessions on oil, fish, and money, the community would rebate part of Britain's financial contribution! Undaunted, she retorted that she simply "wanted her money back, and that was all there was to be said about the matter."[25] Carrington sought to "persuade" her to be more flexible, avoiding a confrontation with the EEC, but she would have none of it, refusing a proffered rebate of 350 million pounds. The Dublin meeting broke up in "deadlock and confusion."

The European press began to refer to Thatcher as a "she-de Gaulle" because of her vigorous pursuit of British national interests.[26] Many thought she had gone too far. As Thatcher noted: "In some circles the very last thing expected of a British prime minister was that he or she should quite so unashamedly defend British interests."[27] This missed the point, however. Of course, she sought the placement of immovable obstacles, intractable problems, and interminable arguments, precisely to prevent closer cooperation with the community. The means chosen was confrontation, but the issue was strategy.

After a series of summit meetings through May 1980, Carrington reached a compromise of sorts in Brussels on the amount of rebate for earlier British contributions. It was also agreed to seek a permanent solution to the budgetary imbalance. The result was that Britain's net contribution was set at just under 200 million pounds annually for 1979–1981. Thatcher was dissatisfied with what she considered to be Carrington's "sleight of hand," but decided not to overrule him.[28] The foreign secretary had taken a stand, informing her that "he would support no other course, knowing that at least half-a-dozen colleagues and seventy Tory MPs would side with him and split the Government...," so she accepted.[29]

This was not the end of it, however. Although she accepted Carrington's compromise on the budget issue, Thatcher subsequently raised more fundamental concerns. From 1982 onward, following her Falklands triumph, the prime minister would insist that both the community's Common Agricultural Policy (CAP) and the general system of EEC financing be reformed "root and branch" before she would permit any further talk of community integration.[30] In other words, Thatcher demanded nothing less than the complete reorganization of the EEC before British membership could even be considered. As it was highly unlikely that the community would consent to such a fundamental reorganization, Thatcher had placed a very effective obstacle to any further British movement into the EEC, which would remain in place for as long as she was prime minister.

The Rhodesian Solution

The Rhodesia issue had bedeviled successive British governments since 1965 when Ian Smith declared independence. Smith's act had immediately triggered a costly guerrilla war with dissident black forces grouped around a Patriotic Front led by Robert Mugabe and Joshua Nkomo. Britain pursued a sanctions policy through the UN, pledging a return to legality and black majority rule. Sanctions, however, proved highly ineffective, as "even the Black African states hardly observed it."[31]

The collapse of the Portuguese Empire, however, exerted effective sanctions on Ian Smith because it led to the cutoff of supplies that had formerly gone through Mozambique. Forced to come to terms with the black majority to remain in power, Smith struck a deal with the black Bishop Abel Muzorewa. Their collaboration centered on establishing the form of black majority rule while safeguarding the reality of white control.[32] Elections were held in April 1979, and Muzorewa became prime minister of Rhodesia. The elections had been reasonably free, but the Patriotic Front had boycotted them, which rendered the outcome ambiguous.

The Conservative Party had committed itself to dropping sanctions against Rhodesia, provided that the elections were free and fair. Margaret Thatcher, while party leader since 1975, had said relatively little about Rhodesia. She had, however, hinted that she favored recognizing the Smith-Muzorewa regime. Thus, it was assumed that, as prime minister, she would accept the recent election results and drop sanctions, which would extricate Britain from a draining entanglement.[33]

Secretary Carrington and the Foreign Office, as well as the United States and Australia, opposed this course on the grounds that it would maintain the status quo, exclude the Black Patriotic Front, perpetuate the violence, and lead to a confrontation between Black Africa and Great Britain. Carrington instead proposed an inclusive settlement as a means of resolving Britain's commitment. Although Carrington saw this effort as a "damage limitation exercise," Thatcher "wanted to do better than that."[34]

Prime Minister Thatcher agreed to back away from the "defective" April election results on the grounds that "the white minority could block all unwelcome constitutional change."[35] Instead, she seized the initiative with a politically aggressive formula that disarmed her critics and led to a successful resolution of an intractable problem. Thatcher proposed to set aside the recent election and, instead, hold a constitutional conference under British chairmanship. Britain would supervise and police new elections, in which all would participate. Smith and Muzorewa would submit to this formula and all dissident forces would lay down their arms (although Rhodesian government forces would not).[36]

The Lancaster House conference in mid-September 1979 produced an agreement to have new elections in which Muzorewa, Nkomo, and Mugabe would be the candidates. The surprising result was the overwhelming victory of the Marxist guerrilla leader Robert Mugabe. On the basis of free, British-sponsored elections, the British colony of Rhodesia was dissolved, and the new, independent state of Zimbabwe was created. The solution fulfilled Britain's pledge to bring about legitimate, black majority rule even while safeguarding parliamentary power for whites in a settlement that would endure for several years. Civil strife would resume, but not until after Britain had quit its responsibility.

Secretary Carrington conducted the negotiations skillfully, effecting a satisfactory conclusion to a nagging foreign policy issue. Although Carrington's reputation as a negotiator was enhanced by his performance, Thatcher emerged with the stature of a decisive stateswoman. As one black African leader noted: "The voice was his voice, the thought was hers." Indeed, Thatcher later declared that the settlement had infused new life in the nation as a whole. Speaking of it a few months later, she said: "We are once more a nation capable of action rather than reaction."[37]

Early Defense Choices

If Thatcher concluded the Rhodesian issue satisfactorily, the decision on British defense policy was a case of an unsatisfactory compromise. In attempting to fulfill the NATO pledge of a 3 percent increase in defense spending, the British leadership was forced to make several tough choices. Determined to preserve Britain's independent deterrent, Thatcher actively negotiated the acquisition of the U.S. Trident submarine to replace the aging Polaris system. Modernization of the nuclear deterrent was necessary and costly—$10 billion overall. It was argued, however, that this would be less than other alternatives, reportedly including the cruise missile alternative. Still, the original decision to acquire five new submarines was revised to four. Even more important, the entire cost of Trident was to come from the navy budget, instead of being spread throughout the defense budget as Polaris had been.[38] The effect was to reduce severely the funds available for the rest of the fleet.

Second, Thatcher strongly supported the December 1979 NATO decision to deploy 572 long-range theater nuclear weapons to counter the large Soviet SS-20 force. For Great Britain, this meant the deployment on British soil of 160 American-owned ground-launched cruise missiles on forty launchers. The original number had been 144, but Helmut Schmidt prevailed upon Thatcher to take an additional flight, so he could reduce the number he would be required to take.[39] The two sites for the deployment were Greenham Common in Berkshire and Molesworth in Cambridgeshire, which quickly became targets for the growing nuclear disarmament movement that surged across Western Europe in the early eighties.

Both the Trident and cruise missile decisions clearly represented Thatcher's determination to pursue policies that would strengthen Atlantic partnership with the United States. Indeed, there was the suggestion of a quid pro quo in the Trident and INF decisions; in return for a favorable price for Trident, Britain supported deployment of ground-launched cruise missiles. There was additional speculation that the quid pro quo included "tilting of future procurement toward the U.S. and British aloofness from any independent European policy that might annoy Washington."[40] Such speculation was premature.

In the spring of 1981, in what was a very unusual, if not unprecedented, step, newly appointed Defense Secretary John Nott decided to revisit the just completed defense review. Within a two-month period ending in June 1981, Nott made a series of sharp cuts in the Royal Navy, which moved sharply counter to both the spirit and the reality of Atlantic partnership. Thatcher was most reluctant to agree to these cuts, reportedly reacting "with almost tearful resentment" against the Treasury, which insisted that defense would have to be "trimmed and rearranged."[41] As such, the defense cuts announced at that time represented an undeniable victory (albeit temporary, as it turned out) for the Continentalists.

The acquisition of Trident had been justified on the grounds that accrued savings would be shifted to strengthen the conventional force, but the reverse occurred. The essence of the defense decision was a significant planned reduction of the British surface navy to permit, it was said, funding of the Trident missile system.[42] The major thrust of Nott's review was Britain's commitment to European defense through NATO—maintaining the forward defense of West Germany—and the newly discovered need to strengthen the defense of Britain itself. Thus, the British Army on the Rhine (BOAR) would be maintained, suffering only a small cut from fifty-seven thousand troops to fifty-five thousand, while the Home Defense would be strengthened, particularly through augmentation of the Royal Air Force and expansion of the territorial army. The total air force was to increase by a third; the territorial army by a fourth.[43]

Reduction of the Royal Navy was a severe blow to American strategy, as Britain would have insufficient naval forces to compensate for the redeployment of U.S. ships to the Persian Gulf area. As it was, the surface force represented "70 percent" of NATO's naval presence in the eastern Atlantic and the English Channel. The planned cutback from sixty-five surface ships to forty-two over four years would severely erode antisubmarine warfare coverage and convoy capability. The reduction was ostensibly to fifty, but eight frigates would be placed on "standby" status—that is, they would be kept in port, assigned only skeleton crews.[44] That represented an immediate and drastic cut, for the number of truly operational escort ships would be in the low thirties, given refit and maintenance rotation schedules.

Carriers, already downsized, would be reduced from three to two, which meant that only one would be operational at any one time. Indeed, during the summer, the sale of HMS *Invincible* was announced to Australia. HMS *Invincible* was one of two then-operational carriers, along with HMS *Hermes*. These two carriers would form the core of the task force sent to repossess the Falkland Islands. (British carriers were barely one-fourth the size of their American counterparts. HMS *Invincible*, for example, was the largest of Britain's modern ASW carriers at nineteen thousand tons. The U.S.S. *Nimitz* weighed in at ninety thousand tons.) The lack of large-deck aircraft carriers meant that the fleet could not mount major operations on the high seas, for it lacked the ability to provide suitable air cover for itself. Air cover would have to be provided by land-based air, limiting the navy's area of operations. Nor could the fleet provide self-contained early airborne warning against attack.

Britain's only two assault ships, HMS *Fearless* and HMS *Intrepid*, were to be decommissioned, meaning that a contested amphibious landing would be nearly impossible. The submarine force was to be reduced from twenty to seventeen and several fleet auxiliary ships were to be disposed of prematurely. To top it all off, HMS *Endurance*, Britain's only naval presence in the South Atlantic, was to be withdrawn in March 1982. The defense cuts, particularly the draconian paring of the Royal Navy, were justified in terms of the need to reduce government spending in a time of economic travail.

Not only would Britain's NATO maritime responsibilities be reduced, but "out of area" operations would be sharply curtailed. The decision, which American leaders attempted to forestall, imposed an increased burden on the United States to maintain sea lane security across the Atlantic.[45] This added burden came just as the Reagan administration was straining to shift naval assets to the Indian Ocean to counter Soviet pressure in Southwest Asia. Worse, London's decision came at the same time that Tokyo was making similar cutbacks. Thus, the United States would find it increasingly difficult to shift ships away from either the Atlantic or the Pacific.

Profoundly disturbing at the time, in light of the subsequent war in the Falkland Islands, the stated rationale—cost effectiveness—for the drastic reduction of Britain's capability to project naval power far beyond home waters became increasingly dubious. Each decision was logical enough, but in toto unnecessarily premature. The entire circumstance of Nott's "review" was extraordinary, immediately following a newly completed defense review. And then, Nott's effort took only two months' time to decide future defense posture for a decade ahead. Was gutting the surface fleet, including carriers, frigates, destroyers, and assault ships, the core of any British ability to project power beyond home waters, economic, or part of the "Falklands Sting"?

"The most cost-effective maritime mix," Secretary Nott said, "will be one which continues to enhance our maritime-air and submarine effort, but accepts a reduction below current plans in the size of our surface fleet."[46] The scale and sophistication of shipbuilding would be reduced and mid-life modernization would be eliminated. "A rather smaller but modern fleet...will give better value for defense resources." The "cost-effective" rationale could not withstand scrutiny, however, and raised the question—If the purpose was not to save money, what was it?

Navy minister Keith Speed objected to the naval cuts and was peremptorily sacked. The principal thrust of his criticism was that the naval drawdown was premature and lost, rather than saved, money. The aircraft carrier, HMS *Invincible*, for example, was only eighteen months old, had a life expectancy of twenty years, would cost $500 million to replace, yet was earmarked for sale to Australia for $250 million.[47] Furthermore, the circumstances surrounding the sale of HMS *Invincible* were unusual. Admiral Sir Henry Leach, First Sea Lord at the time, although present when the decision was made, expressed his complete bafflement about how it was made. When he enquired about it he could "never get any explanation." During lunch with the Australian defense minister, the subject of the sale of HMS *Invincible* "came as a complete surprise." The decision lacked any "rational philosophy, except for this driving thing of saving money [but] what was fundamentally wrong...was that it was not backed by professional argument at all."[48]

Although the decision to sell HMS *Invincible* may have been extraordinary, the effect of the sale upon navy operations was utterly predictable. Reducing the carriers from three to two meant that two would never be operational together. One would always be under repair. One carrier, with but a handful of aircraft, ten on average, had no self-contained airborne early warning capability and would not be able to operate beyond the range of land-based air support. Britain's carrier would be restricted to European waters and to operations in conjunction with other allied navies. There could be no question of conducting independent naval operations on the high seas.

The Antarctic patrol ship, HMS *Endurance*, which was to be withdrawn the following spring, "had many years of good life ahead of her," and cost the nominal sum of $5 million a year to operate. HMS *Endurance* was Britain's only semipermanent presence in the South Atlantic, and its withdrawal broadly signaled British disinterest in maintaining its Antarctic possessions. Furthermore, contrary to Secretary Nott's assertion that the attack submarines were to be part of the "maritime mix," they were also to be reduced. Additionally, several fleet auxiliaries, tankers, and supply ships were to be "prematurely disposed of."

Dockyard closures and reductions at Chatham, Portsmouth, and later at Gibraltar were supposed to effect a net savings of $200 million a year by 1985. But when closing costs were calculated—resettlement payments, unemployment pay for total job losses of thirteen thousand, and special aid to Gibraltar, including retraining and relocation costs, the savings were minimal, if any.[49] Early closures of the dockyards also meant no mid-life modernization for ships, which usually remain in service for twenty years. Without mid-life modernization, Nott's "rather smaller but modern fleet" would either become obsolete in service or require high-cost replacements.

Having decided to change and reduce the composition of the surface fleet, Prime Minister Thatcher obviously understood that there could be no defense of the Falkland Islands, but there was no decision to fortify the islands. Combined with the rapid growth of Argentine military power, the obvious and necessary policy course should have been to reach agreement with Buenos Aires, and the sooner the better. Yet, Margaret Thatcher did neither. Indeed, the Thatcher government backed away from an earlier governmental commitment to negotiate a transfer of sovereignty and came to rest on the position that the "wishes" of the Falkland Islanders would be decisive. In other words, Thatcher's decision was to do nothing—that is, to stall—a decision that would be very provocative.

The Falklands Stall: Thatcher Versus Carrington

The split between Prime Minister Thatcher and the "wets" on European community, Rhodesia, and defense policy issues, was even more manifest on the issue of the Falkland Islands. Foreign Secretary Carrington doggedly sought to resolve the dispute, divesting Britain of the islands. In his view, expressed in a minute to the prime minister on September 20, 1979, lease-back, as opposed to Fortress Falklands or a simple stall, was the "solution best fitted to meet the Government's objectives and the wishes of the Island-ers."[50] Carrington "asked for agreement" to his recommendation that "substantive negotiation on sovereignty" proceed forthwith. Thatcher refused. In her view, "the problem could not be rushed." Instead, the issue should be fully aired in the Cabinet Defence Committee (OD).

Undeterred, Carrington sent another memorandum to Thatcher on October 12 proposing the same argument, but pointing out the consequences if his recommendation were not accepted. Anything other than a transfer of sovereignty through leaseback, he said, would carry "a serious threat of invasion" (para. 75). Prime Minister Thatcher once again demurred, this time arguing for even longer postponement. "Discussion of the Falkland Islands by the Defence Committee," she replied, "should be postponed until after the Rhodesian issue had been settled." The Joint Intelligence Committee (JIC), directly subordinate to the prime minister's office, produced an assessment later in November that reinforced the prime minister's position and undercut that of Carrington. The JIC assessment concluded with the view that:

> While the Argentine Government would prefer to achieve their sovereignty objectives by peaceful means, if negotiations broke down or if for some other reason the Argentine Government calculated that the British Government were not prepared to negotiate seriously on sovereignty, there would be a high-risk of their resorting quickly to more forceful measures against British interests; and that in such circumstances direct military action against British shipping or against the Falkland Islands could not be discounted, although the risk of such action would not be as high as hitherto. (para. 77)

The JIC, in other words, directly contradicted Carrington's view that there was "a serious threat of invasion," unless negotiations on the transfer of sovereignty were begun immediately. It implicitly supported Thatcher's more cautious view of postponing discussion until a more propitious time, since the risk of invasion was "not...as high as hitherto."

The JIC assessment settled the matter for the moment, but, on January 24, 1980, barely a month following the Rhodesia/Zimbabwe elections, Carrington sent another minute to Thatcher. He advised that "exploratory talks... should be started soon since to continue to stall could be risky" (para. 78). As before, however, the decision went against Carrington. The Defence Committee meeting a few days later concluded that "it was undesirable that talks should be resumed on the basis of the terms of reference announced by the previous Government in April 1977."

In other words, Thatcher had decided against holding talks on the transfer of sovereignty, the explicit position of the April 26, 1977, policy statement. That statement read, in part, that the governments of Great Britain and Argentina had "agreed to hold negotiations...which will concern future political relations, including sovereignty, with regard to the Falkland Islands, South Georgia, and South Sandwich Islands." These "negotiations will be directed to the working out of a peaceful solution to the existing dispute on sovereignty between the two states" (para. 60).

Instead, Carrington was instructed to "seek written confirmation from the Falkland Islands Council that it was its wish that talks with the Argentine Government should be resumed" (para. 78). Thatcher may have assumed that the answer would be negative. Surprisingly, the FIC did agree to talks. Before they took place, however, Thatcher ensured that the delegation would reflect her own position. During the April talks in New York, the British delegation now included for the first time a representative from the Falkland Islands Council.

The presence of a "delegate" from the FIC ensured that negotiations between Great Britain and Argentina would reach a stalemate. What emerged from the talks was not surprisingly "a fundamental difference of opinion" over sovereignty. The Argentines insisted on negotiating a transfer of sovereignty while the British delegation attempted to deflect the issue with expressions of hope that their differences would not "inhibit further discussion of the possibility of cooperation on the development and conservation of the resources of the South West Atlantic." But the issue was sovereignty, not resources (para. 79).

Carrington persisted in attempting to change Thatcher's view. In July, he sent "a further memorandum" to the prime minister requesting a review of the position. Now the Defence Committee, in another reversal, agreed "to attempt to reach a solution of the dispute on the basis of a leaseback arrangement." Carrington apparently had won. But had he? Although the Cabinet Defence Committee now agreed on leaseback, Thatcher had not. Under great pressure, the prime minister continued to stall. It would be more than three months before the matter would be addressed again. At a Defence Committee meeting on November 7, it was decided once again to consult the islanders before making a decision. Toward the end of 1980, just as Ronald Reagan was being elected, pressure was clearly building on Thatcher to agree to leaseback for the Falklands.

Junior Minister of State Nicholas Ridley would go to the Falkland Islands, November 22–29, "to discover the level of support there for such an arrangement" (para. 80). Discussing the various options with the inhabitants, he reported that regarding leaseback "Islander opinion appeared to be divided, with a substantial minority opposed to it and the majority undecided" (para. 81). When Ridley returned and appeared in the House of Commons on December 2 to make a statement in favor of leaseback, he received "a very hostile reception from all sides of the House" (para. 82).

Cabinet ministers meeting two days later noted that "Islanders' hostility to Mr. Ridley's approach seemed to have been exaggerated" by members of Parliament. But was it? On January 6, 1981, the Falkland Islands Council met and passed a motion objecting to "any of the ideas put forward by Mr. Ridley," but agreed to hold further talks. The explicit purpose of such talks, however, was to "seek agreement to freeze the dispute over sovereignty" (para. 83). It seemed that both in Great Britain and in the Falkland Islands sentiment was absolutely opposed to leaseback.

Seemingly stymied, Carrington carried on, sending yet another memorandum in mid-January to the Defence Committee asking for yet another review. In his memorandum, Carrington noted that the islanders' response "was less than had been hoped for, but they had given a mandate for future talks, although the idea of a freeze…was unlikely to be acceptable" (para. 84). It was Carrington's recommendation that negotiations should continue "to let the Islanders come to see the need to explore a realistic settlement based on leaseback." The Defence Committee endorsed Carrington's view and the following month Ridley held talks in New York with the Argentines. This time the British delegation included two councillors from the FIC who proposed the freeze—an idea that the Argentines "rejected outright." Following the February 1981 meeting, Carrington hoped that the islanders would "come to see" the necessity of leaseback, but acknowledged that everything would have to await the outcome of FIC elections in the fall.

Meanwhile, in March 1981, a change of government had occurred in Argentina with Robert Viola succeeding the departed Jorge Videla. The transition offered Thatcher an opportunity to delay further through the spring. In mid-year, the Foreign Office held a major review, which occurred parallel to, and simultaneous with, the Defence Policy review. While the Defence Policy decision, as we have seen, was to eliminate progressively Britain's ability to protect the islands, the Foreign Office decision was to "play for time" on the Falklands. A "campaign of public education" was proposed for the islanders, who, according to Gov. Rex Hunt, still "wished to have nothing whatsoever to do with the Argentines" (para. 90–93).

Following the Foreign Office review, and undoubtedly influenced by the Defence Policy Review, the JIC now produced a new assessment of the Falkland Islands in early July, the first since November 1979. In answer to the question of what the Argentines would do if they decided to "resort to direct measures," JIC offered a carefully graduated set of possible responses. Buenos Aires could:

- Denounce Great Britain in the United Nations for "bad faith."
- Place an air and fuel embargo on the islands.
- Take action against British economic interests in Argentina.
- Harass ships using Port Stanley.
- Carry out a landing on South Georgia.
- Execute "pin-prick" incidents, such as a "freelance" landing on the main islands.
- Occupy an uninhabited island of the Falkland group.
- Conduct a full-scale invasion.[51]

The list of options that JIC believed were available to Argentina had not substantially changed since its previous estimate, but its assessment of the junta's willingness to take action had. In the 1979 assessment, JIC had noted that "direct military action against British shipping or against the Falkland Islands could not be discounted, although 'the risk of such action would not be as high as hitherto'." In the July 1981 estimate, JIC had deleted the phrase downgrading the risk of direct military action and inserted a phrase raising the possibility of "full-scale invasion." Thus, the final paragraph read "military action against British shipping or a full-scale invasion of the Falkland Islands could not be discounted" (para. 77 and 95).

On July 20, Minister Ridley now sent a minute to Carrington outlining three options. London could proceed to negotiate with Buenos Aires without islanders' approval but conditional on their ultimate agreement; conduct an educational campaign or stall and "let Argentina conclude that the Government would not discuss sovereignty, and to set in hand contingency action to deal with the consequences" (para. 96). Ridley recommended against the first option on the grounds that it would violate the policy of acting in accordance with the islanders' wishes and opposed the last option on the grounds that it would be too costly and lead to a military confrontation with Argentina. He recommended the second option—an educational campaign—proposing that the matter be discussed at the next Defence Committee meeting scheduled for September.

On September 7, Carrington, Ian Gilmour, and Ridley discussed the issue and prepared a paper for consideration by the Defence Committee, recommending the education campaign. But there the matter ended. Margaret Thatcher now acted to terminate the internal discussion. There would be no meeting to discuss the paper. As the Foreign Office explained in a letter communicating the decision to Ambassador Williams in Buenos Aires: "domestic political constraints...continue to prevent us from taking any steps which might be interpreted either as putting pressure on the Islanders or as overruling their wishes. Specifically that meant that an education campaign...has, at least for the present, been ruled out" (para. 99).

"Domestic political constraints," of course, referred to the prime minister, who had decided against "educating" the Islanders into accepting leaseback. Furthermore, there would be no Defence Committee meeting to discuss the Falkland Islands issue either, because of "the absence of any immediate danger of hostile Argentine reactions" (para. 99). Carrington had been beaten. In a minute to Thatcher on September 14 acknowledging defeat, Carrington declared that he would inform the Argentine government that London could proceed "only in accordance with the wishes of the Islanders" (para. 100).

Meanwhile, Ambassador Williams reacted strongly against "the idea… that the wishes of the islanders could possibly be a paramount consideration in British policy." In his view, the decision against an education campaign "was to have no strategy at all beyond a general Micawberism" (para. 104). It had to be recognized, he said, that the "unguided wishes" of the islanders were unlikely to "provide even a grudging acceptance of sovereignty transfer in any form." Furthermore, he protested that "the OD meeting had not taken place."[52]

> Why…we needed to go to OD, was that we were saying, in these circumstances, that one alternative is to make concessions, the other alternative is to be tougher. But being tougher involves a re-examination of what you're prepared to spend. This is what really needed to be taken into account.[53]

But when Lord Carrington met with Argentine Foreign Minister Oscar Camilion in New York on September 23, he received an unexpected reaction. Carrington dutifully informed Camilion of the British government's position that the islanders' wishes were paramount, and received the standard Argentine reply that the islanders could not be permitted to "veto" the negotiations. Carrington then acknowledged, perhaps going beyond his brief, that "the present status quo is difficult to sustain today" (para. 102–3). Although the Argentine foreign minister insisted that the key question was sovereignty and that negotiations must be between Argentina and Great Britain, the exchange had not been rancorous and Camilion "emerged visibly satisfied from the talks" (para. 103).

After all that had been said over the previous year-and-a-half regarding Argentine determination to recover the Malvinas, including a readiness to invade the islands, it seemed that President Viola was in no hurry. In subsequent discussions, in October, Camilion informed Carrington that "meaningful negotiations would have to be long and difficult," and Buenos Aires was prepared for a "protracted dialogue" (para. 105). Argentina's new position was unmistakable. Viola was far less eager to acquire the islands than Carrington was to divest them. The reasons for the change in Buenos Aires' approach toward the Falklands will be discussed in a later chapter.

The Foreign Office was especially pleased, or rather relieved, at what was thought to be a constructive attitude, not only because it got them off a very painful hook, but because conditions had changed sharply for the worse in the Falkland Islands themselves. The long-awaited elections to the Falkland Islands Council on October 14 had produced a "hardening" of attitude. All of those elected were opposed to transfer of sovereignty, or even discussion of the subject.

By autumn 1981, two fundamental shifts had occurred. Under Prime Minister Thatcher's guidance, the British government had drawn away from the Callaghan government's decision to enter into negotiations for the transfer of sovereignty. The long struggle between Thatcher and Carrington had been resolved in favor of the prime minister. The decision-point in Carrington's campaign in favor of leaseback had come in December 1980, paralleling Ronald Reagan's election in the United States. Perhaps more surprising was the shift in the attitude of the Argentine government. Under President Viola, the Argentine government had accepted the British shift of position on the Falkland Islands and had agreed to lengthy negotiations. But this happy state of affairs would not last. A change of leadership in Buenos Aires in mid-December 1981, marking the rise of Leopoldo Galtieri to power, would quickly lead to yet another change of position.

Reagan and Thatcher: A Coincidence of Interests

The critical period for Margaret Thatcher was the end of 1980, when the prospects for her political longevity were at their gloomiest. At this point, several developments occurred that would change her fortune. There was, literally, a sustaining silver lining in the political and economic gloom. First was the economic windfall of North Sea oil, which offered a secure financial reserve to support any plans she might have for the economy. Then, there was the fundamental weakness of her opposition, in both parties, which had become apparent by then and which meant that there would be no serious challenge to her leadership. Finally, but most important, was the election of Ronald Reagan, whose needs were nearly identical to those of the prime minister.

North Sea oil had come on-line in 1976, but, although production had increased over the next four years, by 1979, Great Britain was still a net, though declining, importer.[54] In 1980, Great Britain achieved self-sufficiency and from 1981 became a net exporter. As Young notes, "the first Thatcher Government would coincide with the swift escalation of production of North Sea oil, the greatest uncovenanted economic blessing the country had ever enjoyed."[55] Becoming an oil exporter at the period of the highest petroleum prices in history was a windfall for both the country and Margaret Thatcher. Not only did it allow her to proceed with her policies reasonably confident about the political limits of economic risk, it also enabled the country to pass through the difficult, wrenching transition she sought to engineer maintaining real income at a "reasonably high level."[56] North Sea oil revenue, in essence, would be a safety net covering short-term balance of payments problems during the period when needed, but destabilizing and painful structural changes were occurring in the economy.

The second development was the absence of a cohesive opposition within Parliament, the Conservative Party, the government, and in the cabinet itself. The opposition Labour Party had split in two, enabling Thatcher, ultimately, to disregard its increasingly strident charges. Careful cultivation of back-bench support in Parliament assured support there for the prime minister, particularly against those opposed to her in the Conservative Party. Clever orchestration of the decision-making process, enabled Thatcher to bypass or outmaneuver what might otherwise be difficult obstacles within government and cabinet. The "wets," as she termed the "moderates," never coalesced into a coherent opposition and, while voicing objections to policies individually, were collectively ineffectual.[57] Thatcher was able to identify her opponents and mark them for eventual removal, or neutralization, or both.

Of utmost significance for Margaret Thatcher and the strategic debate within the British leadership was the election of Ronald Reagan and the support provided by his strong advocacy of the strategy of containment, as well as the policies underpinning it. Reagan's election, which Thatcher saw as "of immediate and fundamental importance," reinforced the tentative turn initiated by Jimmy Carter during the summer of 1979.[58] Reagan would consistently, from the beginning of his administration and during the most troublesome times, associate himself wholeheartedly with Thatcher, rebuilding the tarnished Anglo-American "special relationship."[59]

For American strategy, the return to containment required a change in Great Britain's role. Under the new world order strategy, Britain's future lay in joining and augmenting the defense of the continent, as the United States pulled back. Thus, from 1973, under both conservative and labour governments, Great Britain moved gradually, if haltingly, toward closer union.

Under the strategy of containment, Britain's role was, once again, to act as the bridge to the continent for the United States, and thus to remain separate and independent of the continent. A return to this role naturally presupposed that there were British leaders with similar ideas, which was no easy assumption.

Margaret Thatcher was one of only a handful of Conservative Party politicians still predisposed toward an anti-Soviet strategy. She had come to power in May 1979, just before former President Carter's realization that the new world order strategy would not succeed. Carter's halting turn away from the new world order posture was greeted warmly by Thatcher, particularly after the Soviet invasion of Afghanistan. Thus, by the time of Ronald Reagan's election as president in November 1980, the basis for a coincidence of interests between the United States and Great Britain had already begun to emerge. Indeed, Reagan's immediately proffered support (Thatcher was his first major visitor) was all the more necessary because the prime minister had been weakened by the initial failure of her economic policies.[60] In fact, her popularity would continue to plummet throughout 1981 and by December she would become "the most unpopular prime minister since polls began."[61]

The coincidence of interest between Reagan and Thatcher went beyond the obvious need to bolster NATO and provide for the means by which the United States could reinforce Western European forces in the event of a Soviet invasion. It encompassed Thatcher's own political viability without which Britain's role in containment could not be maintained. Finally, and most important, the Reagan-Thatcher coincidence of interest occurred relative to American strategic objectives in the western hemisphere, specifically and most immediately involving Argentina.

American strategy toward the western hemisphere and Argentina had undergone an unannounced change because of two relatively recent and very ominous developments. Since World War II, the United States had pursued, with varying success, two primary objectives in the hemisphere—promoting the emergence of democratic regimes and maintaining a nuclear weapons-free region.[62] By the late 1970s, aside from Central America and the Caribbean, Washington had become increasingly concerned about both prospects in South America. Particularly in the southern cone, Argentina, Brazil, and Chile were all ruled by military dictatorships, and two of the three were conducting a secret race to construct a nuclear weapons capability. Both Brazil and Argentina had embarked upon ambitious clandestine schemes to develop and produce nuclear weapons under the cover of public nuclear power programs.[63]

The United States had unsuccessfully attempted to prohibit the introduction of nuclear technology into the hemisphere, objecting to a 1975, $2 billion, West German-Brazilian agreement whereby Bonn would provide both enrichment and reprocessing technology in return for Brazilian uranium.[64] Despite American professions of concern regarding the potential for nuclear proliferation, the Bonn government under Chancellor Helmut Schmidt refused to be dissuaded. Indeed, as discussed in the previous chapter, West German, as well as Canadian and Swiss, firms had contracted to build nuclear plants for Argentina, too. The nuclear genie had been let loose in South America.

Indeed, it would be principally the rapid development of Argentina's nuclear and ballistic missile programs that would produce under Ronald Reagan the U.S. side of the coincidence of interests with Great Britain. Margaret Thatcher's political needs would produce the other. It may well be true, as Russell Lewis says, that "Mrs. Thatcher's popular ascendancy was already established before the Falklands crisis broke," but her ascendancy had decidedly not been established when the decision was made to provoke it.[65]

CHAPTER 3

•••

Reagan and Galtieri: Encouraging Delusions of Grandeur

The junta's secret decision to acquire a nuclear weapons capability pushed the issue of the transformation of Argentine politics to the forefront. It goes without saying that the United States, deeply concerned about the prospects of nuclear proliferation worldwide, would not passively acquiesce in the emergence of a nuclear-armed state in its own hemisphere. The question was how to prevent it. The record of American policy toward Argentina, 1980–1982, indicates that the United States pursued a devious, indirect, but highly successful policy that resulted in the overthrow of Argentina's military dictatorship, its replacement by civilian rule, and the latter's decision to make public and abandon the previous regime's secret nuclear weapons program.

Argentine Nuclear Plans and the U.S. Response

Beginning in 1980, following the discovery of the junta's secret weapons program, the United States under President Jimmy Carter reversed the policy of self-estrangement from Buenos Aires initiated by Carter himself. Then, under President Ronald Reagan, the United States embraced the junta, promoting the emergence of a pro-American leadership in Buenos Aires on the explicit grounds of developing an Argentine-American alliance. Finally, on the basis of expectations of American support, the United States encouraged the pro-American junta to embark upon a disastrous military adventure that led to its eclipse.

53

The Reagan administration's effusive embrace of the Argentine junta can hardly be explained by Jeane Kirkpatrick's *Commentary* essay "Dictatorships and Double Standards," in which she distinguished between authoritarian and Communist dictatorships and made the intellectual case for dealing with the former. This was a key justification for the administration's actions, to be sure, as, from the outset, the Reagan administration sought to develop a close and cooperative relationship with the junta. Of course, an improvement in relations was the sine qua non of any attempt to influence the junta's behavior, but President Reagan had not initiated the policy reversal toward Argentina—President Carter had.

Although little was mentioned publicly, from the mid-seventies, the nuclear programs in both Argentina and Brazil raised great U.S. concern about the future prospect of nuclear proliferation in Latin America. This was particularly true when both states embarked upon the construction of reprocessing and enrichment facilities (for which West Germany was supplying technology). The Carter administration was immediately attentive, for it advanced the date when either state would potentially acquire a nuclear weapons capability. Regarding Argentina, for example, a secret State Department report warned:

> Argentina's capability in the nuclear field, announced plans for a national nuclear industry and prospects for nuclear growth, including eventually a nuclear weapons capability, remain a source of concern for the United States.[1]

Although the report is undated, it probably was written after the announcement that Buenos Aires intended to expand its nuclear facilities, but before American intelligence had discovered the parallel secret program. It is, by the way, highly doubtful that the secret enrichment facility at Pilcaniyeu remained hidden from American intelligence for very long. The United States was extremely sensitive to nuclear proliferation issues, particularly the prospect of a nuclear arms race between Latin America's two largest states. In addition, U.S. and British intelligence had long since broken Argentina's code system, which made it highly probable that intelligence agencies would scrutinize Argentine nuclear projects and reach the appropriate conclusions.[2]

Under Jimmy Carter, testifying to proliferation concerns, Washington had sought unsuccessfully to obtain the cancellation of the West German-Brazilian nuclear contract and equally unsuccessfully to pressure Argentina through criticizing its human rights practices. The United States placed an embargo on arms sales (the Humphrey-Kennedy Amendment), stopped sales of all nuclear and nuclear-related equipment to Argentina, and unsuccessfully attempted to ban the reprocessing of irradiated fuel from which plutonium could be recovered.[3]

It was undoubtedly the discovery of Argentina's secret nuclear weapons program that prompted President Carter, in early 1980, to "revise" his policy of critical detachment toward Argentina based on human rights abuses. This revision was made all the more difficult by Argentina's defiance of Carter's grain embargo on the Soviet Union for its invasion of Afghanistan, as Buenos Aires promptly stepped in to replace the grain Moscow lost from the United States. It was also difficult because of the great emphasis placed earlier on human rights criticism. Publicly, Carter's turnabout was attributed to "evidence" that the "military authorities were restraining the worst of the violence by the security forces."[4]

Although it was true that the rate of arbitrary arrests had diminished by 1980, that alone was insufficient to explain Carter's action. Discovery of the scope of Argentina's secret nuclear weapons program is the much more likely explanation. Clearly, Washington's calculation had to be that it was preferable to attempt to influence the Buenos Aires regime from a position of close relations, than remain locked in a self-constructed adversarial relationship with no leverage. (Kirkpatrick, a conservative democrat and Latin American specialist, had published her essay attempting to justify dealing with authoritarian regimes in November 1979, paving the way for Carter's policy change.)

From 1980, the Carter administration subtly, and without fanfare, attempted to improve relations. Washington increased financial assistance to Buenos Aires. U.S. Export-Import Bank credits jumped from $32.7 million to $79.2 million, and Argentina's duty-free exports under GSP (Graduated System of Preferences) more than doubled from $102 million to $231 million.[5] Eximbank credit guarantees and OPIC (Overseas Private Investment Corporation) credits both increased. Before any fundamental change could occur, however, Carter was defeated in his bid for reelection. The new president would continue his predecessor's approach unburdened by the limitations Carter had placed on his foreign policy because of the human rights focus.

The issue of nuclear proliferation in South America was alarmingly real. Neither Argentina nor Brazil was a signatory of the nuclear nonproliferation treaty, which meant that their nuclear programs lay outside the scrutiny of the International Atomic Energy Agency safeguards. Furthermore, although both had signed the treaty of Tlatelolco, specifically intended to preclude the emergence of nuclear weapons states in Latin America, neither had ratified it.[6] Given its repugnant military dictatorship, as well as its aggressive approach to territorial conflicts with Chile and Great Britain, Buenos Aires was an obvious concern.

Although Argentina repeatedly disavowed any intent to become a nuclear weapons state, claiming a desire simply to be "as self-sufficient as possible" in its civilian nuclear power program, global conditions, then extant, belied such claims.[7] From the mid 1970s, major new discoveries of uranium deposits in Canada and Australia, global cutbacks in nuclear power programs, and major advances in enrichment technology, created a worldwide uranium glut and excess enrichment capacity, changing the economics of nuclear power. In addition, Argentina had reached the point of near self-sufficiency in petroleum and natural gas production, which further eroded the rationale for expensive investment in nuclear power construction. Argentina's petroleum production in 1980 was just short of 180 million barrels, while imports were only 15 million barrels.[8]

The global oversupply of uranium and excess enrichment capacity dramatically reduced the costs (by as much as two-thirds) of obtaining enriched uranium on the open market—thereby virtually eliminating the economic incentives to construct an indigenous reprocessing and enrichment capability.[9] It is not the reactor itself that raises nuclear proliferation concerns. No weapons fuel can be diverted from an on-line reactor. The concern is about the enrichment and reprocessing facilities at either end of the reactor where weapons-grade materials can be produced. Uranium is enriched before use in the reactor and reprocessed after it has been used. This process not only doubles the efficiency of the "burn," it also produces weapons-grade material.

The existing supply of uranium, calculated against the worldwide rate of uranium usage, meant that known uranium supplies—without reprocessing or enrichment—were sufficient to fuel 1,000 light water reactors for almost one hundred years. (There were only a few hundred reactors in existence at that time.) Because reprocessing and enrichment facilities are major capital-intensive investments requiring multiyear lead times for construction, a decision to build such capacity could not be justified on economic grounds, particularly considering Argentina's increasing foreign debt, which raised immediate warning flags.

It was, of course, entirely possible that Argentina simply intended to use the extracted plutonium, as proclaimed, to "raise the fissile content of their heavy water reactor fuels and thus increase the burnup."[10] The peaceful protestations were unconvincing, however, because aside from the nuclear weapons states, "the most common technical route to nuclear explosive capability has been the natural-uranium-fueled large research or power reactor coupled with a pilot reprocessing plant."[11] Argentina's public decision to follow that same path, not to mention the secret decision to construct a reprocessing plant at Pilcaniyeu, caused great concern.

By the time that the Reagan administration assumed power, the Argentine nuclear program was well advanced. In late 1981, one source estimated that "Argentina's power reactor has *already* produced enough plutonium, contained in spent fuel, to make several dozen nuclear bombs of the Nagasaki type."[12] What the Argentine junta had not yet managed to develop to a sufficient degree by then was the warhead, trigger, and missile technology to deliver a nuclear weapon, although missile testing had already begun. In late 1981, the British journal *New Scientist* declared that Argentina "will have manufactured its first atom bomb by the end of 1982" and reported that American intelligence believed that it had "already tested a missile capable of carrying a nuclear bomb."[13]

Undoubtedly, the rapid development of Argentina's nuclear capability was the critical factor in the Reagan administration's decision to deepen the relationship with Buenos Aires, far more so than any ideological intent to cozy up to Latin American dictators for whatever reason, or the need for assistance against Nicaragua. As we now know, by early 1982, the junta had come perilously close to achieving its objective of presenting the world with a nuclear fait accompli—and would have succeeded had it not been for the Falkland Islands War. Indeed, after the fact, Reagan's policy was the essence of practicality, but did not appear so at the time.

Another pressing concern involved the difficult political situation surrounding Margaret Thatcher during late 1980. Should she fall, much of what President Reagan hoped to accomplish regarding the resuscitation of containment would collapse with her. A close and revitalized Great Britain under the leadership of Margaret Thatcher was essential to the success of American strategy in Europe and beyond. The problems confronting the Reagan leadership involved ensuring Thatcher's political longevity and forestalling Argentina's plan to produce a nuclear ballistic missile capability. The Falkland Islands dispute offered a golden opportunity to solve both problems.

Economic Woes and Political Factionalism

The world recession in 1980, triggered by the second oil crisis and the tightening of U.S. monetary policy, catapulted Argentina into crisis. Martinez de Hoz's high interest rate, anti-inflationary policies, which had been moderately successful until then, could not be sustained against global deflation and uncontrolled public spending. The result was a rapid appreciation of Argentine debt, which reached $27 billion by the end of 1980—on the way to over $35 billion by the end of 1981.[14] The expanding debt was financed by foreign borrowing, but debt service pressure increased as exports fell and growth slowed.

Public spending, moreover, particularly defense spending, continued at high levels and not only was beyond Martínez de Hoz's control, but, as one study suggests, "probably" even his knowledge.[15] Only continued high interest rates stood a chance of stabilizing the peso, maintaining public confidence, and controlling inflation. It was at this moment, in December 1980, that President Videla announced that his successor would be his close friend and ally, army chief Gen. Roberto Viola. Viola declined to provide reassurances with regard to economic policy, however, which further destabilized the Argentine economy.

Viola declined to make a public commitment to maintaining the exchange rate—that is, to maintaining high interest rates—indicating an expected change in economic policy. "Viola's silence," as it was termed, implied an imminent devaluation and triggered a massive capital flight out of pesos into dollars, facilitated by the earlier removal of capital controls.[16] When Viola formally assumed office in March 1981, Argentina was already careening into crisis. By July, Argentina's reserves had plummeted from \$11 billion to \$1 billion.[17] He had named Lorenzo Sigaut to replace the outgoing finance minister and, as expected, Sigaut reversed Martinez de Hoz's policies, with disastrous consequences.

The Argentine financial system began to collapse and nothing Sigaut did could stabilize the economy, let alone effect recovery. Sigaut pushed through two massive devaluations of the peso through the spring, provided tax and credit relief to industry, and authorized government assumption of private international debt, but capital outflow continued unabated, and inflation soared. The manufacturing sector, especially steel, automobile, and textiles, moved to the point of collapse, as bankruptcies multiplied, and several dozen banks and financial houses collapsed.[18]

It was against this background of economic collapse that opposition to President Viola grew. Viola's response to the very real and deepening economic crisis, as well as to the political recriminations that were accompanying it, was the classic one of divide and conquer. He attempted to strike a bargain with the principal civil political parties and to ostracize those considered beyond the pale. His first step in this direction was the release of Isabela Peron who had been held under house arrest by the junta since it had come to power in 1976.

The five main parties—the Peronists, Radicals, Desarrolistas (industrializers of ex-president Frondizi's MID party), the Intransigentes, and the Christian Democrats—by July 1981 had formed a loosely knit coalition known as the Multipartidaria. In truth, the coalition was fragile and continued to be faction-ridden, which, perhaps, served Viola's purposes. Within the Peronists, the largest party, there were four factions—the main group open to negotiation with the junta, a smaller conservative element that supported retired Admiral Massera, a third opposed to any dialogue whatsoever with the junta, and a fourth, which eventually came to support Viola's successor Gen. Leopoldo Galtieri.[19]

The essence of Viola's approach to the Multipartidaria was to offer a quid pro quo: the parties would "tone down their opposition and give Roberto Viola a breathing space in return for better things later on, possibly free elections in 1984."[20] The offer had perhaps the desired effect of splitting, and thus weakening, the Multipartidaria, as the left wing of the new grouping—the Peronistas Intransigentes—opposed any short-term alliances with the junta, or an electoral solution before the establishment of democracy within the party.[21]

Meanwhile, Viola attempted to undermine likely political threats to his rule, the most prominent of which was Adm. Emelio Massera. Massera had been navy minister under Videla, but retired in September 1979. As a civilian, he continued efforts begun under Videla to build a political bridge to a conservative faction within the Peronist Party, which he planned to employ as the vehicle for a return to politics. Just as Viola was assuming power in March 1981, Massera, on the verge of success, was crippled politically by a scandal originating in Italy.

In Rome, the Italian police broke up a secret society named Propaganda Due (P-2), arrested many of its leaders, and seized its records. Through its international connections, including the Catholic church and the underworld, P-2 had laundered huge sums of money and financed various and sundry political and economic schemes. P-2's Argentine affiliate, to which Massera belonged, was Pro-Patria, an organization with links to the Argentine death squads.[22] Discovery of Pro Patria and its links to the death squads quickly caused suspicion to fall upon Massera. The scandal put him on the defensive for several months during which Viola was able to strengthen his own position.

Before long, however, Massera was back in the game. By midyear, he had assembled a coalition of Peronist and Conservative political figures in support of his cause, arranged for promotion of his views through a magazine (*Cambio*) and a newspaper (*Convicción*), and in August had launched a political party somewhat ironically named the Social Democratic Party.[23] Viola quickly shut down *Cambio*, however, and briefly placed Massera himself under house arrest.[24] The message was clear. Viola would not tolerate any efforts but his own to construct a civil-military opposition group, particularly one involving the Peronistas, as Massera had been attempting to do.

Ironically, as the civilian parties coalesced, factionalism within the military establishment intensified. Three powerful factions emerged within the military. Within the army, the principal grouping was, of course, the Videla-Viola faction, headed from March 1981 by President Roberto Viola. A second faction within the army emerged under the new commander in chief, Leopoldo Fortunato Galtieri, and a third was the hardline group led by Gen. Cristino Nicolaides.[25] Factionalism also thrived within the navy and air force, but was less apparent. In part, the antagonism among these groups reflected service loyalties; for example, Viola from the infantry and Galtieri from the cavalry, but issues of strategy and politics predominated, particularly the issue of a return to civilian rule.

From the outset, Viola appeared to have underestimated the extent of threat that could emanate from within the junta itself. He had not considered his replacement as army chief, General Galtieri, as a political contender. Yet, within weeks of assuming his position, Galtieri openly began to distance himself from the president and to stake out an alternative position that was based initially on no early return to civilian rule. As the issue of Isabela Peron's release arose, Galtieri declared pointedly, "If Viola pardoned the ex-president, the military junta would ask him to resign."[26] His tough stance gained him the support of Gen. Cristino Nicolaides and others, as, during the next several months, opposition to Viola coalesced around Galtieri.

Indeed, Viola's position was tenuous from the beginning. Not a month had passed before there was talk of a coup based upon the presumed "alliance" developing between Galtieri and Gen. Antonio Bussi, powerful commander of the first army. Observers considered these two men to be the "main threat to the stability of Viola's government."[27] By early June, as Viola was opening a dialogue with the civilian politicians, Galtieri was publicly denouncing the president's move. "The ballot boxes are still stored away," he said, openly attacking any notion of a near-term return to elections and civilian control of the government.[28]

A few weeks later he stated even more emphatically that previous military regimes had made the mistake of thinking that elections were the solution to political problems. "We must not make the same mistake."[29] There was now open speculation about a coup to replace Viola and Sigaut, with Galtieri increasingly depicted as the favored alternative who would sponsor a return to policies associated with Martinez de Hoz. The Viola government, banking sources said prophetically, "may not last the year."[30]

Viola's troubles mounted. As the economy continued to crumble, virtually all sectors of Argentine society turned against him. By July, the peso had plummeted to eighty-eight hundred to the dollar. Unemployment—open and disguised—had affected 40 percent of the workforce. Business, labor, and the church all began openly to oppose the regime. Most significant was the church. A July letter from the Catholic Church hierarchy indicated its withdrawal of support. "We must distinguish between the justification for the war against the guerrillas, and the methods used in the war."[31] The implication was clear: the cause was just, the means excessive and indefensible.

Undoubtedly, the split within the junta severely undermined the credibility of the Viola government and called into question every effort made to stabilize the country, economically and politically. It was a vicious circle. The lack of credibility and continuing instability, in turn, increasingly persuaded financial lenders to cut back on loans to Argentina. Obtaining international financing of Argentina's growing debt became more difficult even as the need for it increased. As Argentina spiraled downward, its leaders searched all avenues, including foreign assistance, as a way of effecting recovery. It was under these conditions of extreme internal instability that the United States exercised its influence in Argentine politics.

Reagan's Courtship of Leopoldo Fortunato Galtieri

A close and cooperative relationship with Argentina was an essential precondition for the success of American strategy. Washington's first attempt, however, was less than successful. Immediately after assuming office, President Reagan invited president-designate Roberto Viola to visit Washington in mid-March, amid much public discussion of Argentina's new status. Reagan administration officials "praised recent improvements in Argentina's human rights performance"[32] and emphasized "the strategic importance they attach to Argentina, particularly in terms of South Atlantic naval security."[33]

Gen. Vernon Walters, a former Central Intelligence Agency deputy director, who was also a Latin America expert and fluent in Spanish, would be Reagan's private interface with Argentine leaders. In the Falklands drama, General Walters would play an instrumental, behind-the-scenes, role from beginning to end. He would be an éminence grise in bringing Galtieri to power, act as Secretary of State Alexander Haig's interpreter during the mediation, and, when Argentina was defeated in the war, prepare the way for the reconstitution of civilian rule. Visiting Buenos Aires in February, Walters extended President Reagan's invitation to Viola.[34]

Receiving Viola with all the honors accorded to democratically elected leaders, the Reagan administration declared its intention to end Argentina's isolation and cease criticism of Buenos Aires' human rights policy. During

their talks, administration officials indicated that they would undo legislation (the Humphrey-Kennedy amendment) preventing arms sales.[35] Congressional hearings were held to review policy on military assistance.[36]
Washington sought Argentine participation in several international projects,
including Central America and the Middle East. Meanwhile, however, the
Reagan administration clarified Washington's opposition to "any" Argentine-Soviet "deals...that could in any way threaten the U.S. supply lines with
South America and Africa."[37]

Viola generally welcomed the Reagan administration's positive policy approach, declaring that his reception had exceeded his "most exaggerated
hopes," but he was nevertheless noncommittal with regard to Argentina's
geopolitical position.[38] Grain sales to the Soviet Union would continue, he
said. Furthermore, while interested in arms purchases, he noted that Argentina had found alternative suppliers. Nor was he anxious to associate Argentina with the United States in Central America or the Middle East, preferring
to maintain a nonaligned status.

Viola's reticence, far from discouraging the Reagan administration, galvanized it into a search for a more receptive audience. The split within the
junta, as Galtieri began publicly to oppose Viola, made the army chief an
obvious candidate for courtship. Their attraction was mutual, for Galtieri
held an undisguised affection for the United States, which originated in
1960 when he spent six months in engineering training at Fort Belvoir, Virginia. These had been, he later told Jeane Kirkpatrick, "the happiest months
of his life."[39]

The courtship of Galtieri began in the spring with a procession of unprec-
edented visits to Argentina by several very high-ranking military officers.
These included: Rear Adm. Peter K. Cullins, commander of the United
States South Atlantic Forces; Adm. Harry Train, commander in chief of the
Atlantic Fleet; and Brig. Gen. Richard A. Ingram, commander of the Air
Force Command and Staff School. All spent several days in Buenos Aires.
Most important, however, was the visit of Gen. Edward C. Meyer, the U.S.
Army Chief of Staff.

Meyer spent a week in Buenos Aires in early April. Meyer's public agenda
included the question of advisers to El Salvador, participation in the Sinai
Peace Force, policy toward Bolivia, and nuclear energy. Conveying the
American leadership's views of Argentina as the most "trustworthy"(!) nation

in the cone, he also spoke of American interest in sea lane defense based on a South Atlantic alliance. Galtieri, who formally held the same position as Meyer in the military hierarchy, was "clearly flattered by Meyer's visit," and agreed to "regular consultations."[40] Indeed, Meyer's visit marked the beginning of Galtieri's more assertive posture.

Meyer's visit raised the pressure within the junta for a change of policy. He implicitly posed the question for the Argentine leadership of either closer cooperation with the United States, perhaps including an alliance and treaty relationship, or continued nonaligned status. Galtieri clearly favored an alliance, while Viola opposed one, a fact that undoubtedly sharpened their increasing antagonism, further polarizing the junta. Following Meyer's visit, for example, Foreign Minister Camilion hastened to insist that Argentina would not shift toward the United States, but remain "independent."

In discussions with foreign journalists, Foreign Minister Oscar Camilion declared that "our participation in the Nonaligned Movement is proof of our desire to remain independent from the two blocs."[41] Dismissing questions about improving relations with the Soviet Union, he said that recent contacts were "essentially commercial...to offset the deficit of our trade balance." In the same vein, Camilion flatly rejected another American request to provide troops for the Sinai Peace Force then being assembled as part of the Camp David Accords.[42]

Galtieri, however, as a result of newfound confidence (perhaps from his discussions with General Meyer?), took a tough stand toward Great Britain over the Falkland Islands dispute during his Argentine Army Day speech on May 29. Referring to the Falklands as Argentina's "island territories," Galtieri declared:

> Nobody can or will be able to say that we have not been extremely calm and patient in our handling of international problems, which in no way stem from any appetite for territory on our part. However, after a century and a half, they [these problems] are becoming more and more unbearable.[43]

Acute Polarization—Prelude to the Coup

In midyear, a series of seemingly unrelated events occurred that severely undermined the strategy Viola had been pursuing and strengthened the argument for alliance with the United States. First, on June 7, came the Israeli bombing of the Iraqi nuclear reactor at Osirak. Then, a few days later, the London newspaper *The Guardian* revealed in an exposé that Brazil and Iraq were engaged in a secret program of nuclear cooperation, and that West Germany was secretly an active supplier of the nuclear reprocessing technology that enabled their enterprise. Finally, in mid-June, Great Britain announced a major change in defense policy, which undoubtedly changed Argentine perceptions of their quest for the Falkland Islands.

Brazil, it was revealed, had for some time been sending uranium dioxide to Iraq for irradiation at Osirak into weapons grade plutonium.[44] Iraq retained some of the spent fuel for its own nuclear weapons program, returning the bulk to Brazil. West Germany, it was also revealed, was secretly providing Brazil with an additional reprocessing facility beyond that which had been publicly contracted for in 1975. The facility was scheduled to begin operation in 1983.

These revelations sent shock tremors through the Argentine leadership. They meant that Brazil was playing the same game with Argentina that Buenos Aires was playing with Brasilia—pursuing a cooperative relationship, publicly denying any intent to achieve a nuclear weapons capability, while secretly moving at top speed toward that very objective. The Israeli attack on Osirak was a severe setback to Brazilian and Iraqi plans. Meanwhile, the suggestion of American support for Israeli action intimated oblique support for Argentina.

Then, in late June, came publication of Great Britain's Defense Program. Somewhat ironically titled "The Way Forward," it marked a dramatic retreat in British naval policy.[45] After heated debate throughout the spring, the British government announced a major shift in defense priorities. Based on decisions to emphasize the nuclear deterrent in the Trident submarine program, defense of the British Isles, and NATO, the role of the Royal Navy was dramatically reduced to that of a coastal force. Secretary of Defense John Nott declared both in terms of the high cost of technology and the need for a more rational force structure, "we cannot...sustain a surface fleet of the full present size."[46]

Noted briefly in Nott's announcement, but publicly revealed piecemeal over the next several months, Britain had decided virtually to eliminate its ability to mount independent "out of area" operations at sea. The *Daily*

Telegraph carried an article highlighting the "fundamental" nature of the British shift, making the point that Great Britain was "abandoning the protection of the Falkland Islands."[47] Several Argentine newspapers carried articles paraphrasing the article. Despite British government protestations, the decision to withdraw HMS *Endurance* was not seen as a cost-cutting measure, but rather as a deliberate political signal that the Thatcher government was at last ready to negotiate seriously over the Falkland Islands issue. In Britain, public concern grew, particularly among the Falkland Islands lobby.

What was cause for alarm in Great Britain (Navy minister Keith Speed objected to the cuts and was sacked) was, of course, cause for quiet jubilation in Buenos Aires.[48] Argentine leaders quickly noted that Great Britain would be progressively unable to defend the Falkland Islands. Nicanor Costa Mendez, Argentina's foreign minister during the Falklands crisis, observed that the "sign to which I really paid attention...was the Defence Debate of 1981....the Royal Navy was to be concentrated on the submarines, on the Trident, rather than the surface fleet. To that we paid attention....My conclusion was that it would be very difficult for Britain to maintain the Islands without our cooperation or collaboration."[49]

Combined with Argentina's military buildup, it was simply a matter of time before the crossover point was reached, and Great Britain was forced to accommodate to Argentine wishes. Ultimately, therefore, the inescapable conclusion was that sovereignty over the Falkland Islands would eventually accrue to Argentina. Not initially apparent was the immediate effect of the announced defense cuts. In the short run, Britain's declining capability meant that the decisive factor would be played by the United States, for only if the United States provided the necessary logistical and political support, compensating for Britain's deficiencies, could London maintain a defense of the islands.

Clearly, in logistical terms, this meant the American-leased air and naval bases on the British-owned island of Ascension. Ascension Island lay virtually midway between the British Isles and the Falkland Islands. It was literally the only point from which Britain could project declining military power into the South Atlantic—and only if the United States provided vital support. If, however, Washington could be induced to play a role similar to that which it played during the Suez crisis of 1956, when it refused to support Great Britain, then an earlier-than-planned recovery of the Falklands/Malvinas was possible.

In brief, the revelations of June—the British defense cuts, the Brazilian nuclear gambit, Argentina's deepening economic crisis, and America's evident interest in developing close, strategic relations with Buenos Aires—began to reshape the Argentine leadership's political calculations. The revelations called into question the strategy adopted in 1978 under Videla—and continued by Viola—to pursue friendly relations with Brazil, while remaining neutral "between the two blocs" and continue the slow-paced, outside-in approach to the Falkland Islands.

The new situation precipitated a fierce debate throughout the summer within the Argentine leadership. What emerged publicly was the demand for "shared regional leadership" with Brazil.[50] Privately, the revelations seem to have strengthened the argument in favor of better relations with the United States. Increasingly, it seemed, better relations with the United States was the panacea. A strategic relationship with the United States could not only help Argentina out of its economic doldrums, it could also provide a necessary counterbalance to Brazil. Most of all, American neutrality vis-à-vis the Falklands could open up early recovery of Las Malvinas.

UN Ambassador Jeane Kirkpatrick, on a Latin American tour, continued the courtship of Galtieri. Arriving in Buenos Aires on August 1 for a three-day visit, Kirkpatrick met with "generals, civilian officials, diplomats and scholars."[51] She reiterated the earlier American request for Argentine participation in the multinational peacekeeping force for Sinai, an issue that "divided the Government." Indeed, U.S. ambassador Harry Schlauderman and his deputy Claus Ruser were peddling the U.S. plan so assiduously that Foreign Minister Camilion had considered declaring Ruser "persona non grata." Instead, he went to Schlauderman and requested that he curtail Ruser's activities.[52]

Then, from August 5 through 15, Galtieri went to the United States on the return invitation of General Meyer. The Reagan administration royally feted Galtieri during his visit, sparing no effort. General Walters accompanied him on excursions to Hollywood and Disneyland, while pressing the case for closer cooperation between the two countries—on arms sales, nuclear policy, and particularly involvement in the Sinai scheme.[53] Throughout, Galtieri publicly announced his interest in better relations.

When Galtieri learned of Camilion's attempt to muzzle Ruser, he publicly disparaged the foreign minister, speaking of his grave "defects." And, against the advice of his aides, Galtieri informed General Meyer and others that regarding the matter of providing troops for the Sinai force "there is no problem in giving that support because we can give it and much more."[54] Galtieri believed that Argentine support for the American Sinai scheme would help to restore the complex bilateral relationship with the United States and open the door for a quid pro quo over the Falklands.

Washington and Galtieri's Rise to Power

A few weeks later, Washington increased the pressure for cooperation. While Foreign Minister Camilion was in New York for the annual opening of the United Nations—declaring that Argentina would maintain its "independent stance," continue to trade with the Soviet Union, send no troops to El Salvador, not participate in the Sinai scheme, and not join any South Atlantic Treaty Organization (SATO)—General Walters was in Buenos Aires for a secret meeting with Viola and the junta.[55]

General Walters came armed with a broad agenda. He urged that Argentina not interfere in the internal affairs of Bolivia (Washington was concerned that Buenos Aires would sponsor a coup in La Paz), refrain from increasing tension with Chile over the Beagle Channel, and be very wary of entanglement with Moscow. U.S. assistance in Argentina's nuclear program would follow, he said, if Buenos Aires ratified the Tlatelolco treaty. Similarly, arms sales would be promptly resumed, if Argentina participated in the Sinai plan and supported the United States in El Salvador. Of course, he said, movement toward a more democratic government and release of prisoners would enormously facilitate the improvement of relations.[56]

There was no public reference to SATO, or the Falkland Islands, but it seems unlikely that these issues were not discussed. General Meyer had first raised the subject of a South Atlantic alliance during his April visit, and it had remained on the agenda. Labour MP, Tom Dalyell, a harsh critic of Thatcher's foreign policy, asserted that Walters not only discussed the possibility of establishing a South Atlantic Treaty Organization, but also the "advantages for such an organization of an island-base in the Falklands."[57] The discussion of a U.S.-proposed South Atlantic Treaty Organization with Argentine leaders was a matter of public record. Indeed, Viola's foreign minister had stated a few days before at the United Nations that Argentina would not participate in such a treaty organization.[58] Although discussion of a

Falkland Islands base was unconfirmed, discussion of "scientific and military bases in Patagonia" apparently did occur at some point.[59]

Reportedly, when asked what Britain would do if Argentina seized the islands, Walters "replied to the effect that the British would huff, puff and protest, and do nothing, with the implication that the Americans could soothe ruffled British feathers."[60] And when asked about U.S. receptivity to a request for neutrality in the event of a conflict, Walters intimated that American neutrality would be contingent upon the absence of any British casualties from Argentine military action. (Incidentally, there were no British casualties when Argentina first seized the islands.)

The result of the meeting, as far as the public record shows, was that Argentina would, after all, participate in the Sinai scheme, although not immediately. It would send troops only after the initial rotation, and it would also cooperate with the United States in El Salvador. In exchange, the U.S. Senate, in early October, lifted restrictions on arms sales provided that President Reagan certified progress on human rights. American leaders had very subtly maneuvered to draw the Argentine junta into a closer relationship, split Viola and his foreign minister, Camilion, which would isolate him, and openly tilt toward Galtieri. During the process, Washington had backed away from insistence on the Sinai plan, while encouraging cooperation in El Salvador where Argentina already had a presence.

Meanwhile, as Argentina gradually moved closer to the United States, the composition of the junta itself changed, which further undermined Viola's position. In September, Adm. Jorge Anaya replaced Adm. Amando Lambruschini as navy member of the junta, tilting the balance in favor of Galtieri. Not only was Anaya an old friend of Galtieri's, the navy man held a personal grudge against Viola. They had first crossed swords in 1976, when Anaya had wanted to venture slowly against Isabela Perón, while Viola argued for immediate action. Then, in 1978, Anaya virulently opposed Viola's arguments in favor of opening a dialogue with the political parties. Worst of all, Viola not only "mocked Anaya's political judgment but also made fleeting reference to the navy man's dark skin and his Bolivian background [which] Anaya never forgot...and [he] spent the next three years looking at ways of restoring his self-respect."[61]

Moreover, Anaya and Galtieri favored a more direct approach to the problem of recovering the Malvinas, which drew increasing support from other colleagues in the leadership and sharpened their differences with Viola, who continued to pursue the indirect approach initiated by his predecessor. Galtieri spoke authoritatively about Argentina's tilt toward the United States. In late October, while in the field at Rio Gallegos observing maneuvers, he was asked by reporters about "possible U.S. disapproval" of growing Argentine-Soviet commercial ties. Galtieri replied: "Our comrades in the United States, the U.S. people and all the people of America should rest assured that the traditional Argentine way of life will not change for any commercial issue."[62]

At this point, in early November, fate intervened to open the way for Galtieri's accession to the presidency. The general had traveled to Washington for a second visit to attend the Assembly of American Army Chiefs. He was "treated as a superstar" and flattered repeatedly as "Argentina's General Patton."[63] According to one account based on firsthand information, Galtieri "regarded himself as having a special relationship with the Reagan administration. It was this, evidently, that encouraged him to seize power, and that probably contributed to his decision to embark upon a desperate military adventure in the South Atlantic."[64]

The guest list at his farewell luncheon included Secretary of Defense Casper Weinberger, NSC head Richard Allen, Assistant Secretary of State for Inter-American Affairs Thomas Enders, OAS ambassador William Middendorf, Assistant Secretary of Treasury Paul Craig Roberts, Commander in Chief of the Army Edward Meyer, Secretary of the Army John Marsh, the ubiquitous Vernon Walters, and others. He was described variously by several attending as a "majestic personality," a "shrewd strategist," and a "warm ally of the United States." Before departing, he was received by Vice President Bush.[65] Galtieri could be forgiven for assuming that he was held in special favor by America's highest leaders.

Upon departure on November 7, Galtieri was informed of momentous news; President Viola had been hospitalized with what was being publicly described as a case of acute arterial hypertension. Although initial reports said that he would resume his duties in a few days, he failed to improve, and by mid-November Buenos Aires was abuzz with rumors about his imminent replacement by Galtieri. Viola's illness, which was eventually acknowledged to have been a heart attack, both physically and politically debilitated him.[66] Then, in another blow, the air force representative to the junta, Gen. Omar

Graffigna announced his retirement; he would be replaced by Gen. Basilio Lami Dozo on December 17.

On November 21, as Viola's health worsened, Maj. Gen. Horacio Tomás Liendo was sworn in as "acting" president.[67] Viola's illness, combined with the addition of Anaya and Lami Dozo to the junta, fatally undercut his position. Both Anaya and Lami Dozo, in varying degrees, supported Galtieri in making a shift in Argentina's strategy by moving closer to the United States and taking a more forceful approach toward the Falklands.

Viola's slide was more than matched by the faltering of the economy as the peso hit fifteen thousand to the dollar in November. On November 7, the Peronist-led (and church supported) labor unions marshaled fifty thousand people to demonstrate against the Viola regime demanding Paz, Pan y Trabajo (peace, bread, and work).[68] Galtieri was now seen as "clearly the strongest candidate" to succeed Viola and as "Washington's man."[69] Perhaps to reinforce that latter impression, in mid-November, General Walters made another brief stopover in Buenos Aires on his way home to Washington from Santiago, Chile.[70]

Viola's days were now numbered. Anticipating the eventual outcome by nearly two weeks, on November 29 Chilean radio broadcast December 20 as the date for Galtieri's takeover.[71] (It would actually occur on December 22.) Galtieri, moving with a steady hand, gained Anaya's support for his candidacy and sought to obtain the neutrality, at least, of former president Videla. On December 2, he met with Videla, who took a noncommittal stand, which Galtieri correctly interpreted to mean that he would not support Viola.[72] A few days later, when the crunch came, Videla would publicly declare that he would "in no way...interfere."[73]

The next day, December 3, in a move carefully planned with Anaya, Galtieri announced a purge of the top five generals of the army high command, removing critical support from Viola and a potential rival to himself.[74] Placed on the retirement list were: Antonio Bussi, considered to be a competitor with Galtieri to succeed Viola; Rogelio Villareal, Viola's ally and channel to the political parties; Reynaldo Bignone, who would replace Galtieri after the Falklands War; Eduardo Crespi and Carlos Martínez, who would be involved in the postwar investigation of the Galtieri-led junta's policies.[75]

To replace them, Galtieri named five of his associates from the cavalry, all hard-liners. Generals Cristino Nicolaides, Juan Trimarco, Llamil Reston,

Osvaldo García, and Horacio Ortiz. Only Gen. José Vaquero, of Viola's appointees, was retained, no doubt because of his close ties to the American ambassador.[76] Galtieri's men were not considered to be political sophisticates, but tough-minded military men. They would need to be, for Galtieri planned to use Argentine military power to resolve long-standing, intractable problems.[77]

It would take several days to remove Viola in what became a slow-motion palace coup against the junta, which ironically had itself come into being by means of a palace coup. The problem was that the Proceso's procedures did not anticipate the possibility of the junta demanding the resignation of its own president. Galtieri's solution was for Viola to resign voluntarily for reasons of health and thus preserve the authority of the presidency. He sent Generals Reston, Martello, and Vaquero individually on successive days to broach this formula to the stricken president while he was in the hospital undergoing tests.[78]

But Viola refused. Upon leaving the hospital, he rejected a recommendation to undergo double bypass heart surgery, insisting that he was "perfectly well."[79] When Galtieri himself met with Viola for two days in succession after his return from the hospital, the best he could obtain was a letter of resignation clearly indicating that his action was taken under duress.[80] Viola's decision to force the junta to demand his resignation for political reasons heightened the aura of illegality about his removal and strengthened the sense within the Proceso of sharp division that had become all too apparent during the past year.

That evening, December 9, Galtieri, Anaya, Lami Dozo, and the man he was replacing, Omar Graffigna, gathered for dinner at Anaya's home. Viola's obstinacy had "irritated" them. "They had…hoped to be able to avoid, at least to all appearances, a public display of their palace intrigue and so limit the damage to the Military. But if that was how Viola wanted to be overthrown, then that is how it would have to be."[81] Confident that Viola would not attempt to fight, they decided that "the Military Junta would name the next President" and, late that evening, sent a messenger to invite Viola to meet with them the next day.

The next day, December 11, after Viola reiterated his refusal to resign for health reasons, the junta informed him of his removal from the presidency.[82] They then issued a communiqué declaring that "the junta has decided to remove" General Viola "and has appointed" General Galtieri in his place.[83] Galtieri would take office December 22, 1981, and serve out Viola's term which was to have ended on March 29, 1984.[84] The junta also stipulated that Galtieri would be replaced as army chief in December 1982.

Contrary to popular impression, Galtieri's victory was at best incomplete and carefully hedged. As an "appointed" interim president, he was given neither a mandate nor a full term of office. Worse, he would be required to relinquish his post as army chief of the junta in a year. In essence, he could count on being in a position of considerable, but not unhindered, power for only the next twelve months. Galtieri was planning a long tenure as president, however, and quickly set in motion schemes on both domestic and foreign fronts, which he believed would ensure his longevity in office.

Domestically, Galtieri moved to strengthen the position of the presidency and to weaken the junta. He attempted to end the "feudal" structure by which service loyalties superseded loyalty to the president. He sought to change the relationship between province and center. Instead of governors reporting to military leaders in the junta, henceforth, they would report directly to the president. Finally, he sought to create a national political network, an apparat that would serve and support the president, Leopoldo Fortunato Galtieri.[85] It seems, however, that his efforts backfired—undermining loyalty to the presidency and encouraging defiance. In short, Galtieri's political agenda served mainly to unify other factions against him.

In foreign affairs, Galtieri quickly appointed Nicanor Costa Mendez as foreign minister and established his twin priorities as resolution of the Beagle Channel and Falkland Islands disputes. Costa Mendez had been foreign minister earlier during the sixties under former President Juan Carlos Ongania and had been involved with the Malvinas issue then. The addition of Costa Mendez to the leadership meant that from Galtieri to the junta and including the foreign ministry, all were committed internationalists determined to thrust Argentina into the first rank of nations. The key step to that end was, of course, strengthening ties with the United States.

Galtieri, reportedly, immediately engaged in "secret talks with the U.S." about ways to strengthen Argentine-American relations.[86] Issues under discussion included "possible establishment of U.S. scientific and military bases in Patagonia" (the vast region of southern Argentina), installation of sophisticated communication systems, construction of a three-hundred-mile gas pipeline from Neuquén to Puerto Madryn, and an increased role for American oil companies. Each project appeared to have been an effort to counterpose American and British interests. Clearly, President Leopoldo Fortunato Galtieri believed that he had a special relationship with the United States, which would be fully reciprocated.

The Origins of the Falklands/Malvinas War

Within four days of the junta's decision to replace Viola, on December 15, Admiral Anaya, as part of his pact with Galtieri, ordered Vice Admiral Juan José Lombardo, who had just become Commander of Naval Operations, to begin the planning for the seizure of the Malvinas.[87] Lombardo immediately called together his closest colleagues for initial planning. These were chief of naval air, Rear Adm. Carlos García Boll, chief of the fleet, Rear Adm. Gualter Allara, and chief of the marines, Rear Adm. Carlos Busser. Acting in strictest secrecy, "they took special care not to alert the Naval Intelligence Service," where Viola had allies.[88]

In early January 1982, following initial planning, Lombardo secretly established a "task group" that included representatives from the air force and army. Army Gen. Osvaldo García, one of Galtieri's close colleagues and commander of the Fifth Army Corps, and Air Force Brig. Gen. Sigfrido Plessel, one of Lami Dozo's senior advisers, were added. Although they had begun meeting in the Navy Club in Buenos Aires, to preserve secrecy, they moved to Puerto Belgrano—a naval reserve facility approximately 380 miles south of Buenos Aires near Bahía Blanca.[89] By mid-February, a draft plan had been completed, setting the invasion date of the Malvinas at May 20, with operations to be completed by May 25—Argentine National Day. For internal security purposes, several dates were mentioned—late May, early July, and mid-September, but the junta's choice was May 20.[90]

Ironically, however, the origin of the war lay not in the planning decision of Anaya's task group, but in one taken by President Viola several months earlier. By mid-November 1981, when Viola realized that he would lose his struggle with Galtieri, he activated the plan to establish a base on South Georgia—Davidoff-Alpha—in hopes of derailing a move against the Falklands. Davidoff-Alpha would preempt and preclude the planned operation to take the Falklands/Malvinas. Viola feared that a successful acquisition of the Malvinas would secure Galtieri's tenure as president. Failure to accomplish his declared objective, Viola hoped, would discredit Galtieri and lead to his removal. Viola would thus have his revenge against Galtieri for ousting him and set the stage for the return to power of men of the Videla-Viola faction.

In late November, two high-ranking naval officers and two foreign office officials met with Constantine Davidoff at the Florida Garden, a popular tearoom located in downtown Buenos Aires.[91] One of the navy men was Capt. Adolpho Palau, of naval transport command, and the other was Capt. César Trombetta, of the navy's Antarctic Squadron. Trombetta had taken part in the landing on South Thule in late 1976. The purpose of the meeting was for the navy officers to tell Davidoff that the Argentine navy was now prepared to transport him free of charge to South Georgia and for the foreign office officials to inform him that the scrap metal he brought back would enter duty-free, increasing his profit margin.

Palau and Trombetta were directly subordinate to Adm. Edgardo Otero, commander of naval transport. Otero, in turn, was a close friend of Admiral Eduardo Girling, who was then head of naval intelligence. Both Otero and Girling were responsible for Operation Alpha. Neither would be involved in the planning for the Malvinas seizure, which was kept completely separate. "Davidoff-Alpha" was entirely a project of President Viola, initiated while he was still president and executed by his supporters after he had been ousted—despite explicit subsequent orders to the contrary.

Under President Viola's orders—while he was engaged in a struggle for political power with Galtieri, which he knew he would lose—the government "activated" Davidoff's South Georgia scrap metal enterprise, the precursor to Operation Alpha. Aside from being superficially consistent with the "outside in" approach originated by former President Videla, Viola undoubtedly took this decision with the full understanding that South Georgia would cancel out the Malvinas. Indeed, all concerned in both operations had made the identical assumption—if Argentina took South Georgia, it could not take the Malvinas, for Great Britain would be forewarned and reinforce its island possession. At the very least, Thatcher would have time to repeat her predecessor's maneuver of deploying a nuclear submarine.

Testifying to the ferocity of the factional infighting that characterized Argentine politics, even when Anaya discovered the existence of Alpha and canceled the operation, it was still implemented! Despite its formal cancellation, pro-Viola elements in the navy would carry out Alpha in direct violation of Anaya's orders.[92] An incident on South Georgia, in short, would be a "bitter" Viola time bomb designed to blow up Leopoldo Fortunato Galtieri's plan to recover the Malvinas.[93]

Thus, two operations proceeded simultaneously, each independent of the other, implemented by different personnel, and with markedly different purpose. Each action represented a different strategy. Anaya had begun what he believed would be a several months-long diplomatic and military process to recover the Malvinas, while Viola had set in motion immediate plans to execute a preemptive maneuver designed to preclude that very objective. A landing on South Georgia would alert Great Britain, remove the essential element of surprise, and foreclose action against the Malvinas. Davidoff-Alpha was, in short, Viola's time bomb, which began ticking in December and exploded the following March long after he had been removed.

During the November meeting, Davidoff, never having been to South Georgia, wanted to make a preliminary trip to inspect the stations to be dismantled. Trombetta agreed, for it would provide an opportunity to take a closer look at the island and test the likely British reaction.[94] Thus, on December 16, the day after Admiral Anaya had given the order to begin planning for the seizure of the Malvinas, five days after the junta had removed Viola from power, and six days before Galtieri formally assumed office, Davidoff embarked aboard Captain Trombetta's naval ice-breaker, *Almirante Irizar*, for South Georgia.

Davidoff had sent a letter to the British embassy in Buenos Aires notifying them of his visit, but the letter did not arrive at the embassy until "after he had departed."[95] According to Burns, Davidoff delayed sending the letter to the embassy deliberately, on the advice of Trombetta, who intended it as a "provocation."[96] But Davidoff also sent a telex to Christian Salvesens in Edinburgh, informing the company of his trip, and Salvesens had promptly informed the Foreign Office.[97] The British government had thus been informed of Davidoff's visit well in advance of his arrival.

Further provocations followed. Trombetta traversed the 1,650-mile passage in four days maintaining radio silence, an unusual procedure, and without radioing the magistrate at Grytviken, the official port of entry, of his impending visit. Upon arrival on December 20, Trombetta declined to follow prescribed landing procedures by obtaining clearance at Grytviken. Instead, he proceeded directly to Leith, twenty miles to the west of Grytviken, where the contracted-for abandoned whaling stations were located. Davidoff and a small landing party went ashore to make an inventory and take photographs. During their brief stay of a few hours, one of the party chalked on a wall the slogan "Las Malvinas son Argentinas" along with the date, December 20.[98]

The British government did not interfere in any way with Davidoff, but waited to see what he would do. Three days after the departure of the *Almirante Irizar*, the BAS base commander, Peter Witty, went to Leith, confirming evidence of the Argentine party's unauthorized visit, including the chalked date and message. Witty reported to Falkland Islands Gov. Rex Hunt in Port Stanley, who, in turn, relayed the report to London.[99] Hunt recommended instituting legal proceedings against Davidoff and lodging a strong protest to the Argentine government over the failure to follow established procedures.

London's decision, however, was to deal with the matter through its ambassador in Buenos Aires. Thus, Hunt was told "not to institute proceedings (locally) which would risk provoking a most serious incident," while instructing Ambassador Williams "to deliver a formal protest in the strongest terms at this violation of British sovereignty."[100] On January 6, when Williams delivered his message to the Ministry of Foreign Affairs, newly installed Foreign Minister Costa Mendez professed that "he had no knowledge of Davidoff's journey, nor of what had occurred."[101] Costa Mendez promised Williams that he would conduct an immediate investigation, whereupon the ambassador agreed to withhold the protest until he had done so.[102] Viola's time bomb had begun to tick.

Chapter 4

Crisis on South Georgia:
Britain Poses a Dilemma

By the new year, the situation in Argentina had changed dramatically. The new government of President Galtieri, in office only a few weeks, had already displayed a significantly tougher attitude toward Great Britain and had moved to strengthen relations with the United States. Both changes were clearly observed by British leaders who were then conducting an annual review of British-Argentine relations. Finally, the latest intelligence pointed to a near-term confrontation with Argentina. A climactic finale was being played out on the Falklands drama.

Captain Barker's Observations

Reports from Capt. Nick Barker of the patrol ship HMS *Endurance* indicated that the Argentine navy was not unified and that one segment, localized in the southernmost port of Ushuaia, was openly hostile. As part of its normal work pattern, HMS *Endurance* visited Argentine ports as well as the Antarctic, Falkland Islands, and the Dependencies, South Georgia and South Sandwich Islands. During a two-week layover at the Argentine port of Bahía Blanca in late November, officers and crew of HMS *Endurance* had a "particularly happy" time interacting with their counterparts in the Argentine navy.[1] Thus, immediately before Galtieri's ascension to power, relations seemed quite normal.

HMS *Endurance* departed Bahía Blanca on December 1 for Port Stanley and arrived on December 5. Barker then left Port Stanley for South Georgia on December 9, arriving on December 12. HMS *Endurance*, in fact, was at King Edward Point, South Georgia, when the *Almirante Irizar*, arrived at Leith with Davidoff aboard on December 20, and could have enforced British landing procedures had that been desired. Although the *Almirante Irizar* maintained radio silence while underway, the Davidoff trip was not secret, and the British knew when he would arrive. It was only prudent to ensure that HMS *Endurance* be nearby.

From Grytviken, HMS *Endurance* sailed to Punta Arenas, Chile, at the western end of the Beagle Channel. Arriving at the end of December, Captain Barker was told in no uncertain terms that "the Argentines were up to no good."[2] Then, while heading for the southernmost port of Ushuaia in early January, Barker had been in radio contact with Captain Trombetta of the *Almirante Irizar*. Trombetta declared that he was heading for an Argentine base in Antarctica, but he actually had a different destination. Trombetta was headed for Britain's Dependency of South Thule, where he had no right to be.[3]

Arriving at Ushuaia on January 25, Barker received a "distinctly frigid" reception. HMS *Endurance*, he was told, was "now in a war zone." Was this in reference to Chile, Barker asked? "Yes...but it is also the Las Malvinas war zone," was the reply.[4] Argentine naval personnel there had been ordered "not to fraternize with the British."[5] The base commander, who was on friendly terms with Barker, was not permitted to meet with him.

A few days later, however, when HMS *Endurance* visited the port of Mar del Plata farther north, she was "warmly received." It was impossible not to concur in the sentiment an Argentine harbor pilot had confided to Barker upon departure from Ushuaia that "something was 'very wrong' with the Argentine navy." Certainly, something was wrong with part of it. (Indeed, after the conflict, it would be learned that Ushuaia was the port from which Operation Alpha had been mounted.)[6]

If Captain Barker's reports suggested that "the Argentines were up to no good," as Galtieri was ascending to power, reports from Ambassador Williams and Governor Hunt made plain that the diplomatic route had reached a dead end. Williams had been "sending warnings back that things were getting worse." In his view, the Foreign Office "were by no means convinced that my information was necessarily better than what they were getting through other intelligence sources [that is, signals intelligence, the interception of Argentina's diplomatic cipher traffic by Government Communication Headquarters (GCHQ)]."[7]

Williams also thought that "the Argentines and the Islanders [were] more on each others' nerves than a year ago," while Hunt noted that islander relations with both Argentina and Britain had "deteriorated."[8] The islanders had become suspicious of a sellout by London. The announced withdrawal of HMS *Endurance*, cuts in BAS, planned closure of the Grytviken station, and, above all, the decision not to grant British nationality to the Falkland Islanders in the British Nationality Bill, had seemingly confirmed fears that Britain would no longer support them. Certainly, combined with the defense decisions of June, the evidence was that Great Britain was cutting back its presence in the South Atlantic.

The toughening of Argentina's position raised additional fears. Argentine air service had been abruptly reduced, and harassment increased, particularly of overflights by Argentine aircraft. The result was that the Island Legislative Council had become "unanimously opposed to leaseback," and in "open support of a 'Fortress Falklands' policy."[9] Of course, the debate in the House of Commons the previous December 2 had already made clear that leaseback was dead. During the debate, Minister Ridley was informed in no uncertain terms by one of the members that "whatever the Government and whatever the majority, there will never be a majority in this House to give this historically separate people and separate islands to the Argentine."[10] The council merely, and perhaps happily, echoed this conclusion.

In January, as London's review began, a series of press articles appeared in Buenos Aires regarding the Galtieri regime's new policy toward the Malvinas. The essence of the press commentary was that Argentina would shortly present Great Britain with specific conditions and "very precise time-limits" for resolving the dispute. What was new was the confident assertion of U.S. support of Argentina's policies. Argentina, one writer well-connected to officialdom said, "would receive support from the United States for any action leading to the recovery of the Islands, not excluding military action." Indeed, if negotiations failed, Argentina would recover the islands by force "this year."[11]

Most intriguing, perhaps, was a subtle Argentine attempt to bring nuclear considerations to bear on the dispute. The head of the Argentine National Atomic Energy Commission, Adm. Carlos Castro Madero, declared in an interview that Argentina already "could manufacture an atomic bomb without difficulty."[12] This could be accomplished within three years, following "a few more studies," and construction of additional facilities. Argentina, he explained, was building a pilot plant, which would be completed in August, for recovering plutonium from spent uranium. Argentina, he said, intended to export the plutonium as reactor fuel. But, he was asked, did this not increase the chances for nuclear proliferation?

> No, I do not believe so because proliferation must have a stimulus behind it, a need to have an atomic bomb. Fortunately, on our continent there are no geopolitical conditions to force a country into making significant expenditures of scarce resources on a type of development that offers little to a country. It would confer some prestige upon he who owns the atomic bomb, but that prestige would be short-lived because such a development in Latin America would set off a race among all other countries to catch up.[13]

In response to the reporter's protestation that there were "many pending international conflicts in our continent," Madero replied, "But these conflicts can be solved by peaceful means. Practically all of them can be solved." Madero's interview was with a Brazilian reporter and thus the discussion centered around the issue of Brazilian-Argentine cooperation in the nuclear field. Nevertheless, it was impossible to ignore the implications of his remarks for British-Argentine negotiations over the Falkland Islands.

True to predictions, at the end of the month, on January 27, Buenos Aires delivered a "toughly worded" note containing a proposal for settling the island dispute within one year's time. Calling for "serious and in-depth negotiations" culminating in the recognition of Argentine sovereignty over the disputed islands, the Argentine government proposed the establishment of a "negotiating commission." This commission would meet monthly for one year after which a solution would be reached on the transfer of sovereignty. It was a thinly disguised ultimatum, the first of its kind in the long history of Argentine-British negotiations.[14]

British-Argentine talks regarding the Falkland Islands were scheduled for the end of February in New York. (They originally had been scheduled for December but had been postponed after Galtieri's coup.) On February 9, as

Prime Minister Thatcher was declaring that HMS *Endurance* must be withdrawn, Ambassador Williams delivered a low-key response to the tough January 27 note, but loudly protested Davidoff's three-hour December trip to South Georgia.[15] The Argentine Foreign Ministry responded on February 18 by rejecting the protest. The tough position taken by Buenos Aires did not bode well for the upcoming discussions. Indeed, as we now know, on February 15, the plans for the May 20 invasion of the Falkland Islands had been completed in outline, and the decision to proceed had been made.[16]

The British leadership could be under no illusions that Argentina's new belligerent attitude signaled that a confrontation soon would be inevitable. The next few weeks would confirm that assessment. Even if judged to be a bluff, precautionary measures would have to be taken, but there must be no overt provocation. It was vital that Argentina "fire the first shot" so that Britain's "legal" position would be irreproachable, and all action then taken would be justifiable self-defense. Most important, from the point of view of being able to mount a timely response, it was absolutely imperative that Argentina fire that "shot" well before the onset of winter in mid-June.

One author has said that "the timing of the Argentine invasion indicates a lack of concern for minimizing Britain's ability to respond," but this is simply incorrect.[17] Argentina's planning for the seizure of the Malvinas centered precisely on the best moment to act, to minimize Britain's response time. Timing was everything, determining victory or defeat, but it was not the timing of Britain's defense drawdown that was crucial. Rather, it was the weather in the South Atlantic. In this regard, there were two obvious "windows" for Argentine military action against the Falkland Islands.

The first was in mid-May, a month before the onset of winter, and the second was the following spring—from September onward. No major military operation could be undertaken during the fierce, stormy winter of the South Atlantic where sixty- to seventy-foot waves could capsize even large warships.[18] Assuming continuation of current military trends, action in or after September would offer the advantage of a weaker Britain and a stronger Argentina, perhaps in possession of a small nuclear deterrent. The disadvantage, from Argentina's point of view, was that Britain would have a longer period of time and good weather within which to mount an expedition to recover the islands, assuming it had the wherewithal and determination to do so. (Travel time between Great Britain and the Falkland Islands was approximately three weeks for surface ships and two weeks for nuclear-powered submarines.)

Action immediately before the onset of winter, however, offered essentially the same military advantages without the disadvantages, for no effective British response could possibly come before spring. Perhaps the decisive factor tipping the junta's decision in favor of action just before winter was the prospect of a period of time marked by uncontested Argentine possession of the Falkland Islands, when Britain could not respond militarily, accompanied by attempts to negotiate a resolution. Coupled with an American mediation, a prewinter seizure offered a cooling off period and thus the better prospect for an essentially peaceful transfer of sovereignty. This seems to explain the reason that the junta chose May 20, one month before the arrival of winter, as the invasion date, with completion scheduled for five days later, on Argentine National Day.

It bears restating that the weather factor was critical. Winter would arrive in the Falkland Islands by mid-June. Winter weather in the South Atlantic was so ferocious that no British fleet could maintain itself in the open seas, as British Task Force Commander Sandy Woodward attested during the subsequent military campaign to retake the islands. Speaking of the onset of winter in mid-June, he declared that, by then, "The land battle would have to be over" because "the Task Group would be falling apart...without proper maintenance and with winter setting in."[19]

Indeed, as we now know, the Argentine plan called for a quick, surreptitious takeover of the islands on May 20, less than a month before the onset of winter. This, it was assumed, would not leave Great Britain sufficient time to assemble and dispatch a large-scale, military expedition to recover the islands. A quick-strike fait accompli would also nullify deployment of a nuclear submarine, which had happened in 1977. Britain, according to these calculations, would have no choice but to negotiate a transfer of sovereignty.

Buenos Aires would thus have sufficient time either for the preferred outcome—a negotiated transfer of sovereignty over the winter—or for a defense against a British attempt at forceful recovery in the spring from September onward. In the latter instance, the possibility of Argentina's brandishing of a minimal nuclear weapons deterrent capability should not be discounted. The junta, however, believed that a defense would not be necessary, that Britain would not fight, and that the United States would support Argentina in ensuring a smooth, peaceful transfer of sovereignty.

It must be assumed that British leaders reached essentially the same conclusions as the junta had, that a seizure of the islands immediately before the onset of winter would be the best move for Argentina. How then explain that the invasion of the Falkland Islands occurred on April 2, not May 20, a full seven weeks before it was intended? An invasion in early April made no sense from Argentina's perspective, but it was Britain's only chance, for it offered Britain sufficient, if not ample, time for a full military response before winter set in.

As it turned out, there was literally just enough time. The surrender of Port Stanley occurred on June 14, as the first of the fierce winter storms that annually lash the Falklands began and as Task Force Commander Woodward was preparing to remove his ships from the area. Conversely, it is plain that had the invasion occurred on May 20 as planned, there could have been no timely nor effective British military response. How then can one explain that the invasion of the Falkland Islands occurred at a time maximally to the advantage of Great Britain (under the circumstances) and maximally to the disadvantage of Argentina, given the strike windows chosen?

The explanation of the timing of the invasion lies in the ongoing factional infighting within the Argentine leadership. This continuing struggle was incontestable and, therefore, well-known to British intelligence and Prime Minister Thatcher, who utilized it to supreme advantage. British leaders were acutely aware of the policy differences that had produced the political crisis in Buenos Aires and the new president, Leopoldo Galtieri. As previously mentioned, they had for several years been aware of the political implications of Davidoff's "commercial" enterprise in South Georgia.

Waiting for Davidoff

Thus, when Constantine Davidoff presented himself at the British embassy on February 23 to apologize for the problems caused by his December sojourn and to declare that he intended to return soon to South Georgia to salvage the whaling stations, British leaders were immediately alert to the possibilities. Indeed, activity at South Georgia was increasing. Only a week earlier, BAS personnel had discovered the forty-ton yacht *Caiman* anchored (illegally) at Leith Harbor. Although flying the Panamanian flag, on board were an Italian crew of three and an Argentine bank employee, Adrion Marchessi.[20] Marchessi claimed that his bank was financing Davidoff's enterprise and he was simply inspecting the whaling stations. Suspicions were raised when three "very sophisticated" radios were found aboard the yacht, and more so when Davidoff, contacted by the British embassy to verify Marchessi's story, denied it.

If British leaders did not know the precise invasion date for the Falkland Islands, and all available evidence indicates that they did not, it was because late February was far too soon for any signs of overt preparations for the late May attack. British leaders were, however, alert to the active interest in South Georgia. Given the recent history of Argentine probing in the Dependencies, it certainly must have crossed their minds that some sort of provocation was being prepared.

Winter arrived on South Georgia more than a month earlier than in the Falkland Islands creating difficult, if not impossible, working conditions. Outdoor activity of any kind, let alone the rigorous task of dismantling the heavy iron and steel structures that constituted the whaling stations, during the winter months with barely five hours of daylight and almost continuous snowfall, had to be perceived as an "unlikely scenario," at best. Yet, Davidoff's proposed plan did "not arouse any traceable curiosity in London."[21]

Privately, however, Davidoff's visit had to be understood as the golden opportunity for Margaret Thatcher. Whatever the intention of the Viola faction, the Davidoff enterprise was an opportunity Margaret Thatcher would undoubtedly turn to her own advantage. Britain would use the Davidoff expedition to maneuver Argentina into a lose-lose situation—the junta would be forced either to decide on an earlier-than-planned seizure of the Falklands, giving Britain time to recover them, or to back down in the face of a British threat, thus losing credibility and risking probable overthrow. In either case, Margaret Thatcher's political position would have been strengthened, although only the overthrow of the junta would serve American nonproliferation concerns.

Viola's intention was undoubtedly to place Galtieri in an untenable situation. He had intended Davidoff-Alpha to precipitate a crisis with Great Britain, to be sure, but one that would cause the Galtieri regime to abandon its plans to invade the Falkland Islands. For that reason, South Georgia had to precede it. Backing down in the face of British intransigence, Galtieri would lose credibility and, perhaps, fall from power. It is highly doubtful that Viola expected that his pinprick on South Georgia would ignite a war, resulting in the collapse of military rule in Argentina. There had been nothing in previous British reactions to Argentine pinpricks to suggest a massive response this time.

Both the junta and Margaret Thatcher, however, reacted in ways contrary to Viola's expectations. Galtieri and the junta would correctly interpret the crisis on South Georgia, not only as a threat to the Falklands operation, but also to the credibility of his regime. Cornered, instead of abandoning the junta's plans, Galtieri and Anaya would advance them, assuming that Britain would not fight and that with American support, even neutrality, an earlier-than-planned invasion would still lead to the desired outcome. Presumed American "neutrality" was critical in shaping the junta's decision, for without American support, no British response could succeed—even with sufficient time for action before winter.

In advancing its plans, however, the Argentine junta would play into Thatcher's hands. An earlier-than-planned seizure of the islands would provide the time needed to mount a military recovery operation before the onset of the South Atlantic winter. Britain could also react with military power it would not have six months later. And, decisively, the United States actively and massively would assist Great Britain, not Argentina! The successful military action would enable Margaret Thatcher to solidify her domestic political position as the "Iron Lady." The strengthening of Thatcher's position, in turn, would help to reinforce the American strategic objective of resurrecting containment.

When Davidoff appeared at the British embassy on February 23, therefore, to inform them of his plans, British officials could not have been more cordial in informing him of proper procedures to be followed. He explained that he himself would not be returning to South Georgia. A Sr. Ricardo Cacace would be in charge of the work party, but Davidoff's own nineteen-year-old son would be a member of the group.[22] It would be an opportunity for him to broaden his experience, he said.

The work party would travel to South Georgia aboard the 3,100-ton Argentine naval transport, *Bahía Buen Suceso*, with a four-month store of supplies. Davidoff, recalling the cordiality of his visit, said: "They asked me if I would take medical supplies for the British Antarctic Survey on my next trip, and I agreed."[23] The embassy immediately reported the full details of the Davidoff visit to the Foreign Office, which acknowledged without comment. The British reaction to Davidoff was, of course, nothing less than extraordinary. Perkins's skeptical evaluation is worth quoting at length:

> Despite the furor earlier in the month, despite the Argentine outright rejection, on 18 February, of the British government's formal protest regarding the illegal *Almirante Irizar* visit, London raised no objection to this new visit. Presumably it was felt that he should be given the chance to redeem himself and to fulfill the terms of his contract with Salvesens. The weakness in this line of reasoning was the fact that the workforce would not be under the personal supervision of Davidoff himself. Its movements would be entirely in the hands of an Argentine naval officer, Captain Briatore, captain of the *Bahía Buen Suceso*. Taking account of the behavior of Captain Trombetta in December, and considering the mounting pugnacity of the Argentine navy in general, it was surely somewhat optimistic to suppose that Captain Briatore would in effect acknowledge British sovereignty on South Georgia by meekly asking the Magistrate for permission to land. Optimistic or not, this was the policy adopted.[24]

Four days later, on February 27, Argentine and British representatives met in New York to discuss the demand made by Buenos Aires for the creation of a negotiating commission of one-year's duration to settle the question of sovereignty over the Falkland Islands. The British delegation included two representatives of the Falkland Island Legislative Council, who, of course, were unalterably opposed even to the discussion of the sovereignty question. Moreover, the head of the British delegation, Richard Luce, conveyed to the Argentines that not only would any solution have to take into consideration the interests of the islanders, but their wishes, as well, which would be "paramount."[25]

The Argentine delegation "pressed" for the establishment of a negotiating commission to commence meeting from April 1, 1982. Perhaps to their surprise, London was quite willing to set up a negotiating commission, which would enable discussions to continue. They were unwilling to negotiate under a deadline, however, and thus were averse to the one-year duration. Finally, the British delegation would not commit to any specific starting time for the meetings, referring to "May or June" as a beginning date.[26] At the conclusion of the New York meeting, Great Britain had agreed to talks, but had been vague about an opening date and wanted no terminal date.

It is apparent, in retrospect, that Buenos Aires pressed for an April 1 starting date for the negotiating commission in order to have discussions under way when the Falklands were seized in May. Ongoing discussions would serve to demonstrate Argentine good faith and British intransigence, thus justifying forceful action to bring about acquiescence. The failure of the Argentine delegation to gain agreement for the April 1 starting date produced an immediate denunciation from Buenos Aires. Before the delegation left New York City, the Foreign Ministry issued a strong statement on the just-completed discussions, declaring that: "If a solution [on sovereignty] should not be reached, Argentina maintains the right to end the system and freely choose the procedure which it may deem most convenient to its interests."[27]

The Argentine declaration spurred British leaders into action. As Prime Minister Thatcher was declaring that "we must make contingency plans," Luce was on his way to Washington to brief Assistant Secretary of State Thomas Enders before departing on an official trip to Latin America, which would include Buenos Aires.[28] Luce expressed the hope that Enders would advise the Argentines to "keep things cool." Returning to London, on March 3, Luce appeared before Parliament. In response to questions about the Falklands, he declared that there would be no transfer of sovereignty "without consulting the wishes of the Islanders." When asked whether "all necessary steps were in hand to ensure the protection of the islands against unexpected attack," however, Luce avoided a direct answer, saying only that, "We have no doubts about our sovereignty over the Falkland Islands and no doubt about our duties to the Islanders."[29]

Reviewing the situation on March 5, Carrington instructed that several courses of action be pursued. He wanted a stern note prepared for Costa Mendez to reaffirm the agreement reached during the New York talks. This message would never be sent, as its content would be overtaken by events. He prepared a personal note to Secretary of State Haig expressing the British government's "increasing concern" about Argentina. This would be sent on March 8, while Enders was in Buenos Aires.

Carrington also instructed UN Ambassador Anthony Parsons to be prepared to undertake an initiative at the United Nations should relations suddenly deteriorate. Parsons's early action in the United Nations would gain passage of a resolution that would be instrumental in marshaling international opinion in favor of Britain and in establishing Thatcher's bottom-line negotiating position. Finally, he issued instructions for the preparation of a contingency paper for a meeting of the Defence Committee, to be held "fairly soon."[30] Foreign Office and Ministry of Defence officials immediately began reviewing "various" contingency plans, "in case the Argentines do something silly," including dispatch of a small naval task force.[31]

At this point, Admiral Madero, chairman of Argentina's National Atomic Energy Commission, reentered the picture, increasing the pressure of the nuclear threat. Admiral Madero declared that Argentina would "not promise not to build a nuclear explosive for peaceful purposes."[32] Although maintaining that "nothing is decided yet," he said that "Argentina must make a move towards the use of plutonium which will allow it to double its nuclear energy potential."

Although the British government ignored this statement, the Reagan administration did not. Three days later, while Enders was in Buenos Aires, March 6–9, Washington issued a warning admonishing the Argentine government that the United States "does not differentiate between nuclear weapons and peaceful nuclear explosions."[33] The Argentine government declined to respond, undoubtedly because it was a very sensitive issue. Perhaps no response was made in deference to the sensibilities of their high-ranking visitor. Or, more likely, Buenos Aires declined to respond because Enders had indicated that Washington's "warning" was merely pro forma.

Whatever the reason, Enders's presence in Buenos Aires a few days following the Argentine government's implied threat to break off talks with Great Britain and resort to forceful means, could only be interpreted as encouraging by the Galtieri junta.[34] Certainly, nothing he said during his visit could be construed as discouraging. The *Buenos Aires Herald* reported that Enders, receiving a "lengthy briefing" on the Malvinas, "showed special interest in the subject."[35] Indeed, as Ambassador Williams reported to London: "Enders had *not* taken the opportunity specifically to advise the Argentines to keep the temperature down," as Luce had requested.[36]

On the contrary, British intelligence reported, Enders had been told that "Argentina planned to mount an international diplomatic offensive," if there were no "immediate signs" of British willingness to concede sovereignty. Furthermore, "Enders had indicated that the United States Government would see no problem in this course of action." Its attitude was "hands off."[37] The United States, Enders said, would not "take a position, one way or the other, on the territorial dispute." Whatever Enders said or meant to say, his visit clearly reinforced the junta's belief that the United States would support Argentina.

On March 9, the day of Secretary Enders's departure from Buenos Aires, Constantine Davidoff reappeared at the British embassy. Notifying officials that his men would be sailing for South Georgia in two days' time, he submitted a name list of forty-one persons who would be in his work party.[38] Davidoff had judged that the salvage operation would take two years, so he had requested, and was granted, a one-year extension of his contract with Salvesens to March 31, 1984. Salvesens duly reported the contract extension to the Foreign Office on March 16.

There can be no question that Davidoff's notification alerted British leaders of an imminent crisis. As everyone knew, the time to conduct salvage operations on South Georgia was between November and March, not March and October. Yet, Davidoff's declared plan of operations called for his men to work for the next four months through the worst of South Georgia's winter— late March through late July—when there would be nineteen hours of darkness out of every twenty-four, heavy winds, and several feet of snow.[39] Prospects were highly dubious for what purported to be a purely commercial enterprise involving open-air work tearing down buildings and equipment.

On schedule, the *Bahía Buen Suceso* under the command of Captain Oswaldo Miello departed Buenos Aires on March 11 bound for South Georgia. On the same day an Argentine C-130 aircraft overflew the island on an apparent reconnaissance flight, the third since January. HMS *Endurance*, meanwhile, was also on the way to South Georgia from Antarctica on its final work period before returning to England. Under normal circumstances, both ships would reach the island at approximately the same time. By pure chance, however, it would be yet a third ship that would arrive at South Georgia before either the Argentine or British ships. This was the forty-foot sailing yacht *Cing Gars Pour*.

Unanticipated Complications

Three young Frenchmen, Serge Briez, Olivier Gouon, and Michael Roger, had departed Buenos Aires on February 9 aboard their forty-foot sailing yacht, *Cing Gars Pour*, bound for Antarctica, where they planned to make a film. Off Cape Horn, they encountered a fierce storm with winds gusting to over ninety miles an hour. Their ship capsized, and, although it eventually righted itself, it was badly damaged. "The wheelhouse had been torn off and the tiller smashed."[40] Under bare poles, unable to navigate, and at the mercy of the wind, the three men had been swept approximately 1,300 miles off course. When the storm subsided, they found themselves within sight of South Georgia, where they managed to struggle to safety at Grytviken harbor on March 14.[41]

Under almost any other conceivable circumstances, the BAS personnel would have welcomed and assisted the exhausted trio. But a handful of Frenchmen in position to witness events was the last thing they wanted, precisely when the *Bahía Buen Suceso* was expected to arrive at any moment. The BAS personnel displayed a decided inhospitality, treating the Frenchmen like interlopers, rather than shipwrecked seamen.

> The welcome they gave the Frenchmen was almost as frigid as the climate. There was no offer of help to repair the boat and no offer of food, despite the fact that the Frenchmen had lost almost all of their supplies in the capsize and had survived ever since on a very meagre diet.[42]

Left to fend for themselves after completing landing formalities at King Edward Point, the Frenchmen went over to the abandoned whaling station at Grytviken. There, they scrounged materials to make partial repairs to the yacht and found some twenty-year-old canned food. With a small .22-caliber rifle they shot a reindeer (which was illegal). For the next several days, they attempted to recover from their harrowing experience—consuming the venison with canned carrots and potatoes, washed down with the one consumable item that had not been swept overboard during the storm—a case of cognac. The three Frenchmen were thus accidental, if not entirely sober, firsthand observers to the beginnings of the Falkland Islands War.

Meanwhile, Captain Miello and Captain Barker were playing cat and mouse as they approached South Georgia. Having departed Buenos Aires on

March 11, the *Bahía Buen Suceso* should have reached landfall by March 15. Instead, hearing HMS *Endurance* radio chatter, Miello decided to loiter some distance offshore until Barker left. Barker, however, having arrived early on March 16, hoped to encounter Miello on his way in. Miello, however, was not moving. He maintained radio silence just as Captain Trombetta had in December. Barker could not delay his departure unduly, having to return several passengers to Port Stanley, and so left South Georgia in the late afternoon of March 16.[43]

Before departing, however, Captain Barker used one of his Wasp helicopters to airlift stores and a "substantial wooden noticeboard" to Leith.[44] Large red letters proclaimed:

> British Antarctic Survey,
> Leith Field Station.
> Unauthorized Entry Prohibited.

The last line was repeated in Spanish, Russian, Polish, and French to make absolutely plain that anyone landing at Leith would understand the necessity of following the procedures required to obtain "authorization." Failure to do so would make their presence illegal.

Although HMS *Endurance* had departed, Captain Miello on the *Bahía Buen Suceso* still loitered offshore, probably to ensure that Barker had actually departed and was unable to make a quick return. Waiting in silence for almost a day-and-a-half, Miello finally put in at the deep-water jetty at Leith harbor at nine o'clock on the morning of March 18, bypassing Grytviken and failing to observe landing procedures.

Miello's behavior was completely inconsistent with the original "Davidoff-Alpha" plan of quietly establishing a legal, commercial presence on the island that would eventually be transformed into an Argentine "base" after the British had gone. From Viola's perspective, Alpha was the vehicle for quite a different mission whose ultimate objective was to dethrone Galtieri. As Freedman and Gamba-Stonehouse observe, "there was no need to act as intruders and if the legalities had been observed Operation Alpha could have been implemented later."[45] It is precisely the point that Miello had no intention of observing the legalities, but instead sought to provoke a British response. Miello's behavior was thus fully consistent with the "bitter Viola's revenge" thesis.

Forewarned, the BAS were waiting for their arrival. Next morning, March 19, a four-man BAS party traveled to Leith, partly to secure the station for the winter and to put up the previously delivered signboard. In reality, their purpose was to catch the Argentines in the act of illegal entry. Arriving, they saw "about fifty men" busily engaged in moving an extensive amount of cargo ashore. "It was clear that some of the Argentines were genuine workmen engaged in demolition work." Though somewhat disorganized, their tools and equipment left "no doubt that they were there to fulfill the Davidoff-Salvesens contract." A few of the men wore the "Alpine type" military uniforms of the Argentine marines, making their status "less certain."[46]

As they headed toward the encampment, the BAS men heard gunshots, observed evidence that deer had been killed, but saw no firearms. On the "no-entry" signboard someone had scrawled "Argentine" over "British" and the Argentine flag had been hoisted on a makeshift mast atop the turret of an electric generator.[47] Escorted aboard the *Bahía Buen Suceso*, the British were introduced to a "Captain Briatore." They explained that his presence was "illegal under maritime and Falkland Islands Dependencies law," but "Briatore" cordially reassured them that "he had been granted permission to land by the Foreign Office in London who...had sent a radio message to him only two days before."[48]

This, of course, was utter nonsense and beside the point. Immigration procedures stipulated registration at King Edward Point, under any circumstances. The British embassy in Buenos Aires had reemphasized the need to follow required procedure before the Davidoff work party's departure. There could be no confusion about this, nor special dispensation from London. "Briatore" knew that the BAS magistrate would check out his story with the embassy in Buenos Aires and learn of his prevarication. The object, of course, was to provoke a British reaction, which came promptly.

When apprised of the landing, Governor Hunt at Port Stanley was convinced that Davidoff's operation was simply a cover for the Argentine navy's attempt to establish a presence on the island in the way they had done earlier at South Thule. In a message to the Foreign Office that night—March 19—he urged the termination of the Salvesens contract, eviction of the work party, and deployment of HMS *Endurance* with marines to enforce their removal.[49]

The Foreign Office chose a different course, however, instructing Hunt to draft the following message for the BAS to deliver to "Briatore":

> You have landed illegally at Leith without obtaining proper clearance. You and your party must go back on board the *Bahía Buen Suceso* immediately and report to the Base Commander Grytviken for further instructions. You must remove the Argentine flag from Leith. You must not interfere with the British Antarctic Survey depot at Leith. You must not alter or deface the notices at Leith. No military personnel are allowed to land on South Georgia. No firearms are to be taken ashore. Ends.[50]

Of course, as the British knew, the Argentines had already ransacked the depot, defaced the signboard, landed military personnel, and brought firearms. In short, London had the Argentines hooked and would not let them go. At eight o'clock on the morning of March 20, less than twelve hours later, Trefor Edwards of BAS returned to Leith Harbor, handed the message to "Captain Briatore," and departed. Later that day, in Buenos Aires, Ambassador Williams delivered a different message to the Argentine Ministry of Foreign Affairs, declaring that the British government regarded the incident as "serious." The crux of the communication was that, "if the Bahía Buen Suceso did not leave forthwith, the British Government would have to take whatever action seemed necessary."[51]

London's démarche was deliberately ambiguous, designed to sow confusion in Buenos Aires. The message to "Briatore" demanded that he and his party "report to the Base Commander Grytviken to await further instructions," while Ambassador Williams's message demanded that the "Bahía Buen Suceso...leave forthwith." What were they being asked to do? Should they go or stay, with or without the workers? London was not waiting for an answer. Even before the Argentine government replied, Prime Minister Thatcher personally ordered HMS *Endurance* to depart as quickly as possible for South Georgia, supplementing its own ships' complement of marines with nine additional marines from the Port Stanley detachment.[52]

That night, someone, obviously an islander(s), "using a key," entered the Argentine airline office in Port Stanley, draped the British flag over the Argentine flag and wrote on a desk (in toothpaste) "tit for tat, you buggers."[53] The act was significant and revealing. The use of the flag and the defacement of Argentine property exactly mirrored what the Davidoff party had done at Leith, hoisting a flag and defacing the signboard. Only the governor knew what had happened on South Georgia. Someone closely associated with him had been responsible. Furthermore, the act ensured an Argentine protest.

HMS *Endurance* departed Port Stanley at a quarter of nine the next morning, March 21, a fact that Argentine observers in Stanley quickly noted. At Leith, Briatore lowered the Argentine flag but stayed put. When the three Frenchmen of the *Cing Gars Pour* heard of Governor Hunt's message and its rejection, they decided to sail over to Leith "in the hope of finding a warmer welcome and the materials they needed to finish repairs to their boat."[54] Steve Martin, the BAS magistrate, attempted vainly to dissuade them from going. As they had completed all immigration procedures, there was no reason to detain them, and they left.

The three Frenchmen had found sufficient materials at Grytviken to get their engine running. En route to Leith, they assisted the Argentines by towing back to the pier a barge that had broken loose from its moorings and been cast adrift.[55] Thus, when the *Cing Gars Pour* arrived at Leith with barge in tow, nearly all of the Davidoff work party turned out on the pier to greet them. "They immediately offered the Frenchmen lunch and, during it, all the supplies they needed. They also offered to help with repairs."[56]

In Buenos Aires, meanwhile, the Argentine Foreign Ministry initially professed to have no knowledge of the ship's visit, which was undoubtedly true, and officially expressed the hope that the affair would not be "exaggerated."[57] Later, on March 21, after making a frantic but necessarily cursory investigation, Costa Mendez attempted to comply with the British demands. He formally notified Ambassador Williams that "the party and the ship would be leaving the same day; that they were in no way official; and that the party included no serving service personnel and was not carrying military arms."[58]

The *Bahía Buen Suceso* raised anchor and departed Leith at seven o'clock on the evening of March 21, but, contrary to Costa Mendez's assurances that "the party and the ship" would be withdrawn, the entire party was not withdrawn. Furthermore, and probably unbeknownst to him, ten of the men left behind were "serving service personnel." In fact, they were Argentine marines. It would be the presence of these ten men that would lead directly to crisis and then war over the Falklands. Ironically, these men had been selected months earlier for Operation Alpha, when Viola was still president. It was doubly ironic that they had been selected by none other than Vice Adm. José Lombardo who, at the time, was chief planner for Alpha. Subsequently, after the ascension of Galtieri and the decision to change strategy, Alpha was canceled, and Lombardo was placed in charge of planning for the Malvinas operation.

Now, as part of the effort to investigate the British charges about the illegal landing at Leith, Lombardo began checking over the name list of the Davidoff work party. Stunned, he quickly recognized the names of the ten men whom he himself had chosen and assigned to his Alpha operation. They were highly professional marine tactical divers, who had remained under his command until October 1981, when Vice Adm. Alberto Vigo, chief of the navy staff, had requested their transfer to his command.[59] Lombardo assumed that Vigo needed these men for intelligence work in relation to Chile. Instead, contrary to all instructions, they had been inserted into the Davidoff work party "the night before the *Bahía Buen Suceso* sailed" and then left behind on South Georgia.[60]

The almost immediate realization by both Buenos Aires and London that Argentines, including ten marines, had been left behind on South Georgia, contrary to the foreign minister's assurances, is central to the subsequent unfolding of events. The official Franks report denies that London knew early on March 22 that any personnel had been left behind after the *Bahía Buen Suceso* had sailed, declaring that BAS observers initially saw "no sign" of a shore party. Franks asserts that it was only "later on March 22 that the Base Commander at Grytviken reported that some Argentines were still at Leith."[61]

This misleading (and false) formulation is crucial to the British plan to keep the Argentines on the hook. It explains why, during the morning of March 22, the Foreign Office, ostensibly working to resolve the incident quickly, proposed to negotiate a communiqué with the Argentine chargé d'affaires, Atelio Molteni. The chargé, eager to achieve closure, agreed, but insisted that the communiqué include a paragraph noting that the Argentine ship was not a warship, had no military personnel or weapons aboard, had assisted a legitimate commercial enterprise, and departed. He also expected to be notified when the communiqué would be released.[62]

Instead, the Foreign Office released the communiqué that afternoon, without notifying Molteni beforehand, without including his explanatory paragraph, and focusing entirely on the promised departure of the Argentines from South Georgia. The communiqué declared that "a group" of Argentines had disembarked on South Georgia on March 19, committing an "absolute violation of British sovereignty" by raising the Argentine flag. The British government asked for clarification of this incident. "The Argentine authorities have reported to London that the group of Argentines left the island yesterday [March 21]." The Foreign Office was "waiting for confirmation [of their departure] by the British commander of the Grytviken base."[63]

In other words, if British authorities discovered that the Argentines had not departed as promised, the gravest of issues would arise, for it would confirm Argentine perfidy, requiring the British government to exercise strong measures. The fact was, however, that British authorities in London knew almost immediately that Argentine personnel had been left behind. That is, they knew there were Argentines on South Georgia when negotiating the communiqué. They, therefore, knew that the British commander of the Grytviken base would soon "discover" that "there were an estimated ten Argentines left at Leith."[64]

The facts, according to the detailed Perkins account, confirm British foreknowledge. "Throughout 22 March," he notes, a two-man BAS party equipped with high-powered binoculars, maintained watch of Leith Harbour from an observation post on Jason Peak, a hill (elevation 2200') on the south side of Stromness Bay. From there they could "see the whole of the bay and its sea approaches." They saw that *Bahía Buen Suceso* had left approximately ten men behind. "There were far fewer men working around the jetty. None of them were in uniform."[65]

Not only was the Davidoff group under constant surveillance, but BAS observations were communicated rapidly, if not instantaneously, to London by satellite link.[66] The Jason Peak observation post was in direct radio contact with King Edward Cove. The BAS base at King Edward Cove was in contact with all concerned parties—at Port Stanley, London, Cambridge (BAS headquarters), Northwood, Buenos Aires, and HMS *Endurance*.[67]

In Buenos Aires, the realization that marines had been left behind on South Georgia caused great consternation and confusion in the junta and Foreign Ministry. Captain Briatore had flatly disobeyed the Foreign Ministry's orders to withdraw both "the party and the ship." That matter would eventually have to be addressed. The immediate issue was that of determining a way to reconcile the obvious and provocative contradiction between Costa Mendez's formal assurance to London and the fact of the continued presence of what were now known to be (as a result of Lombardo's examination of the name list) military personnel among the scrapworkers on the island.

The manner in which the communiqué was released, when "Argentinian officials thought that the contents were still under negotiations, and had not been told that the communiqué was about to be issued," thoroughly alarmed Costa Mendez.[68] He saw a trap coming and tried to avert it. First, he called Ambassador Williams to the Foreign Ministry that evening to admit that "some men had been left behind," and then issued his own communiqué to explain it.[69] He also attempted to place the British on the defensive by raising the incident at the Argentine airline office in Port Stanley. But most important, his purpose was to "explain away" the continued presence of Argentines on the island.

Just before midnight on March 22, the Foreign Ministry released its own communiqué including the points that Molteni had made in London. The *Bahía Buen Suceso* was a naval transport, which "customarily sails to ports in Patagonia, the Malvinas and other South Atlantic islands in fulfillment of commercial transport contracts." The ship carried to South Georgia "material loaded by the contractor as well as personnel employed by him...for the work he intended to carry out ashore." After the cargo was unloaded, "on 21 March, the ship continued its normal cruise to other ports."[70]

The communiqué itself did not mention whether any personnel had departed with the ship, identifying them simply as men "employed by" the contractor. But the official Foreign Ministry press spokesman, Massini Ezcurra, who released the communiqué, acknowledged that some Argentines, whom he characterized as "technical personnel...were still on the island."[71] He also said, in reply to a question about the attack on the Argentine state airline office in Port Stanley, that "the event may be serious if the report is true." The British ambassador was being summoned to the Foreign Ministry for an explanation.

These twisted admissions would not suffice. Next morning, March 23, the British government now declared its intention of doing what Buenos Aires would or could not do—"remove the remaining Argentines" from South Georgia. Captain Barker, aboard HMS *Endurance*, still en route to South

Georgia, was instructed to proceed to Leith Harbour. Mr. Luce, reporting on the events to a thoroughly aroused House of Commons, declared that "a small number of men and some equipment remain. We are therefore making arrangements to ensure their early departure."[72]

London instructed Ambassador Williams to deliver the following "oral note," to Costa Gomez:[73]

> Ministers have agreed that HMS *Endurance* should continue to South Georgia in order to remove the remaining Argentines. The continued Argentine presence at Leith...leaves us no option but to take this action. The Argentine workforce are at Leith illegally and we cannot allow them to remain. On present plans HMS *Endurance* will arrive at Leith on 24th March in order to take men on board and return them to Argentina via Port Stanley. Our intention is to conduct this operation correctly, peacefully and in as low a key as possible. We hope that the Argentine Government will, if they are able to do so, advise the Argentine workmen at Leith to cooperate. We have in mind the need to ensure that equipment landed at Leith is properly safeguarded.
>
> We deeply regret that this action is being forced on us. We had hoped that the previous Argentine undertaking that the ship and party would leave, would have allowed the incident to be surmounted with the least political damage. Our hope is that the political consequences, with careful handling on both sides, can continue to be minimized. But it should be quite clear that this situation has not been of our seeking. It has been Davidoff's irresponsible action and the apparent inability of the Argentine Government to take the necessary remedial action which has brought it about.

While Ambassador Williams was delivering the oral note to Costa Mendez, the junta was meeting for the first time to discuss the South Georgia incident. As soon as Williams had delivered his message, Costa Mendez hurried over from the Foreign Ministry to the Casa Rosada to inform the junta of Britain's decision to evict the workers. Williams's oral note was "interpreted virtually as an ultimatum."[74] London had created a painful dilemma for the Argentine leadership. If they acquiesced in Britain's eviction of the men on South Georgia, the regime would be irretrievably weakened and possibly overthrown. Resistance, however, meant confrontation, and confrontation risked war, for which Argentina was unprepared. War meant inevitable defeat, which meant overthrow.

A Hobson's Choice for the Junta

The discussion that followed receipt of the British note of March 23 immediately clarified for the junta the realization that the crisis over South Georgia threatened the viability of the plan to recover the Malvinas. Recall, the reason Operation Alpha was canceled after Galtieri assumed office was that it would preclude seizure of the Malvinas. The decision had been made, and orders issued, canceling Alpha.[75] Yet, here was the very crisis they had sought to avoid. The hoped-for element of surprise was now lost. At the very least, Britain would now have time to fortify the Falkland Islands, precluding any near-term attempt to recover them.

What should they do? What could they do? Viola and Margaret Thatcher had placed the junta in a lose-lose situation. They would be damned if they failed to react to Britain's ultimatum and damned if they did. The junta would lose all credibility should it capitulate—and eventually be toppled. But the junta would also be toppled if any action were taken that resulted in military defeat. The only hope was to implement quickly the original plan for seizure of the Falklands/Malvinas and forestall a British response until June. Crucial to the success of this plan was the two-month period through late May. If Britain could be prevented from attacking until then, the junta stood a better than even chance of success because of the winter weather that would descend upon the South Atlantic and make naval operations impossible. The original timetable would be in force.

After heated discussion, led by Admiral Anaya, the junta reached decisions on both South Georgia and the Falklands/Malvinas issues. First and foremost, regarding the crisis over South Georgia, Argentina "was not going to accept a withdrawal under threats." As Rear Adm. Carlos Busser, who would soon be designated operational commander of the Malvinas seizure, recalled: "We decided to support our presence there, in view of what we considered was an ultimatum and an aggression."[76] Later, Galtieri would view the South Georgia crisis as "the straw that breaks the camel's back."[77]

Anaya proposed, and all concurred, that another ship should be sent to protect the men on South Georgia. He proposed this action, presumably as he was informed that the naval auxiliary *Bahía Paraiso* was close to South Georgia, having delivered supplies to the Argentine base off Laurie Island in the Islas Orcadas, and could get there quickly. There were, he was told, fourteen marines on board. Orders were sent to Captain Trombetta of the *Bahía Paraiso* to take these marines to Leith as quickly as possible to provide protection for the men there.[78] (What Anaya did not know, as will be discussed later, was that *Bahía Paraiso* was actually carrying more than one hundred Argentine special forces commandos, or *buzos tacticos*, and its proximity to South Georgia was not accidental, but part of the plot to provoke an incident.)

Anaya also gained initial agreement to deploy two missile-carrying corvettes, *Granville* and *Drummond*, between South Georgia and the Falkland Islands, to be in position to intercept HMS *Endurance* should the need arise. Although orders were transmitted, this decision was shortly rescinded when Admiral Lombardo declared that those ships would be needed for the revised Falklands invasion plan.[79] With regard to the Malvinas, it was agreed to task Vice Admiral Lombardo and his planners about the possibility of moving the operation up from its scheduled May 20 date.

Finally, Costa Mendez was to engage Ambassador Williams in an attempt to buy time. From this point onward, the main task for Costa Mendez would be to stretch out discussions and later negotiations for as long as possible in an effort to delay action by Britain. This phase of the junta's plans was implemented immediately. The same day, March 23, first Deputy Minister of Foreign Affairs Enrique Ros called Ambassador Williams to the Foreign Ministry to complain about the break-in at the airline office in Port Stanley and to demand an investigation.

A few hours later, Costa Mendez himself called Williams back to the Foreign Ministry to discuss the events at Leith. He "expressed surprise that the British government were proceeding so rapidly to such very grave action, without exhausting the diplomatic options." Then, he said, "if action to remove the party on South Georgia was not postponed, those like himself and Sr. Ros who were trying to deal with the Falklands in a moderate way, would lose control of events."[80]

Meanwhile, British radio intercept operators had picked up Anaya's signals both to Captain Trombetta aboard the *Bahía Paraiso* and to the corvettes of March 23. Whether it was because of what was believed to be an Argentine decision to counter force with force, or because of the Argentine foreign minister's remonstrations, according to the Franks report, London now "decided to make a further attempt to resolve the problem without provocation." HMS *Endurance* was ordered "to wait at Grytviken instead of proceeding to Leith."[81] Captain Barker would drop anchor in King Edward Cove at a quarter past six on the morning of March 24.

Still, on March 23, Carrington passed a message to Costa Mendez, declaring that it remained "essential" for the Argentine personnel still in South Georgia to be evacuated promptly. "If the Argentine government can order the immediate return of the *Bahía Buen Suceso* to Leith Harbour to carry out this action, the use of HMS *Endurance* will not be necessary. If this is not done, we would have no alternative but to proceed [unilaterally]."[82]

Although Carrington's note appeared to be conciliatory, it was inflammatory. British intelligence knew that the *Bahía Buen Suceso* had departed Leith four days earlier and was already nearing Buenos Aires. It was thus approximately four days' sailing time from Leith. Carrington also knew, however, from Anaya's intercepted signal, that the *Bahía Paraiso* was at that moment sailing to South Georgia and would, in fact, arrive late on March 24, that is, within twenty-four hours. Carrington's specific demand that *Bahía Buen Suceso* immediately retrieve those left behind at Leith was impossible to fulfill. Was its purpose to elicit additional communications from the junta, which could be intercepted and analyzed to further disclose Argentine movements, or simply to sow further confusion?

Very late on March 23, Costa Mendez called in Ambassador Williams again (for the third time that day) to say that he "welcomed" Lord Carrington's message and that he had "discussed the issue with the junta." Costa Mendez "assumed it would be possible for another Argentine ship to remove the men, and was about to discuss this with the military."[83] This exchange confirmed what British intelligence had already gathered—that the junta had decided to act in support of the workers rather than to remove them. It meant that as HMS *Endurance* had gone to King Edward Cove, instead of to Leith, that *Bahía Paraiso* would arrive first and unhindered.

Surely, if Costa Mendez had "discussed the issue" of Carrington's message with the junta, the idea of employing *Bahía Paraiso* must have been part of it. To say that he was only now going to raise the issue of "another

Argentine ship" was undoubtedly designed to buy time. When Costa Mendez told Williams the next day, March 24, that "he was hopeful of arranging the removal of the men by another vessel but that the decision would be made at a meeting of the commanders-in-chief," London knew that the die had been cast.[84] They knew—if not through intercepted signals, then through the press leak of March 24—that *Bahía Paraiso* was already en route, with marines on board.[85]

Indeed, on March 24, Carrington sent a minute to the prime minister and members of the Defense Committee saying that "the dispute had developed to a point where an early confrontation with Argentina might need to be faced....It was therefore necessary to recognize that negotiations might be at an end and that the Argentines would turn to other forms of pressure." These included, "in the final analysis, military action against the islands."[86]

Although there is no direct evidence of advance preparations, it would strain credulity to believe that the British government, at this late stage, had not yet gone beyond its "review" of early March. In fact, the departure of the Royal Fleet Auxiliary HMS *Fort Austin* for the South Atlantic on March 26 implied that loading operations must have begun several days earlier. According to Admiral Woodward, formation of the task force began on the evening of March 26.[87] Ironically, the junta only decided that very evening to invade the Malvinas.

By March 24, if not earlier, the junta had confirmed Anaya's earlier proposal to send the *Bahía Paraiso* to Leith to support the men there. By this time, too, the junta had been encouraged to learn—probably from Otero and Girling, the responsible officers in charge—that the *Bahía Paraiso* had on board not fourteen men, but over 100 special forces commandos—*buzos tacticos*. These men were attached to the Antarctic mission at Ushuaia under Capt. César Trombetta, who was also captain of the *Bahía Paraiso*. When the *Bahía Paraiso* left Ushuaia, March 18, the commandos "were handed secret instructions in a sealed envelope which they were ordered to open only after they had put to sea. The orders confirmed that they were to proceed in late March to South Georgia, where they were to establish a military base."[88]

The *Bahía Paraiso*'s itinerary took it to the Argentine army station on the [Antarctic] peninsula, the Argentine naval station at the South Orkney Islands, and the Argentine naval station at South Thule before heading for

South Georgia.[89] The *Bahía Paraiso* departed Ushuaia on March 18, after the *Bahía Buen Suceso* had departed Buenos Aires, but before it arrived at Leith. Captain Trombetta's departure may have been triggered by the cat and mouse game Captain Briatore played with Captain Barker on March 15–16, or planned long before. In either case, departing from Ushuaia with a force of over a hundred men was designed to put sufficient power into a position to reinforce the Argentine government in an anticipated crisis with Great Britain.

The trouble was, of course, that the junta and the Foreign Ministry, at least Costa Mendez, knew nothing of the movements of *Bahía Buen Suceso* and *Bahía Paraiso*, learning of them only after the fact. That the Galtieri regime acted in catch-up mode, responding rather than initiating, seems undeniable. Admiral Otero, for example, had authorized Davidoff's trip without consulting the Ministry of Foreign Affairs—a fact that Costa Mendez later corroborated.[90] The junta was, therefore, led into a confrontation with Great Britain by elements within the Argentine government unsympathetic to the junta under President Galtieri.

The junta, now fully alert to the deepening crisis, began meeting daily. On March 24, Vice Admiral Lombardo reported that it was feasible to advance the date for the invasion of the Malvinas, but there was a complication. Lombardo's original plan had called for a heliborne assault on Port Stanley using the naval transports *Bahía Buen Suceso* and *Bahía Paraiso* as launch platforms. No warships were to be used to ensure deception and surprise, the hallmarks of this plan. The ships originally envisaged for Operation Rosario, however, were all tied up in the South Georgia incident, forcing a change of plans, and making conclusive the argument that the South Georgia and Malvinas operations were not connected.[91]

As an alternative, Lombardo designated Argentina's main fleet assets for an amphibious assault. The fleet could sail on March 28, ensuring some ambiguity of purpose under the guise of previously scheduled naval exercises with Uruguay. Largely sacrificing secrecy, Lombardo's hastily devised alternative plan called for a marine invasion force of just under one thousand men to land at Port Stanley on April 1 or 2.[92] In a "clean," or bloodless, operation designed to take five days, this force would overwhelm the few defenders at Port Stanley and other key posts and establish Argentine control. The invasion force would then be withdrawn and be replaced by a 500 to

700-man army garrison force that would maintain order during what was expected to be a negotiated transfer of sovereignty.

The central assumption in this plan of operations was that Argentina would present, and Great Britain would accept, a fait accompli. Galtieri believed that a British military reaction was "totally improbable."[93] As no British blood would be spilled, the anticipated British response to the seizure would be "in a fashion intended to force negotiations."[94] Nowhere in the Argentine "strategic military directive" for Operation Blue (the now renamed Operation Rosario) is there the concept, let alone plan, to defend the Malvinas against a British attempt to recapture the islands.

In discussion on March 24, the junta could not reach agreement to execute this plan, but Lombardo was instructed to continue with preparations as he had outlined them. Commander of the expeditionary force, Rear Adm. Gualter Allara, was given orders to have all preparations completed for fleet departure by March 28. The junta established, however, that the entire operation could be canceled virtually until the last moment.[95] The junta, in other words, could not decide whether to invade the Malvinas, further indicating that the South Georgia incident was not intended to be a trigger for seizure of the Malvinas.

There were actually powerful arguments against invasion. The Argentine army was at its smallest and weakest point in the annual training cycle.[96] Conscripts, which constitute seventy percent of the army, serve for a maximum of one year. They are inducted in March and released in stages beginning in November through the following February. Thus, some serve less than a full year. In any case, March is the low ebb in the recruitment-training cycle for the Argentine army. No mobilization of the army had yet occurred, and it would take time to recall men to active duty. The counterargument here was that the conscript army was not involved. Only a small professional elite marine commando force was planned for seizure of the Malvinas with an even smaller army unit for garrison duty afterward. Therefore, there would be no strain on the army's existing military capabilities.

More serious were arguments about weapons stocks. Most of the weapons on order from French, West German, and Israeli suppliers had yet to be delivered.[97] The Argentine navy's contract to acquire fourteen Super-Étendard fighter-bombers from France equipped with Exocet antiship missiles had been only partially fulfilled. Only five aircraft with missiles had been delivered (the previous December), and these had not yet been modified for carrier launch. French technicians were in Argentina, however, engaged in this work, and delivery of the remaining nine aircraft was scheduled for July.

Also on order from France were three frigates, additional Mirage fighters, twenty-five Puma helicopters, ninety-six armored cars, and a large quantity of Roland surface-to-surface and surface-to-air missiles. Scheduled for delivery from West Germany were four destroyers, four diesel submarines, and two missile-armed vessels. In addition, Argentina was constructing under West German license four diesel submarines, six frigates, and 220 light tanks. None of this was yet available.

The Argentine air force was only in the beginning phase of its aircraft modernization. Israel had sold twenty-six (some estimates were forty) Dagger fighters to Argentina, but, for the most part, the Argentine air force still relied on its aging American A-4P Skyhawks, which had no radar, and older Mirage IIIs. The Argentine air force had a grand total of eighty-two aircraft available for combat. No aircraft in the Argentinian Buenos Aires' inventory had sufficient range to conduct extended air operations in the Falklands from mainland bases. Clearly, in terms of trained military forces and available weaponry, Argentina was unprepared to fight a war with Great Britain.

There was also the very important factor of the status of Great Britain's forces. Scheduled force reductions in the British fleet had yet to occur. The crisis on South Georgia would undoubtedly interrupt any that were imminent. The critical element of surprise had been lost, assuming that it had ever been possible to achieve. A crucial question was whether, with its existing military capability, Great Britain could expeditiously deploy sufficient forces to recapture the Malvinas once Argentine forces seized them? Did Thatcher have the desire or the will to take her nation to war?

As the junta wrestled with its decision, preparations began. Argentine ports and military installations burst into activity, matched only in intensity by rumors of imminent crisis that began circulating in the Argentine press. "Early on 24 March" Ambassador Williams and the defense attaché, Col. Stephen Love, met to review the latest developments. In a telegram to the Defense Ministry and Foreign Office, they warned that any attempt to evict the scrap metal workers "might give the Argentine government an excuse to mount a 'rescue mission' leading to the occupation of the Falkland

Islands."[98] The possibility that it was all a clever and extremely well coordinated Argentine ploy simply to exert pressure on London was now viewed as highly unlikely.

Britain's naval attaché to Buenos Aires, Julian Mitchell, promptly reported on the intensified naval activities. Much of his information was gleaned from his many contacts "privy—in one way or another—to the activities of the Argentine armed forces."[99] On the night of March 24–25, Mitchell sent a number of signals to London, advising of the sailing from Mar del Plata of submarines and surface ships for the ostensible purpose of joint antisubmarine exercises with the Uruguayan navy. These were scheduled exercises and caused no undue anxiety.

But the departure from the same port of the frigates *Drummond* and *Granville* for South Georgia was "disturbing." More disturbing were reports from Mitchell's "contacts" of "intense activity at the main naval base of Puerto Belgrano...[where] the bulk of the Argentine navy had started to put to sea."[100] Most alarming of all, however, were reports that "soldiers and marines had been seen embarking with full field equipment and armored fighting vehicles," which meant that these ships were probably not engaging in antisubmarine exercises.

Late that same evening of March 24, Costa Mendez summoned Ambassador Williams to tell him that he was having "great difficulty, particularly with Admiral Anaya." The navy member of the junta refused to take "any action under the threat of force implied in the deployment of HMS *Endurance*," a view that British intelligence was at that moment also confirming. The foreign minister was probing, attempting to gain an insight into possible British actions, while continuing to buy time. Costa Mendez said that "he had been reassured to learn that HMS *Endurance* had sailed to Grytviken rather than Leith and undertook to see whether Sr. Davidoff could be persuaded to arrange for the removal of the party, perhaps on a scientific ship which was in the area, but he was doubtful whether he would succeed."[101]

Costa Mendez's professed doubt that he could persuade Davidoff to agree to the government's proposals was hardly credible. He knew by now that Davidoff was a pawn in a larger game, but it served his purpose to assert some independence for the scrap dealer, although he surely had no voice in this matter. The discussion was plainly a subterfuge, designed to string the British along. He also knew that the ship "in the area" was not a "scientific ship," but an Argentine naval vessel on a decidedly unscientific mission. Indeed, at the very moment that Costa Mendez and Williams were engaged in their conversation, close to midnight, the *Bahía Paraiso* anchored in Leith Harbor, South Georgia, and began to debark troops.

Witnesses to Invasion

Serge Briez and his two friends aboard the *Cing Gars Pour* had been at Leith since March 22 and had witnessed the departure of the *Bahía Buen Suceso* that evening. There had been no warning of any new arrival. Now, late on March 24, just as he was going below to bed for the night, Briez was startled by a "shuddering jolt," that

> sent him racing back on deck. He emerged to find himself face to face with a group of men in camouflaged uniforms, faces blackened, their belts festooned with grenades, automatic rifles on their shoulders. Briez just had time to see more men leaping from the landing craft that had bumped the yacht before a strong light dazzled him, and a voice asked in bad English if he had a radio on board.[102]

Briez was told that he was in no danger "so long as he did not use the radio or attempt to take any photographs." Despite that warning, next morning at daylight, Briez hid in his dinghy and "filmed the disembarkation of troops and equipment from Argentina's newest fleet auxiliary, *Bahía Paraiso*."[103] It took, as Franks notes, three landing craft and a military helicopter most of the following day, March 25, to transfer all of the men and cargo from ship to shore.[104] In all, Briez estimated that "there were more than a hundred" troops.[105] They were under the command of Lt. Alfredo Astiz, an infamous navy hatchet man of the days of the dirty war.

But Briez and his two friends were not the only ones to observe the unloading of the *Bahía Paraiso*. The British marines who had accompanied Captain Barker aboard the HMS *Endurance* were also watching. HMS *Endurance* had dropped anchor at Grytviken before daybreak on March 24, at which time the marines had assumed from the BAS personnel the task of keeping tabs on Leith Harbor.[106] They were thus manning the outpost on Jason Peak the following day when the *Bahía Paraiso* unloaded its cargo and personnel.

The next day, after the Argentine ship departed, two of the marines crept to within six hundred yards of the jetty for a close-in reconnaissance. From the amount of cargo and personnel unloaded, it was clear that "the Argentines evidently intended to stay on the island for a long time and in strength."[107] The reports from Leith combined with those from Buenos Aires—not to mention decoded Argentine cipher traffic—made it unmistakably clear that the Argentines were intent upon employing military force to hold onto South Georgia.

Still, no shots had yet been fired. Therefore, under the dictum that the aggressor must fire the first shot, Carrington and the British leadership played out the diplomatic string, while advising Washington of the situation. In a telegram on March 25 to the British ambassador Nicholas Henderson in Washington, Carrington concluded that, although everything was being done to defuse the potentially dangerous situation, "in the final analysis we cannot acquiesce in this infringement of British sovereignty and are bound to take action to restore the status quo."[108]

Later that same afternoon, in Buenos Aires, Costa Mendez met again with Ambassador Williams. Referring to inflammatory articles in the British press about the deployment of HMS *Endurance* to evict the Argentines from South Georgia, he said "there now seemed to be no way in which the Argentines could remove the men, even if they had agreed to do so, without appearing to have responded to threats."[109] Costa Mendez wondered, however, whether the British would revoke the expulsion order, "if Sr. Davidoff ordered his men to complete the necessary landing formalities by having their 'white cards' stamped at Grytviken?"

Costa Mendez knew the "white card" regime did not extend to South Georgia and the other Dependencies. The "white card" system was part of the 1971 Communications Agreement that related only to Argentine travel to and from the Falkland Islands. His proposal was, at best, a delaying tactic and, at worst, an attempt to degrade British sovereignty. Although they were administered from Port Stanley, the Dependencies were politically separate from the Falkland Islands. Acceptance of the "white card" system for South Georgia would signify that Great Britain no longer insisted on sovereignty there, or, at the very least, that they admitted that sovereignty was in question.

Although Ambassador Williams "recommended this course of action in view of the risk of military confrontation," London insisted that rules governing South Georgia be those governing travel to and from sovereign states—that is, that the Argentines would have to have their passports stamped as would any visitor traveling to a foreign country. Williams was thus instructed to inform Costa Mendez that, although Britain was publicly committed to removing the Argentines from Leith, the government was willing to compromise. "If the Argentine party went to Grytviken, documentation would be issued to enable it to return to Leith."[110]

It seems that London, too, was willing to engage in diplomatic play. Costa Mendez, perhaps realizing that the game was up, said that "he could not comment on the proposal without consulting the President."[111] He hoped to be able to report back that same evening, March 25. In the event, there would be no reply that evening, or the next, as Costa Mendez postponed meeting with Williams on the grounds that President Galtieri was scheduled to discuss the South Georgia issue with his military chiefs on the evening of March 26.

The delay in the response from Buenos Aires appears to have made London edgy, and realizing that the junta was on the verge of a fateful decision, Carrington decided to force the issue. Late on Friday, Carrington decided that, after all, HMS *Endurance* "should evacuate the Argentines," but, if challenged, should offer to transfer them at sea.[112] This was an extraordinary proposal. Even if seriously intended for execution, it contained two very problematic assumptions. First, that HMS *Endurance* could simply sail in and force the Argentines to board ship without incident and, second, that, if challenged, the inherently dangerous transfer of personnel at sea could be effected smoothly.

In reality, Carrington had decided to place HMS *Endurance* in harm's way as a last attempt to provoke the Argentines into action. He knew that the *Bahía Paraiso* had unloaded a substantial amount of military matériel and had to assume, even if it could not be confirmed, that additional military personnel had disembarked with the supplies.[113] Thus, the probability was great that Britain would meet resistance. Indeed, it would have been incredible had he assumed otherwise.[114] The essence of Carrington's decision, however, was that Britain had authorized "the use of force" to place the ground party on South Georgia aboard the HMS *Endurance*.[115]

Carrington clearly understood that this was intended to precipitate conflict. Indeed, he sent a message that day to Ambassador Williams to "prepare for the worst," a situation the ambassador had already anticipated. The day before, March 25, Williams had already "authorized the destruction of every sensitive document held in the Embassy filing cabinets."[116] It would take five days, using two shredding machines, to destroy all the classified material held at the embassy. The British leadership's decision to force the issue came at the precise moment that the junta was meeting to decide how to respond—as they no doubt realized.

Amid wild rumors circulating in the Argentine press, the junta met with the military planners responsible for Operation Blue (Rosario) the evening of March 26. Present at the beginning of the meeting were President Galtieri, Navy chief Anaya, and Air Force head, Lami Dozo. With them were chief planner Admiral Lombardo, and his service colleagues Air Force Brigadier Plessel and Army General Garcia. Also present was the head of the Joint Chiefs of Staff, Vice Admiral Juarez del Cerro. Foreign Minister Costa Mendez arrived later.

The military men of the junta made the only decision it was now possible to make—to seize the Malvinas. Although unanimous, it was evidently a difficult decision. Some, like Anaya, were less troubled than others in reaching it. The Galtieri leadership had certainly planned to seize the Malvinas, but in late May, not in early April. Thus, preparations were incomplete, and the conditions were far from optimal. The difference in timing being forced on them by the crisis on South Georgia was the difference between almost certain success as opposed to improbable success.

But it was now or never. That same day, Carrington had issued instructions for HMS *Endurance* to proceed with the eviction of the Argentines on South Georgia. If the junta passively accepted British domination, it would entail a great loss of face and the junta's inevitable demise, for the conflict was now public, and the public expected action. Resistance, however, meant conflict. HMS *Endurance* was proceeding to Leith where Argentines special forces awaited them in strength, far outnumbering the British. The Argentines on South Georgia might win this skirmish, but could they win the war it would produce?

The hue and cry in the British House of Commons, by government supporters and opposition alike, made it apparent that the British government intended to connect the South Georgia incident to the Falkland Islands. The Falkland Islands lobby's demands to "fortify the Falklands" would finally be accepted. A failure to act would mean losing the opportunity for Argentina to recover the Malvinas. But could the crisis be prolonged for an additional few weeks or a month? Clearly, the closer to the original invasion date of late May that the junta could come before taking decisive action, the better the chances were for success because of the winter weather.

A seizure of the Malvinas now meant that Great Britain would have sufficient time to attempt a recovery before winter set in. Britain clearly had the military capability to undertake such an action, but the crucial question was whether Margaret Thatcher had the political courage to use it. Here, one must surmise, is where the argument raged. Would Thatcher fight? And here, it seems, Anaya and Galtieri tipped the balance in favor of the assumption that she would not fight. (The great irony involved the Argentine leadership's limited understanding of British political realities. The actual question was not whether Thatcher had the courage to act, but whether she could fail to act, given her domestic political predicament.)

Thus, on the fundamental question of whether Great Britain would respond to an attack on its territory by means of a counterattack, the junta had persuaded itself that it would not. Reinforcing this basic decision was the conviction of American neutrality, the product of assiduous American cultivation for the past year. It seems very likely that the American courtship of Galtieri helped shape his view that Thatcher would not go to war over the Malvinas. Furthermore, Galtieri and Anaya believed Washington's neutrality would reinforce Britain's predisposition to avoid a fight. It would be a replay of Suez in 1956.

Moreover, there were several recent precedents for what they planned. Iran had taken several islands at the mouth of the Persian Gulf; China had seized the Paracel Islands; Vietnam had occupied the Spratleys; Indonesia had assumed control of East Timor; and Turkey had appropriated a part of Cyprus. Twenty years before, India had invaded Goa. Although protest had accompanied each of these actions, it had reversed none of them.[117] Then, there was Rhodesia where Britain, indeed, the Thatcher government itself, had arranged a smooth transition. Was not Great Britain attempting to divest itself of the remnants of empire?

Margaret Thatcher, meanwhile, would not tolerate prolonging the crisis, which convinced the junta that it must either act now or never. Carrington's order to HMS *Endurance* to evict the Argentines from South Georgia required a response; and Costa Mendez would announce the Argentine government's decision to provide "protection" for the scrap metal workers. But it was another British step that finally prodded the junta into immediate action on the Malvinas. This was the passage of information, or disinformation, that convinced the junta that its window of opportunity was closing swiftly and that the opportunity to recover the Malvinas would be irretrievably lost if there were not immediate action.

The information in question was a purported ITN (Independent Television News) broadcast late on the evening of March 26–27, announcing that the British nuclear-powered submarine, HMS *Superb*, had sailed from Gibraltar for the South Atlantic.[118] To Anaya this meant that "when this nuclear-powered submarine arrived on the scene, it would not be possible to execute the surface operations that would be required to place Argentinian troops ashore at Port Stanley. The window of opportunity was limited by the steaming time it would take HMS *Superb* to get from Gibraltar to the vicinity of the Falklands."[119]

It would take a nuclear-powered submarine two weeks to travel from Gibraltar to the Falkland Islands. Once there, any amphibious assault on the islands would involve extreme risk. In other words, to Anaya and the junta, the plan to recover the Malvinas would have to be executed before the submarine arrived, on or about April 7–8. Within two hours of receiving the ITN broadcast, Anaya testified, he ordered the fleet to sail. Indeed, Anaya referred to news of the dispatch of a submarine as the "war-starter."[120]

Of course, it is beside the point to declaim—as British authorities do—that the decision to deploy a submarine was taken only on March 29, three days *after* the junta's decision to invade.[121] Nor does the claim that there is no record of a broadcast regarding the departure of HMS *Superb* meet the point.[122] The point is that Anaya did receive a report that a nuclear submarine had sailed for the Falklands. Was it disinformation cooked by British (or American) intelligence, designed specifically to prod the Argentine junta into action? Or, did it really occur? In any case, Anaya is not to be excused for acting on this report without confirming it. The Argentine junta allowed itself to be spooked.

To Anaya, in particular, dispatch of a submarine brought back memories of 1977 when Britain had executed the same maneuver and forestalled an Argentine attempt to fortify South Thule (discussed in chapter 1). He had been the naval attaché in London at that time and was one of a few Argentines (and Britons) who knew that a submarine had been sent. But it had been sent, which left an indelible imprint on his mind. It was either a quirk of fate that Anaya was now the navy member of the junta susceptible to influence in this way, or very sophisticated reasoning on the part of the British leadership who, understanding Anaya's role in 1977, sought to play tricks with his mind now. Either way, it succeeded.

There are three possibilities. Either no submarine was sent at all, one departed and then returned to British waters, or one was actually sent. There is apparent "evidence," perhaps disinformation is the best term, for all three interpretations of this decisive action. The Franks report maintains that no submarine was sent. "The decision to sail the first nuclear-powered submarine was taken only on Monday 29 March."[123] Freedman & Gamba-Stonehouse acknowledge the "wrong" report that HMS *Superb* left base on March 25, but then note the submarine's return on April 16.[124] The implication is that it departed and then returned, having achieved its provocative purpose.

Following the invasion, however, on April 7, British "military sources" passed on information to reporters that the HMS *Superb* "has already arrived off the South American archipelago," while *Spartan*, *Splendid*, and *Conqueror*, the three submarines officially dispatched on March 29, "were believed to be within two days' sailing time of the islands."[125] As all authors agree that for nuclear-powered submarines the sailing time from Britain to the Falklands is two weeks, if "military sources" were correct that HMS *Superb* had in fact arrived on April 7, that would mean departure from British waters fourteen days earlier—on or about March 25. London had, in fact, withdrawn nuclear submarines and support vessels from NATO patrols "the week before the Argentine invasion."[126]

Whatever the truth of the matter, the junta's belief that London had dispatched a nuclear submarine was the last straw and persuaded them to execute hastily devised plans for the seizure of the Malvinas. Britain had finally provoked the junta into "firing the first shot."[127] The invasion force sailed on March 28 on a course directly south between the Malvinas and the mainland. Final instructions for the attack were sent on March 31 to forces while at sea. British intelligence picked up these signals. Of course, by this time, London had decided to send the first of three nuclear-powered submarines that were deployed to the Falklands. The HMS *Spartan* sailed on March 31; HMS *Splendid* and HMS *Conqueror* followed shortly thereafter.[128]

British intelligence, or, rather, the Latin America Current Intelligence Group, had made a precisely accurate assessment of the origins of the conflict—an assessment fully supported by the author's own analysis. On March 31, it circulated the view that

> the landing on South Georgia had not been contrived by the Argentine Government, but that the Junta was taking full advantage of the incident to speed up negotiations on the transfer of sovereignty. Despite Sr. Davidoff's close contacts with some senior Argentine naval officers, the unauthorized landing was not considered to be part of the navy's plans. There was no central coordination of Argentine policy and the Junta's intentions were not known.[129]

Implied was the notion that neither the Argentine government nor navy had "contrived" the South Georgia incident. That someone else within the government had done so was the further implication in the assessment that there had been "no central coordination of Argentine policy." What was quite rightly omitted was the British side of the equation, which was, of course, that it was Margaret Thatcher who was "taking full advantage of the incident" to advance the timing of the conflict to serve her own interests.

In her memoir, Margaret Thatcher completely ignores the period March 20–28, and with good reason.[130] To discuss this period would necessarily include the subject of warning. Thatcher maintained that the invasion came without warning, which, as this study demonstrates, was not remotely close to the truth. Even Defense Minister Nott, responding to criticism in the House of Commons, acknowledged on April 5 that "preparation [had] been in progress for several weeks. We were not unprepared."[131]

PART II

... The Sting ...

CHAPTER 5

Mediation:
The American Sting

When the conflict began, the Reagan administration moved quickly to control the dispute. The instrument employed was the mediation by Alexander Haig—or, rather, the intense and extremely complex political struggle that occurred in the name of mediation. It was actually a multifaceted affair involving the conflicting interests of President Reagan and Secretary Haig, Prime Minister Margaret Thatcher and Secretary Pym, and the Argentine junta, which, for all its disagreements, had a more focused approach toward its objective than either the American or British leaderships.

From the outset, President Reagan maneuvered to provide clandestine support to Great Britain, while dissembling with Argentina. It was not, as represented, a case of attempting to reach a fair settlement and, failing that, siding with Great Britain. American support for Great Britain began immediately and was continuous, although this fact would not be acknowledged until much later.[1] Only a select few within the administration were aware of the secret supply program centered at tiny, barren, remote Ascension Island, roughly midway between Britain and Argentina. Thus, there were those within the administration who acted in good faith, seeking a "fair" solution to the dispute, but there were also those who did not share President Reagan's objectives.

Policy Fault Lines

The mediation was, in its effect, a triple sting by Reagan and Thatcher directed in the first instance against the junta, but also against internal adversaries in each leadership—Alexander Haig and Francis Pym, respectively. Within a week and a half after the end of the Falkland Islands War, Reagan would "accept" Haig's unwilling resignation; following Thatcher's reelection, she would dismiss Francis Pym; and, of course, the entire junta would be replaced by civilian political rule. Raul Alfonsín, Argentina's president from 1983 to 1987, would expose and abolish Argentina's clandestine nuclear weapons program.

The split in the Reagan administration was universally recognized, but its fault line was misperceived. During the Falklands crisis, the split was perceived to be between "Latinos" and "Atlanticists," personified in press accounts as conflicts between UN Ambassador Jeane Kirkpatrick, a Latin American specialist, and Alexander Haig, who had strong ties to Europe. These differences clearly existed and should not be minimized, but they did not drive events. The governing division was not based on personalities and was not "Latinos" versus "Atlanticists," but was the continuing battle over strategy between the president and his secretary of state.

From its inception, the Reagan administration was a coalition government composed of representatives from the two principal wings of the Republican political establishment. The main division between the two groups concerned grand strategy—should the United States continue to pursue détente with the Soviet Union, or revert to the containment strategy that had been in place since the beginning of the cold war? There was no question where Reagan stood, having campaigned against the failed détente strategy of Henry Kissinger and Jimmy Carter. Alexander Haig, however, was part of the Kissinger détente-wing of the Republican Party.

To ensure a unified election campaign, Ronald Reagan had reached a compromise with the prodétente wing of the Republican Party led by Henry Kissinger and Alan Greenspan at the party convention in July 1980.[2] In return for establishment support for his election bid, Reagan agreed to several key personnel appointments from the Kissinger wing. From the outset, therefore, the incoming Reagan administration was a coalition government of procontainment Reagan supporters and prodétente Kissinger supporters. The prodétente group now professed to favor "hard-headed détente," requiring a greater degree of equality in the relationship with Moscow, a shift that made short-term cooperation between the two groups possible, while their long-term objectives remained irreconcilable.

President Reagan had publicly vilified Henry Kissinger as the architect of the failed détente policy. Therefore, it was impossible for Kissinger to be a part of the Reagan administration, although a brief attempt to include him had been made during the party convention where the original compromise "compact" had been struck, and afterward when the new administration was being assembled. The recommendations for Kissinger's surrogate as secretary of state were his close colleagues from the Nixon administration—George Shultz and Alexander Haig.

In adhering to his "compact" with the Kissinger wing, Reagan selected Haig as secretary of state. Unquestionably, Haig opposed Reagan on the fundamental issue of grand strategy. While the president planned to rebuild American economic and military power to confront the "evil empire," Haig sought an accommodation with it. In a speech delivered after he became secretary of state, Haig described his objectives. In return for Soviet "restraint and reciprocity," said Haig, "we offer the possibility of Western trade and technology."[3] What he sought was "a working relationship with the Soviet Union," precisely the quid pro quo proffered by his mentor Kissinger.

The first year of the Reagan administration thus witnessed a public and protracted struggle for control of foreign policy and the machinery that formulated it. The president eventually won this battle, establishing control over the foreign policy-making apparatus with the appointment of his close friend and colleague William Clark as National Security Adviser in January 1982. The conflict between Reagan and Haig would not be resolved until six months later, however, shortly after the British victory in the Falkland Islands when the president forced Haig's resignation. Indeed, by the time that the Falkland Islands crisis broke, both the White House and Haig himself expected, as Barrett notes, that "there might well be a new Secretary of State before the new year."[4] As Haig put it, by then "it was clear enough that there were men and women around the President who would urge my departure."[5]

Although he was publicly neutral on the subject of the Falklands, President Reagan was strongly pro-Thatcher—and not only because she was a kindred philosophical spirit. "We were staunch allies of the United Kingdom and supported its right to defend its colony. We also assured Margaret Thatcher that we were fully behind Britain. Publicly, however, I decided it was wisest to mute our reaction while extending the good offices of the United States."[6]

For the resuscitation of Reagan's policy of containment to succeed, British cooperation was essential. Britain was America's gateway to Western Europe in any future conflict—as true in 1980 as it was in 1940. Conversely, Thatcher's fall from power would seriously question the feasibility of Reagan's strategy, at least toward Europe. Margaret Thatcher's fate, in a very real sense, would determine the fate of Reagan's strategy. For this strategic reason, support for Thatcher would supersede support for Galtieri.

UN Ambassador Jeane Kirkpatrick, widely perceived to be a Latino, considered herself neutral in the Falkland Islands dispute—not pro-Argentina.[7] Whatever her actual views, about which she was not reticent, she appears from the record to have acted under the president's instructions. The year-long embrace of Argentina by the Reagan administration, in which Kirkpatrick played a prominent role, generated the clear expectation on the part of the Galtieri leadership that the United States would, at a minimum, act as an honest broker in Argentina's dispute with Great Britain. Indeed, Argentine president Galtieri, at the outset, believed that Reagan's pro-Argentine sentiments would prevail in a test of preferences.

Secretary of State Haig, however, unanimously identified as an Atlanticist, was profuse in his statements of support for Great Britain, though not necessarily for Prime Minister Thatcher. In fact, as we shall see, Haig attempted to reach a negotiated settlement that would have kept Galtieri in power—and resulted in Margaret Thatcher's fall and replacement by Francis Pym. Perhaps only Casper Weinberger, who was also uniformly viewed as a staunch supporter of Thatcher's, was correctly role-cast in the eyes of contemporary reporters. Yet, even he had been publicly at odds earlier with the prime minister over British naval policy.

In Thatcher's government, the division was clearly defined between the prime minister and the "wets." This division, too, was an extension of earlier strategic differences, as we have seen. When Lord Carrington resigned after the Argentine invasion of the Falklands, he was replaced as foreign secretary by Francis Pym. Earlier, in January 1981, Thatcher had removed Pym, "the man she least respected and least liked" in a "limited reshuffle" to change the cabinet balance in favor of her economic policies, which he had opposed.[8] She had transferred him from defense to the relatively innocuous post of leader of the House of Commons.[9] Now, to unify the party, Thatcher brought Pym back into the cabinet. In a rare misjudgment,

Thatcher believed Pym to be "a good tactician, but no strategist."[10] In fact, however, during the mediation Pym would advance an opposing strategy that would present "serious difficulties" for the prime minister.

From the beginning, the crisis was zero-sum for Prime Minister Thatcher. Any outcome short of her declared objective of complete recovery of the Falkland Islands and reestablishment of British authority would mean her removal from office and replacement by Francis Pym. And Pym pressed hard within the cabinet for an outcome far short of Thatcher's declared minimum. As the *Sunday Times* Insight Team described him: "He actually wanted the peace missions to succeed even when she felt that they were becoming a farce, and he was the last of the war cabinet to concede that war was inevitable."[11]

Privately, Pym proposed acceptance of a negotiated settlement and a delayed transfer of sovereignty over the Falkland Islands to Argentina, just as Carrington had urged, while publicly supporting a harder line. Pym was greatly assisted in his efforts by Secretary of State Alexander Haig, who even more vigorously pursued a similar objective from the American side. Indeed, as Hastings and Jenkins observe, by the end of the Haig mediation a "yawning gulf" had emerged between Thatcher and Pym.[12]

While the Reagan administration was equally divided, the president was "fully behind" Thatcher, as he notes in his memoir.[13] Their collaboration, after all, was the "sting" this book recounts. The clearest expression of Reagan's support was the extensive and secret military, logistical, and intelligence assistance provided by the United States to Great Britain from the outset of the crisis, "before the task force even set sail."[14] Naturally, that decision could not be publicized because the United States was involved as a mediator, but the decision was clearly made by the president, although it was attributed to Defense Secretary Weinberger for obvious reasons of plausible deniability. Weinberger, who vigorously advocated aid to Britain and skillfully managed to provide that assistance, as the *Economist* delicately phrased it, "privately cleared his approval of this help with President Reagan."[15]

Thus, from the beginning, while publicly assuming a "neutral" stance, President Reagan actually loaded the outcome in favor of British military victory, which would sustain Margaret Thatcher. Not only was the amount of support crucial, its timeliness was decisive. Recovery of the islands had to be completed by the onset of winter—by mid-June; without timely American assistance, this schedule could not have been maintained. Had Argentina been able to hold on through the winter, avoiding immediate military defeat, it would have enhanced, if not forced, a negotiated solution, and led to Thatcher's replacement by Pym. That was the reason both Haig and Pym urged revival of the negotiating track each time it collapsed—even after the mediation had ended.

Alexander Haig's assignment as mediator cast him in a dual role. As mediator, Haig aggressively sought to achieve a negotiated solution to the conflict by a formula that would have enabled Argentina to reap the rewards of its aggression, leaving Galtieri the victor (and Thatcher the loser). Haig's mediation, however, also cast him in the role of unwilling and, certainly initially, unwitting instrument of the "sting," for the protracted mediation bought Britain the time required to field and deploy the forces necessary to recover the islands. There is also some evidence that Haig was initially unaware of the magnitude and scope of American assistance to Great Britain.

The outcome of the conflict would have ramifications far beyond what Ronald Reagan called that "ice-cold bunch of land down there." From Haig's point of view, a "successful" mediation would have cost Thatcher her office because it would have fallen short of her declared terms requiring full British recovery of the islands. Thatcher's fall, moreover, would undermine Reagan's overall strategy of containment that so heavily depended on her support. A "successful" mediation, of course, also would have reinforced Secretary Haig's rather tenuous position in the administration.

The Argentine leadership's objective was strategically the most straightforward, but tactically complicated. In seizing the Malvinas earlier than planned, Galtieri sought to take advantage of a closing window of opportunity to prod Great Britain into a negotiated transfer of sovereignty under the auspices of an American mediation. If negotiation should unexpectedly fail, the junta would attempt to defend its conquest. In either case, a protracted negotiation would move inexorably toward winter. Thus, Argentine strategy was to buy as much time as possible. At no point in this process does it seem that the junta was prepared to make genuine compromises. For them, too, it was a zero-sum contest.

This two-pronged objective explains Argentine eagerness to accept an American mediation effort. It also explains protracted negotiating tactics that sought the objective of an outright transfer, or an eventual transfer after a fixed term of negotiation. What appeared to be confusing and contradictory negotiating procedure actually served the purpose of delaying decision while continuing talks. If the approach of the British fleet gave leverage to Great Britain, the approach of winter offered leverage to Argentina.

Preinvasion Maneuvers

American strategy, from the eve of the invasion, embraced four goals. Initially, it sought to delay Argentine recognition of the nature of Britain's immediate response, particularly in the United Nations, which would enable London to take the diplomatic high ground with passage of a resolution demanding Argentina's withdrawal; then, it sought simultaneously to reassure Argentina of U.S. support in the conflict, reinforcing Argentine expectations, even while stating U.S. objections to the use of force; it also attempted to secure control of the dispute through the role of an "honest broker," thereby shaping the structure of the conflict and determining the parties who would be involved in it; and finally, it was intended to determine the outcome.

The trigger date, both American and British sources agree, was Lord Carrington's plea of March 28 to Secretary of State Haig to intervene with Buenos Aires "to defuse the situation."[16] Sent in the knowledge that the Argentine fleet had set sail that day, it could only have been a signal alerting the United States to be prepared to act in the event that the Argentines did decide to expand the South Georgian crisis, as anticipated, into an invasion of the Falklands/Malvinas.

In light of this action, Prime Minister Thatcher's position is untenable when she insists that for her the invasion came "out of the blue" three days later on the evening of March 31.[17] While insupportable factually, it is fully understandable politically. Admission of early warning would, of course, lead directly to questions regarding the failure to take preventive measures and thus avoid the subsequent conflict with all its costs. Thatcher's related position—that there was no surprise regarding the South Georgia crisis, on which she was kept informed, but only of the connection to the Falkland Islands, which came "out of the blue"—is equally untenable. Such a distinction was never made by British intelligence, which in every assessment related Falkland Islands and Dependencies issues.

The contextual record also argues against the "out of the blue" thesis. Carrington had minuted the prime minister on March 24 that "military action against the [Falkland] islands" was a likely consequence of the growing dispute over South Georgia.[18] On March 26, Carrington had instructed Ambassador Williams in Buenos Aires to "prepare for the worst" and burn all secret documents, hardly the appropriate response to a dispute over scrap metal dealers on South Georgia. When the Argentine fleet sailed on March 28 fully loaded with troops and equipment, an invasion had to be presumed.

For President Reagan, the signal of imminent invasion meant that it was time to ensure that Great Britain gain passage of a favorable resolution in the United Nations that would legitimize counteraction against Argentina. In practical terms, this meant throwing Argentina's UN representatives off guard, providing assurances of American support, giving Britain's representatives a chance to steal a march, and, above all, not interfering with the invasion.

UN Ambassador Jeane Kirkpatrick would play a key role in this effort— whether wittingly or unwittingly. The Argentines were convinced that she spoke with the president's voice, a view that was reinforced by her cabinet rank and the common belief that she had the president's ear. Her disarming role came in the context of rumors on March 31 that Argentina was preparing to invade the Falklands. Kirkpatrick, on her last day as rotating president of the Security Council, telephoned Argentina's ambassador to the United Nations, Eduardo Roca, who had only arrived in New York the previous week. She extended an invitation to tea so that he and British ambassador Anthony Parsons could meet.[19]

Realizing that the invasion fleet was on its way, Roca did not know at first how to respond to Kirkpatrick's invitation. He also assumed that Buenos Aires would look unfavorably upon any meeting with Parsons. After some deliberation, however, he spoke with Kirkpatrick, saying that they had better "leave the visit pending for the present."[20] He also said that his government was contemplating bringing the question of South Georgia before the Security Council.

Kirkpatrick immediately attempted to dissuade him from taking the South Georgia issue to the United Nations. She said that "Britain did not like to put this sort of issue before the United Nations because the Organization was so unpredictable and anything which hinted of colonialism tended to work against the Western powers."[21] She also believed it "impossible that Great

Britain would bring a crisis in the Falklands to the United Nations." Roca was persuaded. On the strength of Kirkpatrick's remarks, he reported back to Buenos Aires of the "British decision not to refer the matter to the UN."[22]

Kirkpatrick then suggested that Roca go to the United Nations the following day for an informal meeting with Parsons, a suggestion that he accepted. Next day, on April 1, Roca and Parsons met in a small room off the main hall of the Security Council. Their meeting was "extremely brief" (Parsons says the "meeting never took place").[23] After exchanging greetings, Parsons abruptly excused himself saying that he had to return to his office to receive a message from London, but offered to meet the following day. The message from London, however, was that an invasion was imminent and that he, Parsons, should "call an emergency meeting of the Security Council to take pre-emptive action."[24]

Parsons went immediately to see Ambassador Kamanda of Zaire, who had replaced Kirkpatrick as president of the Security Council. After some difficulty in rounding up the council members, some of whom thought that he was playing an April Fool's Day joke, Parsons succeeded in convincing them that the issue was deadly serious. The council met for "informal consultations" that afternoon during which Parsons suggested that Kamanda issue a presidential statement urging restraint. He agreed.

Meanwhile, Kirkpatrick confronted Parsons, saying that she would "block" him if he attempted to take the issue to the Security Council.[25] Although this display probably reinforced her credibility with the Argentines, she certainly had to know that Parsons was acting under instructions. Furthermore, Kirkpatrick knew that the invasion was imminent, as she had telephoned Ambassador Estaban Takacs that morning in Washington to tell him so.[26] It would seem, therefore, that the entire "block you" exchange was a charade, for, in the case of an aggression, appealing to the United Nations was the appropriate, indeed, mandatory, move. In any case, Parsons was not deterred.

Kamanda convened the Security Council in public session later that evening proposing for adoption a presidential statement appealing to both parties to exercise restraint. After a brief exchange between Parsons and Roca, Kamanda read the statement aloud. Parsons "immediately took the floor to assure the Security Council that my government would be guided by the presidential appeal and challenged Ambassador Roca to respond similarly. He remained silent."[27]

Parsons had seized the initiative, establishing the proposition, even if by implication, that Argentina was about to commit aggression against Great Britain. When the attack materialized the next day, Parsons was ready to secure Britain's immediate diplomatic objective. As Thatcher put it:

> We needed to win our case against Argentina in the UN Security Council and to secure a resolution denouncing their aggression and demanding withdrawal. On the basis of such a resolution we would find it far easier to win the support of other nations for practical measures to pressurize Argentina.[28]

Roca had been "taken by surprise" by Great Britain's prompt move to the Security Council largely because of Kirkpatrick.[29] Kirkpatrick's effort to dissuade Roca from raising the issue in the United Nations and her attempt to put him into informal personal contact with Parsons, had thrown the Argentine representative off guard and bought Parsons and Great Britain a brief but invaluable moment to seize the initiative. In short, Roca had been left "less well prepared when the issue broke [than he should have been]."[30]

Meanwhile, "in the early evening of 31 March," British intelligence had learned that Buenos Aires had set the early morning of April 2 as the day and time for the attack. Six o'clock the evening of April 1 was the deadline for calling off the invasion. There followed a curious sequence, which guaranteed that there would be no interference with the invasion. Instead of calling Galtieri directly, Thatcher sent a message to Reagan, asking him to contact the Argentine leader.[31] She declared that, although Britain would not escalate the dispute, neither would she acquiesce in an aggression. Thatcher professed that Reagan was Britain's "only hope" of dissuading Galtieri from invading, but took no action herself.[32]

Neither did President Reagan. Instead of immediately intervening, Reagan instructed Secretary Haig to contact the Argentines through diplomatic channels, which guaranteed delay. Haig then delayed further, until "late afternoon," before instructing Ambassador Schlaudeman to deliver a strong warning to Costa Mendez.[33] The Argentine foreign ministry, also playing for time, stalled, and it was several hours before a meeting was arranged. When they did meet, on the morning of April 1, Costa Mendez stonewalled, declining to provide any assurances that an attack was not imminent.

Haig then instructed Schlaudeman to see President Galtieri to warn that in the event of an attack on the Falkland Islands, the newly developed relationship between the United States and Argentina would be abandoned. Schlaudeman met with Galtieri later that morning on April 1.[34] In response to Schlaudeman's direct inquiry regarding Argentina's intention to invade the Falkland Islands, Galtieri snapped: "We are not going to tell you, Ambassador!"[35] Schlaudeman immediately called Haig to express his conviction that invasion was a certainty.

Meanwhile, Haig urged President Reagan to telephone Galtieri, as Thatcher had originally requested, and issue a "strong personal warning."[36] Still, the president delayed. Reagan did not place the call until 6:30 that evening, at least six hours after learning of Galtieri's reply to Schlaudeman, but, more important, after the junta's "go no go" deadline had passed. Reagan had not wanted to make the call to Galtieri before the deadline precisely because, as Cardoso observes, "it might result in him having to cancel the plans to recover the archipelago."[37] Presumably, this was the same reason why Thatcher herself had not attempted to contact Galtieri directly.

Galtieri finally agreed to accept President Reagan's call at 10:10 PM on Thursday, April 1, four hours after the deadline had passed. Their conversation began at 10: 21 PM Buenos Aires time.[38] There was now no possibility of calling off the invasion. The conversation between Reagan and Galtieri, therefore, must be interpreted as being "for the record," considering that both knew that the Argentine invasion was beyond cancellation. Reagan's objective in making the call was not to convince Galtieri to cancel the invasion, but to establish the basis for an American role afterward and lay the groundwork for a shift of position to provide full support to Great Britain. Galtieri, however, sought to involve the United States as a mediator. It was, after all, Argentina's plan from the beginning to employ an American mediation to effect a negotiated transfer of sovereignty.

President Reagan opened their conversation with the observation that he had "reliable news that Argentina [was] about to adopt force in the Falkland Islands" and expressed his concern about the "repercussions such an action would have."[39] In his reply, in which he avoided the issue of the imminent invasion, Galtieri twice declared his country's "favorable attitude towards negotiations," a stance which "has not changed." But, he said, Britain has threatened its citizens "legitimately going about their business on South Georgia," and the Argentine government has "an obligation to protect" them.

Reagan declared that it was "essential to continue the discussions and to seek an alternative to force" because, he went on, "I have good reason to assure you that Great Britain would respond with force to any Argentine military action." Galtieri reaffirmed Argentina's peaceful intent, but "the alternative you seek," that is, a resumption of negotiations, would only be possible if Great Britain agreed to "explicit and public" recognition of Argentine sovereignty over the Falkland Islands.

Reagan then offered the "good offices" of the U.S. government "to get the discussions going again." He offered to send Vice President Bush to Buenos Aires "to hold discussions," or "we could find an adequate formula under the aegis of the United Nations." Ambassador Kirkpatrick, whom you know well, "is ready to assist both parties." Galtieri replied that "I appreciate your offer Mr. President, but I want you to understand that we have been negotiating fruitlessly for seventeen years in the United Nations," with no result. Indeed, Britain had not even responded to Argentina's latest proposal, delivered in February. Galtieri thus clearly rejected a UN role, but not Vice President Bush.[40]

President Reagan then noted that a conflict would have "grave repercussions" in the hemisphere and particularly upon the "special relationship" that he had attempted to cultivate with Argentina. At this point, Reagan briefly and abruptly shifted the topic, attempting to discover Argentine intentions regarding the Falkland Islanders. "What will happen to those two thousand islanders," he asked? Galtieri responded: "Rest assured...the Argentine Government will expressly offer all guarantees to the inhabitants in the Falkland Islands. They will keep their liberty, their free will, and their property."[41] This reply seemed to satisfy the president that Argentina had no plans to hold the Islanders as hostages.[42]

Reagan repeated his earlier notice that Great Britain would "respond militarily to an Argentine landing." Furthermore, he went on: "Mrs. Thatcher, a friend of mine...would have no other alternative than to make a military response." Galtieri was unmoved, however, reaffirming his earlier position, saying: "Argentina did not seek this situation, and the desire of Argentina to negotiate has been unmistakably demonstrated over seventeen years of discussions." President Reagan now stated plainly that he understood that

Argentina "reserves the right to use force. I want to make clear, therefore, that the relationship between your country and mine will suffer gravely." It would, he said, be "irremediably prejudiced."

Galtieri reiterated that "we have not been responsible for this situation," and immediately pleaded for American mediation to resolve the conflict.

> The English are not, nor have they ever been, our enemies. I would like to ask, Mr. President, if the United States could lend all its support so that the situation can be overcome in the best way possible. It is essential that the United States understand the extremity to which Argentina has now arrived. My country and government hope that the United States may act as a friend of Britain and Argentina equally in order to be able to resolve the present situation.[43]

Invasion and Response

Less than an hour and a half after Reagan's call to Galtieri had ended, advance units of marine special forces and commandos began to land on the Falkland Islands. By six-thirty on the morning of April 2, the first wave of the makeshift and hastily improvised invasion force, variously estimated to be between 2,800 and 4,500 men, but actually numbering fewer than a thousand, had swept ashore.[44] By 11:30 AM the capture of the islands was complete and the Argentine flag hoisted above Government House in Port Stanley. A remarkably clean operation, there had been no British casualties and only one Argentine death.

Then, according to the plan, which called for negotiations to follow the seizure, Galtieri and the junta immediately began to remove the entire invasion force and return it to the mainland. Gen. Mario Benjamin Menéndez was installed as provincial governor and a small, 630-man army garrison force was deployed to keep order.[45] An effort was made to maintain a "business as usual" approach to the islanders, but recalcitrant persons were unceremoniously deported, and troop needs tended to impinge on food supplies. For the islanders, the occupation was mainly an inconvenience, for example, requiring cars to drive on the right side of the road instead of the left, but Argentina's military presence hung like an oppressive cloud.[46]

In Buenos Aires, the morning news that Argentina had recovered the Malvinas struck like an unexpected thunderclap. The junta, which only three days before was besieged by an angry mob in the Plaza de Mayo protesting deteriorating economic conditions, was now being cheered by many of the same people, who saw long-cherished dreams materializing. Galtieri, unable to resist addressing the gathered and chanting multitude, appeared on the balcony of the Casa Rosada to declare that Argentina "will accept a dialogue after this forceful stand."[47]

In New York, news of the invasion galvanized Ambassador Parsons into action at the United Nations. At a hastily convened Security Council meeting, Parsons circumvented an established—and time-consuming—procedure for tabling a resolution. In lieu of circulating a working paper and developing a preliminary draft, he read the text of the resolution he was tabling.[48] Known as "black drafts," they entitled the presenter to a vote within twenty-four hours of tabling.[49] Indeed, Parsons's "first intention was to demand a vote the same day," but he "readily acceded to pressure from members of the Council" to wait until Costa Mendez arrived the next day.[50] The text of the Parsons resolution read:

> The Security Council, recalling the statement made by the President of the Security Council at the 2345th meeting of the Security Council on 1 April 1982 calling on the Governments of Argentina and the United Kingdom of Great Britain and Northern Ireland to refrain from the use or threat of force in the region of the Falkland Islands.
>
> Deeply disturbed at reports of an invasion on 2 April 1982 by armed forces of Argentina,
> Determining that there exists a breach of the peace in the region of the Falkland Islands,
>
> 1. Demands an immediate cessation of hostilities.
> 2. Demands an immediate withdrawal of all Argentine forces from the Falkland Islands.
> 3. Calls on the Governments of Argentina and the United Kingdom to seek a diplomatic solution to their differences and to respect fully the purposes and principles of the Charter of the United Nations.

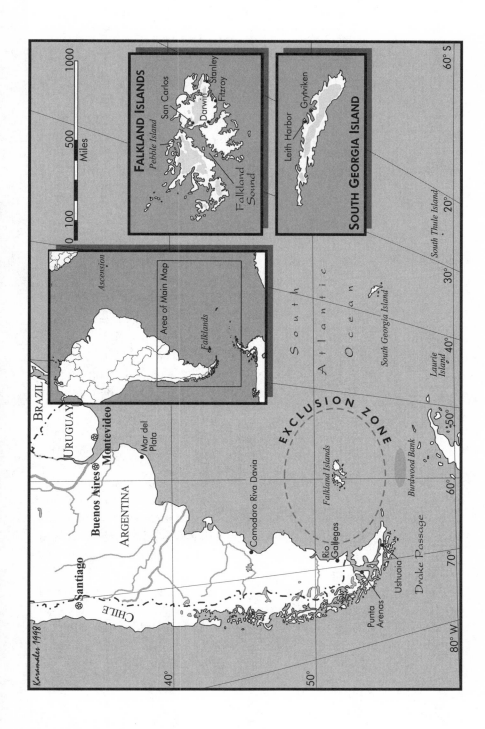

Argentina had managed to postpone the vote on the Parsons resolution until the next day when Costa Mendez would arrive to state his nation's case. The odds that the resolution would be defeated, given the anticolonial bent of the United Nations, seemed to favor Buenos Aires. Indeed, for twenty-four hours, the Argentine leadership experienced a "false euphoria" based on the assumption that Britain would not be able to marshal the ten votes required in the Security Council.

A two-thirds majority was required for passage of a resolution by the fifteen-member Security Council. The membership of the council consisted of the five permanent members (United States, Great Britain, France, China, and the Soviet Union), who could veto any resolution, and ten rotating members drawn from the General Assembly for two-year stints on the council. In 1982 these were: Japan, Poland, Ireland, Spain, Jordan, Togo, Zaire, Uganda, Panama, and Guyana.

To defeat the British resolution, Argentina needed either six nay votes (or abstentions) or a veto from one of the permanent members. Five countries would clearly not support the British resolution on principle: the Soviet Union, China, and Poland would not support Britain. The question was: would Moscow cast a veto or merely abstain? Panama and Spain supported Argentina's case. Thus, Buenos Aires needed but one vote to defeat the British resolution.

Would it be Jordan? The Jordanian ambassador, Hazem Nuseibeh, had assured Ambassador Roca that "Britain will not get the necessary votes."[51] Would it be the Soviet Union? Costa Mendez believed there was the strong possibility that the Soviet Union would cast a veto. Would the United States abstain, to be consistent with its professed neutral position? Finally, would one or more of the nonaligned states abstain in view of their anti-imperialist antipathies? In short, there seemed every likelihood that Argentina would obtain the one additional vote necessary in the Security Council to block passage of the Parsons resolution.

The hope that the United States would abstain on the vote centered around Ambassador Jeane Kirkpatrick. That night of April 2, Argentine ambassador Takacs was hosting a dinner for Kirkpatrick in honor of her just-completed month-long stint as Security Council president. Although the dinner had been scheduled long in advance, there was considerable trepidation that because of the invasion she and the other invited Americans would cancel. At midday, however, Kirkpatrick called to confirm. The question had been referred to the White House, she said, and the president had decided that to cancel would damage later efforts to mediate.[52] She and nine other senior officials would attend, raising hopes that Washington would support Argentina.[53]

During dinner, while discussing the obvious topic of the events in the South Atlantic, the guests tiptoed around the crucial question of what the United States would do the next day in the Security Council. Kirkpatrick waited until after dinner was over, during dessert, to inform Takacs that the United States would be voting in favor of Great Britain the next day.[54] She immediately offered the stunned ambassador her personal assistance and invited him, Roca, and the soon-to-arrive Costa Mendez, to dine with her the next evening in New York following the vote in the Security Council.

Also on April 2, Jordanian ambassador to the United Nations Hazem Nuseibeh had reassured Roca that Britain "will not get the necessary votes" to secure passage of its resolution.[55] Nuseibeh had been instructed by Amman not to vote in favor of any "colonialist cause."[56] But colonialist cause or not, the long history of British-Jordanian friendship manifested itself when, in the course of being lobbied for the vote, Nuseibeh told Parsons—as they conversed in Arabic—of his instructions. Parsons quickly contacted Thatcher, who called King Hussein; within the hour the "old friend of Britain" had agreed to vote in favor.[57]

Meanwhile, Foreign Minister Costa Mendez arrived early on the morning of April 3, the day of the vote. He quickly went into a meeting with the non-aligned ambassadors. As time was short, he spent most of his talk exhorting his listeners to vote against Britain rather than detailing the merits of Argentina's case. Most of his listeners knew precious little about the Falkland Islands, but were well informed about human rights violations in Argentina, Buenos Aires' links to South Africa, military assistance to El Salvador, Guatemala, and Honduras, and, on Middle East issues, Argentina's consistent support for Israel. The Ugandan delegate summed up his performance: "Costa Mendez was a man who came to a place in which he did not believe, to say things in which he did not believe—and we didn't believe him either."[58]

Argentina's last hope was a Soviet veto. Immediately before the vote on the morning of April 3, Costa Mendez, now desperate, sought out Soviet representative Oleg Troyanovsky, who readily rose from his seat to accompany Costa Mendez to a lobby off the main Security Council chamber. In response to the Argentine's question about whether Moscow had sent instructions to veto, Troyanovsky said: "The wheels of time do not favour us, sir.... You will understand that a veto in the Security Council is a matter of extreme importance; I do not decide it, nor even an assistant secretary in Moscow, and it is now 2 o'clock in the morning over there."[59] In the event, Moscow abstained.

The vote, following deflection of several procedural motions and a delay to insert the words "Islas Malvinas" beside "Falkland Islands" in the resolution text, was ten in favor, one against, and four abstentions. The resolution had passed. Only Panama had voted against; the Soviet Union, China, Poland, and Spain had abstained. The rest—France, Ireland, Jordan, Zaire, Togo, Uganda, Guyana, Japan, and the United States—had all voted with Great Britain. Charles Lichtenstein, subbing for Kirkpatrick, offered the good offices of the United States to help resolve the dispute.

The wording of the resolution was the key to its passage. Even those nations that would not normally support Great Britain could vote in favor of a cessation of hostilities. Implicitly, by reference to the "principles of the Charter," UNR502 legitimized British action under Article 51, which permits the use of force in self-defense. Finally, it called on both parties to seek a diplomatic solution, but made no mention of a UN role. Britain wanted the UN legitimization without the pressure for a negotiated settlement it would be bound to insist upon, if directly involved.

Although Britain had stolen a march on Argentina in the United Nations, handing Buenos Aires a diplomatic defeat, the terms of UNR502 were not unacceptable. The resolution had not condemned Argentina as an aggressor. Hostilities had ended on the islands; and a negotiated settlement was the objective, after all. The absence of a UN negotiating role did not trouble Argentine leaders, who expected and preferred an American mediation. Even the demand for the immediate withdrawal of forces was consistent with Argentina's plans and could be complied with if negotiations commenced promptly. The invasion force was already being withdrawn.

The gaping loophole in UN502 was that it said nothing about the restoration of British administration in the islands—an omission that would plague later negotiations. It meant that Argentina theoretically could withdraw its "forces" but still maintain control of the islands—that is, if British forces could be kept away. Indeed, the troubling part of the resolution was the absence of any requirement for Britain to refrain from using force to retake the islands.

The evening following news of the invasion, April 2, Thatcher had convened the entire cabinet. It was crucial to put the issue of sending a task force to recover the islands to a full cabinet vote. This would commit both Thatcherites and "wets" alike to a common course of action—at least at the outset. It would also enable the government to face Parliament the next day united and resolved. The prime minister polled each cabinet member on the question and each, with the exception of Trade Secretary John Biffen, gave approval for the dispatch of the task force.[60]

The full cabinet would play but a minor role thereafter. Thatcher determined that all subsequent decision-making would take place in a subgrouping of the overseas and defense committee, designated ODSA, the SA for South Atlantic. The structure of opinion in what came to be referred to as the "war cabinet" was much more favorable to the prime minister, but roughly representative of the balance in the cabinet.

The war cabinet was composed of Thatcher, John Nott, Francis Pym, Cecil Parkinson, and William Whitelaw. Included as nonvoting members were the Chief of the Defense Staff Sir Terence Lewin; Cabinet Secretary Sir Robert Armstrong; Permanent Secretary to the Foreign Office Sir Antony Acland; and the Cabinet Office Chief of Foreign and Defense Liaison Robert Wade-Gery. Also in virtual continuous attendance were Attorney General Sir Michael Havers and Foreign Office legal adviser Sir Ian Sinclair.[61]

News of the Argentine invasion of the Falklands stunned a largely unsuspecting nation. The House of Commons convened an extraordinary (and raucous) meeting next day, on Saturday, April 3, as news also arrived of Argentina's seizure of South Georgia. It was the first such Saturday meeting since the Suez crisis in 1956. Prime Minister Thatcher announced that a task force would sail on Monday, April 5, and declared:

> The Falkland Islands and their dependencies remain British territory. No aggression and no invasion can alter that simple fact. It is the Government's objective to see that the Islands are freed from occupation and returned to British administration at the earliest possible moment.[62]

Thatcher, of course, was under no illusions that the "growls of approval" accompanying her announcement in the House signified clear sailing. She "knew that not everybody was cheering the same thing. Some saw the task force as a purely diplomatic armada that would get the Argentinians back to the negotiating table. They never intended that it should actually fight."[63] But she needed to demonstrate a "united national will" to both ally and enemy alike. And, for the moment, she had.

Prelude to "Mediation"

In Washington, the weekend of April 2–4 was filled with frenzied activity, as the Reagan administration prepared to manage the next phase of the conflict. Haig speaks of "a series of conversations with the British and the Argentineans" and "a series of intensive staff meetings."[64] The weekend also saw President Reagan make the highly secret decision to begin to provide extensive aid to Great Britain in the form of logistics, weapons, equipment, and intelligence "before the task force even set sail."[65] He also acted to tighten security to prevent any information leaks.[66]

Secretary of Defense Casper Weinberger was assigned the task of managing the highly secret assistance program. As Navy Secretary John Lehman noted: "There had been a massive de facto tilt towards Britain from the very first day."[67] Secrecy was of the utmost importance, and only a handful of people knew of the program. Indeed, its very existence was "concealed from senior members of both governments."[68] Nor in the early days did the issue come before the National Security Council.

> Washington observers doubt that much of it was made known…to Mr. Haig, embroiled throughout the conflict in the role of honest broker between the two sides. The assistance certainly went beyond Mr. Haig's "customary channels." Since the bulk of it was sent direct to Ascension, the island had to be surrounded by a tight security net. Journalists with the taskforce assumed this was to prevent military information reaching Argentina. It was also to prevent the world (and the state department?) knowing the scale of American help.[69]

That weekend, two other decisions were made that would define the internal politics in both Washington and London. The first was President Reagan's offer to mediate the dispute accompanied by the decision to give Secretary of State Alexander Haig the responsibility of exploring the prospects of a negotiated solution to the conflict.[70] Haig claims that he volunteered for the mission after conversations with British and Argentine representatives. "It became clear that both sides hoped that I would serve as intermediary."[71] That Haig had not sought the assignment, however, is suggested by his immediate consultation of Henry Kissinger over that weekend, who counseled against his acceptance.

> Haig, before taking on the job, consulted me. I told him not to take it, that it would not be convenient for him, that it was difficult and that in any case no one in Latin America would believe that he would be impartial. I told him that should he take it, he should go first to Buenos Aires and then to London.[72]

Haig decided to accept the challenge, and on Tuesday evening, April 6, "called the President and suggested that [he] go to Buenos Aires and London in an attempt to find a solution."[73] President Reagan formalized Haig's assignment at a brief meeting of the NSPG (National Security Planning Group) the next morning, but decided to send him to London first and then to Buenos Aires (the opposite of Kissinger's suggestion).[74] According to press accounts, "Reagan has instructed Haig to look for ways of satisfying Argentina's demand for sovereignty over the Falklands…while allaying Britain's concern" for the Islanders.[75]

The story the White House put out on Haig's selection was that as Galtieri had rejected Reagan's offer of Vice-President Bush and Jeane Kirkpatrick during his telephone conversation before the invasion, that left Haig as the only remaining high-level official. The fact is, however, that Galtieri had not rejected Bush, but only a UN role (see above). Galtieri had expected Bush to be named the intermediary—he was the crisis manager, after all—and was surprised when Haig was named, raising suspicions that the United States did not consider this a genuine crisis.[76]

Some within the administration believed that "Haig was being handed a rope to hang himself with—if the mission failed then Haig's position might be fatally undermined."[77] In fact, however, Haig's position was apparently already tenuous. His selection placed the secretary of state on a toboggan that hastened his descent down the slippery slope on which he was already sliding.

Placing Haig in charge of the "mediation," however, gave him an outside chance to achieve a negotiated solution that would strengthen his position within the administration and undercut Reagan's containment strategy by damaging the relationship with Britain—the outcome of any negotiated settlement that failed to reestablish British rule in the Falklands and reinforce Margaret Thatcher's position as prime minister. Of course, unbeknownst to Haig, Reagan had already stacked the deck against him with the secret military assistance program to Britain.

The second decision was Prime Minister Thatcher's choice of Francis Pym as foreign secretary to replace Lord Peter Carrington, who resigned.[78] Carrington had resigned ostensibly because he had "incorrectly judged the Argentine military buildup that led to the lightning assault on the Falklands."[79] That explanation, however, was only for public consumption. The record as demonstrated clearly indicates that Carrington, of all people, had actually consistently predicted the likelihood of an invasion. Nor was he the sacrificial lamb thrown out to appease the backbenchers, who criticized him roundly. Criticism of the Foreign Office was not new and could hardly have been the reason for his resignation. Why, then, did Carrington resign?

The crisis over the Falklands raised the prospect of Thatcher's resignation should a Suez-like fiasco ensue, or the outcome fall significantly short of her objective of restoring the islands to British rule. Carrington would have been the likely successor to Thatcher had it not been for his hereditary peerage, which effectively barred him from consideration for the prime ministership.[80] For the "wets," therefore, it was imperative to replace Carrington with someone who could succeed Thatcher should that prospect emerge.

That someone was former defense minister Francis Pym, the man most widely believed to be Thatcher's potential successor.[81] Pym, in fact, would privately attempt to reach a negotiated solution that would result in the eventual transfer of sovereignty over the Falkland Islands to the Argentines. Such a solution would have forced Thatcher's resignation, as Thatcher herself notes, and opened the door to Pym's ascendancy—and the ascendancy of the "wets" over the Thatcherites in the Conservative Party.[82] Pym's appointment, thus, did temporarily unite the party, but it gave the "wets" an opportunity to bring down Thatcher.

There was symmetry in the fact that in both capitals the leaders were preparing for the forceful recovery of the Falkland Islands, while those second in command pursued the opposite policy of a negotiated settlement. Each was tempted by the prospect of the opportunity to assume control of his respective nation's foreign policy leadership, but each initially was unaware of the secret American assistance to the task force and the collusion of Reagan and Thatcher. Thus, both Haig and Pym argued against the use of military force and worked together to achieve a negotiated solution.

Thus, on the American side, Reagan, Weinberger, and a few trusted officials in the defense department were privy to the secret aid program, but Haig initially was not told.[83] It may be assumed that on the British side, Thatcher and Nott were privy, but initially Pym was not. It seems that the secret was kept from them for roughly two weeks, when rumors began to leak to the press. At that point, Haig unsuccessfully attempted to place constraints on the Ascension Island program, but failed. More about that later.

Even as President Reagan was authorizing massive, clandestine military assistance to Great Britain, he was publicly offering to help effect a peaceful resolution of the conflict. At what was described as an "impromptu meeting with reporters at the White House," on Monday, April 5, Reagan was asked whether he would support "Britain's efforts to free its hostages in the Falklands?" He replied:

> It's a very difficult situation for the United States, because we're friends with both of the countries engaged in this dispute. And we stand ready to do anything we can to help them. And what we hope for and would like to help in doing is have a peaceful resolution of this, with no forceful action or no bloodshed.[85]

A reporter asked Reagan directly whether "America [was] prepared to offer military assistance if the British ask for it?" Clearly uncomfortable, having just authorized massive military assistance, he sidestepped the question and began to stumble through an answer saying: "Again, as I said, we're friends with both sides in this. And we're going to try, strive for—and I think that they will be willing to meet in the idea of a peaceful resolution."[86]

Press commentary further misled both the Argentines and those within the American and British governments seeking a negotiated solution. Unidentified "administration sources" suggested that the invasion had been a fait accompli. They told reporters that "Argentina's occupation of the Falklands appears to be an accomplished fact that cannot be reversed unless Britain resorts to force on a scale that would cause tensions for years."[87] Even if Great Britain succeeded, it "would leave bitterness throughout Latin America and put Britain in the position of having to maintain a huge, long-term protective...presence in the Falklands." It was for these reasons, the sources said, "the United States hopes to find a formula that will acknowledge Argentine sovereignty over the islands and still be sufficiently acceptable to Prime Minister Margaret Thatcher's government."

Thus, at the outset, all of the public information available in Washington, from the president to the press accounts, was highly supportive of Argentina, but also sensitive to the British government in an effort to present a balanced position. The problem appeared to be a diplomatic one—"to find a formula"—although the wheels had been secretly set in motion to supply Great Britain with everything it would require to achieve the military recapture of the Falkland Islands.

Haig's "Mediation"

From the first discussions Secretary Haig held on April 6 with Argentine Foreign Minister Nicanor Costa Mendez and British Ambassador Nicholas Henderson, he advanced a formula that he would urge on both sides—frequently adjusted—throughout the conflict. This formula was completely consistent with Argentine expectations and, if accepted, would have ensured eventual Argentine acquisition of the Falkland Islands and the downfall of Margaret Thatcher.

He proposed to Costa Mendez that, in accordance with UN502, all Argentine forces be withdrawn from the Falkland Islands. In return, the British task force would return or be diverted. A multinational interim administration, including a peacekeeping force, would manage the islands, during negotiations to resolve the dispute. Haig proposed the United States, Canada, Brazil, and Colombia for the peacekeeping force, but Costa Mendez quickly suggested a tripartite administration of the United States, Great Britain, and Argentina, which Haig immediately accepted.[88]

When Haig broached this formula to Henderson, the British ambassador thought it was "inopportune to think in terms of some multilateral administration of the islands. We were prepared to talk about the future of the islands and their relations with Argentina only when Argentine troops had withdrawn and our administration had been restored."[89] Furthermore, he declared unequivocally: "Anything less would mean the fall of the Thatcher government."[90]

Henderson said that London "was not asking the United States to take a position on the sovereignty of the islands, but was maintaining that it would not be reasonable for Washington to be neutral on matters such as self-determination and the use of force."[91] Clearly, Haig's proposal would rule out the return of the British administration, Thatcher's sine qua non for the beginning of negotiations. Negotiations on the future disposition of the islands would occur under the impetus of Argentine aggression and not provide for the exercise of islander self-determination.

On the basis of that uneasy exchange, Haig flew to London to meet a prime minister who, press accounts blared, had "nailed her colors to the mast," staking her reputation as the Iron Lady of British politics on the restoration of British rule in the Falkland Islands.[92] Polls reflected public pessimism. A "substantial segment of British public opinion [had] been alienated." *The Daily Mail* poll, for example, showed that 80 percent blamed the government for what had happened, 36 percent blamed Thatcher herself, and 25 percent believed she should resign.

While Haig was en route, the Thatcher government announced the imposition of a Maritime Exclusion Zone (MEZ) of two hundred miles around the Falkland Islands, to be in effect from April 12. The announcement preemptorily conveyed to Haig Thatcher's determination to proceed with the recovery of British territory. Military sources reported simultaneously that the British submarine HMS *Superb* had already arrived off the Falklands.[93] The phantom voyage of HMS *Superb* was undoubtedly designed to confuse Argentine leaders and upset their calculations.

The White House pointedly refused to describe Haig's mission as a "mediation," instead insisting publicly that his objective was to hold "preliminary discussions."[94] The small team he took with him tended to reinforce that notion. Accompanying Haig were Assistant Secretary for Latin American Affairs Thomas Enders, Gen. Vernon Walters, and several aides. No members of the press were permitted to travel with Haig, which infuriated a foreign press corps accustomed to accompanying American officials on trips.

Haig arrived in London on April 8. After initially speaking with Pym for an hour, he went to No. 10 Downing Street for discussions with the prime minister, followed by a five-hour working dinner.[95] Thatcher echoed the White House view that Haig was not there as a mediator. She insisted on making "quite clear to him...that he was not being received in London as a mediator but as a friend and ally, here to discuss ways in which the United States could most effectively support us in our efforts to secure Argentine withdrawal."[96]

Despite Haig's assurances that there would be no repetition of Suez, and that he had come purely to discuss the issues, it was clear to Thatcher that Haig "had come to mediate."[97] Haig revealed his three-part proposal—mutual withdrawal, an interim authority, and negotiated settlement. Thatcher insisted upon Argentine adherence to UN502—that is, Argentine withdrawal before any negotiations began. Her reaction to Haig's proposal of an interim authority was that it was "too wooly."[98] Thatcher correctly interpreted the notion of an interim authority as "something other than the British administration which I was publicly pledged to restore."[99] Haig got nowhere.

Haig attempted to employ the Soviet threat as a way of generating some flexibility, but Thatcher countered with the view that "the West might be stretched, but so were the Soviets." Thatcher held firm. Argentina must withdraw in compliance with UN502, and British administration must be reestablished before any negotiations began. British sovereignty must continue; the islanders must be permitted to exercise self-determination. Aggression must not be rewarded. The task force would proceed.

To Haig, it seemed that, although Thatcher was "strongly backed by Nott and also by Admiral Lewin, [she] did not enjoy the full support of the other members of her government."[100] Because, in his discussions, Haig had met only with Thatcher, Pym, Nott, and Lewin, in addition to the head of the Foreign Office, Sir Antony Acland, and Thatcher's personal secretary Clive Whitmore, it is plain to whom he referred when he spoke of "other members of her government." He was referring to Francis Pym. The implication was that if there were to be any British "flexibility," it would have to come from Pym and his associates among the Conservative Party's "wets."

Reporting to President Reagan afterward, Haig observed that Thatcher's "irreducible requirement for settlement" was self-determination for the islanders. Haig "emphasized that unless some way could be found to alter British authority and provide for an Argentinean role in the government of the Falklands, Mrs. Thatcher's terms ruled out Argentinean acceptance. If Galtieri accepted her terms, it would be the end of him. Just as Mrs. Thatcher must show that the junta got nothing for its use of force, Galtieri must be able to show that he got something."

Haig had accomplished little in London beyond a reaffirmation of Britain's original stand on UN502. In an effort to soften up the Argentine leadership before his arrival, Haig sent Vernon Walters on a quick trip to Paris to see his friend, the Argentine ambassador to France, Gerardo Schamis. Walters briefed Schamis on Haig's discussions with Thatcher, emphasizing Thatcher's uncompromising stand, and her domestic political need to fulfill her public pledge to restore British authority in the islands. Finally, he said that the United States would ultimately back Britain because President Reagan could not risk Thatcher's fall from power.[101] Schamis, of course, immediately sent this information to Buenos Aires, his cable preceding Haig's arrival by only a few hours.

Haig's departure from London for Buenos Aires occurred simultaneously with that of the first ships of the task force, carrying three thousand troops.[102] Some early reports said that the task force would "contain fewer than the 36 ships originally planned—perhaps as few as 20—because of the need to keep ships in reserve in case the Government decides upon a blockade." Moreover, the task force possessed few aircraft and no airborne early warning capability. Rumors were rife that London "might be hoping to work out a deal, similar to the one that fell through in 1981" on leaseback.[103]

Thus, the early indications for Argentina were contradictory, but implied that expectations were being fulfilled. On the one hand, Thatcher was being portrayed as totally inflexible and determined to fight, if necessary. Yet, on the other hand, the initial force dispatched to the Falkland Islands was not sufficiently large to succeed in recovering the islands. The Argentine leadership, therefore, concluded that the British government was bluffing, conducting a display of force as a prelude to negotiations, with no intention of actually fighting. The United States also appeared to be fulfilling expectations as mediator in support of Argentina's cause.

Meanwhile, reflecting this judgment, Costa Mendez had returned to Buenos Aires to await Haig's arrival from London. Speaking at the airport, he declared himself "very optimistic" about the chances of a peaceful settlement, saying that "the danger of war with Britain is fading."[104] Argentine officials staked out their own hard bargaining position before Haig's arrival. Declaring their readiness to negotiate, they said, "withdrawal was out of the question until Britain recognize[d] Argentine sovereignty over the islands." Moreover, Argentina would defend the islands "at any cost."[105]

The junta prepared a warm reception for the American secretary of state, lining the streets and circling the Casa Rosada with throngs of shouting people, to "show Haig the spirit of Argentina."[106] Indeed, the boisterousness of the crowd was more than matched by the aggressiveness of Galtieri and Costa Mendez in discussions with Haig—an aggressiveness that was reciprocated.

During the first day of talks, April 10, Haig adopted the "tough guy" approach. He warned Costa Mendez that, if Argentina failed to comply with UN502, there would be war. In that event, the United States would side with Britain, and all the effort to develop good relations with Argentina would be in vain. Costa Mendez was "disgusted" with the "vehemence" of Haig's demeanor, but was careful not to overreact.[107]

Haig's first meeting with Galtieri later that day was less acrimonious, but now it was the Argentine leader's turn to issue a warning. There was no question of Argentine sovereignty; his forces were prepared and "would not hesitate to respond militarily to any British aggression, although that possibility was certainly not desired by Argentina."[108] Furthermore, Galtieri said, he had "received offers of aircraft, pilots, and armaments from countries not of the West."[109] Interpreting Galtieri's remark as a reference to Moscow, Haig felt that it was "hardly astonishing" that the Soviets would attempt to take advantage of such a tempting "target of opportunity."

As the two sides got down to business the second day, April 11, the Argentines responded to Haig's three-part scheme. On UN502, Argentina would withdraw only if the task force also withdrew. If it moved beyond Ascension Island, the half-way point in the Atlantic between England and Argentina, then Buenos Aires would call for a meeting of the Rio Treaty of 1947. The treaty called upon signatory states to assist a member state attacked by another state. Haig countered with the view that, as Argentina had initiated the use of force, the treaty did not apply.

Argentina agreed to the concept of an interim authority, but refused to accept the return of British administration. Argentina wanted to use the military government just established on the islands as the administrative core, with "some appropriate participation of the islanders," whose rights and interests would be guaranteed.[110] In response, Haig abandoned his offer of the tripartite commission concept including the United States, Britain, and Argentina, and returned to his original suggestion of a broader-based commission to include Brazil, Colombia, Peru, and Canada, which would dilute Washington's role.

Costa Mendez insisted that the negotiations have as an "explicit objective the recognition of Argentine sovereignty over the archipelago and its dependencies."[111] Moreover, the negotiations should be completed by December 31 of that year, at which time the "transfer of sovereignty of the islands to Argentina would have to be automatic." Finally, he said, the United States should "guarantee" the outcome. Haig countered that the negotiations could not be prejudged in advance, Britain would not accept a time limit, and the United States could not guarantee the outcome.

Upon having reached a complete impasse, Haig later told Walters to see Galtieri alone to impart some realism to the junta's thinking. In a private meeting with Galtieri, Walters emphasized that if there were a war, "the British would fight and win—and that the United States would support Britain."[112] But Galtieri was "absolutely, viscerally, convinced that the British would not fight." He believed not only that the two countries were militarily "equal," but persisted in the notion that Thatcher was weak-willed. "That woman wouldn't dare," he declared, to which Walters replied: "I would not count on that if I were you."[113]

The Argentines were intransigent. Haig declared the futility of continuing to London with "utterly unacceptable" proposals.[114] He would have to return to Washington and perhaps cancel the negotiations. At this, Costa Mendez realized that they had gone too far—that if a negotiating rupture occurred, there would be no way of deterring Britain from commencing hostilities. Therefore, he hastily arranged another meeting between Haig and Galtieri.

In a lengthy session that lasted past one o'clock the next morning, Haig went through his list of arguments again, now buttressed by the announcement that the EEC had placed a trade embargo on Argentina. Without concessions from Argentina, his mission would fail; war was "absurd"; if it came, the United States would side with Britain; Britain would win. Galtieri countered by questioning Haig about a report that Washington was permitting Britain's task force the use of a satellite for communications purposes. Haig denied it "categorically."[115]

Midway through their discussions, as impasse loomed, Galtieri excused himself to meet with the other two members of the junta—Jorge Anaya and Basilio Lami Dozo. Anaya took the hard line, arguing that the United States could not afford to abandon Argentina; therefore, Haig's threats were mere bluffs. Lami Dozo, however, argued that some concessions were necessary in any negotiation. Finally, they agreed to formulate their "minimum requirements" so that Haig "might have something to show the British."[116]

Haig's Machinations

At this point, the record becomes murky. Haig presents a contradictory account. He claims that "between midnight and one in the morning, the impasse broke." Galtieri, Haig avers, said "he could not withdraw both his military and his administrative presence from the Malvinas and last a week." On the basis of this statement, Haig says, "Now that we knew Galtieri's requirements, the work went quickly. In less than an hour, we produced a new draft that was essentially the same as the one I had brought from London, except for two important modifications. Argentine troops would leave the islands and the British administration would be restored."[117]

The contradiction is self-evident. Galtieri said he could not remove both his military and administrative presence, implying that one, at least, must remain. Haig then modified his draft to produce both an Argentine military withdrawal and the restoration of British administration! Obviously, there had been no breakthrough, for there had been no change in the Argentine position.

Another source, Gavshon and Rice, supports the Argentine account. They claim, on the basis of an unidentified transcript of the session, that Haig in desperation proposed "a secret protocol" in which Mrs. Thatcher would commit to, and President Reagan would guarantee, the conclusion of negotiations before the end of the year, if only Argentina would agree to permit the reestablishment of the British administration. But they point out that both Costa Mendez and Galtieri refused. Galtieri observed: "They took away our flag for 150 years. Now that we've reinstalled it we can't ask the Argentine people to accept our taking it away again."[118]

The Argentine side had produced its "minimum requirements"—a five-point document that they bid Haig to present to Thatcher. It called for the immediate and simultaneous implementation of UN502, which involved cessation of hostilities, withdrawal of forces, and commencement of negotiations; an interim administration under Argentine control in which islander participation might be possible; and an international body to oversee and guarantee the new procedures.[119] Britain would cancel the MEZ and suspend all economic sanctions.

The Argentines were evidently concerned that Haig either may have misunderstood what had happened, or had decided to proceed on another basis than the one they had discussed.[120] Therefore, the next morning at the airport, just before Haig enplaned, Costa Mendez handed him a paper, which according to Haig "contained some personal thoughts."[121] Actually, the paper contained the official position of the Argentine government and was obviously designed to correct any misimpressions and, hopefully, deter Haig from taking a different tack.

Haig claims that the paper "constituted a retreat from everything we had accomplished at the Casa Rosada the night before."

> The Argentineans were demanding either de facto authority over the islands through administrative arrangements that would give them immediate control of its government, or a British promise that sovereignty would be transferred to Argentina no later than December 31, 1982, regardless of the outcome of negotiations. This was a formula for war.[122]

When Haig arrived back in London on April 12, however, he disregarded Costa Mendez's paper and proceeded on the basis of his own draft, which reflected none of the junta's positions, but nevertheless subtly served Buenos Aires' interests. Superficially, Haig's proposals appeared to be highly favorable to Margaret Thatcher. Haig proposed:

- Mutual withdrawal within a two-week period.
- No reintroduction of military forces and forces withdrawn to "return to normal duties."
- A tripartite commission (U.S., UK, A) would replace the governor to ensure compliance. Commission members could fly their flags at headquarters.
- The commission would promote travel, trade, and communications with Argentina, but Britain would have a veto over its operations.
- The "traditional local administration...would be restored," to which Argentine representatives drawn from the local Argentine population "would be added."
- Economic and financial sanctions against Argentina would be lifted.

- Negotiations for a lasting settlement to be pursued consistent with the purposes and principles of the UN charter and to be concluded by December 31, 1982.[123]

To Thatcher, Haig's proposals were "full of holes," but "if we could really get the Argentine forces off the islands by conceding what seemed a fairly powerless commission, very limited Argentine representation on each council...and an Argentine flag flown alongside others at Headquarters there was something to be said for these ideas."[124] Upon closer inspection, however, Thatcher saw "formidable difficulties."

She bombarded Haig with questions: What would happen if there were no agreement by December 31? Would the United States offer any guarantees against renewed invasion? Would the principle of self-determination be enforced? Would the Islanders' "wishes" be paramount? What would prevent the Argentines from packing the islands with their own people and gaining a majority? Where would the Argentine flag fly? Where would British forces be when withdrawn?

She observed, however, "the main issue was always bound to be the military one." For Thatcher, "the only reason the Argentinians were prepared to negotiate at all was because they feared our task force." Therefore, the "task force must continue to proceed southwards, though it would not enter the demilitarized zone." The one concession that Thatcher was prepared to allow was that "the task force could be stood off at a point no closer to the Falklands than Argentine forces were based. Anything less would be unacceptable to Parliament."[125]

At this point, the session adjourned for lunch, which was early morning in Washington, D.C. The morning edition of the *New York Times* contained an article that completely exposed Haig's ploy. As it happened, the Argentines not only had reaffirmed their position in the paper Costa Mendez had handed to Haig just before his takeoff from Buenos Aires, they had also leaked their position to *New York Times* reporter Edward Schumacher in Buenos Aires, who promptly transmitted it to the *Times*, which placed it on the front page.

"Argentine officials," Schumacher reported, said that "the package of ideas Mr. Haig took to London...includes a simultaneous pullback of the British Navy and a withdrawal of Argentine forces from the islands, but only after Britain recognizes Argentine sovereignty." Furthermore, the Argentine package "rules out" the restoration of British administration on the islands. At most, it "would allow for some form of limited local autonomy such as letting the islanders share in local government."[126]

When Haig learned of the article, he realized that it "threw everything into doubt."[127] He was now forced to acknowledge that the article reiterated the position contained in the document Costa Mendez had handed to him in Buenos Aires, which he had chosen to disregard. Indeed, Thatcher observed that terms in the two documents were "utterly inconsistent with the terms [Haig] presented to us."[128] It was apparent that Haig had presented to Thatcher a set of proposals to which the Argentines had not agreed and about which they may not even have had any knowledge.

Haig immediately placed a call to Costa Mendez to ask for an explanation, but the Argentine foreign minister put him off, saying that they would talk later after he had consulted with Galtieri. Of course, what Costa Mendez was doing was waiting to see what effect the disclosures would have on Haig's discussions in London. He would wait until they were concluded before speaking again with Haig.

Whatever doubts Thatcher and the British leadership may have had as a result of the *Times* article exposing Haig's manipulations, that afternoon and evening's talks proceeded on the basis of the secretary of state's draft. Most important was the position of the task force. Haig wanted to halt the task force once an agreement had been reached. Thatcher replied: "I would not survive in the House of Commons if I stopped the task force before Argentine withdrawal had been completed." She was prepared to "let the troop ships proceed more slowly...but the main task force must maintain its progress towards the Falkland Islands." Thatcher was prepared to halt the task force the same distance from the islands "as that between Argentina and the islands, but I could go no further than that."[129]

After making their views "absolutely clear," Thatcher agreed to pursue further negotiations on Haig's "somewhat wooly text." They had nothing to lose. Haig had been hoist on his own petard. If in the now highly unlikely possibility that the Argentines agreed to what had been discussed, Thatcher could achieve her objectives effortlessly. She no doubt surmised, however, that the Argentines had no intention of accepting terms that would require them both to withdraw their forces and permit the return of British administration. That, however, was Haig's problem.

Later that evening, after midnight, Costa Mendez called Haig to reiterate for the third time the Argentine position. There was no reason for him to return to Buenos Aires, unless Britain agreed to permit Argentina to both appoint the governor and fly the Argentine flag there. If that were unacceptable, he said, then Britain must provide assurances that "at the end of negotiations with Britain there would be a recognition of Argentine sovereignty over the Falkland Islands."[130] The junta, he said, "could not tell the Argentinian people that it would discuss self-determination after all the risks they had taken. These two points are essential, either one or the other."[131]

Haig professed to be "shattered" and "depressed." He said to Costa Mendez: "I didn't understand that from your president. All I got from him was the importance of flying the flag. This is a tragedy for everyone."[132] Although Haig claimed it was a "double cross," as this account shows, it would be more accurate to describe it as a double exposure. The Argentine position had not changed, not here, not in the *New York Times* article, not in Costa Mendez's "paper," and not in Buenos Aires. Haig could not possibly have believed that Galtieri was simply interested in "flying the flag."

CHAPTER 6

From Mediation to War

What had Haig hoped to gain by presenting his own formula for a settlement to Thatcher? He knew that if he presented the junta's "minimum requirements" the negotiations would be over immediately. Hoping to gain time, he advanced a proposal that would be very enticing to the "wets" in the Conservative Party, deepening the division between Thatcher and Pym. If they accepted, he would then return to the junta and plead misunderstanding or double-cross—anything to keep the negotiations going. Haig was hoping to gain time.

Haig understood the time problem as well as did the British and Argentines. The arrival of winter by mid-June was the key factor. The British timetable called for a landing on the Falkland Islands no later than the end of May, with military operations to be completed by no later than mid-June.[1] The fierce South Atlantic winter would preclude any continued naval presence in Falkland waters after that. That timetable dictated the limits of negotiation. If, through the promise of a successful negotiation, Haig could delay a landing in May, he could very likely avert any conflict whatsoever.

The fact was that should Thatcher agree to recall the fleet to England, domestic political pressures—not the least from the "wets" in her own cabinet—would preclude its return. This would be true even if the negotiation subsequently collapsed. The cost of mobilizing and outfitting the fleet a second time would be prohibitive and the pressure for a settlement overwhelming. Thus, Thatcher would have found herself hard-pressed to remain in office after failing to produce the objective she had set. Like the Duke of York, she would have marched the army up the hill and marched it down again. She would have replicated Anthony Eden's disastrous climb down at Suez. And, she would suffer the same fate.

The Argentines had exposed Haig's ploy. Thatcher told him that "if those are the conditions, you cannot return" to Buenos Aires. Although Haig agreed, after sleeping on it, he tried a new tack. The following morning, he requested another meeting where he now produced for the first time the five-point document embodying Argentina's "minimum requirements." He noted that the practical effect of the Argentine tactics was to buy time, to which Thatcher responded: "I always thought that this was their main purpose in negotiating." Galtieri, she said, "wanted to claim victory by force of arms." Driving her point home, Thatcher declared, impatiently: "The question now was whether he could be diverted from his course by economic sanctions or, as I had suspected all along, only by military force."[2]

They discussed the advisability of terminating the negotiations, and both agreed to continue. Haig observed that, if the negotiations were brought to an end now, "other less helpful people might try to intervene." Thatcher replied that she was "keenly aware of that and...also felt that public opinion here required us not to give up on negotiations yet."[3] But a public opinion poll published that day belied Thatcher's sentiment, indicating strong support for a military response as well as for her government. The poll indicated that 83 percent of the British people approved of sending the task force; 67 percent favored landing troops; 51 percent thought casualties justified; 60 percent were satisfied with the government's handling of the conflict thus far—a remarkable turnaround from the initial public reaction to the Argentine invasion.[4]

Reading the same polls, the junta now also had second thoughts. Concerned that the talks were about to be terminated, Costa Mendez called Haig just before noon on April 13 to say that his government was now willing to modify its demands. Buenos Aires, he said, "would not insist on an Argentinian governor if the agreement contained a British acknowledgment that it intended to 'decolonize' the Falklands in compliance with the 1964 United Nations Declaration on Decolonization."[5]

Costa Mendez's reference was to chapter XI, article 73, of the UN Charter that stipulates the obligations of those countries administering "territories whose peoples have not yet attained a full measure of self-government."[6] Haig loosely "interpreted the Argentine proposal to mean that Buenos Aires accepted autonomy and self-determination for the Falklanders."[7] In fact, however, chapter XI is vague and susceptible to various interpretations. In an attempt to circumvent Thatcher's insistence upon the paramountcy of the islanders "wishes," Costa Mendez sought to emphasize a different clause that stressed that the "interests of the inhabitants are paramount," not their "wishes."[8] Emphasis on "interests" would permit outside parties, not the inhabitants, to determine the outcome.

Haig spoke to Pym and the two agreed "there was a basis for hope that we might keep the dialogue going."[9] In discussion with Thatcher, Haig now professed to believe that there was a chance of a settlement along the lines we had been discussing "if we would agree to language about decolonization," and, Thatcher interjected, "subject to the wishes of the islanders."[10] Of course, the Argentines did not interpret decolonization as self-determination, but as another way of getting around Thatcher's "wishes" roadblock.

It is impossible to believe that Haig, Thatcher, and Pym were not fully briefed regarding the ambiguity in chapter XI, but, for different reasons, each wished to continue the negotiations and seized on the ambiguity to do so. Haig and Pym wanted to continue the negotiations because it was their only hope of reaching a negotiated settlement, while Thatcher needed more time for the fleet to get into position for the assault.

Although Costa Mendez now agreed that Haig should return to Buenos Aires, the secretary decided to stop over in Washington, partly to get a good night's rest (his team was getting fairly scruffy by this time), and partly to arrange for a more suitable arrival time in Buenos Aires. Before his departure from Heathrow, Haig said that his talks with British leaders had been useful and that he now had some unspecified "new ideas" for continuing the negotiation.[11] He refused, however, to disclose these ideas.

Thatcher appeared before the House of Commons to restate her position, which appeared to be unchanged. She insisted that UN502 must come first. There must be Argentine withdrawal before any negotiations. Britain reserved the right to employ force based on article 51 of the UN Charter. The task force would sail on. The government stood ready, if necessary, to employ force to recover the islands. The "wishes" of the Islanders remained paramount. Self-determination was the governing principle. There were no "new ideas" here.

Troubles in Washington

If Haig was hoping for a respite, his stopover in Washington did not provide one. The next day, April 14, the *Washington Post* greeted Haig's return with a front-page story that threatened to sink the talks altogether. "Senior administration officials...confirmed" an ABC-TV report of the night before that the United States was providing assistance to the British task force.[12] At British request, the article said, the United States had provided the use of a channel on a U.S. communications satellite, passed satellite reconnaissance and weather data to London, and made available approximately two million gallons of jet fuel at Ascension Island for British warplanes.

The Argentines were furious and demanded an explanation. Haig spent his day in Washington "trying to convince an outraged and deeply nervous junta that the U.S. government was telling the truth." He claimed that the report was false, a "mischievous press report based on a mendacious leak," but, of course, it was much more.[13] Upon investigating, Haig discovered that the report was correct—the United States was actually secretly aiding Great Britain. The newspaper article had mentioned only communications, intelligence, and fuel—elements of a long-standing pattern of cooperation. Haig, no doubt, now discovered to his dismay the enormous amount of military equipment that was also being supplied through Ascension Island, and he attempted to stop it, as well as the leaks.

In a call to Thatcher, Haig wanted to mollify Argentine concerns by issuing a statement regarding American impartiality. But the statement he proposed struck directly at Reagan's secret aid program. The proposed wording was:

> Since the outset of the crisis the United States had not acceded to requests that go beyond the scope of customary patterns of cooperation. That would continue to be its stand while peace efforts were under way. Britain's use of U.S. facilities on Ascension Island had been restricted accordingly.[14]

Thatcher was "very unhappy about what he wanted to say and...told him so." She pointed out that Ascension Island "was our island." Of course, "a great deal was being done to help us...within those 'customary patterns of cooperation.' " But, she argued, "to link this with the use of Ascension Island was wrong and misleading. Moreover, to make such a statement would have a very adverse reaction on UK opinion." In the end, thwarted, Haig "agreed to remove all mention of Ascension Island from his statement."[15]

Haig now turned to stop the leaks, "extremely upset both about the reports and about the willingness of unidentified administration officials to confirm them to the press."[16] He enjoined the president to say nothing about the Falklands during his press conference that morning.[17] (In fact, during his press conference, Reagan declined comment on the grounds that "the situation is too critical.")[18] Haig also obtained Reagan's agreement to "impose a ban on statements by U.S. officials about any aspect of the Falklands situation."[19]

Having stabilized things for the moment, Haig took off for Buenos Aires, arriving late on April 15. While he was aloft, flouting the secretary's injunctions against further commentary on the Falklands, the *New York Times* published an article that quoted "administration officials" reiterating the same points contained in the *Washington Post* article of the previous day. The United States was indeed providing Britain with satellite communications, photoreconnaissance, and fuel. "All of that assistance," officials said, "came under the definition of 'customary patterns' as described by Secretary of State Alexander M. Haig."[20] But there was no mention of military assistance.

Meanwhile, while Haig was still en route, Galtieri telephoned Reagan to voice his concern about American neutrality and to convey the tacit threat of Argentine cooperation with the Soviet Union. The advance of the British fleet, he said, was "not only making the situation ...more and more dangerous...but there is also the danger of involving other nations in this matter." Galtieri feared that "things could get out of hand and out of our control, becoming an extremely delicate matter for the whole world."[21]

President Reagan hastened to reassure the Argentine president that he "personally remain[ed] committed to a peaceful solution to this dispute." Reagan said that he realized that there was a "propaganda effort to seek or perhaps provoke hostility between our two countries. We have done nothing ...at variance with the role we have assumed as neutral and objective intermediaries. Peace is our cause and our only objective." Then he said:

> We must be careful to continue to be even-handed. There must be neutrality and friendship for both nations, because not to take this attitude would naturally prejudice our role as helper.... Therefore

> I want you to know, Mr. President, that we shall continue to play a
> neutral part in this matter....My intention is to continue with this
> neutrality while the negotiations proceed.[22]

President Reagan's professions of "neutrality and friendship" combined
with reports from London of a split in Thatcher's governing Conservative Party
and the possibility of a no-confidence vote against the prime minister in the
House of Commons, momentarily boosted the junta's spirits.[23] But Thatcher
received House support with passage of a resolution urging recovery of the
islands "by the diplomatic route, but with strong military support."[24]

When Haig arrived in Buenos Aires to present his "new ideas," he found
that the Argentines had developed some new ideas of their own. Meeting
with Galtieri for roughly an hour during the morning of April 16, Haig offered
his new ideas, which, he said, were "approved by Mrs. Thatcher."[25] A settlement package would now include:

- Mutual withdrawal within a two-week period and demilitarization of the
  islands for the interim period.
- Tripartite interim administration; decisions by majority rule, and right
  of Argentina to fly its flag.
- Considerable expansion of the Argentine role in the island councils.
- Guaranteed conclusion of negotiations by year's end.
- Negotiations to be guided by Chapter XI of the UN Charter on de-
  colonization.
- Normalization of communications with the mainland.
- Removal of all sanctions against Argentina.[26]

Galtieri "showed interest" but indicated that the Argentine foreign minister had already developed a counterproposal, which he would be sharing
with Haig later. Galtieri was concerned about other developments on the
American side. What was the meaning, he asked, of requests by "all of the
officials in the American embassy" for visa applications to Uruguay? "It was
as if," said Galtieri, "they had an instruction from Washington to prepare for
the evacuation of the embassy." Was it a reflection of an "Iran syndrome," or
a subtle attempt to exert pressure?[27]

Declaring that that was "terrible," Haig began to say that "I don't need to
go back to the U.S. to recognize that there are people of bad faith who are
trying..." before breaking off in mid-sentence. Galtieri moved to reassure

him saying, "We know that this is not the work of the American Government," but then said, "but there are also the statements of the Secretary of Defense, Weinberger, which were not very encouraging." (Weinberger had forcefully expressed his support for Great Britain the previous day.) Haig said, "Weinberger speaks without authority, Mr. President. You know what President Reagan said."[28]

To compound Galtieri's confusion about American intentions, at this point, Vernon Walters, who had been acting as Haig's interpreter, requested Galtieri's approval for a visit he wished to make with ex-President Arturo Frondizi, an old acquaintance. Galtieri immediately agreed, but could not but wonder at the reason Walters would choose this moment to seek out Frondizi, old acquaintance or not. Frondizi was head of one of the opposition parties, MID (Movimiento de Integracion y Desarrollo), which had strong links to big business and the multinationals. As it turned out, less than a week after the Walters-Frondizi meeting, MID published the first of several arguments critical of the war and opened what would become a widening gulf between the civilian parties and the military junta.[29]

Following Haig's meeting with Galtieri, he accompanied Costa Mendez to the Foreign Ministry where they attempted to delineate the differences between Haig's proposal and the junta's counterproposal. The Argentines realized that Haig and Thatcher had not interpreted chapter XI of the UN Charter in the same way that they had, emphasizing self-determination rather than the inhabitants' interests. Haig, in short, had turned the Argentines' ploy against them, for self-determination was simply another term for "wishes."

To avoid entrapment, the junta sought to return to square one and therefore proposed a patently unacceptable counterproposal.[30] They retained the decolonization formula, but extended it to include the dependencies of South Georgia and the South Sandwich Islands. This was obviously unacceptable because Britain held clear title to these territories, which were unconnected to the Falkland Islands and, moreover, were uninhabited. In addition, the junta now not only demanded the right to appoint the governor during the interim period, but also insisted that the governor appoint and control the police force.[31] They also demanded equal representation of Argentines and islanders on the legislative and executive councils and equal property and residence rights on the islands for continental Argentines.

The junta relegated the tripartite interim authority to a marginal role of verifying the execution of the agreements and called upon the United States to guarantee a settlement—that is, that to assure that the negotiation would result in a declaration of Argentine sovereignty by the end of the year. Finally, regarding withdrawal from the islands, the junta wanted the task force to withdraw not less than three thousand miles in the first week and to disperse entirely by the end of the second, returning all units to usual operational duties.

As Haig observed, "I am sure the British will shoot when they receive this message."[32] But Haig's "pessimism" was misplaced. It was not that, as he claimed, the Argentines were not bargaining in "good faith." The Argentine counterproposal was obviously extreme and a negotiating ploy. Indeed, it was a prelude to a dramatic reformulation within forty-eight hours, for their real objective was to drag out the negotiations beyond the point when British military operations would no longer be feasible. To have maintained the extreme position of the counterproposal would indeed have ensured an early British decision to "shoot."[33]

Costa Mendez asked Haig whether he would like to see Galtieri or the junta? Haig replied that, as he had not yet met either Anaya or Lami Dozo, he "believed [he] had earned the opportunity" to see the junta to tell them the consequences of their decision. Then the foreign minister said: "My advice is to wait until you see the junta before you send the British any messages....I am truly surprised...that the British will go to war for such a small problem as these few rocky islands."[34]

The British task force, now renamed Operation Corporate, had now set off from Ascension for the Falkland Islands and was no longer the "diplomatic" force that had sailed from England less than two weeks before. Key components had been added. The *Atlantic Conveyor*, an eighteen thousand-ton container ship capable of twenty-four knots, had been commissioned to transport additional Harrier aircraft, doubling the initial complement to forty. Second, the *Intrepid*, an eleven thousand-ton assault ship, was recommissioned to take additional troops and supplies. Along with *Fearless*, already en route, the two ships gave Britain a far more powerful assault capability. Finally, the Royal Air Force announced that Nimrod reconnaissance aircraft were commencing scouting patrols from Ascension Island. Still, it was thought, with only approximately five thousand men, the task force did not have enough men to defeat what were believed to be eleven thousand entrenched Argentines.[35]

Haig Meets the Junta

When Haig met the junta on April 17, he spoke against the background of a growing specter of conflict. Throughout the day, he resorted to bluff and bluster in an attempt to browbeat the junta into concessions. But they gave as good as they got. In what was a "tense" discussion, led by Anaya, the junta adopted a very hard and uncompromising line. They termed Haig pro-British, a liar, and a spy.[36] Typical of the exchanges was this between Haig and Anaya. Anaya said that he would be honored to see his own son, an army helicopter pilot assigned to the islands, give his life in the struggle. To which Haig retorted, "You don't know the meaning of war until you see the corpses of young men being put into body bags."[37]

For his part, Haig repeated his earlier argument that the United States could not accept the use of force to resolve international disputes. War was horrible; many would die, unnecessarily, on both sides. If there were war, American public opinion would force the United States to side with its long-time ally, Britain. Britain would win and the junta, he said ominously, could very well be destabilized. United States relations with its Latin neighbors would suffer lasting damage, too.

There was, however, a way out, he said, revealing his own agenda for the first time. He urged them to trust him and to settle for a restructuring of the island government along the lines they had been negotiating. This was the best chance of achieving their objective. Any negotiated outcome that avoided war now would inevitably lead to the transfer of sovereignty later. This was so because Britain would never again be able to mount a military operation of this kind.[38] Besides, he argued, Britain genuinely wished to divest itself of the islands, but could not do so under threat of force.

After hours of frustrating and fruitless haggling, the two sides agreed to break until the next day. It was at this point, late on the evening of April 17, that the Argentines decided to shift gears and present their most attractive package to date. Haig believed that his late-night call to Judge Clark at the White House had something to do with the decision. Playing a "wild card," he told Clark on an open line, which he knew was being monitored by the

Argentines, that British military operations were imminent. The result, says Haig, was that within a few hours "new proposals were delivered to me at the hotel together with an invitation to resume the negotiations at the Casa Rosada at two o'clock in the afternoon."[39]

While Haig was calling Clark in an effort to soften up the junta, that same evening, President Reagan telephoned Prime Minister Thatcher to caution her against accepting any compromise. As Thatcher reveals, Reagan said that "it would not be reasonable to ask us to move further towards the Argentine position."[40] Did Reagan know through American intelligence that the Argentines had decided to present their most attractive proposal to date? Was that part of Haig's call to Clark? In any case, it was extraordinary timing for the president of the United States to call the British prime minister to tell her not to agree to any compromise proposals just before they were sent.

Negotiations resumed the next day, April 18, at two o'clock in the afternoon. Twelve hours later, after inching forward by "syllables and centimeters," the Argentines had produced a new proposal.[41] It was a marked shift in position indicating that at least some of Haig's arguments had been persuasive. UN502 would receive full compliance. There would be a cessation of hostilities, withdrawal of forces (the task force would withdraw two thousand miles instead of three thousand), and negotiations would commence within fifteen days of signing. All sanctions would be removed.

So much was only marginally different from earlier positions, but what followed was a major departure. No explicit demand was made for the transfer of sovereignty, although December 31, 1982, remained the end-date for the transition period. Thatcher's principal demand for the restoration of British administration, the legislative and executive councils, would be honored. To each would be added two representatives selected by Argentina and at least one elected by the local Argentine population.[42] The councils would continue to control the police.

There would be no governor. The tripartite administration would be reestablished as the special interim authority to govern the islands and make all "decisions, laws and regulations." In the decolonization clause, the Argentines now substituted the term "rights" for "interests" and "wishes." And the term "Argentine" was removed from the earlier objectionable phrase "principle of Argentine territorial integrity applicable to this dispute."[43]

As it had evolved by 2:40 AM on April 19, the Argentine position was eminently reasonable. Had a negotiated settlement been desired, unquestionably the Argentine position, as it then had been formulated, could have provided the basis for agreement. At this point, however, Secretary Haig made what was, perhaps, the worst mistake a negotiator can make. He failed to perceive when his opposite numbers had reached the limits of their ability to compromise and persisted in demanding additional concessions.

Haig insisted that "more concessions were needed."[44] In his view, "Mrs. Thatcher would have great difficulty in accepting this text."[45] But Haig's attempt to pressure the Argentines backfired, producing intense suspicion and resentment. Argentine disillusionment with Secretary Haig was now complete. Galtieri, in an emotional outburst, once again warned Haig that should he attempt "to fence me in," he would be forced to seek assistance from the Soviet Union.[46]

Haig's argument was that a vaguely worded settlement would persuade Britain to hand over the islands. To the Argentines, this meant that, if there were no exact wording to this effect, the United States would have to guarantee the outcome. But when they questioned Haig closely on this point, it became clear that Washington would do nothing of the sort. Moreover, he waffled on British reactions, as well. "I do not say that this agreement will represent British acceptance of an eventual transference of sovereignty at the end of the negotiations, but that Great Britain will accept the inevitable end of this long process."[47] Argentine suspicions were heightened to the extreme.

At this point, Costa Mendez voiced Argentine fears that they had negotiated themselves out of their gains. If, he said, sovereignty were not transferred at the end of the year, "the terms that we have agreed to use here, which are so diffuse and ambiguous so as to be acceptable to the British Government today, will add a very risky threat to our position as of 31 December."[48] Indeed, those terms amounted to almost complete capitulation to Thatcher's fundamental position of Argentine withdrawal and restoration of British administration.

Retiring to discuss their predicament, after an "agitated debate" during which "Anaya brought all his influence," the junta decided to add one more sentence to the proposal thus far negotiated. Designed to ensure that, if there were no final resolution by December 31, Argentina would still gain de facto control of the islands, it read:

> As from December 31st 1982, and until such time as the agreement on the final status comes into force, the leadership of the government and administration will be exercised by an official appointed by the Argentine Government.[49]

In other words, if there were no resolution to final status by December 31, Buenos Aires would appoint a governor of the islands! Costa Mendez immediately realized that this would not fly, but it was inserted, he said, "so we could later negotiate it." Afterward, he acknowledged that he thought they had "made a mistake."[50] Others in the Argentine negotiating group that had the same opinion dubbed this last sentence the "mad clause."[51]

When he saw it, Haig blew up. Rejecting the final clause, he angrily declared war imminent. Pulling out all stops, he said the junta could fall with only itself to blame. After spending a sleepless night, Haig was back at the negotiating table the next morning attempting to dissuade the Argentines from insisting on the final clause. They refused. He set a deadline, declaring he would leave by four o'clock in the afternoon. Costa Mendez said he would meet him at two o'clock, but then was "delayed," and promised to meet Haig at the airport.

Costa Mendez arrived at the airport with the engines of Haig's jet turning. As he escorted Haig to his waiting aircraft, Costa Mendez told him that "there would be no revision of the final clause of the proposal."[52] Moreover, he informed him, "in the next few hours," Buenos Aires would be formally requesting a meeting of the Rio Pact foreign ministers. Thoroughly alarmed, Haig said, "Don't do it." Attempting to bluff, he warned, "Something is going to happen in Central America." Nicaragua was about to attack Honduras. If the two problems exploded in the OAS simultaneously, it would be chaos. Haig's bluff failed. Costa Mendez was unmoved. There would still be no change in the Argentine position, nor did Nicaragua attack Honduras.

Haig's account of his final twenty-four hours in Buenos Aires is markedly different, suggesting an attempt to cover up his negotiating faux pas. He blames the Argentines and describes an incoherent decision-making process in which, because no one is in charge, there is, therefore, no one with whom to negotiate. "If Galtieri did not hold the power of decision, neither did the junta. On every decision, the government apparently had to secure the unanimous consent of every corps commander in the army and of their equivalents in the navy and air force."[53]

If one were to accept this at face value, it is more a testimony to the Argentines' ability to conceal their decision-making process than an indictment of its incoherence. Asserting Argentine incoherence, however, permitted Haig to shift the blame for the breakdown. The structure of the Argentine negotiating team, aside from Costa Mendez and the junta, was divided into two groups. One was the Malvinas Working Group with which Haig interacted, but the other was the Military Committee, which was hidden from him. Thus, there were negotiating inputs, which Haig misperceived, from outside the Malvinas Working Group. Nevertheless, it was the junta that decided, not "every corps commander."[54]

Haig also omitted from his account the final sentence of the April 19 proposal—the "mad clause" by which the Argentines sought to protect themselves. Here, he resorted to the same device he used to explain the end of his first trip to Buenos Aires—that of Costa Mendez handing him a paper to be read only when airborne. Haig says Costa Mendez's message read, the result of the negotiations on December 31, 1982, "must include a recognition of Argentinian sovereignty over the islands."[55] Haig's account is completely different from the Argentine account cited above.

This was, Haig says, "an exercise of bad faith that is unique in my experience as a negotiator, the Argentinians had gone back on their word." The British must "either give Argentina sovereignty...or approve an arrangement for governing the island that amounted to de facto Argentine sovereignty."[56] Of course, when Haig wrote his memoir, the text of the Argentine proposal of April 19 was not public, as it is now. The April 19 proposal contains no explicit demand for sovereignty, although the "mad clause" would amount to de facto sovereignty by insisting on a governor after December 31, if no agreement had been reached.[57]

That Haig sought to manipulate the record is also evident from his next action. While airborne, he sent the Argentine proposal to London—but omitted the "mad clause!" Haig also sent a message back to Costa Mendez of his decision, adding that "he knew this was not the final Argentine position but that he hoped that Costa Mendez' Government would understand his reasons."[58] Of course, Costa Mendez's government did not understand. Outraged, the foreign minister immediately complained to Ambassador Schlaudemann, to no avail.

So Costa Mendez resorted to the same tactic that the junta had used after Haig's first trip to ensure that the Argentine position would be faithfully conveyed. Costa Mendez issued a public statement while Haig was still airborne. "Argentina," he said, "would move to invoke the Rio Treaty of 1947 in the Organization of American States." Furthermore, with regard to the proposals that Haig was carrying, Costa Mendez foresaw:

> the possibility of a limited period during which diverse alternatives would be contemplated and negotiated for a final solution, and which would lead swiftly to the recognition of genuine Argentine sovereignty in the region.[59]

But the basic Argentine position on sovereignty "had not changed and would not change."[60] In short, Costa Mendez had publicly reasserted the essence of the last sentence that Haig had omitted in transmitting the Argentine position to London.

Haig and Pym Collude

The proposal that Margaret Thatcher received from Haig, therefore, was the Argentine proposal minus the last sentence, although Costa Mendez's remarks undoubtedly alerted her to the probability that Haig had transmitted an incomplete proposal this time as he had previously. Nevertheless, although she immediately categorized it as "quite unacceptable" and "poor," she knew that even within the war cabinet, not to mention the entire cabinet, this was an eminently negotiable document because of its crucial omission.[61]

Thatcher's immediate reaction was to buy time to consider her next move. Haig was told not to proceed to London, but to return to Washington. And so as not to be considered responsible for the breakdown in negotiations—an indication in itself that there was great internal pressure to reach a negotiated solution—she did not immediately reject the Buenos Aires proposal. Indeed, she appeared before the House to announce that Britain (for the first time in the negotiations) would advance its own proposals.

The reason that Haig omitted the last sentence of the Argentine proposal is that to have done otherwise would have promptly ended the negotiations.

Haig's only hope was to drive a wedge in the war cabinet, isolate Thatcher, and appeal to Pym and the "wets." The Argentine proposal—minus the last sentence—superficially seemed to comply with the essence of Thatcher's position of restoring British administration to the islands and her requirements for self-determination. In truth, however, it was nothing more than a thinly disguised formula for the eventual transfer of sovereignty. The fact that it was couched in vague and seemingly reasonable terms, however, made it even more dangerous for Thatcher.

Reagan's call, cautioning against further compromise, had forewarned and forearmed the prime minister. She knew now, if she had not realized it earlier, that Haig and Reagan were on opposite sides. Haig had requested, and Thatcher had reluctantly agreed, that Pym go to Washington to discuss the Argentine text. It was imperative to ensure that Pym and Haig would not cobble together an agreement. Thatcher would henceforth take one step toward an increase in military pressure for every one she was required to take toward further negotiations—to undercut the prospects for a negotiated settlement.[62]

First, in an attempt to constrict Pym's negotiating flexibility, Thatcher forwarded to Haig "detailed comments and essential amendments" to the Buenos Aires text. An outline of Thatcher's position was also passed to the press, and an article delineating her views appeared in the *New York Times* on the day Pym arrived in Washington.[63] Pym was instructed to seek an "American guarantee" and to "be guided by these counterproposals during his visit."[64] The counterproposals amounted to insistence on compliance with UN502, restoration of British administration on the islands, and recognition that the wishes of the Islanders were paramount, which represented Thatcher's fundamental position.[65]

That Pym refused to be "guided by these counterproposals" became obvious almost immediately. During questions at Commons the day before he left for Washington, he implied that force would not be used as long as negotiations continued. Thatcher demanded that he recant, as such a position could allow the Argentines to "string us along indefinitely." Pym returned to the House to retract the remark.

Following receipt of the Argentine proposal, Thatcher also gained war cabinet agreement authorizing military action to retake South Georgia. The question of whether to retake South Georgia had been disputed within the military high command from the beginning. Some considered it a risky and unnecessary diversion, which would expend scarce resources, while others believed that the island could serve as a forward base from which to mount the attack on the Falkland Islands. Thatcher and the war cabinet now decided in favor of recovery.

The day before Pym traveled to Washington, April 21, Haig was informed of the decision, which "surprised and concerned" him. He told Ambassador Henderson that "he thought he would have to give the Argentine junta advance notice of our intended operation."[66] Thatcher was appalled and registered a strong dissent through Henderson, who believed that he had persuaded Haig "to think better of it." In fact, Haig had not been persuaded, warning publicly of the probability of imminent British military action.

Britain had hoped to retake South Georgia, swiftly, secretly, "with minimum loss of life and with minimum damage to property."[67] Haig's warning had alerted the junta, which immediately directed the submarine *Santa Fe*, already in the area with nearly fifty troops on board, to reinforce South Georgia.[68] The "mere presence" of the *Santa Fe* complicated "all British plans," eliminating any possibility of a swift, secret operation. Not only would recovery be more difficult because of the reinforcements, the presence of the submarine would be a threat to British ships.

In an attempt to deter the junta from reinforcing South Georgia, the British government issued a "general warning" to Argentina on April 23. Without mentioning South Georgia by name, which, of course, was not included in the MEZ, the British government warned that "any approach" by Argentine warships, submarines, or aircraft "to British forces in the South Atlantic" would be regarded as a hostile act and the units in question subject to attack.[69]

Thatcher Versus Pym

Pym had spent April 22–23 in Washington conferring with Haig. Upon his return, he confronted Thatcher with the proposal that he and Haig had composed, the so-called American proposal, and urged its acceptance. To Thatcher, Pym's document was tantamount to "conditional surrender." Their day-long struggle "at loggerheads" on April 24, Thatcher recounts, was "one of the most crucial days in the Falklands story and a critical one for me personally."[70]

The decisive moment came that evening during a meeting of the war cabinet. At issue were Thatcher's plan and Pym's "American proposal," which Thatcher refers to in her memoir as "the texts of 22 and 24 April." It was "the differences between" these texts that "went to the heart of why we were prepared to fight a war for the Falklands." There were three broad issues in dispute—the nature and timing of the withdrawal of forces, the length and composition of the interim administration, and the terms and conditions of the negotiations after Argentine withdrawal.

On the question of withdrawal of forces, the crucial issue was the kind of leverage Britain would maintain to ensure Argentine compliance with UN502. Pym's proposal would have required the task force "to stand off even further than in the Buenos Aires proposals" and "disperse altogether" after fifteen days. This would deprive London "of any effective military leverage over the withdrawal process." Argentine forces, however, were to be held to "less than 7 days' readiness to invade again," but there was no definition of "readiness," nor any assurance that Argentina would honor the concept.[71]

To ensure continued leverage, Thatcher insisted upon maintaining the integrity of the task force until the Argentine withdrawal was complete. She held to the same principle regarding the lifting of sanctions. Pym wanted sanctions to be removed when the agreement was signed, "rather than as in our counterproposals on completion of withdrawal." Their differences on withdrawal, however, paled in comparison to their differences concerning the interim regime that would govern the Falkland Islands after Argentina withdrew.

Pym had agreed to the Argentine proposal of April 19 establishing joint administration of the islands. This involved "two representatives of the Argentine Government on the Islands' Councils, as well as at least one representative of the local Argentine population." (The local Argentine population on the Falkland Islands totaled thirty.) Pym also agreed to the extension of residence and property rights to Argentines on the islands "which would effectively have allowed them to swamp the existing population with Argentinians."

Although Thatcher does not note in her memoir her own position on the interim administration for the islands, it was revealed in contemporary press reports.[72] Thatcher wanted the full restoration of the British administration as originally demanded following the Argentine invasion. There would be no joint administration with the Argentines, who would be required to remove the Argentine flag. In Thatcher's proposal, during the interim period, "only the British flag would fly over the disputed South Atlantic archipelago and only British officials and policemen would be involved in its administration."[73]

Finally, regarding negotiations of the final status of the islands, Pym had "ruled out the possibility of a return to the situation enjoyed by the islanders before the invasion." For Thatcher, this meant that "we would have gone against our commitment to the principle that the islanders' wishes were paramount and would have abandoned all possibility of their staying with us. Did Francis realize," Thatcher asked, "how much he had signed away?"[74]

Thatcher's proposal emphasized the Islanders' right of self-determination. Their "wishes would be paramount," a position that she had also staked out immediately following the invasion. She did allow, however, for the possibility of a "quite short" interim period during which the Islanders' wishes would be expressed.[75] Once the Islanders had expressed their wishes—either to remain under British rule, accept Argentine rule, or emigrate (with due compensation), then negotiations on the subject of sovereignty would commence, but without prejudice and without a deadline.

Before the war cabinet meeting, Thatcher had successfully lobbied for the support of the other members of the committee—Nott, Parkinson, and Whitelaw. Whitelaw, in particular, was believed to be Pym's ally, but Thatcher took him aside, gave him her "reasons" for opposing Pym's views, and won him over. "As always," she said, "on crucial occasions he backed my judgment."[76] The war cabinet stood with Thatcher, outvoting Pym four-to-one. Thatcher had won. There would be no retreat from UN502, the demand for restoration of full British sovereignty on the islands, and the stipulation that the wishes of the Islanders were paramount.

> And so a great crisis passed. I could not have stayed as Prime Minister had the War Cabinet accepted Francis Pym's proposals. I would have resigned.[77]

The crisis of April 24, however, would not be the last. The war cabinet had rejected Pym's American proposal, but had decided not to reveal that fact. Instead, it was decided—at Nott's suggestion—to require the junta to respond publicly to the proposal first. If they accepted it, Thatcher would "undoubtedly be in difficulties," but the matter could be placed before

Parliament in view of their acceptance. In other words, it would not be her decision alone, and her position would not be at risk.

The prime minister considered Argentine acceptance unlikely "because it is almost impossible for any military junta to withdraw." In that case, London would urge the United States to "come down firmly on our side." Nevertheless, Thatcher acted to ensure against Argentine acceptance of Haig's proposal by reducing to a minimum the time that the junta would have to consider it. In a message to Haig late on April 24, she insisted that he "establish urgently whether Buenos Aires would accept."[78]

Thatcher's message to Haig indicated that she had deemed the negotiation to have ended. Whatever Argentina decided, a new phase would begin. Acceptance would put the issue squarely in Britain's court. The resulting Parliamentary debate would undoubtedly involve great pressure for a negotiated settlement. Labour had already broken away and the "wets," as Pym's readiness to accept Haig's proposal indicated, also wished to settle.

Rejection, however, would—at least momentarily—clear the way for military action. Indeed, military operations to recover South Georgia were already underway, and a British victory would be certain to inhibit further negotiations in any case. Time was growing short, and winter was fast approaching. The task force, which was now in position to begin operations, would have to be either employed or withdrawn. No one doubted for a moment, however, that the negotiating impulse was still viable. Thatcher sought to force the issue.

A British force of seventy-five men retook South Georgia on April 25, after an intense shore bombardment. Argentine forces had offered little resistance, although Argentina had reinforced its garrisons at Grytviken and Leith in anticipation of a British attempt to recover the island. Indeed, British forces had also located, attacked, and disabled the submarine employed to send in reinforcements–the *Santa Fe*. Its crew abandoned it after piloting it into Grytviken. By the afternoon of April 25, South Georgia was once again in British hands.

Costa Mendez was scheduled to arrive in Washington on April 25 for an OAS meeting where he planned to invoke the Rio Treaty. Haig had intended to deliver his proposal to him then. Just as Costa Mendez arrived, however, news of the British recapture of South Georgia, and the surrender of approximately 180 Argentines, threw a roadblock into Haig's plan.[79] Costa Mendez canceled his meeting with Haig, but said he would contact him after the OAS meeting the next day. Meanwhile, Francis Pym called Haig early on April 26 before the meeting to say that "new ideas were coming from London."[80] So the push-pull in London continued, with Thatcher attempting to end the negotiations and Pym striving to continue them.

The OAS meeting produced a less than satisfactory outcome for Buenos Aires. Canvassing the delegates, Costa Mendez learned that Argentina would be able to obtain neither the necessary two-thirds majority needed for joint action against Britain, nor explicit recognition of Argentine sovereignty over the Falkland Islands. He pressed, therefore, for British withdrawal based on the argument that Britain was about to commit aggression against Argentine territory. His speech to the assembly on April 26 was greeted with a standing ovation, suggesting that he would obtain some support.[81]

Haig spoke after Costa Mendez, reiterating his view that the United States had "perhaps a unique ability" to be the mediator in the dispute. He noted, without mentioning Argentina by name, that "there has been a use of force by an American state already." Therefore, the provisions for collective defense in the Rio Treaty did not apply. "This organization, and the world community," he said, "long ago made the determination that force shall not be used to settle international disputes. We shall all suffer if this principle…is ignored."[82] His remarks elicited an embarrassing "stony silence" from the gathered foreign ministers and ambassadors, leaving the impression that the OAS would repudiate the United States.

Afterward, Haig and Costa Mendez met in OAS secretary-general Alejandro Orfila's office. Sensing Costa Mendez's "reluctance to forward the U.S. proposal," he offered to go to Buenos Aires again to deliver the text personally to Galtieri. Haig believed that the British would withhold further attacks while he was in direct negotiations with the Argentines and asked that the junta receive him. Haig says that he gave Costa Mendez twenty-four hours to reply, but as the hours passed and no reply came, he then instructed Ambassador Schlaudeman to deliver the proposal to Galtieri, setting midnight April 27 as the deadline for a reply.[83]

Haig's account, however, here as in so many places, conflicts with the Argentine account, as well as with the contemporary record. In the Argentine account, there was no "reluctance" to forward the proposal, no unilateral action by Haig, and no Argentine agreement to respond to a deadline. There were "no grounds for proposing a new visit by Haig," so "both men agreed that the text of the proposal would be simultaneously delivered to the Argentines in Washington through Ambassador Takacs, and in Buenos Aires, through Schlaudeman." Concerning the deadline, "Costa Mendez made only one promise: the reply would be sent 'as early as possible.' "[84] Indeed, State Department spokesman Dean Fischer, said: "We are awaiting a response. There is no ultimatum, no deadline other than what is imposed by the reality of the situation."[85]

Thatcher Ends the Negotiations

Meanwhile, that evening of April 26, Thatcher acted again to foreclose any further negotiation. First, the war cabinet approved the establishment of a total exclusion zone (TEZ) of a two-hundred-mile radius around the Falkland Islands to enter into force on April 30. During Prime Minister's Questions she pointed out that "time is getting extremely short." Political choices and military options were narrowing "with the task force in the wild and stormy weathers of that area."[86]

Pressure in Parliament was strong from the Left in favor of continuing negotiations. Social Democratic leader David Owen argued that "it is right to give Secretary Haig a few more days." Labour leader Michael Foot wanted to know whether Thatcher would ask for help from the United Nations if Haig's mission failed and declared, "the search for peace should never be torpedoed by us." He asked Thatcher: "How are we to be assured there will be no dangerous escalation of the crisis?"[87]

Afterward, during a television appearance, Thatcher elaborated on her negotiating position for the first time. "Negotiations," she said, "cannot just go on indefinitely."

> All Argentine forces would have to be withdrawn from the Falklands before the British task force would be pulled back, complete British civil administration would have to be restored, and self-determination would have to be maintained for the 1,800 "British" residents in negotiations about the Falklands' long-term sovereignty.[88]

Argentine leaders most certainly compared Thatcher's position with Haig's proposal and drew the obvious conclusion that one bore no relationship to the other. Haig's proposal, dated April 27, called for simultaneous withdrawal, a joint administration of the islands, and "due regard for the rights of the inhabitants," but not self-determination.[89] Haig's special interim authority of Britain, Argentina, and the United States included the right to fly national flags. Thatcher would "not allow the Argentine flag to fly on the Falklands," as a sign of sovereignty, although one could fly over an Argentine mission there.[90]

Costa Mendez met with Haig at the State Department on Wednesday afternoon, April 28, following the OAS vote earlier that day. The OAS vote was a mixed blessing for Buenos Aires. It had not, as Costa Mendez had hoped, called for British withdrawal, but only urged Britain to "cease hostilities...within the security region defined by the Rio Treaty." It also called upon Argentina "to refrain from any act that may affect inter-American peace and security." While offering OAS assistance in the search for a peaceful solution, the resolution supported UNR502 and the Haig mediation.[91]

The purpose of Costa Mendez's visit was to say that "Argentina had not rejected the latest American proposals and that he expected a formal response to them shortly."[92] Costa Mendez outlined several points that the junta needed to clarify, but Haig was not satisfied. His "deadline" had passed, and he reproached Costa Mendez for condemning his mission to failure. In a heated exchange, which reflected Haig's panic, he declared that if conflict came "it will not be Great Britain alone....The United States will support her, and together with NATO we will bring pressure to bear so that inevitably the Argentine Military Government is going to fall. Be sure of that." Costa Mendez replied, "That threat, Sir, is unworthy of a Secretary of State."[93]

After their meeting, Haig called Pym to inform him that there was still no answer from Buenos Aires. Pym now divulged his "new idea." Taking as a point of departure an offer by Mexican president Lopez Portillo to provide a venue for negotiations, Pym proposed to turn back the task force, if the Argentines first withdrew from the islands. Then, if the United States would guarantee the security of the islands, London would not return their governor and would accept an Argentine resident to look after the interests of the Argentines living in the islands.[94]

Haig was "surprised" by the Mexican-American idea, but unreceptive. Quickly transmitting the foreign minister's idea to the Argentines, Haig received a prompt reply. "The Argentines regarded this offer as surrender terms dictated by the British," bringing to an end yet another attempt by Pym to reach a negotiated settlement.[95] In truth, Pym's rather quixotic offer implied a willingness to dispense with Haig as an interlocutor and only served to complicate Argentina's response to Haig's proposal. It was a rather blatant attempt to circumvent the prime minister's position. It would not be the last of Pym's attempts—nor of Haig's, for that matter—to reach a negotiated settlement.

That evening, Haig appeared before a closed-door session of the Senate to brief the more than seventy senators who attended on the course of the negotiations. Haig described the Argentines as "intransigent," and the differences between Buenos Aires and London as "irreconcilable."[96] Haig's briefing strengthened the pro-British resolution sponsored by Senators Biden and Moynihan, which passed the following evening by a margin of 79 to 1, with only Senator Helms voting against.

On the morning of April 29, Thatcher, thoroughly vexed by Haig's apparent willingness to stretch his own proclaimed deadline and, no doubt, Pym's persistent efforts to reach a settlement, sent a message to President Reagan declaring that "in our view the Argentines must now be regarded as having rejected the American proposals."[97] Before Reagan could respond, a "troubled" Ambassador Takacs delivered the Argentine reply.[98] Contrary to the impression that Costa Mendez had left with Haig, it was an unmistakable rejection of the latter's entire negotiating effort.

The original Argentine position had been for either an immediate formal British transfer of sovereignty over the Falkland Islands to Argentina or de facto transfer through Argentine control of the island administration. The essence of Haig's negotiation had been to persuade Buenos Aires to drop its demand for the immediate transfer of sovereignty, accept an enlarged role in the British administration of the islands, and seek a favorable outcome through U.S.-sponsored negotiations. The unstated presumption was that there would be a negotiated transfer of sovereignty sometime in 1983.

The Argentine reply of April 29 repudiated the Haig approach and reverted to its original claims, demanding a prejudgment of the outcome. The recognition of Argentine sovereignty over the Falkland Islands, the note said, "constitutes for us an unrenounceable goal." The negotiations have focused on two points—"recognition of sovereignty and a provisional administrative regime."

> The two are intimately connected to each other. To the extent that the provisions relating to the recognition of our sovereignty are imprecise, for us it is necessary…to establish mechanisms that give us broader powers in administration of the islands. On the other side of the coin, if it were clear that Argentina's sovereignty would be recognized in the end, then we could be more flexible regarding the matter of temporary administration.[99]

Haig's proposal, the reply continued, "falls short of Argentina's demands and does not satisfy its minimal aspirations for either of the two points." It would bar Argentina from strengthening its administrative control, if negotiations faltered, and the introduction of a "virtual referendum" to determine the "wishes" of the Islanders threatened to foreclose any possibility of eventual transfer of sovereignty. "Thus we are faced with the real possibility of establishing a predominantly British administration with no fixed expiration date." Making the rejection of Haig's formula unambiguously clear, the note concluded: "The Secretary knows that we cannot accept these changes. …Other formulas must be found."[100]

In an attempt to soften the impact of the Argentine rejection, Alfredo Saint Jean, who was managing the Foreign Ministry in Costa Mendez's absence, attempted to keep open the lines of communication. He declared that Argentina had not rejected Haig's proposal, it was simply not accepting it. "There is a difference between rejecting and not accepting. With the latter, we can at least keep the Americans in that middle position."[101] It was actually a distinction without a difference. In short, the junta had reverted to its original position—either prior recognition of Argentine sovereignty or a "gradually larger" Argentine role in the administration of the islands. Henceforth, with one exception, Buenos Aires would focus its diplomatic efforts in the United Nations. Haig's "mediation" had ended, but, as we shall see, his efforts to produce a negotiated settlement had by no means ceased.

After Haig briefed the president, the White House and the State Department issued terse identical statements couched in diplomatic language, but no less clear because of it. "The situation remains very serious. There is no movement and very little basis for optimism."[102] In a statement Thatcher described as "very satisfactory," Reagan now replied to her earlier message:

I am sure you agree that it is essential now to make clear to the world that every effort was made to achieve a fair and peaceful solution, and that the Argentine Government was offered a choice between such a solution and further hostilities. We will therefore make public a general account of the efforts we have made. While we will describe the U.S. proposal in broad terms, we will not release it because of the difficulty that might cause you. I recognize that while you see fundamental difficulties in the proposal, you have not rejected it. We will leave no doubt that Her Majesty's Government worked with us in good faith and was left with no choice but to proceed with military action based on the right of self-defence.[103]

While Reagan was giving the green light for British military action against Argentina, Haig was delivering a different message to a closed-door meeting of the House Foreign Affairs Committee. He said that, although he had not completely abandoned hope for a diplomatic solution, there was little chance that fighting could be averted. The Royal Navy, having come so far, was not going to stop before capturing the islands. But, he said, "even if fighting began, there might still be an opportunity for a diplomatic solution."[104] By voice vote, the committee adopted a resolution to give Britain "full diplomatic support," if the dispute could not be resolved peacefully.

That evening, April 29, following the overwhelming Senate vote in favor of supporting Great Britain, Haig called Ambassador Takacs to inform him that the United States would declare its backing for Great Britain the next day. The next morning, Friday, April 30, following what was reported to have been a "bitterly contested" National Security Council (NSC) meeting, the decision was made to "tilt" toward Britain.[105] Haig read a statement recapitulating the mediation effort and described the American proposal. He said that "we had reason to hope that the United Kingdom would consider a settlement along the lines of our proposal, but Argentina informed us yesterday that it could not accept it."[106]

Then, he said, "In light of Argentina's failure to accept a compromise, we must take concrete steps to underscore that the United States cannot and will not condone the use of unlawful force to resolve disputes." The president has ordered, he said, the suspension of military exports, withholding of certification for military sales, suspension of Ex-Im Bank credits and guarantees, and suspension of Commodity Credit Corporation guarantees. The president has also directed that the United States will respond positively to British requests for matériel support.

In closing, Haig kept open the door to negotiation. He declared that American policy will continue to be guided by our concern for the rule of law and "our desire to facilitate an early and fair settlement." A strictly military outcome, he said, "cannot endure over time. In the end, there will have to be a negotiated outcome acceptable to the interested parties." Otherwise, we will all face "unending hostility and insecurity" in the South Atlantic. The United States remains ready to assist the parties in finding that settlement.

President Reagan, speaking to a luncheon group of Midwest editors, also spoke hopefully of a diplomatic settlement "before action takes place," but, he said, the United States had "gone as far as we can go" in trying to mediate.[107] Reagan placed the blame for the breakdown of the negotiations entirely on Argentina. "We must remember that the aggression was on the part of Argentina in this dispute over the sovereignty of that little ice-cold bunch of land down there, and...aggression of that kind must not be allowed to succeed."

Meanwhile, in London, Francis Pym quickly welcomed the announcement of American support and said that he would again visit Washington and New York as well over the weekend, "to continue the search for a peaceful solution."[108] As Thatcher notes of the period following the end of Haig's mediation, while "military considerations loomed ever larger in my mind...this did not mean that the pressure for negotiations eased—far from it." The prime minister found herself "under an almost intolerable pressure to negotiate for the sake of negotiations and because so many politicians were desperately anxious to avoid the use of force."[109] Foremost among them were, of course, Foreign Minister Pym and Secretary of State Haig.

CHAPTER 7

After the "Tilt":
The Politics of War

The climax of the political struggle between Reagan and Haig, on the one hand, and Thatcher and Pym, on the other, occurred as British forces commenced military operations. As the political fates of both Haig and Pym hinged on a negotiated settlement, their efforts to achieve one reached fever pitch after the "tilt." The first of these centered around the so-called Peruvian Initiative, which was actually the continuation of Haig's mediation through a Latin American intermediary. Haig and Pym colluded on the Peruvian Initiative in an attempt to arrange a peace settlement behind the scenes and present Reagan and Thatcher with a fait accompli.

The first major military engagement of the war sank their scheme. The British torpedo attack on the Argentine cruiser *General Belgrano* on May 2 ended the Peruvian Initiative and seemed to clear the way for resolution of the dispute on the field of battle. The successful Argentine exocet strike on the *HMS Sheffield* two days later, however, which disabled the British destroyer, immediately revived the prospects for negotiations. Haig and Pym, thereafter, resumed their efforts separately for a negotiated settlement—in Haig's case, virtually until the last days of the fighting.

The irony in attempts to reach a negotiated settlement was the disinclination of the junta to accept any compromise that would deny them control of the Falkland Islands. For the junta, the purpose of negotiations—aside from those that would confer outright sovereignty or control—was principally to delay the beginning of landing operations on the islands. Each day of delay brought them one step closer to winter, making British military operations increasingly difficult and strengthening the prospects for victory. Significantly, Argentina's not inconsiderable forces remained largely intact and were poised to deliver a lethal blow. The junta remained confident that Argentine forces would either thwart a landing attempt or make the price of a landing so prohibitively expensive in men and matériel that Britain would sue for peace. The junta's confidence in its ability to defeat a British landing reinforced intransigence at the bargaining table.

The War Cabinet Meeting of April 30 and the Events of May 1

By the end of April, the task force was largely assembled, except for most ground force units still held in reserve at Ascension Island. With negotiations at an impasse, naval headquarters at Northwood sent a message to task force commander Sandy Woodward, "In all respects prepare for war by midnight, April 29th."[1] Deployed at the eastern edge of the TEZ, approximately two hundred miles from the Falkland Islands, the task force was beyond the range of Argentina's land-based aircraft and open only to the relatively insignificant threat of submarine attack.

Only two circumstances could seriously threaten the task force. The first would occur if Argentina decided to send its single aircraft carrier, the *25 de Mayo*, out to sea. Then, if it could elude Britain's nuclear-powered hunter-killer submarines, its aircraft—A4 Skyhawks and Mirage jets—could mount a potentially devastating attack. The second, and more likely, circumstance under which the task force would come under threat could occur when British forces attempted to land on the islands. Then the task force would come within range of land-based, bomb-carrying aircraft as well as the Exocet-laden Super Étendard. Both British and Argentine leaders were well aware of this circumstance and of the fact that the task force had no aerial early warning capability. Britain's deficiency in this regard was slightly mitigated by forward-deployed submarine spotters, special forces units inserted onto the mainland to provide some advance warning, and by the very fact that everyone knew that Argentina would attack when British forces attempted to land.

Argentine leaders decided from the outset not to present a naval challenge to Britain on the high seas, realizing that the Royal Navy was superior to theirs. They knew, too, that a sea battle, or battles, would occur at the limits of the range of their aircraft, the majority of which was land based. This meant only a short time on target, reducing their superior numerical advantage. They determined, instead, to attack the task force when it came within range and was most vulnerable—when Britain attempted to land troops on the islands. They chose, therefore, to husband their forces and wait for the landing.

For their part, British leaders realized that, unless they could reduce superior Argentine force levels beforehand, the landing would be at risk. They chose, therefore, to feign landings in hopes of drawing a response. Their plan was, through attrition, to gradually reduce, if not eliminate, Argentine air superiority to facilitate a landing on the islands. These tactics would at least enable them to determine the manner in which the Argentines sought to respond when the landing actually occurred. A related objective was to create opportunities to insert special forces units on the islands to develop critically necessary tactical intelligence about Argentine defense dispositions. Woodward later described his military objectives:

> My initial plan was to lay on a major demonstration of force well inside the Exclusion Zone to make the Argentines believe that landings were about to take place and thus provoke a reaction that would allow me to conduct a major attrition exercise....And at the very least, I might discover whether they had a coherent defensive plan.[2]

The War Cabinet met on Friday afternoon, April 30, following Haig's "tilt" statement. Intelligence indicated that the Argentine fleet had deployed to sea three days earlier and the day before had divided into three groups, designated Task Force 79. The Argentine carrier, *25 de Mayo*, and four escorts, were deployed to a position 270 miles due east of the Cape of Tres Puntas immediately beyond the northern perimeter of the TEZ. That put the carrier less than 400 miles away from the task force situated at the eastern edge of the TEZ. A second group of three corvettes was deployed to the Gulf of San Jorge as a reserve. The third group, also of three ships, included the cruiser *Belgrano* and two destroyer escorts, *Bouchard* and *Piedrabueno*. This group was deployed to patrol off the southern rim of the TEZ along Drake Passage.[3] Task Force 79's general orders were to "find and destroy the British *if* they attacked the Islands or mainland."[4]

The War Cabinet decided to execute the attrition exercise the next day, May 1, but was not unified about its ultimate purpose. Thatcher viewed the day's attacks as the preparatory steps to a landing of British forces on the islands, leading to their ultimate recovery. Pym, on the other hand, saw the attacks as a demonstration of British power that could lead quickly to a possible Argentine withdrawal from the islands and a negotiated settlement of the conflict, which very likely would not result in their recovery. Toward this end, he gained the war cabinet's agreement to make another trip to Washington for consultation with Haig and Weinberger and to New York for consultation with UN Secretary General Perez de Cuellar.

Militarily, the British high command hoped that the day-long series of attacks would convince the Argentines that British forces were attempting to land on the islands and provoke a response. The attacks would consist of a long-range bomber strike from Ascension Island against the airfield at Stanley to render it useless to Argentine aircraft. Carrier-based Harriers would conduct a series of attacks against the airfields at Stanley and Darwin with the same objective. Ships from the task force would maneuver close to the islands to bombard military installations around Stanley as well as to insert by helicopter numerous special forces units to conduct reconnaissance of Argentine military dispositions on the islands.

The strikes on Stanley were bait for the trap the War Cabinet now set with the submarines *Splendid* and *Conqueror*. Both were ordered to assume blocking positions between their quarry and the main elements of the task force. *Splendid* was ordered to take a position to intercept the *25 de Mayo* should the carrier attempt to move into aircraft launching position within range of the task force. If *Splendid* were to encounter *25 de Mayo*, it would constitute "incontrovertible evidence" that the carrier was a threat according to the April 23 rules of engagement and should, therefore, be attacked.[25] *Conqueror* was sent the same orders to take up a blocking position vis-à-vis the *Belgrano* group. If the *Belgrano* were encountered moving toward the task force, it, too, was to be attacked.[6]

The orders were crafted to satisfy explicitly the declaration of April 23—the rules of engagement—warning Argentina that "any approach on the part of Argentine warships, including submarines, naval auxiliaries, or military aircraft, which could amount to a threat to interfere with the mission of the British Forces in the South Atlantic will encounter the appropriate response." Thus, the submarines were positioned so that British action would be a legitimate defensive response to an Argentine offensive threat anywhere in the South Atlantic—inside or outside the TEZ—should any warships "approach."

Pym disagreed with this plan, particularly with the trap being set for the carrier, *25 de Mayo*. He argued that fair warning should be given to Buenos Aires that its ships could be attacked outside the TEZ. In this he obtained the support of Attorney General Sir Michael Havers, but he nevertheless lost the argument.[7] Thatcher argued persuasively that "no further warning was required." An "attack would be based upon the right of self-defence...be within Article 51 of the UN Charter [and be] in accordance with the notification which had been given on 23 April."[8] Pym remained dissatisfied with this decision.

After consulting with Havers again, Pym registered what amounted to a formal dissent, which he sent to Thatcher before his departure for Washington. He reiterated that the government should give "a warning to the Argentine government, requiring the aircraft carrier to stay within [a] narrow range." Furthermore, Pym argued, British forces should not initiate, but only respond to, an Argentine attack. Should an attack occur, he conceded, "all other Argentine naval units operating on the high seas, including the carrier 'The 25th of May,' would be considered hostile and...dealt with accordingly."[9]

Thatcher remained firm, refusing to restrict the task force to a purely defensive position. When Pym left for Washington to consult with Secretary Haig, the rules of engagement remained those expressed in the April 23 declaration. "Any approach on the part of Argentine warships...which could amount to a threat to interfere with the mission of British Forces in the South Atlantic" would permit a British attack. This formulation meant that British forces could shoot first, if Argentine warships crossed a predetermined line constituting a "threat to interfere." They could not initiate an attack, however, if Argentine ships failed to "approach." It was a crucial distinction that would shortly precipitate a crisis within the War Cabinet.

The attrition exercise of May 1 disappointed British leaders for the Argentines did not fall for the trap. Just before 4:30 AM (local time) a single British Vulcan bomber, on a long-range mission from Ascension Island involving multiple aerial refueling, released twenty-one one thousand-pound bombs in an attempt to destroy the airfield at Stanley. Except for a single hit at the end of the runway, all missed the target entirely, leaving it slightly damaged but still serviceable.[10] London claimed, however, that the attack had "severely cratered" the runway, a claim that generated immediate skepticism, was not substantiated, and later was proven incorrect.[11] The Argentines piled dirt on the runway during the day to "simulate craters," and removed it at night to permit supply aircraft to land.[12]

Immediately following the Vulcan bombing attack, Harriers from the carrier *Hermes*, which had moved to within seventy miles of the islands, struck in five attack waves spaced approximately forty-five minutes apart at military facilities in and around Stanley and at Argentine bases at Darwin and Goose Green. Harriers aboard the *Invincible*, which accompanied *Hermes*, performed the task of combat air patrol. By noon, their mission completed, the Harriers recovered to the carrier, and the group moved eastward back to the edge of the TEZ. Meanwhile, Woodward rearmed his planes with air-to-air Sidewinder missiles (the U.S.-supplied Aim 9L) in preparation for the anticipated Argentine response. That afternoon and evening, the destroyer *Glamorgan* and the frigates *Arrow* and *Alacrity* sailed to within sight of Stanley to conduct a several-hour-long shore bombardment of military installations around the town to reinforce the idea that a landing was imminent.

That afternoon, as expected, the Argentines responded, sending four Mirage III fighter-bombers to the attack. One Harrier was lost, and the ships suffered only minor cannon damage from the attack. While the Mirages missed with their bombs, some came very close. Two one thousand-pound bombs fell within fifty yards on either side of *Glamorgan*.[13] A hit by either bomb would have sunk the destroyer. The Harrier combat air patrol knocked out two of the Mirages, a third was mistakenly downed by Argentine antiaircraft shore batteries, and the fourth escaped. Then, frigates *Yarmouth* and *Brilliant*, on antisubmarine patrol, encountered two Canberra bombers (but no submarines). A Harrier destroyed one, and the other retreated. Toward midnight, special forces teams were inserted by small craft and helicopter, ending the day's activities.

Woodward had reason to be satisfied with the performance of his forces, particularly his Harriers, but the Argentine response to the British trap had been disappointing. Argentina had sent only six aircraft against the task force, suffering four losses. Woodward had expected far more. The Argentine plan, deciphered by British intelligence, was for "a coordinated attack on the task force to be conducted by aircraft from the mainland, from carrier-based aircraft, and from surface ships equipped with Exocets," but it had not materialized.[14]

In fact, the Argentine command had attempted to mount a massive response to what they initially perceived to be a British landing. As reports came in from the Falklands and from aerial reconnaissance of the British air attacks and the concentration of ships offshore, the Argentine high command began to overcome its doubts that the British were attempting a landing. Admiral Lombardo, now commander in chief of South Atlantic Forces, had been skeptical of an early landing, much less one at Stanley, location of the heaviest concentration of Argentine defenses.[15] After rechecking his intelligence, speaking twice with General Menéndez, governor and ground forces commander in the islands, and conferring with his aides, Lombardo concluded that this was, indeed, "the day of the landing."[16]

According to plan, the Argentine high command ordered a coordinated air and naval attack. In the air, the Argentines mounted a massive strike of fifty planes from mainland bases and the *25 de Mayo* in an attempt to overwhelm British defenses and defeat the landing. But the inexperienced Argentines botched their attack. Fully a third of the aircraft launched missed connections with their refueling air tankers and were forced to turn back, including two Super Étendards armed with Exocet missiles.[17] Of the more than thirty planes that reached the Falklands, only six actually encountered the enemy, as British accounts confirm.

Twenty-four Skyhawks were dispatched, in six flights of four aircraft, but only one flight found a target—and that was one of their own ships. One of the Skyhawk flights spotted the Argentine supply ship *Formosa* off the south coast of East Falkland, mistaking it for a British ship. The planes bombed and strafed the merchantman, but did not sink it. Four Daggers were assigned the mission of attacking Britain's antisubmarine group, but encountered *Glamorgan*, *Alacrity*, and *Arrow*, instead. Attacking them, they missed on all counts. As previously noted, Harriers knocked off two of the attackers, while Argentine ground fire downed a third.[18] Finally, of six Canberra bombers sent, only two made contact with British forces, and one was shot down by a Harrier.

At sea, it was no better. At 3:55 PM Admiral Lombardo sent a message to Rear Admiral Allara, on board the *25 de Mayo*: "Enemy at anchor. You have liberty of action,"[19] which, liberally translated, meant "the ships are vulnerable; attack at your discretion." From that point, all three Argentine task groups, including the submarine *San Luis*, began to move toward the eastern shore of the Falkland Islands where the British fleet was presumably anchored, but several developments occurred that evening of May 1 to force a cancellation of plans.

Argentine intelligence failed to substantiate initial reports of a landing, which then was confirmed when British ships broke off their attacks and withdrew. Argentine naval forces performed no more competently than its air forces. Worst of all, British forces had detected the location of the carrier. The submarine *San Luis* botched an attack when her homing torpedo's guidance wire broke. When the carrier *25 de Mayo* neared its launch point, the head winds required for the launch of fully armed and fueled aircraft were insufficient, and the mission was aborted. Furthermore, Admiral Allara was informed shortly after midnight that his carrier had been detected. A Harrier had come to within sixty to seventy miles—and perhaps closer—before flying off.[20]

Admiral Lombardo, at headquarters, also recognized—as he would later report—that the British had carried out a "dummy run...to test our capacity and training."[21] Therefore, at 1:19 AM on May 2, Lombardo sent Allara a warning message to break off the attack:

> There have been no aerial attacks over the Falklands since 1900 hours. I don't know the position of the aircraft carrier. The enemy is not at anchor and so constitutes a serious threat for the fleet.[22]

Although this was not a direct order to withdraw, the warning was clear. Beware of a trap. There was no landing! The British fleet could be anywhere, and his own force was in danger; therefore, he should consider withdrawing to a safer position. Allara understood, replying to Lombardo at 1:45 AM, less than half an hour later. He agreed that there was little point in continuing. It was already dark, and the carrier was incapable of conducting night operations (they could launch but not recover aircraft at night). As the next day's forecast was for a continued lull, he would still be unable to launch his aircraft.

Allara immediately issued orders for the three groups of the task force to "go back to their former positions."[23] Lombardo, with Anaya's approval, reconfirmed Allara's message, sending coded telex orders to the captains of the three task groups and other participating units. The attack was off. To

Captain Bonzo of the *Belgrano* he sent: "Bring Luis to Miguel," which meant to return his ship to the relatively shallow waters around Staten Island, off the southern tip of Argentina, where he would be less vulnerable to submarine attack.[24] By six o'clock in the morning (ten o'clock in the morning British time) on May 2, the *Belgrano* had completed its course turn and was headed westward.[25]

By dawn on May 2, Margaret Thatcher feared that the worst of all possible situations had arisen. The British plan to trap and destroy key elements of the Argentine air force and navy had failed. Only a handful of planes had actually been committed, and its ships were steaming out of harm's way. Buenos Aires' main threats to the task force remained intact. From the British viewpoint, the Argentines had, in effect, sniffed at the bait and backed off. Meanwhile, a more ominous threat was developing in Washington, where Secretary Haig was engaged in a secret, behind-the-scenes peace initiative with the president of Peru, Belaunde Terry.

Worst of all, Thatcher feared that Foreign Secretary Pym, now in Washington, was plotting with Haig for a repeat performance of the past week's peace initiative. Suspicion was heightened when, the previous morning, the British ambassador, Charles Wallace, had gone to the Peruvian foreign ministry on instructions to brief the foreign minister on the state of affairs. The Peruvian foreign minister failed to "give any hint at all" to Wallace that any peace discussions were under way.[26] The outlook was grim. The likelihood was that Pym would return to London with yet another "peace proposal" in hand, demanding that the cabinet consider this one as it had the one the previous week. Was the prime minister condemned to consider a peace proposal a week until she accepted one? Would peace proposal follow peace proposal until the opportunity to make a landing was lost? What was to be done?

The Peruvian Initiative: Aborted Coup?

Pym traveled to Washington on the understanding that the attacks of May 1 were a one-time demonstration of British power to "concentrate the minds" of Argentine leaders and induce them to agree to a negotiated settlement. He assumed there would be no further military activity while he was on his "mission." Upon arrival Saturday afternoon, May 1, aboard a British Concord, he immediately became deeply involved in what might euphemistically be termed a "back channel" peace ploy with Alexander Haig, or as Ambassador

Jeane Kirkpatrick termed it, "a new undercover Haig mission."[27] This was the so-called Peruvian Initiative.

As with most "back channel" maneuvers that circumvent regular diplomatic procedure, records are scarce. The essentials, however, can be deduced. The essence of the Peruvian Initiative was yet another, and the most serious, attempt by Alexander Haig to effect a negotiated peace. It bears reiterating that Haig's settlement scheme would have propped up the junta and dealt a probable fatal blow to Thatcher's prime ministership. Pym, the obvious beneficiary of Haig's scheme, was more than happy to collude with him, until it backfired. Then, he distanced himself from Haig. Suspicious, both President Reagan and Prime Minister Thatcher were alerted to Haig's ploy, and each attempted to preempt it.

The Haig-Pym scheme was to use President Belaunde Terry of Peru as a middleman to craft an agreement in secret, keeping it from the Foreign Office and its representatives, as well as the White House, and present it to Thatcher as a fait accompli. Pym had learned his lesson from the previous week's confrontation with Thatcher. He had relayed the Argentine-Haig proposal before his own return, enabling Thatcher to prepare for a showdown, which he lost. (Henderson notes that during Pym's April 22–23 visit, "messages whizzed between the three capitals."[28]) Thatcher may have assumed he would send a message again, but the evidence suggests that, this time, Pym planned to deny Thatcher any advance warning and return with an agreement.

No sooner had Secretary Haig publicly announced the "tilt" to Great Britain on the morning of April 30, than he began to search for a viable third party through whom to continue efforts to produce a settlement. He explored the possibility of employing first Colombia, then the OAS (through its Argentine chief, Alejandro Orfila), before deciding upon President Belaunde Terry of Peru. Belaunde had already indicated a willingness to become involved, having demanded a cessation of hostilities shortly after the passage of UNR502, which had been ignored.[29] Peru, an ally of Argentina along with Bolivia in the triple alliance against Chile, was an obvious choice in any case. As early as April 30, as Freedman & Gamba-Stonehouse note, "there appears to have been some contact between Peruvian and American diplomats."[30]

It was from Saturday, May 1, however, that the discussions evolved into what became the Peruvian Initiative. According to Belaunde's press conference of May 2, as reported by the Associated Press, "long and continuous contacts between the two sides began yesterday, continued last night and early this morning."[31] Of the May 1 discussions, Haig's collaborator, Assistant Secretary Thomas Enders says flatly: "We drafted that proposal and negotiated it with the British."[32] Enders's reference to a negotiation with "the British" must be understood to refer to Foreign Secretary Francis Pym. It could not be a reference to Ambassador Henderson, who makes no mention of any discussions on May 1, nor of any "proposal." Indeed, Henderson denied that a proposal even existed, a point that will be discussed in more detail later.[33] Besides, Henderson did not have the authority to "negotiate" a proposal, if there had been one. Nor does Thatcher mention negotiation of a proposal with Haig on May 1, to which she would in any case have been averse.[34]

Enders continues: "Our impression of the British [Pym's] view of this initiative was 'Try it on the Argentines, and see what they say.' Them first, in other words. Belaunde made it his own. Haig and I had drafted it, at Haig's house in Washington, on an early Sunday afternoon and we passed it on to Belaunde in those terms."[35] It would seem, then, that after his arrival on May 1, since his official schedule did not begin until the following day, Secretary Pym joined Haig and Enders to "negotiate" the proposal that would be passed on to Belaunde. (Pym was to meet with Haig in the State Department at ten o'clock the next morning and then have lunch with him at the British embassy. After lunch, he would meet with Secretary Weinberger and hold a press conference before departing to New York for dinner with the UN secretary Perez de Cuellar.[36])

Having negotiated a proposal, Haig "passed it on to Belaunde." How that occurred is disputed by the participants. Haig, in his predictably muddled account, claims that Belaunde called him on Sunday at home. "Speaking over an open line, we worked all day on a new draft."[37] The call was, of course, on Saturday, as Haig later admitted.[38] Nor did Belaunde call Haig. The Peruvian president says he called his ambassador to Washington, Fernando Schwalb, not Secretary Haig, on Saturday night to express his concern that "if no solution emerged from the meeting between Haig and Pym [scheduled for the next morning] a disaster could follow."[39] Schwalb apparently attempted to reach the president; instead, Haig called Belaunde, and said:

President Reagan's not in Washington right now. He's in Knox-
ville, opening an exhibition. But I know you are very concerned,
and so are we. What can we do? How can you help us?

It is not self-evident that a call made to the president of the United States
would automatically be transferred to the secretary of state. The White
House telephone operator would normally transfer a call from the president
of another country to President Reagan wherever he happened to be. Nor
did Haig say that he was calling on behalf of the president. It is a mystery
how Haig came to take Belaunde's call, unless he had been expecting it, but
not surprising that he took the initiative. In any case, during a forty-five
minute discussion, Haig passed on the proposal negotiated with Pym.
Belaunde, in turn, "told him what word was unsatisfactory and what condition unacceptable for Argentina. We finally agreed on a plan which covered
seven points, and I left it that I should call President Galtieri at once to put
that formula to him."[40]

Belaunde telephoned President Galtieri later that same evening, at 11:30
PM (1:30 AM Buenos Aires time). He passed on the seven-point proposal and
urged Galtieri to consider it immediately and be prepared to respond positively early the next morning. Belaunde knew that Haig and Pym were
scheduled to meet the next morning at ten o'clock and proposed to call
Galtieri then. Belaunde was attempting to arrange a three-way negotiation by
telephone whereby he would be the interlocutor between Haig and Pym in
Washington and Galtieri and Costa Mendez in Buenos Aires. In this way, the
final details of a mutually acceptable settlement could be worked out. Pym
would return to London with a "peace proposal" in his pocket—his instrument in a silent coup against Margaret Thatcher.

There was every reason for Belaunde to be optimistic about the junta's
reaction to the seven-point Haig-Pym proposal. It could not be much more
favorable to Argentina, nor less favorable to Great Britain. It called for an
immediate cease-fire, mutual withdrawal of all forces, and removal of all
sanctions. That much was common to all proposals, but what followed was
stunning in its deviation from the prime minister's position. Third parties
would temporarily govern the islands until a settlement had been reached.
Negotiations would begin at once under the auspices of a contact group

consisting of the United States, Brazil, West Germany, and Peru. The viewpoints and interests of the Islanders would be taken into account, but not their "wishes."[41]

The seven-point proposal has been variously referred to as a "rehash" of Haig's previous proposal that the Argentines had rejected, or not a proposal at all. Given the controversy that surrounded it in the aftermath of the sinking of the *Belgrano*, it is not surprising to find that the source of the "rehash" interpretation is none other than the two men who concocted it—Haig and Pym—evidently intending to divert attention from it. Not only was the seven-point proposal a proposal, it was markedly different from Haig's previous proposals. While favoring Argentina, the proposal embodied the "wet" position and was the very antithesis of the position upon which Margaret Thatcher had staked her prime ministership.

The seven-point proposal represented the abandonment of Thatcher's long-held demands for a return of British administration to the Falkland Islands and self-determination for the Islanders. Instead, it would preclude the return of any British administration; there would be no self-determination for the Islanders, and there was a "guarantee" that the issue would be resolved by April 1983, a deadline under which Thatcher had refused to negotiate. Third-party rule meant a UN trusteeship—a proposal first suggested by Labour leader Dennis Healey and Social Democrat leader David Owen—and the effective end of British rule. Britain and Argentina would "take into account the viewpoints and interests of the Islanders," but not their "wishes."

The Argentines could hardly have wished for a better offer. The seven-point proposal was a mechanism for transferring sovereignty to Argentina. If accepted, this "solution" would mean victory for Argentina, reinforce junta rule, and lead to the fall of the Thatcher leadership. Moreover, it would strengthen the proposition that boundaries could be changed by force of arms. It is no wonder that Pym hastened to distance himself from it as soon as the scheme was foiled, because it demonstrated that he was working to undermine his leader.

By dawn on May 2, Margaret Thatcher faced a dilemma. On the one hand, Argentine armed forces had eluded the trap set by the Royal Navy. The Argentine navy was steaming to safer waters, and the air force remained intact, ready to deliver a deadly blow against any attempted landing on the islands.

Indeed, the Argentine air force's quantitative advantage—at least on paper—combined with the task force's relative lack of aerial early warning capability, threatened to render an amphibious landing on the islands an act of folly. Thatcher would obviously not survive a military debacle.

On the other hand, British and American intelligence had monitored Haig's telephone conversation with Belaunde (it was on an open line) as well as Belaunde's late-night call to Galtieri. American officials boasted that "there is almost nothing that is said in Argentina that we don't know about."[42] (The CIA's Buenos Aires station was located in the same office block housing the Argentine high command.)[43] Other informed sources indicated that "Argentine military communications are continuously being intercepted and used to British advantage."[44] And a former British minister stated publicly that British intelligence "had been reading [Argentina's] telegrams for many years."[45]

Thatcher knew, therefore, that Belaunde would be calling the Argentines later that day. The call was scheduled for three o'clock that afternoon, British time (ten o'clock in the morning in Washington). She also knew that Pym was scheduled to meet with Haig in Washington at the same time. It took no great leap of imagination to deduce that her foreign secretary was secretly colluding with Secretary Haig for the second week running, this time using the Peruvian president as an intermediary to reach an agreement with the Argentines that very day. Could she withstand another political challenge to reach a negotiated settlement?

It would take time to reduce Argentina's military capability to defeat a landing, but Pym's back-channel maneuver had to be dealt with immediately. It was a question of how to sink Pym's secret scheme and foil his attempted coup. Her opportunity grew out of the previous day's attempt to trap the Argentine navy. Recall that, as part of the trap, the submarines *Splendid* and *Conqueror* had been deployed to intercept the carrier *25 de Mayo* and *Belgrano*, respectively, if they took the bait and converged on the presumed location of the task force at the eastern shore of the islands. Although Argentina had eluded the trap, the submarines were still in position. Thatcher's decision was to escalate militarily the way she had the previous week, at South Georgia, hoping for the same results. Therefore, she hurriedly authorized *Conqueror*'s attack on the *Belgrano*, hoping to preempt any secret peace initiative by her foreign secretary.

Sinking of the *General Belgrano*

Thatcher's problem was threefold—how to convince her cabinet colleagues to agree to an immediate, escalatory attack; how to justify attacking the *Belgrano*, instead of the more lucrative target, the *25 de Mayo*; and how to gain cabinet agreement for a major change in the rules of engagement with little more than perfunctory discussion, and without all members of the War Cabinet present—namely, Secretary Pym? Obviously, the only grounds for a hurried decision was military exigency. It was also obvious that such a case could be made only by the man on the spot—task force commander Woodward. Woodward would make the case, but his manner of compliance suggests that he was not happy to be drawn into a political fight. Woodward constructed a case for immediate action on grounds that he knew (and knew other knowledgeable observers would know) were patently specious. Woodward argued:

> Early on the morning of 2 May, all the indications were that *25 de Mayo*, the Argentinian carrier, and a group of escorts had slipped past my forward SSN [submarine service nuclear] barrier to the north, while the cruiser *General Belgrano* and her escorts were attempting to complete the pincer movement from the south, still outside the Total Exclusion Zone. But *Belgrano* still had *Conqueror* on the trail. My fear was that *Belgrano* would lose the SSN as she ran over the shallow water of the Burdwood Bank, and that my forward SSN barrier would be evaded there too. I therefore sought, for the first and only time throughout the campaign, a major change to the Rules of Engagement (ROE) to enable *Conqueror* to attack *Belgrano* outside the Exclusion Zone.[46]

Woodward's case consisted of six propositions: (1) the imminence of an Argentine attack on the task force by means of a pincer movement; (2) the *25 de Mayo*'s evasion of *Splendid*; (3) the *Conqueror*'s potential loss of *Belgrano*; (4) the direction of the *Belgrano*; (5) the difficulty of submarine navigation over the Burdwood Bank; (6) and the need for a change in the ROE to attack outside the TEZ. As Woodward well knew, not one of these propositions could stand close scrutiny, yet each proposition was designed to satisfy a particular political expedient.

First, there was no pincer movement. If British intelligence had not intercepted the Argentine navy's orders to break off the attack and return to bases, which was very unlikely, then intelligence certainly saw the fleet turn. Even more unlikely was the argument that messages had been intercepted but not decoded in time. Captain Wreford-Brown of *Conqueror* was in regular, periodic contact with Northwood detailing his observations of the *Belgrano* since the previous morning.[47] The conclusion was straightforward. If there were no pincer movement; there was no imminent threat of attack, and, therefore, no need for an immediate response. Certainly, there was no need for a rush to decision without due deliberation.

Second, *Splendid* did not "lose" the *25 de Mayo* and its four escorting ships. Both Argentine and British sources note that Sea Harriers from *Hermes* had detected the carrier at least twice. Once at shortly after eight o'clock in the evening on May 1 and again at 12:30 AM on May 2.[48] Obviously, if the Harriers detected the carrier, then *Splendid* could not have "lost it." The reason this argument had to be made was because of Pym's formal objection to attacking the carrier without warning. His objection effectively meant that an attack on the *25 de Mayo* could not be made without the foreign secretary's concurrence. "Losing" the Argentine carrier opened up the possibility of hitting the next most important target—the *Belgrano*—and deciding in Pym's absence.

Third, there was little possibility of the noisy *Belgrano* evading *Conqueror*. The swift nuclear submarine, capable of speeds up to twenty-eight knots while submerged, had stayed close on the trail of the World War II vintage cruiser since early morning of May 1. On Sunday morning, Captain Wreford-Brown had reported to Northwood that "I have the *Belgrano* in sight."[49] But arguing that the Argentine cruiser might escape strengthened the proposal for attacking it as soon as possible.

Fourth, *Conqueror* observed *Belgrano*'s course change that morning at six o'clock, and there can be little doubt that Wreford-Brown reported his observations as soon as possible. Because this information was absolutely critical to determining whether or not a pincer movement was occurring—the very basis for insisting on an immediate decision to attack—the argument that it did not reach the prime minister, or was not "assessed as significant," is simply not credible.[50]

Fifth, the Burdwood Bank argument was a red herring. Ocean depths within the confines of the bank would not unduly impede submarine operations. Minimum depths were 150 feet. At telescope depth, the *Conqueror* drew around sixty feet.[51] More to the point, the *Belgrano* was southwest of the bank and moving westward away from it. *Conqueror*'s position was to the south of *Belgrano*. If *Belgrano* were to sail over the Burdwood Bank, it would be on a northeasterly heading and take it directly toward the task force, not to mention directly contradicting orders to return to base. Thus, the assertion that *Belgrano* could sail over the Burdwood Bank and lose *Conqueror* was nonsensical.

Finally, the argument that the rules of engagement had to be changed to permit attack outside the TEZ was a diversion. The TEZ restriction had already been lifted by the April 23 rules of engagement notice. The criterion for attack would be satisfied if an Argentine warship "approached" and "constituted a threat" to the task force anywhere in the South Atlantic— inside or outside the TEZ. The reason the ROE had to be changed to strike the *Belgrano* was precisely because its action did not fit the April 23 criterion. *Belgrano* was not approaching and was not a threat to the task force. All of this was transparent, as Woodward knew, to anyone familiar with the data, but it was his way of complying with orders without compromising his integrity.

Nevertheless, this was undoubtedly the argument Prime Minister Thatcher put to her ministers assembled for lunch that Sunday, May 2. An attack on the task force was imminent, and they must immediately decide what to do. Although the Argentine carrier had evaded *Splendid*, and Pym had anyway objected to striking it, *Conqueror* had *Belgrano* in its sights. To defeat the pincer attack, they must strike quickly at *Belgrano*, before it, too, slipped past and evaded the submarine. In the event, the decision to attack the *Belgrano* was taken quickly. There was no formal War Cabinet discussion and there were no minutes taken. As Freedman & Gamba-Stonehouse observe:

> Because the matter was urgent, Thatcher brought together those ministers and officials who had been invited for lunch before the formal body met in the afternoon. There was therefore no minuted record.[52]

Still, this explanation begs the question: Why the rush and why no record of what was clearly the most momentous decision of the conflict thus far? It would take over five hours to transmit the decision to *Conqueror* and three hours after that before the attack. Surely, so momentous a decision could have waited until after lunch when the War Cabinet would meet. And why were the chiefs of staff excluded from a matter clearly within their domain? Was it because they would immediately rip holes in the specious rationale for action? The answer is painfully obvious. No record meant that no one would be implicated. Thatcher rushed to decide before any objection could be raised and before the argument on which the decision was based could be examined closely and verified. Her urgency sprang from the desire to act before any unwanted news came from Pym in Washington.

The decision made, Northwood signaled the orders for the attack at 1:30 PM (8:30 AM in Washington). But Wreford-Brown in *Conqueror* replied that the signal was "garbled." *Conqueror* had had some damage to its mast and had experienced communications problems the previous day. Still, in all probability, Wreford-Brown wanted to hear the message twice. This would give him time to consider its implications in advance and also give its sender the same opportunity. To provide more food for thought, at 3 PM Wreford-Brown employed the available slot on the U.S. communications satellite to emphasize that *Belgrano* had "reversed course," a message that also indicated that the initial signal had not been garbled beyond recognition.[53]

Of course, at the very least, the fact that *Belgrano* had reversed course meant that there was no rush. It further indicated that there was no pincer movement and, therefore, ample time for the War Cabinet, if not the full cabinet, to gather and consider the broader implications of a change in the rules of engagement. Margaret Thatcher, however, would brook no delay. There would be no reconsideration of the order. Two hours after receiving *Conqueror*'s "reversed course" message, at 5 PM in London (noon in Washington), Thatcher sent through Northwood confirmation of the earlier signal changing the rules of engagement and ordering the attack.

It is instructive to compare the timing of Margaret Thatcher's decision to attack the *Belgrano* with the progress of the Peruvian Initiative. The comparison explains the prime minister's urgency, although she asserts that she "did not at that time know anything about the Peruvian proposals."[54] It was Belaunde's midnight call to transmit the seven-point peace proposal (early morning May 2 in London) that alerted Thatcher. The urgency surrounding the decision to sink the *Belgrano* (and to justify doing so) was undoubtedly owing to the need to escalate the conflict and disrupt the negotiation before any unwanted results were produced by the three-way international call between Haig and Pym in Washington, Belaunde in Lima, and Galtieri and Costa Mendez in Buenos Aires, scheduled for ten o'clock that morning Washington time.

One can well imagine Thatcher's exasperation and incredulous reaction when Wreford-Brown reported that the initial signal had been garbled. Time was of the essence. The message had been sent an hour and a half before Pym and Haig were scheduled to meet, and in plenty of time to preempt any news from Washington. Wreford-Brown's second message at 3 PM that *Belgrano* had reversed course apparently gave Thatcher pause. That message came just as the Haig-Pym meeting began, and Thatcher decided to wait to see what occurred. If intelligence were monitoring the Washington–Lima–Buenos Aires conversation, as one must assume it was, the air must have fairly crackled with tension, tinged with apprehension, as the intercontinental discussion began.

Ambassador Henderson accompanied Secretary Pym to Haig's office at the State Department that morning. In the ambassador's presence, Haig "relayed President Reagan's conviction that British forces were 'doing the work of the free world,'" but immediately contradicted the president's statement of support for Britain "with an ardent plea that we could and should avoid a large-scale battle."[55] Haig then proceeded to tell Henderson a completely false story to conceal the real purpose of Pym's visit. According to Henderson, Haig:

> briefly outlined certain ideas which had originated in a Peruvian initiative and which had not been formulated in any definitive way. These were very similar to those he himself had advanced earlier and he thought they would be more acceptable in Buenos Aires if they were put forward by a South American government.[56]

Choosing his words carefully, Pym observed that "while he was very ready to consider any new ideas," he would have to see how the Argentines reacted. "He would of course need to discuss any new ideas with his colleagues in

London on his return." Haig immediately said that he "fully agreed that more time and more detailed work were needed."

The only truthful parts in this exchange were Haig's point about involving a South American government to put forward the initiative and Pym's declaration that he would need to "discuss any new ideas with his colleagues…on his return." As we have seen, the Peruvian Initiative, which was actually Haig's undercover initiative, was quite far advanced, very specific, and not at all similar to the ideas he had previously presented. Haig showed Henderson no text, which led the British ambassador to conclude that what the American secretary had outlined "could not possibly be described as 'proposals.'" But, as we shall see, there was actually a proposal already formulated in text.

Haig's dissemblance to Henderson was, of course, designed to keep the Foreign Office ignorant of what he and Pym were about to do. Haig knew that, if he informed Henderson of the seven-point proposal in detail, the British ambassador would naturally send a report back to London, which would immediately alert the prime minister—a development that Pym wished to avoid. Nor would Pym himself send any reports back to London. If all worked as planned, he would return to London proposal in hand. The episode with Henderson confirms beyond doubt that Haig and Pym were colluding to spring a peace agreement on the presumably unsuspecting Reagan and Thatcher.

After this exchange, Henderson notes, Pym went off with Haig "for a tête-à-tête that lasted two hours." What the ambassador did not know, and was not told, was that the two secretaries then engaged in a lengthy negotiation involving Belaunde as intermediary between Haig and Pym in Washington and Galtieri and Costa Mendez in Buenos Aires.[57] In the course of their discussions, the Argentines insisted on two changes. Most important, Costa Mendez, who was conducting the negotiations with Belaunde while Galtieri listened, refused to accept the United States as one of the members of the contact group. America had betrayed Argentina and could not be trusted. Remarkably, he proposed Britain's ally, Canada, as an alternative. Belaunde, relaying this change to Haig, was told (no doubt after Haig had conferred with Pym, sitting beside him in his office) that Britain also objected to Peru's participation. It was agreed that the United States and Peru would be replaced in the contact group.[58]

The issue that prolonged the discussion and actually prevented any agreement that morning was Costa Mendez's objection to the phrase "viewpoints and interests of the islanders." Searching for an acceptable alternative, Costa Mendez suggested: "points of view concerning the interests of the islanders," to get around the idea of "wishes," which was implied in the word "viewpoints." But when Belaunde passed this on, Haig responded (after consulting with Pym) that the British side now insisted on retaining the original term "wishes." Later in the day, the Argentines would move to the term "aspirations" as a less politically loaded substitute for "wishes." When the conversation ended around noon, however, they were still stuck on one word. Belaunde said: "With the sole exception of this word 'wishes,' which the UK has just insisted on, the rest is acceptable?" Costa Mendez replied: "Correct."

Belaunde had made several understandable but unwarranted assumptions. He assumed, and was led by Haig to assume, that whatever was acceptable to Haig was acceptable to Pym. He further assumed that "Pym spoke with London's voice." Finally, he assumed that since "Haig himself had been involved in formulating the proposal...[and] with Haig conferring with Pym in his own office, and conveying no British objections, peace must be within sight."[59]

The Argentine foreign minister, too, believed that they were on the brink of agreement. Costa Mendez reportedly declared to his staff: "We have an agreement! We can live with this!" None of this, however, had been transmitted either to London or to the junta. The Argentine leadership had committed to nothing; nor had Thatcher. Had the Peruvian proposal been sent to London, as Pym well understood, Thatcher would have immediately rejected it. That was the very point of Pym's secrecy. Pym and the "wets," however, underestimated the strength of will of the Iron Lady.

The *Belgrano* and Its Consequences

There was no time to lose. Galtieri had told Belaunde that the junta would consider the proposal that evening at seven and reply promptly. Thatcher had no doubt concerning what that answer would be, for the seven-point proposal was an offer the Argentines could not refuse (and she could not accept). With but a single word standing in the way of agreement, Pym would be able to return to London and present the prime minister with a fait accompli. Therefore, the negotiations must be disrupted without delay. Noon in Washington was five in the afternoon in London—and the moment that

Thatcher reconfirmed the initial signal to *Conqueror* to sink the *Belgrano*. Francis Pym was neither consulted nor informed of the decision.

Captain Wreford-Brown executed his attack at eight o'clock in the evening London time (four o'clock in the afternoon Buenos Aires time), reporting to Northwood a successful hit half an hour later.[60] The destroyer *Bouchard*, accompanying *Belgrano*, also reported the strike at 4:35 PM.[61] Incredibly, the Argentine cruiser sank within an hour involving a heavy loss of life. Carrying a crew of 1,138, initial reports were of between 400 and 500 deaths, an extraordinarily high loss rate for a ship presumably on combat-alert status. The final death toll of 321 did not alleviate the magnitude and shock of the sinking. Rather, it seemed to contradict the idea that Britain was intent on staging "limited military actions designed to pressure Argentina into resuming negotiations without a major loss of life on either side."[62] One immediate consequence of the attack was that the Argentine fleet continued back to port and remained there for the duration of the conflict.

Undoubtedly, both American and British intelligence had monitored the attack and the signal traffic that accompanied it. Haig learned of the attack within a short time thereafter, between three and four o'clock in the afternoon Washington time, either directly through satellite monitoring, or through radio intercepts. As soon as he heard of the attack, he realized its significance for his Peruvian Initiative. Therefore, he immediately called Belaunde to inform him and, it seems, to urge him to announce an imminent cease-fire agreement. Thus, Belaunde called a press conference earlier than planned in an attempt to forestall the collapse of the negotiation. (Belaunde revealed Haig's call in a conversation with Galtieri later that night. Haig, he said, "called me in the afternoon, very mortified, and told me something about the loss of a ship."[63])

Shortly after 5 o'clock in the afternoon in Lima, President Belaunde held a press conference to announce the imminence of a cease-fire agreement, although he said he could not divulge its contents. "The proposal which Peru has put forward," he said, "with the firm support of the U.S. government is to get peace very quickly, if possible tonight."[64] Belaunde made clear that the initiative was actually Haig's—with Pym's active collaboration—and with himself as intermediary between Argentina and Great Britain. "In the palace we're in direct contact with Buenos Aires and Washington, where Foreign Minister Pym has spent the whole day in the

State Department." The mediation "has reached a climax with the arrival of Mr. Pym, because both are in Washington and so he can transmit all the wishes for or possibilities of an agreement from the side of the government of Great Britain."

Belaunde's press conference was curiously ill-timed and devoid of content save for the announcement of an imminent cease-fire. He had originally scheduled it for later in the day, after what he expected to be the junta's decision to accept the seven-point proposal. The junta was scheduled to meet at seven o'clock in the evening (five o'clock in Lima) and had not yet convened when Belaunde opened his news conference. (Anaya was late arriving, delayed by news of the *Belgrano*.) Whatever Belaunde's expectations, the junta had not made its decision. Why hold a press conference to announce something that had yet to be decided? The only reason, it seems, was to attempt to use the news of an impending cease-fire to negate the news of the sinking of the *Belgrano*, which Belaunde and Haig realized would effectively terminate any negotiations the moment that information became public.

Belaunde also attempted to bypass Pym and communicate directly with London. Immediately after the press conference had ended, the Peruvian foreign minister, Arias Stella, summoned Ambassador Wallace to lay out the entire negotiation, of which he had refused to provide "any hint at all" the previous day. Ambassador Stella "claimed that the formula had the approval of Costa Mendez, that Galtieri had told Belaunde that he was well disposed towards it but that he had his 'senate' to consult and convince. The junta were meeting then to consider the terms and their reply was expected hourly."[65] Both the premature press conference and the attempt to communicate directly with London were efforts to sustain the initiative, which would have unexpected consequences.

Although Belaunde already had been informed of the attack on the *Belgrano*, Pym had not. At approximately the same time, Pym had just emerged from his meeting with Secretary of Defense Weinberger in Washington to hold a brief press conference before traveling on to New York. Using a phrase which, perhaps, contained double meaning, Pym declared that "last week I came here to see Mr. Haig in his role as a mediator....Today I have come back to consult with him as an ally." While he had not come to "ask for this, that or the other," all support "will be helpful." A spokesman for Secretary Weinberger acknowledged that Pym "had submitted no list and no specific requests for military help." But the defense secretary said that the United States "would be looking for ways to be of help."[66]

Pym indicated that, in the attacks of the day before, Britain had "taught the junta a lesson." The solution now was for Argentina "to withdraw its troops and negotiate." Reflecting the understanding with which he had left London, but unaware of the latest news about the *Belgrano*, Pym declared that "there had been no new military activity in the Falklands today," and "there is no other military action envisaged at this moment." Pym emphasized "Britain's determination now to explore political solutions." According to one press account, Pym "clearly was not aware of the submarine attack at the time of his late-afternoon press conference."[67]

Undoubtedly, immediately after what was an embarrassing circumstance for Pym, he was informed of the attack on the *Belgrano* and concluded that Haig's back-channel ploy had failed. Pym now moved quickly to get to New York for a meeting with Perez de Cuellar, who seemed to be the last hope for a negotiated settlement. As he was departing, however, Haig called, perhaps to alert him of news of the *Belgrano* and of his call to Belaunde. But Pym, now hastily attempting to distance himself from the failed scheme, would not take his call. He instructed Ambassador Henderson to take it, instead, and to give a message to Haig.[68] The message was that "he was of course ready to consider new ideas if they amounted to anything but what had been put forward so far seemed only vague and indeterminate and provided no basis on which to do business."[69] As Pym knew he would, Henderson immediately "reported this by telegram to London."

Haig was incensed at Pym's timidity, and in subsequent conversations with the Peruvians that day, accused him of having "no interest in peace."[70] But Pym's decision to refer to the seven-point proposal only as a set of vague and indeterminate "ideas" providing "no basis on which to do business" was a carefully calculated self-defense. Were he to have acknowledged that there had, indeed, been a proposal, he would have been bound to report it to London, which he had not done. But Pym had been too clever by half. It was only a matter of time—and a short time at that—before he was found out. There can be little doubt that Wallace's reporting cable from Lima about Pym's role in the negotiations contrasted sharply with Henderson's reports of the secretary's activities. Henderson's cables also included Haig's misleading briefing of the status of the negotiation.[71] It made obvious to Thatcher and her closest advisers that Pym had been engaged in a behind-the-scenes as well as behind-the-back attempt to execute a peace coup against the prime minister—and that Haig was in league with him.

It was also clear that, although Pym had now disavowed the Belaunde initiative, he was still pursuing a negotiation through the United Nations. There would, of course, be nothing furtive about a UN initiative, but Pym would have to be headed off there, too. In fact, President Reagan had already set wheels turning in the United Nations. He, too, had been concerned that Pym and Haig were colluding to precipitate a "coup." Therefore, as soon as he learned of Haig's discussions with Belaunde, instructions went out from the White House to Ambassador Kirkpatrick to prod Perez de Cuellar into proffering an initiative. Having two initiatives on the table simultaneously would present a confusing spectacle and, at the very least, provide opportunities for further delay. At any rate, "on May 1st Kirkpatrick began whispering exclusive information in the ear of Perez de Cuellar...to advise him of Belaunde Terry's intervention."[72] Perez de Cuellar, who was an old rival of Belaunde's, was more than happy to cooperate, and, when Pym arrived in New York, Perez de Cuellar was ready to greet him with an initiative of his own, as Thatcher observes, "much to the irritation of Mr. Haig."[73]

Exocet Strike on *Sheffield* Revives Hopes for a Settlement

After the sinking of the *Belgrano*, both Pym and the Argentines exhibited considerable confusion over the negotiating vehicle they wished to pursue, shifting hesitatingly from Belaunde to Perez de Cuellar. Meanwhile, Thatcher kept them off balance by shifting to the opposite side each time they moved, demonstrating the utility of having two negotiating channels available. Haig, however, became increasingly shrill in his persistent demands that the British government accept a settlement short of military defeat for Buenos Aires. Even President Reagan appeared to waver momentarily at Haig's verbal onslaught. Thatcher, however, adroitly turned the pressure for a negotiated settlement into a "reasonable ultimatum," which the junta rejected, clearing the way for a resolution of the issue on the battlefield.

When Pym arrived in New York the evening of May 2, he proceeded to UN ambassador Anthony Parsons's home for dinner with him and the secretary general. Perez de Cuellar had already passed on a "set of ideas" for a negotiated settlement to the Argentine ambassador and discussed them with Pym that evening. The secretary general's ideas were less concrete than Belaunde's, but were probably more attractive because of their ambiguity. They called for mutual withdrawal, resolution negotiations, lifting of sanctions and exclusion zones, and the establishment of nonspecific "transitional arrangements" pending the outcome of the negotiations.[74] Their discussion centered on the advisability of convening the Security Council to formalize the peace effort.

Perez de Cuellar argued in favor of obtaining the Security Council's mandate, but Pym opposed it. He believed that London "would accept a new unofficial peace effort, but not a new Security Council pronouncement."[75] Great Britain had gotten what it wanted from the United Nations in Resolution 502 and was concerned that, "if the Council discussed the granting of the mandate, there might be an attempt to promote a cease-fire." A cease-fire resolution in the United Nations would place Britain's military forces at a great disadvantage and require the exercise of its veto power, which London hoped to avoid. In fact, the Irish representative, Noel Dorr, tried to do just that, attempting to convene the Security Council that very evening. It took some intense argument on the part of Ambassador Parsons to forestall the move, but not before the Irish defense minister had described Britain as "the aggressor."[76]

That same evening of May 2, Argentina decided to shelve the Peruvian Initiative and accept the UN offer in principle, although it would be another forty-eight hours before the UN offer was formally accepted. In a conversation with Belaunde at midnight, Galtieri declared that the junta had "analyzed in depth" the seven-point proposal. He pointedly avoided saying that the junta would have accepted it, noting only that "we were going to go on deepening our analysis." All that had been "overturned," however, by the sinking of the *Belgrano*. "The Argentine government will not...accept any negotiation...in these circumstances." With theatrical bravado, he repeated the phrase first uttered by Dolores Ibarruri during the Spanish civil war: "We would rather die on our feet than live on our knees." Galtieri said he would send a personal representative to Lima to "explain the Argentine position."

The next day, May 3, Haig and Pym made a strong effort to revive the Peruvian Initiative. Peruvian Foreign Minister Stella told Ambassador Wallace that "the Argentines had not entirely closed the door" to the seven-point proposal.[78] Pym thereupon immediately instructed his private secretary to contact Ambassador Wallace "in the middle of the night," tell him to "acknowledge the Peruvian proposals," but say that time was required to consider them.[79] Wallace spoke to Stella, and, in very carefully veiled language that actually paraphrased the same analogy Stella had used, said: "The door is not totally closed within the framework of what has been proposed."

On the same day that Pym was conveying British interest to the Peruvians, Haig confronted Ambassador Henderson in Washington, intent upon bringing Britain to the negotiating table by issuing several veiled threats. Haig said that Belaunde had "complained bitterly about the torpedoing which he said had wrecked the chance of peace." Haig was worried that Argentina might return to the OAS for "sanctions against Britain." Of course, he said, the United States would veto any sanctions proposal, but "it would divide the hemisphere." Buenos Aires was letting it be known that it had been American intelligence and special weapons that had enabled Britain to sink the *Belgrano*, and Haig "feared" that if Britain continued military operations, "American opinion…might become less favorable towards the United Kingdom. People might say that Britain was overreacting."[80]

Continuing in an increasingly strident manner, Haig declared that, "It was difficult to know whether hitting the Argentines was the only thing that would bring them to negotiate, or whether it made them more inflexible." Henderson retorted, "For three weeks we had made no attack upon them and they had shown no flexibility." But Haig persisted, insisting that "Mrs Thatcher…come forward with some declaration expressing readiness to stop hostilities at a certain time provided the Argentines said they would do the same and undertake to withdraw." This was too much for Henderson, who ended their conversation by saying, "We could not…let up on the military pressure unless there was a categorical assurance that the Argentines were going to stop military action and leave the islands."

Haig, however, would not be put off. He met with Henderson later the same day to tell him that he had once again spoken to Belaunde. Galtieri's representatives had arrived in Lima, and Haig believed that "the Argentines would accept the seven-point proposal." Describing the direst consequences, Haig "insisted that military action must be stopped. He did not think that the Argentines could do anything to prevent the British sinking the whole of their fleet. This would bring about the collapse of any authority in Buenos Aires; the whole of Latin America would be alienated." Britain was "driving things too far." But Henderson, however, retorted that "Latin America would not be alienated just because we were prepared to defend our rights by force." London was not going to relent "just because the Argentines were doing badly militarily."

In response to Haig's assertion that the Argentines would accept the seven-point proposal, Henderson questioned its existence, in light of Haig's own description of it the day before as merely some "ideas…which had not been formulated in any definitive way." Hoist on his own petard, Haig was forced to show his hand, so he sent Enders to see Henderson "with a document containing the seven-point plan." This document was accompanied by a "suggested cease-fire statement" he wished Mrs. Thatcher to issue, which was a close paraphrase of what he had said in the "tilt" announcement of April 30. "Whatever happens militarily there must be a negotiated solution to the Falklands crisis if we are to avoid open-ended hostility and instability."

Needless to say, Prime Minister Thatcher "did not like the US/Peruvian proposals" and moved to accelerate preparations for further military action.[81] London announced that the luxury liner *Queen Elizabeth II (QEII)* and two cargo ferries would be taken up as troop and equipment carriers.[82] American military specialists thought Britain would "probably land forces on the islands soon" because of "increasingly severe weather conditions" in the South Atlantic. These sources estimated that "within two or three weeks both sides could be hurting severely because of the cold and the sizeable costs of the faceoff."[83] Others thought the task force could endure indefinitely, citing Britain's worldwide logistical system. On the other hand, "the longer you remain in harm's way, the more likely you are to get harmed," said one. "Submarines could penetrate your defenses or an aircraft could score a lucky shot."[84] A British official said, "Now it is their move."[85]

On May 4, hoping to draw a response from the Argentines, British leaders replicated the scenario played out on May 1. It began with another early morning Vulcan mission from Ascension Island. The result was worse this time than the last, with no hits on the runway at all. Woodward's carrier group had moved to within seventy miles of the islands to facilitate Harrier attacks on Stanley, Goose Green, and Darwin. These strikes began after the Vulcan mission, accompanied by shore bombardment. Results were mixed here, as Britain suffered the loss of a Sea Harrier downed over Goose Green. An added twist to the May 4 feint was the use of computer technology to make it appear on Argentine radar that a troop landing was in progress. The British used "decoys and computers which interfered with the radar signal that the Argentine detection equipment was tuned to—similar in fact to the video games in evidence all over the world."[86]

In moving his carriers forward, Commander Woodward had in standard fashion deployed three of his destroyers in an arc twenty miles ahead as a picket screen. The function of the picket ship is to protect the carriers by intercepting and engaging any threat. On May 4, Woodward's selection of ships for picket duty was particularly unfortunate. *Sheffield, Covington,* and *Glasgow* were Type-42 destroyers equipped with Sea Dart missiles capable of engaging long-range, high-altitude aerial threats up to forty miles away, but they possessed no close-in, low-level air defense below two thousand feet.[87] In fact, only two ships in the entire task force were then equipped with close-in defense. These were the Type-22 destroyers, *Broadsword* and *Brilliant*, equipped with Sea Wolf missiles. Complicating things that morning, *Sheffield* had taken over *Coventry*'s place at the southernmost point of the picket screen because *Coventry* had experienced difficulty with its 965 acquisition radar.

When the attacks began, Argentine forces in the Falkland Islands went to "red alert," but Buenos Aires refused to be drawn into a major response. The sinking of the *Belgrano* had dramatically emphasized Argentine naval inferiority; the entire surface fleet was at risk and was unable to participate in the conflict. Moreover, the lone functioning submarine had been useless. Unless Buenos Aires could severely cripple the task force, the junta would be unable to prevent a landing. There were only two target sets that could potentially defeat a landing—Britain's two carriers and the troop ships. The bulk of the landing force aboard troop ships had been kept safely at Ascension Island, but the carriers had ventured to within range of Argentina's land-based air power during the May 1 attacks. Argentine leaders decided—either out of a sense of desperation, a desire for revenge for the *Belgrano*, stark military necessity, or a little of all of these—that, if the carriers came within range again, they would attempt to attack them.

When Woodward moved his carrier group close to the islands on May 4 and deployed the Type-42s as his picket screen, Argentine leaders saw an opportunity to activate their own plan. They were familiar with the Type-42's low-level radar scanning deficiency because they had two of their own, purchased from Britain, and in previous weeks had practiced mock attacks against them.[88] Their plan was to slip underneath the Type-42's radar coverage with two of their Mach 1 speed Super Étendard fighter-bombers, each carrying a single Exocet missile, in an attempt to get close enough to knock out one or both of Britain's irreplaceable carriers. It was well worth the risk, for a successful attack on even one of the carriers would in all likelihood cause a British retreat.

A Neptune reconnaissance plane had identified the Type-42s in the picket screen at seven o'clock in the morning, and at 9:45 AM two Super Étendard Mirage jets had taken off from Rio Grande air base. After midair refueling, around noon the two aircraft approached the task force patrol area, closing to within twelve miles (one account says to "point blank range, around 6 miles").[89] The Argentine pilots on the mission, Sublieutenant Armando Mayora, and Lt. Comdr. Augusto Bedacarratz, identified two target sets, one large and one smaller, and assumed that the larger set was a carrier. They decided that they should "both" attack the carrier to increase their chances of hitting it.[90]

Glasgow had detected the oncoming jets and alerted the others, firing chaff as a diversionary maneuver. *Sheffield*, however, was at that moment engaged in transmitting on its satellite communications terminal and failed to detect the attack in time. Traveling at a speed of 680 miles an hour, it took only a few seconds before one of the Exocet missiles struck the *Sheffield* amidships, which immediately knocked it out of commission. The other missile sailed on (the frigate *Yarmouth*, in the second echelon of the screen, reported "seeing a missile fly past her") and, most probably, ran out of propellant and fell into the sea before reaching *Hermes* more than twenty miles away.[91] (When interviewed after the conflict, Capt. Jorge Colombo, leader of Argentina's second attack squadron was "still puzzled as to how *Hermes* had escaped....We remained almost certain that it went towards *Hermes*—or at least an aircraft carrier.")[92]

Although the Argentines had failed to disable a carrier, they had hit and decommissioned a British ship and made the most of their accomplishment. Indeed, their spirits soared. Their representatives scoured the international arms markets for Exocet missiles to replenish their remaining inventory of three.[93] Diplomatically, now that they had demonstrated an ability to hurt the task force, the junta was even less inclined than before to enter into negotiations. They sought to buy time on the negotiating front, while they strengthened their military position. If they could string out the negotiations for another two weeks, a landing on the islands—in terms of weather alone—would become very problematical; if they could acquire additional Exocets, it would be entirely preventable. These were fears that clearly animated discussions in London.

CHAPTER 8

•••

Reagan and Thatcher
Victorious

As much as Argentina trumpeted a successful attack, "equalizing" the sinking of the *Belgrano*, Pym, and others who were bent on pursuing a negotiated settlement of the war, did far more. With the sinking of the *Sheffield*, Pym pressed hard for the resumption of negotiations. That very afternoon, he insisted that London convey to Haig a willingness to continue negotiations in the Peruvian channel, evidently ignorant of the Argentine decision to drop the Peruvian venue and shift to the United Nations. Instructed to reach the secretary, Ambassador Henderson found him at Andrews Air Force Base outside Washington en route to New York for a dinner speech. After an intense telephone discussion before his departure, Haig immediately "changed his plans in order to return to the State Department to meet with...Henderson." A State Department spokesman said that the talks had now entered "an extremely delicate and critical phase."[1] Haig was back in business.

Pym, the "Wets," and Thatcher's Gamble

Thatcher was "deeply unhappy about the U.S./Peruvian proposals" Pym brought back with him from Washington. But Pym "believed that in view of the battle in the South Atlantic it would be damaging to reject what were in effect Al Haig's proposals." Thus, she "had to make some response," but insisted on changes. That evening of May 4 in Washington, stretching over to the next morning, Henderson and Haig argued over proposed British "amendments." In a transatlantic negotiation involving Pym and Thatcher,

211

the prime minister insisted upon including respect for the "wishes" of the Islanders in any agreement and excluding South Georgia and the other Falklands Dependencies.[2]

She also wanted to retain the original composition of the contact group to include the United States; she demanded that there be clear limitation on the scope of changes that a third party administration could enact. Thus, a third party could govern only "in consultation with the elected representatives of the islands." She devised a very tight timetable to prevent the Argentines from using a cease-fire simply to reinforce their position on the islands.[3] Finally, Thatcher sought a security guarantee from the United States. All of this was preconditioned upon not only a cease-fire, but also upon Argentine withdrawal, and Thatcher "knew that the Argentine Junta could not withdraw and survive."[4]

Haig claimed that "the British amendments would be rejected out of hand."[5] Pym agreed. Responding to Haig's objections, Thatcher broadened the phrase "wishes" into "wishes and aspirations," the very word the Argentines had settled on, but Haig demanded that only the word "interests" be used.[6] Earlier that day, before the Senate Armed Services Committee, Haig had said that:

> The United States did not completely share Britain's insistence that the fate of the island be decided by the self-determination of the overwhelmingly pro-British inhabitants....The United States believed that their views should be considered but that Argentina should have the opportunity of demonstrating to them "the advantages of other alternatives to the current arrangement."[7]

Thatcher finally agreed to compromise with the formulation "aspirations and interests" of the Islanders.[8] The discussions with Haig on May 5 paralleled the War Cabinet and full cabinet sessions on that morning, followed by questions in the House of Commons. Although Thatcher claims that she had "firm" Cabinet support that the Islanders "wishes" be respected and that South Georgia and the other dependencies be excluded, the record only partially supports her claim.[9] Pym openly repudiated the self-determination thesis, saying before a "hushed and somber House of Commons" that a UN trusteeship "might very well prove a highly suitable" long-term solution.[10] Labor's Dennis Healey agreed, saying: "I think we all feel if military escalation continues as it has in the past few days there will be more casualties than there are inhabitants of the islands."

Thatcher, however, would not be deflected. Announcing that Britain had made a "very constructive response" to the Peruvian proposals, she stepped back from the UN venue. "If [Perez de Cuellar's proposals] are to be acceptable and to command confidence, they must be precise as to the timing and the sequence of verification of events."[11] She had taken an enormous calculated risk that the Argentines would not now accept a venue they had just rejected. She had also demonstrated a willingness to reach a negotiated solution by agreeing that British administration would not return and that the islanders would not be able to determine their own fates—the very antithesis of her long-held position. The prime minister had just undertaken a major gamble, comforted only by "the fact that I had never believed that the Argentine Junta would be prepared to withdraw on these or any other terms."[12] And she was right.

When Belaunde called Galtieri that night to discuss the British counterproposal, he found him in a feisty mood. Speaking for the record, in case there were "leaks," Galtieri peppered their discussion with bluster: "Hundreds and thousands more Argentines are ready to die....We'll wait for Queen Elizabeth and all her fleet....There are many Argentines ready to fight to the end."[13] Consumed by what he considered to have been President Reagan's "betrayal," Galtieri refused point-blank to accept any American role.[14] Argentina had "lost all belief in the government of the U.S." Furthermore, he objected to the tight timetable as "too brief for real negotiations." Galtieri adamantly refused to permit the British to "put us between the sword and the wall." The two presidents agreed that "it was time to transfer the problem to the UN and to Perez de Cuellar."[15]

Remarkably, there had been no discussion, indeed, no recognition, of the fundamental changes in Thatcher's position. Acceptance of Britain's proposal would have been not only a major advance for Buenos Aires, it would also have created havoc in London. The junta disdained, or perhaps did not perceive, the opportunity to widen further the growing cleavage in the Thatcher administration. As *New York Times* columnist James Reston put it, "The Argentinians have won but don't seem to know it—and they keep insisting on trying to settle the controversy over sovereignty by force of arms."[16]

It was becoming increasingly obvious to all but the wettest of the "wets" that the junta was not interested in a negotiated settlement that involved anything less than an immediate zero-sum payoff. Even they, however, could not sell an immediate transfer of sovereignty to the British people. Indeed, Galtieri did not even bother to go through the formality of presenting the proposal to the junta for discussion. He immediately dismissed it, which confirmed that the decision apparently had already been made to stall, wait for winter, more weapons—particularly Exocet—and to force an ignominious retreat and defeat upon Great Britain.

The Argentine calculus was becoming apparent. Shifting the venue to the United Nations meant opting for a larger forum where sensitive discussions would be more difficult, stalling would be easier, and, they believed, the United States would be less of a factor. The junta had decided to begin laying the propaganda groundwork for blaming Britain for the conflict. Moreover, they felt confident about obtaining a UN resolution in support of their position. Their decision to stall was immediately evident. While agreeing to the UN forum, Argentine officials said that they would "not negotiate any substantive points—including an Argentine troop withdrawal—until Britain agree[d] to halt military activities."[17]

Prime Minister Thatcher announced in Parliament on May 6 that Britain would use UN Secretary General Perez de Cuellar's proposal as a "framework" for further talks, but she warned that Britain would not cease its military activity while discussions continued.[18] Thatcher demanded that a guaranteed Argentine withdrawal accompany any cease-fire, as required by UNR502. Pym, of course, was furious over Buenos Aires' rejection of the Peruvian proposal. He said he was "deeply disappointed that Argentine intransigence has once again frustrated a constructive initiative." Britain would have accepted the plan that had the backing of the United States and that "would have led to a cease-fire at noon EDT today."[19]

Before agreeing to shift back to the UN forum, Thatcher sought to coordinate action with President Reagan. Upset over the "constant pressure to weaken our stance, [an obvious reference to Haig, she] drafted a personal letter to President Reagan." There was, she believed, "little prospect of a diplomatic 'breakthrough,' yet still the apparently endless negotiations continued."[20] Reagan responded rapidly. As the decision to accept a UN mediation was being announced, Reagan was asked for his reaction.

Commenting briefly to reporters, he offered support for Thatcher, saying that a settlement must be within the framework of UNR502, which required a cease-fire coupled with an Argentine withdrawal. As yet, he said, "there has not been agreement."[21]

The Perez plan, while similar to the Peruvian proposal, was more general, envisaging a cease-fire, mutual withdrawal, removal of sanctions, UN provided or overseen interim administration during negotiations, and a fixed conclusion date for the talks. The secretary general asked for more concrete replies to this formula from both nations. UN Ambassador Parsons, in delivering the British response, declared that it "is substantial and constructive and addresses all aspects of the secretary general's ideas." The Argentines, however, delivered a much less specific response that urged an immediate cease-fire. In Parliament, Thatcher said that it "may be very likely" that Argentina was using the United Nations to gain a cease-fire without being forced to withdraw militarily. "That would be a very evident ploy to keep them in possession of their ill-gotten gains, and we are right to be very wary of it," she said.[22]

> [Thatcher] was not prepared to hold up military progress for negotiations. We were all aware that we were coming to a critical period. If we were to land and repossess the islands it would have to be done some time between 16 and 30 May. We could not leave it later because of the weather. That meant that negotiations at the UN must be completed within ten days or so. If they were successful and our principles and minimum requirements were met, well and good. If not, or they were still dragging on, then—if the Chiefs of Staff so advised—we would have to go ahead.[23]

As soon as the negotiations commenced, it became apparent that the Argentines were intent upon using the UN temporary administration for the islands as the instrument of transition to Argentine sovereignty. Thus, they insisted that the UN interim administration govern the islands exclusively, taking over "all executive, legislative, judicial and security functions."[24] The United Nations would govern without reference to the islands' democratic mechanisms—the executive and legislative councils—and appoint "equal numbers" of British and Argentine citizens as advisers, despite the huge disparity in local residents (roughly eighteen hundred to thirty). Argentine nationals would enjoy "freedom of movement and equality of access with regard to residence, work and property...on an equal basis with the Falkland Islanders."

Moreover, the junta sought to accomplish this objective quickly, insisting that the interim period and the negotiations be ended by December 31, 1982. If there were no agreement by the end of the year, Buenos Aires demanded that the UN General Assembly, where Argentina could count on overwhelming support, determine the final status of the islands. They demanded that the British Dependencies of South Georgia and South Sandwich Islands be included in the negotiation and that the task force withdraw to British waters and be disbanded. The transparent objective was to exclude any form of British rule, flood the islands with Argentine settlers during the interim period, change the nature of Falkland society, and thereby predetermine the outcome of the negotiations in favor of Buenos Aires.

London's position, although markedly different from Thatcher's initial, flat demand for the return of British administration and self-determination for the islanders, made it plain that a negotiated settlement was impossible. Departure of Argentine forces from the islands would be matched by withdrawal of the task force, but no further than 150 nautical miles from the islands. The dependencies were to be excluded from the negotiations, as they were unrelated to the Falkland Islands, except as an administrative convenience of British rule in the South Atlantic. A UN "administrator" would "verify the withdrawal of all forces from the islands and...prevent their reintroduction." A "small but effective force" from three or four countries other than Britain and Argentina would assist in this function.

Britain agreed to the substitution of a UN administrator for the restoration of British rule in the islands during the interim period, but sought to provide a voice for the islanders by insisting that the administrator act "in conformity with the laws and the practices traditionally obtaining in the islands." The administrator would "consult" the islands' legislative and executive councils, to each of which would be added one Argentine resident. This provision was specifically drawn "so that the interim administration [could] not make changes in the law and customs of the islands that would prejudge the outcome of the negotiations on a long-term settlement." It would prevent an influx of Argentine settlers during the negotiations and negate any possibility that the interim administration could be employed as "an instrument of change." If there were no agreement by the end of the year, then "the interim agreement would remain in force."

Time Runs Out on the Junta

Although the discussions with Perez de Cuellar would continue for two more weeks, after two days—by May 8—Prime Minister Thatcher had decided that "the negotiations would fail."[25] Her objective became threefold. First, the scheduled landings would continue with all deliberate speed. Thus, on May 8, she ordered the landing force south from Ascension, despite the lack of air superiority.[26] Second, ensure that when the talks failed, Argentina "did not manage to shift the blame on to us." Because it was vital to bring the talks to "a definite conclusion before the landings took place....An ultimatum was obviously necessary." Finally, within her own government she "had to stand firm against the pressure for making unacceptable compromises while avoiding the appearance of intransigence."[27]

Pym was the main source of that "pressure," and he strove to head Thatcher off. His opportunity came in the context of an intensification of British military action. For three days after the Exocet attack on the *Sheffield*, Woodward had entered "a state of profound depression" because of the dilemma the Argentines had created for him. The Exocet attack meant that he could not move the task force close to the Falkland Islands during daylight hours and draw out the Argentine air force. The risk to the carriers was too great. Yet, unless he got close to the islands, his Harriers could neither contend effectively with Argentine air power, nor provide adequate support for a landing. What to do? How could he, as Hastings and Jenkins asked, "solve the conundrum of defeating an air threat without in turn being destroyed by it."[28]

At last, he arrived at a solution. He could guard against both the high-altitude bomb threat and low-level Exocet attack by combining ships in complementary ways. Specifically, he would team his Type-42 and Type-22 destroyers. The Sea Dart surface-to-air missile on the Type-42s gave high-altitude defense out to forty miles, while the Sea Wolf missile on the Type-22s provided protection in close and low. Together, they provided the best available all-around defense. London provided another answer regarding early detection of the air threat by deploying Nimrod surveillance aircraft to

Ascension, from whence they could patrol south. Nimrod was Britain's less capable version of the U.S. AWACS (airborne warning and control), but its main shortcoming was a relatively limited range of operation. The Nimrod could track low-flying aircraft as far away as 200 miles, thus providing ample warning time for defense. To extend its range to provide coverage of the Falkland Islands, London requested a loan of air tankers from the United States.[29]

Even the mere discussion of this issue, which appeared in the press, may have had a deterrent effect on Argentine planning. Thus, "Reagan administration sources" said that the United States and Britain "were discussing the possible loan…of some KC135 aerial tanker planes." The United States is committed to assisting the British, but "sources said" the Pentagon might prefer to offer the tankers for use in Europe, thus enabling Britain to move its own planes to Ascension. If U.S. planes were operated directly out of Ascension, "they might have to be flown by British crews to avoid involving U.S. forces." In addition, it was suggested that Britain "may seek to obtain portable, long-range U.S. radar gear for use on the islands in any enclave they may seize there." Such ground-based radar "would vastly improve Britain's ability to detect and repel air attacks from mainland Argentina."[30]

Thus, from May 9 onward, confident in both his ability to detect and defend against the Argentine air threat, Woodward employed his new tactics. Alternately, he sent *Coventry* (Type-42) and *Broadsword* (Type-22) and *Glasgow* (Type-42) and *Brilliant* (Type-22) to within sight of the islands for the first time to conduct intensive shore bombardment, hoping his aggressive actions would provoke an Argentine response. The new tactics ended the lull of the previous few days. On May 9, *Coventry* and *Broadsword* detected an Argentine Hercules transport, escorted by two Skyhawks, on its daily shuttle into Stanley. *Coventry* fired Sea Dart missiles from a range of thirty-eight miles knocking out both Skyhawks. Then *Coventry* destroyed a Puma helicopter in flight at a range of thirteen miles. It was the beginning of much more naval and air activity around and over the islands and portended an imminent landing.[31]

On Sunday, May 9, hoping to delay British planning, Costa Mendez said on CBS's *Face the Nation* that Argentine sovereignty over the Falklands had to be the "objective" of the negotiations, but not, as previously, "a prior condition."[32] His remark seemed to suggest a change of position. Pym immediately picked up on this hint and attempted to show British flexibility. The next day, May 10, he told the Foreign Affairs Committee of the House of Commons that "we have not taken the line that this is British sovereignty forever and a day. It could be, but it need not be."[33]

Backing away from previous government statements about self-determination for the Islanders, Pym said that British negotiators "would bear in mind their wishes" after consulting them, but they would have no veto. Britain, he said, was "inflexible" on only two points—a "supervised Argentine withdrawal" and a "prejudged outcome" of the negotiations, insisting on the former and rejecting the latter. As of yet, however, "we do not see from the Argentines the sort of flexibility we have been looking for." A senior official observed that "the government would have to decide, within a day or two, whether the UN talks are likely to produce a settlement."

The junta responded immediately to clarify its position. Perhaps sensing that the crisis point was at hand and attempting to buy more time, Argentine spokesmen offered what was taken to be (but was not, in fact) a major concession. That day, Gustavo Figueroa, a high official in the foreign ministry and a key figure in the UN negotiations, attempted to state the shift more plainly. "Argentina had dropped its insistence that its sovereignty be recognized before it withdraws its troops and administrators from the islands."[34] Figueroa declared that "we want to maintain negotiations with Great Britain through the Secretary General....To facilitate that, we have said, 'Sirs, we do not want you to give us sovereignty now.' " However, he said, in the negotiations that follow Argentine withdrawal from the islands, there must be "precautions" that "inexorably lead to the recognition of our sovereignty."

Prime Minister Thatcher immediately objected that the "new" Argentine position was "a distinction without a difference." In the House of Commons, on May 11, she indicated that she was willing to wait "a bit longer to see if Mr. Perez de Cuellar could work out an agreement," but there remained "certain fundamental principles that we cannot fudge in any way."[35] Thatcher declared that "any cease-fire must be accompanied by a withdrawal according to a specific timetable, and in a comparatively short time." Then, "we must make it absolutely clear that the Argentines must not enter into negotiations in the belief or on the condition that by the end of the discussions sovereignty will be ceded to them." Finally, she reiterated that the continuance of talks at the United Nations "does not close off any military options."

Thatcher reacted strongly to a suggestion by Labour opposition leader Michael Foot that the Parliament should be given a chance to "judge" any peace proposal produced by Perez de Cuellar before the government did. "No, sir," the Prime Minister nearly shouted in reply. "The Government has the responsibility—will shoulder that responsibility—and will stand before this House and defend its decision."[36] An aide to Thatcher noted privately that "it would be quite wrong to suppose that we are necessarily going places in these negotiations."[37] The time was fast approaching when, as one Conservative politician put it, the prime minister "will have to decide whether to take what she can get or to fight for what she wants."

At this critical moment, Secretary of State Haig entered the picture once again through his enigmatic envoy Vernon Walters. In his determination to initiate negotiations, Haig sent Walters to Buenos Aires incognito and uninvited, May 10–11, to consult with the three members of the junta as well as other military and business leaders. His immediate purpose, it appears, was to elicit an unambiguous statement from the leadership regarding its willingness to enter into negotiations without prejudging the outcome. Walters may also have intimated that Thatcher was willing to make "significant concessions to Argentina on the sovereignty issue." That, at least, is what they were led to believe.[38] The result was that late on May 11 the junta sent "a private note" to Perez de Cuellar affirming that "a transfer of sovereignty to a fixed deadline would no longer be a precondition of settlement." Argentina, it said, would merely "negotiate in search of a recognition of its sovereignty."[39]

Publicly, however, Argentine leaders refused to retreat from their original position, making plain their expectations that "negotiations after withdrawal should be structured to lead eventually to Argentine sovereignty." Galtieri himself, in an interview on May 12 with three British journalists (who were literally coerced into the meeting), said that Britain would have to make the compromises. Galtieri was asked "if Argentina was willing to lower its flag on the Falklands and discuss the sovereignty issue freely with Britain. The president answered with a quick 'no,' " adding: "There are other ways to make available to Great Britain an honorable and acceptable solution for its country."[40] And, at a public rally, Galtieri "swore" that "the Argentine flag will never come down over the Malvinas."[41]

Nevertheless, this wholly artificial "concession" was enough to galvanize Pym and his allies into a last-ditch effort to avert a landing. In a stormy

Parliament debate on May 13, the "wets" took out all the stops. "The Government retains an open mind," said Pym, on the negotiations. While having "no doubt whatever about the British title to sovereignty....We did not, before the invasion, rule out discussion of sovereignty in negotiations with Argentina. Again, successive governments of both parties have taken the same position. We still remain willing to discuss it as one of the factors in negotiations about the long-term future."[42] Former Prime Minister Edward Heath, becoming involved in the policy controversy for the first time, sided with Pym, paying him "a series of pointed compliments...for his peace efforts."[43] Thatcher fumed. The split between the prime minister and the "wets" in the Conservative Party could not have been wider.

Thatcher, however, was not without allies in the debate. Indeed, one source of support was quite unexpected. Denis Healey, foreign affairs spokesman for the Labour Party, drew apart from the "wets" to give Thatcher his strongest support to date in the crisis. He declared that the government was right to make "some important concessions" in the negotiations and blamed Argentina for its intransigence. He also rejected the calls from his own party's left wing for a unilateral cease-fire and withdrawal, which he said would be tantamount to "handing the Falklands to Argentine President Leopoldo Galtieri on a platter."[44]

It was Thatcher's backbench supporters, however, who rallied strongly to her cause. Speaking to her theme that "we are working for a peaceful settlement, not a peaceful sellout," her backbench allies warned Pym against making any more concessions. Indeed, they were critical of previously made concessions—namely, withdrawal of the task force, the proposed international administration of the islands, and Pym's willingness to deny the islanders their veto in the negotiations over sovereignty. Maurice MacMillan, a former Conservative cabinet minister, crystallized their sentiments, saying "the British people would accept casualties resulting from firm action, after the failure of negotiations and a genuine attempt to reach a peaceful solution, more readily than they would accept terms they would take to be a surrender of the principles on which [Britain's] task force set off."[45] Pym left the House of Commons that evening with cries of "No Surrender!" ringing in his ears.[46]

President Reagan, led to believe that the positions were close, called Prime Minister Thatcher after the debate. Thatcher "had to tell him that unfortunately this was not the case."[47] The president, she felt, "had been misinformed about the Argentinians' alleged concessions." "Major obstacles remained," she said, running through the list of issues still in disagreement, particularly the Argentine attempt to employ the interim administration as a Trojan horse. Thatcher complained that "we just did not know with whom we were really negotiating," as different statements were being made by different people in Buenos Aires. "We could not," she told him, "delay military options simply because of negotiations. The truth was that it was only our military measures which had produced a diplomatic response, highly unsatisfactory as this was." Reagan was persuaded.

In attempting to identify the source of the impetus behind Reagan's call, Ambassador Henderson "discussed this telephone call afterwards with the national security adviser, Mr. William Clark." From him, Henderson gathered that, in Haig's absence (he was in Europe), Ambassador Kirkpatrick had "managed to convince President Reagan that the Argentines were ready to be forthcoming and persuaded him to telephone the prime minister."[48] Reagan had also been talking to visiting President Figueiredo of Brazil, who was concerned about a British attack on Argentine mainland bases (which Thatcher characterized as "entirely misplaced"). Clark himself intimated, surprisingly, that Reagan was concerned that the United States "had already impaired its relations with the Latin American countries." But, he added, the president felt that "there would be serious problems in the [western] alliance if hostilities became intensified *and if there were feelings in Britain that America was not being supportive enough.*" (Emphasis added)

Reagan remained a staunch ally. During a press conference that evening, he was asked about the prospects for a negotiated settlement. "Well, I think there's a tendency on the part of many of the countries of South America to feel that their sympathies are more with Argentina than ours. [But] I don't think there's been irreparable damage done."[49] The president noted that "there are reports that some of the issues between the two have been agreed upon." But, he said, it still comes "down to a situation of withdrawal, of what will be the interim administration on the island itself and what will be the period of negotiations then of what the ultimate settlement is supposed to be (sic.). Up until now the intransigence had been on one side, and that is in wanting a guarantee of sovereignty before the negotiations took place... which doesn't make much sense."

The next morning, May 14, Thatcher convened two meetings of the War Cabinet—one military and the other diplomatic. The prime minister chaired a full review of the military position, preparations, and options following briefs by each of the responsible chiefs of operations. The decision was made to proceed with plans for the landing. It was also decided to attack the Argentine garrison and air field on Pebble Island, which lay just outside Falkland Sound and posed a threat to the chosen landing site at San Carlos. Pebble Island had been previously identified as a possible target based on radio intercepts, but permission for a raid had been denied, until now. Thus, early on May 15, a forty-five-man SAS raiding party landed by helicopter on the island and, completely surprising the approximately 100 defenders, blew up eleven Pucara turboprop ground support aircraft, an ammunition dump, and other installations before departing.[50]

In the diplomatic meeting, Thatcher "decided to prepare our own terms to put to the Argentinians as an ultimatum."[51] Ambassadors Parsons and Henderson were called to London to discuss the formulation of the proposal. For Thatcher, "the vital consideration was that we bring the negotiating process to an end—ideally, before the landings—but in such a way as to avoid appearing intransigent." As she discussed the issues that weekend at Chequers, particularly with Parsons, who believed that the positions were not necessarily "unbridgeable," she realized that "we would have to make a very reasonable offer."[52] So Thatcher decided to put forth a reasonable ultimatum on a take-it-or-leave-it basis. "The Argentinians must accept the offer as a whole, or not at all, and once rejected, it would be withdrawn. We would set a time limit for their response."

The final proposal "hardened" terms for the interim administration, "ensuring something close to self-government for the islanders and denying any role to the Argentine Government." South Georgia and the other Dependencies were "excluded." Reference was made to UN Article 73, which implied self-determination and made it clear that "the wishes of the islanders would be paramount in long-term negotiations." Of course, the proposed terms were but a thinly disguised formula for the return to Thatcher's position of a "recognizably British administration" and self-determination for the Islanders.[53] But they did, in fact, offer Buenos Aires the long-term prospect for creeping Argentine sovereignty over the islands. Thatcher "accepted this because I was convinced that the Argentinians would reject it."

Presented to Perez de Cuellar on May 17, Argentina was given forty-eight hours to respond.

Meanwhile, Thatcher authorized Pym to brief Haig, who was in Brussels. Haig "thought that the British proposal was fair enough, though he doubted whether the Argentines would accept it."[54] He seemed to have realized that his hopes had been dashed of reaching a negotiated settlement before a British landing, although he instructed his Deputy Secretary of State, Walter Stoessel, to ask whether "in the likely event of Argentine rejection...we would want Haig to come forward with another proposal." Henderson replied, "Most emphatically not." Despite this, once the landings occurred, Haig would continue his attempts to bring about a cease-fire on one pretext or another on at least six occasions.

Henderson went to see Clark, "sensing a current in the White House in favor of some last-minute activity by the president." Clark told him that Kirkpatrick was indeed attempting to reach the president to suggest a new negotiating initiative. Her view was that "the British proposal was made to be accepted....We must force that acceptance."[55] Henderson "reminded [Clark] of the president's telephone call to the prime minister on May 13th" and stressed the "inappropriateness of yet another American negotiating initiative."[56] Clark said that "he accepted the position." Britain, he said, "could rely on American support. There was no doubt where the president's sympathies lay." Indeed, Clark was at that moment drafting the speech the president was to deliver to the British Parliament on June 8, when he intended to reaffirm his support in a most unmistakable manner.

The Argentine reply was exactly what Thatcher expected. Refusing to accept the take-it-or-leave-it proposal, Buenos Aires countered with its initial, and only slightly amended, position. They insisted on the "unequal...withdrawal of forces," the Trojan horse scheme of exclusive UN administration of the islands, the inclusion of South Georgia and the South Sandwich Islands, reference to previous favorable UN resolutions as the negotiating framework, instead of Article 73, and the position that the UN General Assembly resolve the dispute, if negotiations failed by mid 1983. The only concession was agreement that the UN administrator would govern the islands "on the basis of legislation in force on April 1st 1982."[57] The Argentine leadership had not expected the British to issue an ultimatum and their reply, in effect, constituted a comprehensive rejection of the British proposal.[58]

The Argentines hoped to gain more time and agreed with Perez de Cuellar's attempt to obtain British agreement for additional discussions. When the War Cabinet met on May 20, "once again, Pym urged a compromise," urging a delay in the landings while responding to Perez de Cuellar.[59] But Thatcher moved to close off further negotiations, insisting that the secretary general's proposals were "sketchy and unclear." Publishing the British proposals that day ended the negotiating phase with Argentina. At the same time, she concluded: "There could be no question of holding up the military timetable. It could be fatal for our forces. If the weather was right the landing would go ahead. The War Cabinet and later the full Cabinet agreed." As in the quotation from Macbeth, " 'Twere well it were done quickly," before dawn on the morning of May 21, British forces began to land at San Carlos, East Falklands.

An amphibious landing is a lengthy and vulnerable exercise, and the operation in the Falkland Islands was no exception. According to their strategic plans, the junta mounted a determined effort to prevent the landing, but exclusively by means of air attacks from the mainland. In a fatal mistake, whatever may have been their hopes or intentions, Argentine forces did not attempt to contest the British landing on the ground, nor mount a counterattack to defeat or contain British forces at the beaches. After five days, British forces had established a secure beachhead and, thereafter, were able ultimately to concentrate superior firepower from land, air, and sea against isolated Argentine defenses.

Once British forces had landed and consolidated the beachhead at San Carlos, it would be only a matter of weeks before the Argentines were defeated. It would not be exactly the "walkover" task force commander Woodward predicted, but it would be victory, nonetheless. Indeed, mesmerized by the mobility of British forces and, perhaps, overly conscious of their own lack of mobility, Argentine troops never initiated an attack against British forces, maintaining a defensive stance throughout. Argentine air attacks from the mainland continued but focused on the ships of the task force. Moreover, with two fortuitous exceptions, the air attacks failed to strike supply ships, troop transports, or the carriers.[60]

Endgame: Reagan, Thatcher, and Latin America

Although he publicly urged a "peaceful solution" to the conflict, President Reagan fully supported Britain, while acting to isolate Argentina and allay the fears of other Latin American nations. U.S. opposition to the use of force to seize territory made Argentine defeat inevitable. The only question in dispute was over the scale of the defeat to be inflicted on Buenos Aires. Haig and Kirkpatrick, while vehemently opposed to each other, argued persistently, but separately, in favor of ending the conflict short of total Argentine defeat on the grounds that irreparable damage would be done to American relations with the rest of Latin America. Haig, as we have seen, had additional motives for his behavior. The president pointedly rejected the thesis that "irreparable damage" had been done to America's relations with its Latin neighbors, expressed no opinion on the "right moment for a negotiated settlement," and acted to ensure Britain's victory.[61]

From the beginning, as noted earlier, long before the public "tilt," President Reagan authorized Secretary Weinberger to extend the provision of decisive American support for Great Britain behind the scenes. Without that assistance, as Thatcher has said, "we could not have retaken the Falklands."[62] It was far more than was ever publicly acknowledged during the conflict.[63] The United States was prepared to provide whatever was needed for Britain to win. Secretary Weinberger, at one point "even proposed sending down the carrier *USS Eisenhower* to act as a mobile runway," a proposal Thatcher considered "more encouraging than practical."[64] Were either of Britain's carriers knocked out of commission, Weinberger also "proposed that an amphibious assault ship of about the same size, *USS Guam*, with capacity to handle helicopters and Harriers, would simply be turned over to the Royal Navy."[65]

Most significantly, Reagan won over, or otherwise neutralized, countries that could have made a difference in the outcome of the conflict, had true Latin solidarity prevailed. Of crucial significance was Brazil. Indeed, Argentina's defeat would lead inexorably to Brazil's unchallenged ascendancy to a hegemonic position in South America—a prospect that Brazil's leaders recognized early on and which undoubtedly was discussed when the president of Brazil, João Figueiredo, made an official visit to Washington in mid-May. While paying lip service to Argentina, calling for an early settlement "with neither victors nor defeated, but with the honorable and just requirements on both sides having been met," Figueiredo's main purpose was to establish "balanced relations" with the United States.[66] Reagan's aim, however, was to enlist Brazil as a stabilizing force in the region, thereby reducing Rio's support for Buenos Aires. He did not seek Brazil's assistance in negotiating a settlement of the conflict before Argentina's defeat—much to the discomfiture of Ambassador Kirkpatrick, who wished to enlist Figueiredo in the quest for a negotiated settlement.

Worsening global economic conditions and Brazil's own deteriorating economy made Figueiredo receptive to Reagan's ideas. By the spring of 1982, the dollar was appreciating, global recession was beginning, overall economic activity was slowing, exports and imports were declining. Inflation in Brazil was rising, GDP was hovering around zero, and Brasilia was encountering increasing difficulties financing its huge $70 billion debt.[67] The United States had supported the World Bank's decision to disqualify Brazil for subsidized loans as an underdeveloped country on the grounds of a $2,300 per capita income. Figueiredo sought Reagan's support to reverse this decision. He also sought relief from a recently imposed quota on imported sugar. Brazil had had a bumper crop, and the quota threatened to reduce exports by as much as two-thirds. Reagan responded to Figueiredo's entreaties with the view that the two countries should be able to reach a "pragmatic compromise."[68]

Reagan's "pragmatic compromise" encompassed more than mere economic matters, as the president and Figueiredo reached an understanding on the Falkland Islands, as well. Brazil was in a quandary about the precedent set by Argentina's seizure of the islands. If Buenos Aires succeeded, then others might emulate that behavior. Venezuela, for example, which supported Argentina, might seize Essequibo in Guyana, which, in Figueiredo's view, "would be a much more dangerous development than the occupation of the Falkland/Malvinas."[69] There was also Brazil's own territorial dispute with Argentina, which Buenos Aires would undoubtedly pursue more vigorously. If Argentina were defeated, however, there was concern about the impact the fall of the junta would have on Brazil's own military government. This quandary was what impelled the hope that a settlement could be reached with "neither victors nor defeated." That, of course, was a hope; not a policy.

Meanwhile, Brazil provided some political, economic, and military assistance to its beleaguered neighbor. Brazil was reexporting Argentine products to bypass the embargo, assisting in the financing of Argentine debt, and providing some military equipment (three reconnaissance planes). At the same time, the embargo opened Argentine markets to Brazilian exports. Brasilia's policy was to do just enough to develop some Argentine dependence on

Brazil (Argentina had entrusted Brazil with the management of its affairs with embargoing nations) and ensure that Argentina not move toward better relations with the Soviet Union. Figueiredo did not expect the Soviet Union to make major inroads into South America as a result of the conflict, although he did expect to see more of a Soviet ship presence in the South Atlantic.

The Brazilian president also sought to ensure against any British attacks on the Argentine mainland, which, as previously noted, Thatcher had no intention of authorizing in any case. Reagan was undoubtedly supportive here, for Washington agreed with that position. Brazilian concern was genuine, however, for such attacks would compel greater Brazilian support for Argentina than it wished to give. For that reason, Reagan also declined to accept Ambassador Kirkpatrick's proposal to employ Brazil as an interlocutor with Argentina the way Haig had enlisted Peru.[70] Reagan's objective was the opposite—to ameliorate the support Brazil had been giving to Argentina, particularly in Buenos Aires' earlier efforts in the OAS. Reagan's "pragmatic compromise" with Brazil centered around greater American financial and economic support for Brazil in return for muted Brazilian political support for Argentina—a bargain readily struck as it both coincided with Brasilia's interests and served Washington's purposes.

President Reagan appeared to be quite sanguine about the results of his meetings with Figueiredo. At a fund-raiser in Philadelphia the evening of the Brazilian president's departure, he declared that "he had just seen Figueiredo off." There has been, he said, "some ill feeling between" the United States and Brazil. The president continued, however, "I think I can safely say they realize there's a whole new relationship now there (sic.)."[71] On this occasion, Reagan took the opportunity to reassert that, although the United States was doing its best to broker a peace, "at the same time we can't ignore the fact that the aggressor was...Argentina." The president insisted that "the rule of law prevails, not the rule of force. Where would we draw the line if we say, 'Well, it's all right there'? Then how many other places are there where there are boundary disputes?" Closing his remarks on the subject, Reagan spoke of "a dream I nurse above all," which was to see all of the Americas as "friendly allies bound together within the Western Hemisphere."

The results of the Figueiredo-Reagan meeting appeared rapidly as Brasilia began to acknowledge its growing leadership role in the hemisphere as a result of the war. Still hoping for a settlement of the conflict that kept the junta in and the Peronists out, Brazil nevertheless began to depict its role as a "moderating force," rather than a disruptive one. And Figueiredo began to emphasize his intent to "revive" the inter-American system rather than replace it, a view with which Brazilian spokesmen had expressed sympathy earlier.[72] Indeed, Brazil's moderating influence would be felt during the Rio Treaty meeting in Washington, on May 27–29, where Argentina's allies, Peru, Venezuela, and Panama sought passage of a resolution that not only condemned Britain and the United States, but that would clear the way for "other countries to send aid to Argentina."[73] The "other countries" formula was a code word for the Soviet Union. The best Argentina could obtain was a weakly worded resolution stating that only member states of the Rio Treaty "should lend the Argentine Republic the support that each judges appropriate."[74]

However much Brazil contributed to the OAS outcome, the weaknesses in the Argentine position were too apparent to be papered over with rhetoric. At bottom, the Argentine junta was asking support from its neighbors to legitimize the principle of irredentism. As every nation in Latin America either held claim to the territory of a neighbor, or was the object of such a claim, Latin "solidarity" was limited to verbal condemnation of the colossus of the north. As a *New York Times* editorial put it, Latin American support for Argentina was "as wide as the River Plate, but only a centimeter deep."[75] The junta was asking for sanction of the principle that aggression should be rewarded in flagrant disregard of international law. Argentina's Latin neighbors understood full well the precedents that would be established for themselves by support of these "principles."

Trapped by their own virulent anticommunism, the junta threatened but never established relations with the Soviet Union, although tentative contacts were made through Cuba and Libya. Indeed, Costa Mendez's trip to Cuba to confer with Castro in early June on the occasion of a meeting of the so-called nonaligned movement caused more dissension within the Argentine military—indeed, within the junta itself, than it produced in support of the Argentine cause. Threatening to break relations with the United States, the junta only precipitated a cutoff in American aid programs and ultimately declined to take that drastic step. The junta let it be known that it would develop nuclear weapons (which they had been doing secretly for some time), but the nuclear threat never materialized.

The Argentine campaign to generate Latin American opposition to the United States was far more effective inside the Reagan administration than in Latin America, because it offered Haig—and, to some extent, Kirkpatrick—further opportunity to press for a negotiated end to the conflict. It appeared to have little effect on the Thatcher administration, which now seemed to close ranks behind its men fighting in battle. President Reagan, of course, was concerned about both immediate and long-term consequences of the conflict, conditions in Latin America, deterioration of the inter-American system, the prospects for greater Soviet inroads, and the loss of American influence. He had no intention, however, of snatching defeat from the jaws of victory; nor did Margaret Thatcher.

As defeat loomed for the junta, Reagan administration officials expressed growing concern at the possible negative impact of a British victory. They feared that "a humiliating defeat for Argentina will sour American as well as British and European relations with much of Latin America for a long time to come."[76] It was not difficult to identify the inspiration of these fears and concerns. It was Secretary Haig, as well as Ambassador Kirkpatrick, who continued to attempt to provide dramatic overemphasis to worst-case outcomes. In fact, the public expression of views that seemed to distance the United States from Britain and to indicate an American interest in bringing the conflict to an end short of a "humiliating Argentine defeat," actually served Reagan's interests—insofar as a public airing of these concerns forestalled any actual negative developments. Reagan himself, however, never publicly voiced a lack of confidence in Thatcher.

On the day of the landings, the president convened a meeting of the National Security Council. After heated argument, the White House issued a statement that reflected a compromise between the president and the secretary of state that reaffirmed support for Margaret Thatcher. It also, however, authorized Haig to continue to seek a negotiated settlement and reassured Latin nations of U.S. determination not to become involved with any military personnel. In releasing the statement, Deputy Press Secretary Larry Speakes emphasized the president's view that the United States, "will meet our commitments to Great Britain."[77] British requests would be evaluated on a "case by case basis," but the administration would not publicly discuss "specific requests for assistance or how we will respond." Haig's view was also included with the sentence: "Every step, every action of the President and the United States Government shall be taken with one thought in mind—a peaceful solution." And Speakes declared emphatically that, "there will be no involvement whatsoever of U.S. military personnel in the conflict."

A spate of newspaper articles, based on conversations with unidentified "high administrative officials," accompanied the publication of this decision. Articles by Michael Getler in the *Washington Post* and Charles Corddry in the *Baltimore Sun* generally reflected the president's position, emphasizing support for Britain, while two articles in the *New York Times* by Bernard Gwertzman reflected Haig's determination to reach a settlement and outlined the dire consequences of a failure to do so.[78] All of the articles noted that the landing of British troops on the islands indicated that the conflict had entered its final phase, and implicitly signified that intense argument was occurring within the Reagan administration over the issue of how to conclude the Falkland Islands War.

As reflected in the press, the Reagan view was that "the military edge could tip within days." A British victory might come "rather quickly," or turn into a disaster, but the latter possibility "was not the view of American experts." Of genuine concern was the outside possibility "under intense study in the White House" that the battle would be "inconclusive," facing Britain with "long-term supply difficulties and continuing casualties." Haig's view, reflected in the *New York Times* articles, was that "once the military situation tilted decisively in one side's favor, another opportunity for a diplomatic settlement would probably open up rapidly." Indeed, Haig was ready to resume his mediating mission at any time and had discussed possible initiatives with both ambassadors. While Takacs had been noncommittal, Henderson made it clear that, although he knew that Haig would "always be ready," he emphasized that "the British Government was not seeking any new initiatives at this time."

Haig's Frenzied Last Campaign

Haig's campaign was based upon the worst of worst-case, long-term scenarios. The conflict was "creating a long-term, major shift in attitudes and policies throughout South America that will inevitably be harmful to United States interests."[79] This "gloomy analysis" was not only the reason the administration attempted to mediate the dispute, but also "why it has done as little as possible publicly for the British." No matter what the outcome of the war, Argentina "is now more likely than ever to develop an atomic bomb." If this happens, Brazil "will be psychologically pressed to do the same." Of course, both countries were secretly already well on the road to development of both nuclear weapons and the systems needed to deliver them, but it served Haig's interests to publicize this apocalyptic vision.

Furthermore, the argument continued, the United States would no longer be able to "limit sales of conventional weapons to Latin America." All Latin leaders will argue that the "lessons of Argentina" require that every country have the "most advanced weapons in large quantities." American leadership in the hemisphere has been dealt a serious blow by the decision to side with Britain, "and that blow may be irreparable." Washington's support for Britain was already being regarded in "racial terms," the "Anglo-American-Europeans" were all against the "Latins," who must band together in solidarity. And finally, the Soviet Union, which has "for years been seeking opportunities to gain influence in South America," will receive its opportunity. One could not have conceived a more negative scenario.

As soon as British forces landed on the islands, Haig commenced his campaign with British Ambassador Henderson. Repeating his general theme ad nauseam over the next three weeks, he insisted that Britain seize the first moment of military success to show "magnanimity," a code word for a readiness to reach a negotiated settlement. Without British magnanimity, Haig claimed, there would be "long-term bitterness in Latin America, and the opportunity for the Soviets to increase their influence there."

With British forces now lodged in force on the islands, however, London was no longer interested in diplomatic formulas that would undercut its position. On May 24, Henderson told Haig "on instructions...that the establishment of the British bridgehead in the Falklands was bound to have a major effect on our diplomatic position. We could not in present circumstances consider the idea of British withdrawal from the Falklands or the establishment of an interim administration."[80] The only negotiations Britain was interested in now were those that effected the rapid withdrawal of Argentina from the islands "within a fixed time limit"—that is, surrender.

Haig proposed a plan involving a cease-fire and withdrawal of both sides from the islands and their temporary administration by the United States and Brazil. He wished to "keep the Brazilians in play so as to prevent the OAS from getting out of control" especially during the coming Rio Treaty meeting. If the OAS got out of control, he went on apocalyptically, it "would spell the end of the inter-American system for which the United States would be blamed." Here, Haig was either uninformed about Reagan's understanding with Figueiredo, or thought he could mislead Henderson about the forthcoming meeting.

Haig also expressed fears about the expansion of Soviet influence in the region. Henderson responded equally emphatically, however, that "these ideas would be unacceptable [in London] in current circumstances," and he reminded Haig "how often he had assured me that this would not be another Suez."[81] News of this conversation quickly got back to the president, who instructed Haig to correct any misapprehensions of any lessening of American support. Thus, "later the same day [May 24], Haig telephoned to say that the president supported Britain solidly."

On May 25, Argentine National Day, Buenos Aires ordered massive air strikes against the San Carlos beachhead and task force culminating a five-day-long effort to defeat the landing attempt.[82] Although several ships were sunk, including the Type-42 destroyer *Coventry* and the large, eighteen thousand-ton general cargo ship, the *Atlantic Conveyer*, carrying additional Harriers (which had all been flown to safety before the attack), helicopters, and vital equipment for the ground force, the Argentines suffered substantial losses of aircraft. Of the more than ninety sorties flown during the week of May 21, Argentina lost twenty-one planes. Forty-five were sent on May 25 alone, ten of which were lost.[83]

Most significantly, the Argentine air attacks failed to strike either the carriers or the troop ships. The failure to target the troop ships was a serious oversight, for the landings would be the Argentines' only opportunity to sink them. The two Exocet missiles that struck the *Atlantic Conveyer* were targeted on *Hermes*, which had been positioned behind the supply ship.[84] On the ground, Argentine troops never mounted attacks against British forces, passively awaiting British attacks throughout the conflict.[85] Not even commando operations were conducted to disrupt British operations.

Again, on the evening of May 25, in the context of the large-scale battles then raging over San Carlos, Haig urged Thatcher "not to try to crush the Argentines." He predicted that "the Argentines would look for a scapegoat for a British victory, and that scapegoat would probably be the United

States."[86] Having secured the bridgehead on the islands, Thatcher responded to Haig's gloom and doom ideas before Parliament. "Our objective," she said, "is to retake the Falklands....They are British sovereign territory, and we wish to restore British administration."[87] Henderson made the same point to Haig personally. "On instructions from the Prime Minister and Pym, I rubbed it home...that we were determined to repossess the Falklands." He did acknowledge, however, "the desirability eventually of having some kind of international security arrangement involving the Americans," but only after Argentina had been defeated.[88]

President Reagan said that "the Falklands fighting presented no reason for him to cancel a planned visit to London during a 10-day European trip next month."[89] His London visit would include a two-night stay at Windsor Castle with the Queen. The Pope also reaffirmed that his trip to London would take place on schedule, but be curtailed because of the fighting. He would also visit Argentina after leaving Great Britain. On May 26, the United Nations passed resolution UN505, reaffirming UN502 and authorizing Perez de Cuellar to undertake one more effort in using his good offices to obtain a cease-fire.[90] The resolution was carefully worded to urge British and Argentine cooperation in negotiating a cease-fire, which made it innocuous and, therefore, acceptable to London. In its original form as tabled by Ireland, the resolution called for an immediate cessation of hostilities and resumption of negotiations, but after Parsons threatened a veto, the resolution was watered down. Perez de Cuellar was given a week to try.

During that week, as the OAS meeting produced only a tepid resolution of support for Argentina and British forces won a major battle at Goose Green, a blow-up occurred between Haig and Kirkpatrick. Kirkpatrick was genuinely dismayed by the negative impact of U.S. support for Britain on Latin America and publicly flayed Haig and his aides as "Brits in American clothes." These and other steamy remarks of their increasingly negative interaction found their way into a *Newsweek* article, which Haig hoped would be enough to bring about Kirkpatrick's removal from office. Instead, the president called Haig to the White House to tell him he not only wanted Kirkpatrick to remain in office, he personally wanted to know more about what was happening at the United Nations. Reagan told Haig that "the UN ambassador should report *through* the State Department, not *to* it."[91]

Kirkpatrick's standing with the president was, therefore, high that last week of May when junta member Lami Dozo embarked upon an independent attempt to terminate the conflict—through Ambassador Kirkpatrick. Lami Dozo's motive apparently was intended to preempt any move by Costa Mendez to open ties to Cuba and the Soviet Union—a move that was creating dissension within the ranks of the Argentine military.[92] His proposal was for the establishment of a UN trusteeship on the islands as a compromise solution. Although this "compromise" had no chance of succeeding with Britain on the verge of complete victory, Kirkpatrick attempted to sell it to President Reagan on the grounds that it would prevent the complete wreckage of American relations with Latin America, forestall any Argentine move to the Soviets, and avoid a "bloodbath" in the final battle for Port Stanley.[93]

During a forty-minute meeting, on May 31, Kirkpatrick insisted and the president agreed to pass on Lami Dozo's proposal to Thatcher. Thus, without any preliminary communication regarding the subject he wished to discuss (which indicated that the proposal had not been staffed internally), Reagan called the prime minister to register his concern about Latin American opinion and to float the idea passed on by Kirkpatrick.[94] Thatcher was clearly taken aback and upset that she "should not have had advance warning of what he was likely to say" and her response was "more forceful than friendly."[95] The president suggested that, now that Britain held the upper hand, the time was ripe to "strike a deal." But Thatcher "could not accept this," and "told him that we could not contemplate a cease-fire without Argentine withdrawal." Referring obliquely to the UN trusteeship scheme proposed by Lami Dozo, Thatcher said "we would not consider handing the islands over to a third party," likening such a proposal to the United States agreeing to a UN trusteeship for Alaska under similar circumstances.

Immediately following this conversation, Thatcher instructed Henderson "to see Clark at the White House and ensure that the president and he understood the British attitude."[96] In a meeting with Clark the next day, June 1, Henderson emphasized that Thatcher would not agree to any UN trusteeship scheme. Britain "having negotiated in good faith for weeks, during which time the Argentines had shown no sign of being ready to talk business, was not prepared now, when we were back in the islands after considerable sacrifice, simply to pull out and make way for an umbrella or contact group including countries from Latin America."

Meanwhile, Haig had heard of Reagan's conversation with Thatcher and sought to utilize it for his own ends. In discussion with Henderson, even while declaring his admiration for Thatcher, Haig said that he saw "great difficulties ahead in our relations. Opinion was moving against [Britain]. I asked him if he meant in Congress or the media. No, he said, he meant the President and himself." "We are on your side," but, "we can't accept intransigence." And if Mrs. Thatcher insisted on that, he said, "the U.S. would have to reassess its attitude." But surely, Henderson asked, Britain could rely on the United States in the Security Council? Foreshadowing what was to occur, Haig replied: "Perhaps not."⁹⁷

Henderson's conversation with Haig, reinforced by his reading of the press, left him with the impression that Reagan would want to discuss with Thatcher ways to mend fences in Latin America. Indeed, he thought that there was "a widespread expectation that Reagan...would urge magnanimity on the British government," the code word for reaching a negotiated settlement before Argentina's complete defeat.⁹⁸

But the president once again confounded those attempting to determine his policy views and came out strongly in support of Britain. In an interview with European journalists the day before departure for Europe, a British correspondent asked about the extent of U.S. commitment to Britain. "Are you asking us to hold back, for there to be a negotiation and Argentina be left with some of the fruits of aggression?" Reagan said that it would be "presumptuous" of him to insist that Britain seek a negotiated settlement. England, he said, was responding to "a threat that all of us must oppose, and that is the idea that armed aggression can succeed in the world today." The president did not know when "the right moment for a negotiated settlement" would be. "Whether that can take place without further military action or not, I don't know."⁹⁹

Asked about Latin American criticism of American support for Britain, Reagan said that the United States "had tried to be a peace broker," but Argentine intransigence had made that impossible. Furthermore, "we could not deny the principle involved, that we cannot approve of armed aggression being allowed to succeed, certainly with regard to territorial claims."¹⁰⁰ The president hoped that "after" the conflict was resolved the United States would be able to proceed with efforts "to improve relations with our neighbors...in the Americas." At a news conference earlier that day, Haig was "noncommittal" when asked specifically whether the United States would like to see a British victory before Reagan arrived in London for a meeting with Prime Minister Margaret Thatcher and an address to Parliament.[101]

Prime Minister Thatcher responded to Reagan's interview with European newsmen with one of her own with *Washington Post* reporter Leonard Downie, her first since British forces landed on the islands. She called on Argentina "to withdraw its troops from the Falkland Islands within the next few days to avoid a bloody battle for the capital of Stanley."[102] So far, she said, "when they've talked about withdrawal, they've talked about it only in the sense that they want to keep some of the fruits of their occupation." That, she said, "is not acceptable to me." While taking a firm line regarding the present, Thatcher offered a hopeful future, promising that "once Britain regained control of the Falklands, she would consider negotiations with Argentina on the long-range future of the islands and the role that Argentina might play there."

Thatcher insisted that she was "not seeking to humiliate anyone." She was "just asking that the invader return his troops to the mainland. That is not humiliation. It is a restoration of the rule of law." She commended Reagan's recent interview. The president has been "absolutely marvelous on one of the supreme things, that aggression must not be seen to pay." If it does, she said, "there are 50 to 100 other territories that would be in danger." Asked about Secretary Haig's suggestion that she show "magnanimity" in victory, Thatcher said: "It is not a word I use in connection with the Falklands." Besides, she said: "I'm not talking so much of victory, but of a return of Argentine forces to the mainland." After that was achieved, she said, echoing the president's view, "we shall start to make special efforts to restore the most friendly relations throughout Latin America."

On June 4, Reagan and Thatcher conferred privately for an hour and a half at the American embassy in Paris. A key vote was to be taken in the Security Council. Following the collapse of Perez de Cuellar's week-long attempt to resolve the Falklands conflict, Spain and Panama had tabled a resolution calling for a cease-fire, which had just enough votes to pass. The vote had been postponed to give Reagan and Thatcher an opportunity to discuss the issue. Britain would veto the resolution because it failed to include a call for Argentine withdrawal as required by UN502. As Britain's single veto would be sufficient to defeat the resolution, Kirkpatrick favored abstention as a gesture of conciliation to the Latin Americans. But Thatcher "requested that the American vote should support us at the Security Council."[103] The president agreed, and Kirkpatrick dutifully, if reluctantly, cast the American veto along with Britain's.

No sooner had Kirkpatrick cast her veto than an aide delivered a message which prompted her to state: "Mr. President....I have been told that it is impossible for a country to change its vote once it has made it known but my Government has asked me to put it on record that if it were possible to change votes, I should change it from a no to an abstention. Thank you."[104] Kirkpatrick's extraordinary act in the first instance served to distract attention from Britain's veto, as reporters clamored for an explanation. Was it a clumsy attempt to take both sides of the issue and offer a small gesture toward repairing relations with Latin America? If so, it failed. Thatcher was astounded at the retreat from an agreement made only hours before. The president was enraged that his decision had been countermanded. How could this be explained?

Secretary Haig made the decision to put the U.S. government on record as wishing to abstain "if it were possible," in direct contravention of the president's agreement with Prime Minister Thatcher. Haig admitted that he took the decision while the president was asleep, explaining that he did so because it was "a nuance vote," presumably not requiring presidential approval.[105] More controversy surrounded the manner in which he communicated the decision, than the decision itself. Haig instructed the State Department to convey the message to Kirkpatrick instead of communicating with her directly, although he had spoken with her twice before on that day. He explained away this odd procedure on the grounds that "you don't talk to a company commander when you have a corps in between."

The attempted vote change was more than a nuance vote; it was a reversal. Haig's "corps in between" maneuver was an attempt to circumvent the president's injunction of a few days before that Kirkpatrick was to report "*through* the State Department not *to* it." Presumably, the reverse was also true, that Haig was not to give orders to Kirkpatrick. Had Haig sent the message to abstain in the president's name? The decision itself clearly conveyed a lessening of support for Britain just as the final assault on Stanley was about to commence. It brought no cheers from Latin America, not even from Argentina. Nor did it open an opportunity to bring about a last-minute negotiation of the conflict, although that appears to have been its immediate purpose. Indeed, as Henderson suggests, it was to open the way for "one more attempt...to instill reason into the Argentines" before the final assault on Stanley that Haig orchestrated his UN maneuver.[106]

It was a mark of his own desperation that Haig was prompted openly to defy the president. Indeed, the president's European trip represented the penultimate stage of Haig's role as secretary of state, and his actions over the Falklands must be seen in the wider context of ongoing policy disputes—over policy toward the Soviet Union, the gas pipeline, and Israel's invasion of Lebanon, which had just begun. On all of these issues he and the president differed to the point that Secretary Haig and the president's advisers, especially Bill Clark, argued publicly over everything from symbol to substance.

Most of all, the trip was intended to showcase the president to European leaders and peoples as a "sensible and reliable ally rather than the simpleminded, trigger-happy cowboy that many of them still consider him to be."[107] Haig's public disparagement of the president not only made plain their fundamental disagreement, but revealed a leadership in disarray and a president who, as William Safire observed, "was not master in his own house much less in the Atlantic alliance."[108] When Reagan said the next day that he "had not been told" and "did not know anything about" the change in the UN vote, it was as if the last nails were being hammered into Haig's secretaryship.[109]

When, a few days later, the president made his official visit to London, he clarified his position of complete support for Great Britain and Prime Minister Margaret Thatcher in both actions and words. In addition to a horseback ride with the Queen and a two-night stay at Windsor Castle, the president also declared his support. During a luncheon toast, President Reagan said: "We...have crossed the ocean with a message. America stands with Britain, and I mean that." To which the prime minister replied: "I know that."[110] (Reagan's remark echoed Thatcher's own words spoken to him the previous year during her Washington visit, when she had said: "The message I have brought across the Atlantic is that we in Britain stand with you....Your problems will be our problems, and when you look for friends we will be there.")

Later that same day, the president addressed both houses of Parliament in the Royal Gallery in the palace of Westminster and reinforced his point. In the course of a lengthy speech denouncing communism and urging support for a campaign for democracy around the world, the president said:

On distant islands in the South Atlantic young men are fighting for Britain. And, yes, voices have been raised protesting their sacrifices for lumps of rock and earth so far away. But these young men aren't fighting for mere real estate. They fight for a cause, for the belief that armed aggression must not be allowed to succeed and that the people must participate in the decisions of governments under the rule of law.[111]

President Reagan's highly publicized visit and demonstration of support for Britain's fighting men at last ended the varied machinations executed by both governments to change the outcome of the battle. British ground forces, with air and naval support, pressed forward the final assault on the high ground around Stanley two days after Reagan's departure and, by June 14, had left General Menéndez no alternatives but surrender or destruction. After hurried discussions with Galtieri, who quixotically urged a fight to the last man, the other members of the junta, supported by the military committee and field commanders, overruled him. The decision was reached to accept surrender late that evening. The war was over. British administration would be fully restored to the Falkland Islands. Margaret Thatcher had won.

The Strategic Significance of the Falkland Islands War

Wars affect the destiny of victors and vanquished alike in varied and sometimes unanticipated ways. Although Great Britain and Argentina fought a war over the issue of sovereignty over the Falkland Islands, the great irony was that it did not settle the issue of sovereignty, which still remains in dispute. The outcome of the war determined who would control the islands, but not the question of sovereignty. On the other hand, the war decided crucial issues that were never part of the public discourse on the conflict.

In November 1982, the United Nations voted ninety to twelve in favor of a resolution requesting the governments of Great Britain and Argentina to "resume negotiations in order to find as soon as possible a peaceful solution to the sovereignty dispute relating to the question of the Falkland Islands (Malvinas)." The United States voted in favor of the resolution, and fifty-two other nations abstained. As recently as mid-1996, the UN Decolonization Committee called on Britain and Argentina to resume negotiations to resolve their dispute over the sovereignty of the Falkland Islands.[1]

Although the sovereignty dispute is hardly trivial, the war settled issues that were far more important than sovereignty over the Falkland Islands. The conflict resolved crucial issues of historic significance on three continents. Indeed, it would be accurate to state that the Falkland Islands War was the quintessential example of the right war, at the right time, and in the right place, whose outcome indirectly altered the historic paths of Argentina and Britain and directly benefited the Argentine people, Margaret Thatcher, and

Ronald Reagan. The Falkland Islands War marked a historic turning point at several levels of analysis.

In terms of the secret nuclear arms race between Argentina and Brazil, which, from the point of view of the United States was the deep origin of the conflict, Argentine defeat brought the end of the military junta that concocted the nuclear program and the return of civilian government. Galtieri was forced to resign on June 17—three days after the surrender at Port Stanley. A caretaker military government under Gen. Reynaldo Bignone, entrusted to manage the return to civilian rule, held elections in October 1983. President Raul Alfonsín, in turn, revealed and abandoned the Argentine nuclear weapons program, and in 1986 reached agreement with Brazil to do likewise (an agreement that has continued as of this writing).[2] Thus, the conflict served major United States foreign policy objectives—civilian rule and nuclear nonproliferation in Latin America.

No less important is the fact that the conflict marked a fundamental repudiation of the junta's decision to build Argentina into a world-class military power. Instead, it has followed a path of peaceful, democratic development. A few statistics make the point. In the decade following the conflict, 1983–1993, Argentine military expenditures were cut by more than half, from $9.2 billion to $4.2 billion, up from a low of $2.4 billion in 1991. Total armed forces were reduced from 175 thousand to 65 thousand. Military expenditures per capita were reduced from $311 to $127. Arms imports plummeted from $1.4 billion to $10 million. Finally, the percentage of arms imports to total imports dropped from 22.2 to 0.1.[3] Thus, the return of civilian government, the rejection of nuclear weapons, and the repudiation of militarism were truly historic changes directly attributable to the Falkland Islands War.

For Margaret Thatcher, the end of the war enabled her to become the very embodiment of her reputation—the "Iron Lady" whose reelection would now be a foregone conclusion. She would actually be reelected yet a third time and remain prime minister for eleven and a half years. During that tenure, she would undertake a vigorous and largely successful effort to shift Britain to a market economy, what she would term an "enterprise economy," while attempting to strengthen the special Atlantic partnership with the United States, at least through 1988.[4] It is highly unlikely that Britain would have maintained Thatcher's course under any other leadership. After all, Francis Pym and the "wets" had vigorously opposed her on both foreign and domestic policy from the beginning. And the Labour Party remained committed to a welfare state.

The British economy would grow faster during the eighties than all of the other European economies except for Spain.[5] Fundamental restructuring occurred. Trade unions were reduced in size and influence, business deregulated, private home ownership encouraged. Government-owned industry and public utilities were privatized, taxes were cut, and a tight rein on monetary policy brought down the inflation rate from over 10 percent to less than 4 percent. Margaret Thatcher thus presided over a historic change in the very structure of Britain's economy.

Victory would strengthen her personal friendship with President Reagan and the Atlantic partnership with the United States. Despite sharp disagreements over the issue of the Siberian pipeline and the U.S. invasion of Grenada, Thatcher would solidly support Reagan in his strategy of containment, which strengthened Britain's role. Britain acquired the Trident submarine, deployed the cruise missile, and increased overall defense spending. Although the long-term goals of John Nott's 1981 defense review were upheld, key decisions were made to ensure that Britain would retain and strengthen the out-of-area force projection capability of the Royal Navy.

All war losses were replaced and additional forces acquired, using funds over and above those already allocated to the 3 percent annual increase in defense spending. The decision was made to move to a Fortress Falklands policy, by stationing of a permanent garrison force—a squadron of F-4 Phantoms acquired from the United States—and associated support elements. HMS *Endurance* would be retained in service as would be the amphibious assault ships HMS *Fearless* and HMS *Intrepid*.

Strengthening out-of-area capability obviously enhanced Britain's NATO contribution as well as the ability to reinforce the Falkland Islands. At the command level, a "two-star" headquarters was established "committed" to support of out-of-area operations.[6] One of the most visible of force reversals following the conflict was the decision to maintain three aircraft carriers instead of only two. This meant that Britain would always have two carriers capable of operating together, with one in reserve or refit. Self-contained early airborne warning and point defense were added.

Planning ship levels through the eighties saw an increase in frontline destroyers and frigates, maintaining the number at fifty-five, instead of the

1981 decision to reduce it to below fifty. Instead of keeping eight ships in drydock, only four would remain in reserve. Wide-body transport/tanker aircraft would be acquired to improve strategic mobility for rapid troop deployment and to extend the range of combat aircraft. Ammunition and stores stockpiles for out-of-area operations would also be enlarged. Response time for any future challenge to British control of the Falkland Islands would be dramatically reduced.

As a result of combat operations analysis, several additional improvements were made. All ships would be fitted with close-in defense capability, particularly Sea Wolf. Additional Rapier air defense systems would be acquired for ground forces. The Harrier would be upgraded to be able to fire four Aim 9L missiles instead of two. The Aim 9L would become standard in British air forces. Numbers of helicopters of all varieties (especially Sea King, Lynx, Chinook) would be increased. Antiship missiles (Sea Skua) would undergo "accelerated introduction into service" on helicopters and submarines. Electronic countermeasures and chaff for ships and aircraft were to be developed further to counter the Exocet threat. Antisubmarine capability would be upgraded. In short, Britain emerged from the war with a substantial upgrading of all forces, particularly the Royal Navy.

For the United States, Britain's military victory in the Falklands conferred special victories of a different sort. Aside from dramatically changing the nature of Argentine politics and putting the nuclear genie back into the bottle in South America, which were unprecedented outcomes, the dismissal of Alexander Haig freed Reagan to pursue more vigorously his strategy of containment. Had Haig's (and Pym's) policy prescription of a negotiated settlement prevailed, undoubtedly the junta's oppressive dictatorship would have survived and Thatcher fallen. A strengthened Haig, in turn, would have severely inhibited Reagan's freedom of action regarding containment—a strategy that Haig did not support. It is not difficult to imagine the consequences had Haig and Pym succeeded.

Of course, no victories are final in politics. Reagan and Thatcher were unable to maintain their respective strategic courses throughout the remainder of their terms of office, not to mention beyond them. The end of the Cold War led to the eclipse of the strategy of containment, which had become outmoded—a victim of its own success. It is mildly ironic that the outcome for Argentina was more lasting. At least, as of this writing, Buenos

Aires remains a civilian-controlled, peaceful, nonnuclear, democratic state, and Latin America remains a nuclear-free area. The "Falklands Sting" succeeded.

Notes

INTRODUCTION

1. For a discussion of Argentina's and Brazil's nuclear power and weapons programs, see Leonard S. Spector and Jacqueline R. Smith, *Nuclear Ambitions: The Spread of Nuclear Weapons* (Boulder: Westview, 1990), 223–41. See also *World Armaments and Disarmament: SIPRI-1982* (Stockholm, 1982), 414–18.

2. See David Rock, *Argentina, 1516–1987: From Spanish Colonization to Alfonsín* (Berkeley: University of California Press, 1987).

3. R. Hon. The Lord Franks, *Falkland Islands Review: Report of a Committee of Privy Counsellors* (London: HMSO, 1983), para. 67–69.

4. "British Magazine: Argentina To Make A-Bomb," in *FBIS-LAT*, 3 December 1981, B4.

5. Jack Anderson, "Argentines May Go Ahead With the Bomb," *Washington Post*, 7 June 1982, C15.

6. U.S. Arms Control and Disarmament Agency, *World Military Expenditures and Arms Transfers: 1986* (Washington: GPO, 1987), 65.

7. Franks, *Falkland Islands Review*, chap. 1.

8. Oscar Cardoso, Ricardo Kirschbaum, and Eduardo Van Der Kooy, *Falklands: The Secret Plot*, translated by Bernard Ethell (Surrey: Preston Editions, 1987), 62.

9. Publicly, Callaghan denied it, but privately admitted that "he had told the head of MI6, Sir Maurice Oldfield, of the committee's action but did not know whether this information was passed on." See Richard Deacon, *'C' A Biography of Sir Maurice Oldfield* (London: Macdonald, 1984), 204, who confirms Oldfield's role in arranging to pass the information to Buenos Aires by various means. Dennis Healey, Callaghan's Chancellor of the Exchequer also said in his memoir, *The Time of My Life* (New York: W.W. Norton, 1989), 494, that Callaghan "allowed the Argentine Government to discover this through secret channels. This deterrent was sufficient. There was no invasion."

10. Roger Perkins, *Operation Paraquat: The Battle for South Georgia* (Chippenham: Picton Publishing, 1986), 30–32.

11. Ibid.

12. Margaret Thatcher, *Downing Street Years* (New York: Harper Collins, 1993), 153. Hugo Young, *The Iron Lady: A Biography of Margaret Thatcher* (New York: Farrar, Straus, Giroux, 1989), 241, notes that her job approval rating at that point was a mere 23 percent.

13. Patrick Cosgrave, *Thatcher: The First Term* (London: The Bodly Head, 1985), 114.

14. In fact, both Argentina and Brazil agreed to abjure the search for a nuclear weapons capability. See Tom Zamora Collina and Gernando de Souza Barros, "Transplanting Brazil and Argentina's Success," *ISIS REPORT* (Institute for Science and International Security, Washington, D.C., February 1995).

15. Carlos Escude, "Argentina: The Costs of Contradiction," in Abraham F. Lowenthal, ed., *Exporting Democracy: The United States and Latin America* (Baltimore: Johns Hopkins Press, 1991), 23–25.

16. "U.S. Lauds Argentina For Improvements on Human Rights," *Baltimore Sun*, 19 March 1981, p.6.

17. Steven R. Weisman, "President May Repeal Argentine Military Embargo," *New York Times*, 18 March 1981, p.1 and *FBIS-LAT*, 19 March 1981, p.B1.

18. "General Meyer Leads U.S. Military on Pilgrimage to Buenos Aires," *Latin America Weekly Report*, 17 April 1981, p.1.

19. "Military Diplomacy Tilts Argentine Foreign Policy Toward Washington," *Latin America Weekly Report*, 11 September 1981, p.1.

20. "President Roberto Viola Suffers Heart Attack," *FBIS-LAT*, 20 November 1981, p.B1. For Viola's "bitterness" against Galtieri, see Cardoso, et al., *Falklands: Secret Plot*, 19.

21. "Galtieri Takes the Presidency and Retains Control of the Army," *Latin America Weekly Report*, 18 December 1981, p.1.

22. Jimmy Burns, *The Land That Lost Its Heroes: The Falklands, The Post-War, and Alfonsín* (London: Bloomsbury, 1987), 41–43 and Cardoso, et al., *Falklands: Secret Plot*, 66.

23. Michael Charlton, *Little Platoon: Diplomacy and the Falklands Dispute* (Oxford: Basil Blackwell, 1989), 118–19.

24. Perkins, *Operation Paraquat*, 35ff.

25. In remarks before Parliament, Ted Rowlands, the Labour Party's former Minister of State at the Foreign Office, said: "As well as trying to read the mind of the enemy, we have been reading its telegrams for many years." See *The Times*, 8 May 1984, and Lawrence Freedman and Virginia Gamba-Stonehouse, *Signals of War: The Falklands Conflict of 1982* (Princeton: Princeton University Press, 1991), 131.

26. Franks, *Falkland Islands Review*, para. 180 and Cardoso, et al., *Falklands: Secret Plot*, 71.

27. Derrick Mercer, Geoff Mungham, and Kevin Williams, *The Fog of War* (London: Heineman, 1987), 199.

28. Charlton, *Little Platoon*, 116.

29. Franks, *Falkland Islands Review*, para. 230. (emphasis supplied)

CHAPTER 1

1. Paul Lewis, "The Right and Military Rule, 1955–1983," in Sandra McGee Deutsch and Ronald H. Dolkart, eds., *The Argentine Right: Its History and Intellectual Origins, 1910 to the Present* (Wilmington: Scholarly Resources, 1993), 171.

2. I.M.D. Little, Richard N. Cooper, W. Max Corden, and Sarath Rajapatirana, *Boom, Crisis, and Adjustment: The Macroeconomic Experience of Developing Countries* (Washington, D.C.: IBRD, 1993), 186.

3. Jimmy Burns, *The Land That Lost Its Heroes: The Falklands, The Post-War, and Alfonsín* (London: Bloomsbury, 1987), 11.

4. David Rock, *Argentina, 1516-1987: From Spanish Colonization to Alfonsín* (Berkeley: University of California Press, 1987), 366.

5. Ibid., 367–68.

6. Joseph S. Tulchin, *Argentina and the United States: A Conflicted Relationship* (Boston: Twayne, 1990), 144.

7. Rock, *Argentina*, 368.

8. Recent official reports place the number at "over 13,000," while human rights advocates insist that "more than 30,000 people vanished." See Carl Honore, "Confessions Air 'Dirty War's' Dirty Laundry," and Ian Phillips, "Air Force, Navy Accept Blame for 'Horrors'; Cite Leftist Abuses," *Washington Times*, 7 May 1995, p.A10.

9. Lewis, "The Right and Military Rule," 172.

10. Rock, *Argentina*, 368.

11. Little, Cooper, et al., *Boom, Crisis, and Adjustment*, 187.

12. Martin Honeywell and Jenny Pearce, *Falklands/Malvinas: Whose Crisis?* (London: Latin American Bureau, 1982), 69–70.

13. Rock, *Argentina*, 368–69.

14. Burns, *Land That Lost Its Heroes*, 15–16.

15. Ibid., 15.

16. Ibid.

17. Ibid., 18.

18. U.S. Arms Control and Disarmament Agency, *World Military Expenditures and Arms Transfers: 1986* (Washington, D.C.: GPO, 1987), 65 and Amex Bank Review, *International Debt: Banks and the LDCs, Supplement—October 1984*, Special Paper no.10 (London: American Express International Banking Corporation, 1984), 3–4.

19. Leonard S. Spector and Jacqueline R. Smith, *Nuclear Ambitions: The Spread of Nuclear Weapons* (Boulder: Westview, 1990), 224.

20. Rock, *Argentina*, 371.

21. Lewis, "The Right and Military Rule," 173–74 and Honeywell and Pearce, *Falklands/Malvinas: Whose Crisis?*, 72-73.

22. Oscar Cardoso, Ricardo Kirschbaum, and Eduardo Van Der Kooy, *Falklands—The Secret Plot*, trans. Bernard Ethell (London: Preston Editions, 1983), 4.

23. Rock, *Argentina*, 370.

24. Ibid., 371 and Lewis, "The Right and Military Rule," 172.

25. Honeywell and Pearce, *Falklands/Malvinas: Whose Crisis?*, 73.

26. Cardoso, et al., *Falklands: Secret Plot*, 4.

27. Mark Falcoff, *A Tale of Two Policies: U.S. Relations With The Argentine Junta, 1976–1983* (Philadelphia: Foreign Policy Research Institute, 1989), 40.

28. Lewis, "The Right and Military Rule," 173.

29. *World Armaments and Disarmament, SIPRI-1982 Yearbook* (London: Taylor & Francis Ltd., 1982), 418. See also, Spector and Smith, *Nuclear Ambitions*, 242–62.

30. *World Armaments and Disarmament, 1982*, 488.

31. Oscar Antonio Montes, "Montes Issues Declaration Rejecting Ruling," *Translations on Law of the Sea*, no. 71 (Joint Publications Research Service, 70818, March 22, 1978), 75.

32. Marshall Van Sant Hall, Commander USN, *Argentine Policy In The Falklands War: The Political Results* (Newport, R.I.: Naval War College, 1983), 16.

33. U.S. Department of State, *Conference on Antarctica* (Washington, D.C.: GPO, 1960).

34. Honeywell and Pearce, *Falklands/Malvinas: Whose Crisis?*, 36, cite a closed Foreign Office file titled: "Proposed offer by His Majesty's Government to reunite Falkland Islands with Argentina and acceptance of lease."

35. United Nations Resolution 2065, The Question of the Falkland Islands (Malvinas), December 16, 1965.

36. R. Hon. The Lord Franks, *Falkland Islands Review: Report of a Committee of Privy Counsellors* (London: HMSO, 1983), para. 26.

37. Michael Charlton, *The Little Platoon: Diplomacy and the Falklands Dispute* (Oxford: Basil Blackwell, 1989), 22–23.

38. Roger Perkins, *Operation Paraquat: The Battle for South Georgia* (Chippenham: Picton Publishing, 1986), 26.

39. Honeywell and Pearce, *Falklands/Malvinas: Whose Crisis?*, 15, 40.

40. Perkins, *Operation Paraquat*, 20.

41. Honeywell and Pearce, *Falklands/Malvinas: Whose Crisis?*, 15.

42. Perkins, *Operation Paraquat*, 26.

43. Franks, *Falkland Islands Review*, para.29.

44. Ibid.

45. Perkins, *Operation Paraquat*, 26.

46. Franks, *Falkland Islands Review*, para. 33.

47. Ibid.

48. Guillermo A. Makin, "Argentine Approaches to the Falklands/Malvinas: Was the Resort to Violence Foreseeable?," *International Affairs*, 59, no.3 (summer 1983): 397.

49. Cardoso, et al., *Falklands: Secret Plot*, 62.

50. Charlton, *Little Platoon*, 61.

51. Lawrence Freedman and Virginia Gamba-Stonehouse, *Signals of War: The Falklands Conflict of 1982* (Princeton: Princeton University Press, 1991), 131. In remarks before Parliament, Ted Rowlands, Labour Party's former Minister of State at the Foreign Office, said: "As well as trying to read the mind of the enemy, we have been reading its telegrams for many years." See *The Times*, 8 May 1984.

52. Peterborough, "Frankly Speaking," *Daily Telegraph*, 29 December 1987, 13.

53. Franks, *Falkland Islands Review*, para. 54.

54. Ibid., para.51.

55. Ibid., para. 54.

56. Cardoso, et al., *Falklands: Secret Plot*, 62–63.

57. Franks, *Falkland Islands Review*, para. 58. It was also in February 1977 that the international court announced the outcome of its arbitration of the Beagle Channel dispute. Great Britain denied any involvement in the "Queen's award" of the islands to Chile, but the timing is suggestive of an attempt to divert Argentina from the Falklands. See Charlton, *Little Platoon*, 62.

58. Franks, *Falkland Islands Review*, para. 60.

59. Ibid., para. 61.

60. Charlton, *Little Platoon*, 60.

61. Franks, *Falkland Islands Review*, para. 62.

62. Ibid.

63. Ibid., para. 63.

64. Ibid., para. 65.

65. Dennis Healey, *The Time of My Life* (New York: W.W. Norton, 1989), 494.

66. Hastings and Jenkins, *Battle for the Falklands*, 36. Richard Deacon, *'C' A Biography of Sir Maurice Oldfield* (London: Macdonald, 1984), 204, confirms Oldfield's role in arranging to pass the information on to Buenos Aires.

67. Charlton, *Little Platoon*, 116–17.

68. Franks, *Falkland Islands Review*, para. 62.

69. The Sunday Times Insight Team, *The Falklands War: The Full Story* (London: Sphere Books, 1982), 51, while acknowledging the secret channel, say it was "a businessman with extensive contacts among Latin American regimes." A June 19, 1982, *Guardian* report asserted that the Americans informed the Argentines, "at Britain's request."

70. Franks, *Falkland Islands Review*, para. 65.

71. Ibid., para. 68.

72. Ibid.

73. Charlton, *Little Platoon*, 40.

74. Jack Anderson, "Argentines May Go Ahead With the Bomb," *Washington Post*, 7 June 1982, C15.

75. Spector and Smith, *Nuclear Ambitions*, 224.

76. Ibid.

77. Anderson, "Argentines May Go Ahead With the Bomb."

78. Spector and Smith, *Nuclear Ambitions*, 229.

79. Charlton, *Little Platoon*, 62 and Tulchin, *Argentina and the United States*, 146.

80. "CNEA Chairman Discusses Nuclear Capabilities," an interview by the *Jornal Do Brasil* with Argentina's atomic energy chairman, Castro Madero, in *FBIS-LAT*, 15 January 1982, B2.

81. "Beagle Channel Issue International Problem," *Translations on Law of the Sea*, no. 88, JPRS72285, 22 November 1978, 52.

82. Hall, *Argentine Policy in the Falklands War*, 19.

83. Charlton, *Little Platoon*, 62.

84. Admiral Anaya later claimed that it had not been a bluff and that the United States, learning of Argentine plans through its intelligence systems, "rapidly informed the pope so that he could intervene to try to avoid a clash." See "Anaya Emphasizes Secrecy," *FBIS-LAT*, 8 December 1983, B2.

85. Franks, *Falkland Islands Review*, para. 44 and Charlton, *Little Platoon*, 64.

86. See the Argentine Foreign Ministry's "statement on the South Georgia incident," in *FBIS-LAT* 25 March 1982, B2.

87. Perkins, *Operation Paraquat*, 30.

88. Ibid.

89. Ibid., 30–31.

90. Ibid., 28.

91. Burns, *Land That Lost Its Heroes*, 41.

92. Freedman & Gamba-Stonehouse, *Signals*, 40.

93. Franks, *Falkland Islands Review*, para. 161.

94. Charlton, *Little Platoon*, 112n.

95. Sunday Times Insight Team, *The Falklands War*, 76.

96. Perkins, *Operation Paraquat*, 31.

97. Ibid.

98. Franks, *Falkland Islands Review*, para. 161.

99. Between 1950 and 1978 the average annual price per ton was only $44.

100. Perkins, *Operation Paraquat*, 32. Franks, *Falkland Islands Review*, para. 161, says he was "occasionally in contact with the British embassy" during this period.

101. Burns, *Land That Lost Its Heroes*, 41–42. Burns also notes Davidoff's extensive contacts with the navy.

102. Honeywell and Pearce, *Falklands/Malvinas: Whose Crisis?*, 16.

103. Perkins, *Operation Paraquat*, 26.

104. Ibid., 26–27.

105. Honeywell and Pearce, *Falklands/Malvinas: Whose Crisis?*, 16.

CHAPTER 2

1. John Collins, *U.S.-Soviet Military Balance: Concepts and Capabilities, 1960–1980* (New York: McGraw-Hill, 1980), 251, 255, 520.

2. Drew Middleton, "Navy's Plight: Too Many Seas To Cover," *New York Times*, 1 February 1981, C1.

3. See Paul H. Nitze and Leonard Sullivan, *Securing The Seas: The Soviet Naval Challenge and Western Alliance Options* (Boulder: Westview Press, 1990).

4. For a survey of military readiness at the end of 1980, see James D. Hessman, "Laird: Only Six Percent of U.S. Forces 'Ready Now'," *Sea Power* (October 1980), 39–48.

5. John Allen Williams, "The U.S. Navy Under the Reagan Administration and Global Forward Strategy," in *Defense Policy in the Reagan Administration*, ed. William P. Snyder and James Brown (Washington: NDU Press, 1988), 273–304.

6. "The Allies and Defense Spending," *National Security Record* (March 1981): 1–5. Bonn was asked to contribute naval units to allied patrols of the seas around Greenland, Iceland, and Norway, or what is called the GIN-gap (also the GIUK gap).

7. U.S. Congress, House Committee on Appropriations, Subcommittee on Defense, *Department of Defense Appropriations for 1982: Hearings*, 97th Congress, 1st Sess., Part 9 (Washington, D.C.: GPO, 1981), 8–9.

8. Ibid.

9. For a succinct analysis and critique of Thatcher's economic policies, see the Joint Economic Committee staff study *Monetary Policy, Selective Credit Policy, and Industrial Policy in France, Britain, West Germany, and Sweden,* 26 June 1981 (Washington: GPO, 1981), 36–91.

10. For excellent surveys, see Patrick Cosgrave, *Thatcher: The First Term* (London: The Bodly Head, 1985); Hugo Young, *The Iron Lady: A Biography of Margaret Thatcher* (New York: Farrar, Straus, Giroux, 1989); and Peter Riddell, *The Thatcher Government* (London: Basil Blackwell, 1983).

11. Riddell, *Thatcher Government,* 62–63.

12. Cosgrave, *Thatcher: The First Term,* 98–99.

13. Ibid., 99.

14. Ibid., 114.

15. Margaret Thatcher, *The Downing Street Years* (New York: Harper-Collins, 1993), 122.

16. Young, *Iron Lady,* 199.

17. Thatcher, *Downing Street Years,* 122.

18. Young, *Iron Lady,* 204–5.

19. Thatcher, *Downing Street Years,* 129.

20. Patrick Cosgrave, *Carrington: A Life and a Policy* (London: J.M. Dent and Son, 1985), 125, 157–58.

21. Cosgrave, *Thatcher: The First Term,* 85.

22. Thatcher, *Downing Street Years,* 79.

23. Cosgrave, *Thatcher: The First Term,* 85–86.

24. Young, *Iron Lady,* 188.

25. Cosgrave, *Thatcher: The First Term,* 87.

26. Young, *Iron Lady,* 189.

27. Thatcher, *Downing Street Years,* 85.

28. Ibid., 86.

29. Young, *Iron Lady,* 190.

30. Cosgrave, *Thatcher: The First Term,* 89.

31. Russell Lewis, *Margaret Thatcher: A Personal and Political Biography* (London: Routledge & Kegan Paul, 1983), 171.

32. Cosgrave, *Carrington: A Life,* 141.

33. Riddell, *The Thatcher Government,* 209.

34. Thatcher, *Downing Street Years,* 74.

35. Ibid., 75.

36. Cosgrave, *Carrington: A Life,* 145–46.

37. Riddell, *The Thatcher Government,* 211.

38. Michael Charlton, *The Little Platoon: Diplomacy and the Falklands Dispute* (London: Basil Blackwell, 1989), 148.

39. Thatcher, *Downing Street Years,* 241.

40. Bruce George and Karl Pieragostini, "British Defense in the 1980's: What Price Trident?," *International Security Review* (Winter 1980–1981), 443.

41. Cosgrove, *Thatcher: The First Term,* 112.

42. Steven Rattner, "Britain Plans to Make Sharp Cuts in Navy to Pay for New Trident System," *New York Times*, 26 June 1981, 8.

43. John Nott, *The United Kingdom Defence Programme: The Way Forward* (London: HMSO, 1981), 5–6.

44. Leonard Downie, "Britain Sets Cuts In Military, Adjusts Navy's NATO Role," *Washington Post*, 26 June 1981, p.20.

45. Richard Halloran, "U.S. Admiral Says Britain Erred in Cutting Navy," *New York Times*, 22 May 1982, p.7.

46. Nott, *The Way Forward*, 9.

47. Keith Speed, *Sea Change: The Battle for the Falklands and the Future of Britain's Navy* (Ashgrove: Bath, 1982), 110–11.

48. Charlton, *Little Platoon*, 149.

49. Speed, *Sea Change*, 112–13.

50. The Rt. Hon. Lord Franks, *Falkland Islands Review: Report of a Committee of Privy Counsellors* (London: HMSO, 1983), para.73.

51. Sunday Times Insight Team, *The Falklands War* (London: Sphere Books, 1982), 54. Franks, *Falkland Islands Review*, para. 94–95, provides a lengthy paraphrase.

52. Charlton, *Little Platoon*, 126.

53. Ibid., 127.

54. Geoffrey Maynard, *The Economy Under Mrs. Thatcher* (London: Basil Blackwell, 1988), 48.

55. Young, *Iron Lady*, 144.

56. Maynard, *Economy Under Mrs. Thatcher*, 161–62.

57. Riddell, *The Thatcher Government*, 44–45.

58. Thatcher, *Downing Street Years*, 157.

59. Geoffrey Smith, *Reagan and Thatcher* (New York: W.W. Norton and Co., 1991), 41–43.

60. Ibid., 41. Reagan went to unusual lengths to symbolize his friendship. Not only did the president host the customary White House dinner, "but against all precedent he attended the return dinner at the British Embassy the following evening…staying much later than he normally did at any function."

61. Thatcher, *Downing Street Years*, 153. Young, *Iron Lady*, 241, notes that her job approval rating at that point was a mere 23 percent.

62. For an illuminating case-study approach that develops the general thesis of America's promotion of democracy in Latin America, see Abraham F. Lowenthal, *Exporting Democracy: The United States and Latin America* (Baltimore: Johns Hopkins, 1991).

63. For a discussion of Argentina's and Brazil's nuclear power and weapons programs, see Leonard S. Spector with Jacqueline R. Smith, *Nuclear Ambitions: The Spread of Nuclear Weapons* (Boulder: Westview, 1990), esp. 223–41.

64. Zdenek Cervenka and Barbara Rogers, *The Nuclear Axis: Secret Collaboration Between West Germany and South Africa* (New York: Times Books, 1978), 337–40.

65. Russell Lewis, *Margaret Thatcher*, 194.

CHAPTER 3

1. Jack Anderson, "Argentines May Go Ahead With the Bomb," *Washington Post*, 7 June 1982, p.C15.

2. See "America's Falklands War," *Economist*, 3 March 1984, p.29 and Freedman & Gamba-Stonehouse, *Signals*, 131.

3. Alvin Weinberg, Marcelo Alonso, and Jack Barkenbus, *The Nuclear Connection: A Reassessment of Nuclear Power and Nuclear Proliferation* (New York Paragon, 1985), 227.

4. Juan de Onis, "Four Years After the Coup," *New York Times*, 26 March 1980, p.1.

5. Carlos Escude, "Argentina: The Costs of Contradiction," in *Exporting Democracy: The United States and Latin America*, ed. Abraham F. Lowenthal (Baltimore: Johns Hopkins Press, 1991), 23–25.

6. *World Armaments and Disarmament: SIPRI-1982*, 414–18.

7. Weinberg, et al., *The Nuclear Connection*, 174.

8. George T. Kurian, ed., "Argentina," Vol. 1 of *Encyclopedia of the Third World* (New York: Facts on File, 1982), 91. See also "Argentina Basks in the Afterglow of Martinez de Hoz's 'New Image,' " *Latin America Weekly Report*, 8 May 1981, 6. The *Report* is published in London.

9. Weinberg, et al., *The Nuclear Connection*, 106f.

10. Ibid., 40.

11. Ibid., 140 and 33.

12. *SIPRI-1982*, 420 (my emphasis).

13. "British Magazine: Argentina To Make A-Bomb," in *FBIS-LAT*, 3 December 1981, B4.

14. IADB, *Economic and Social Progress in Latin America: 1983 Report*, 144.

15. Little, Cooper, et al., *Boom, Crisis, and Adjustment*, 46.

16. Ibid., 189.

17. "Low Reserves and High Debts Sound Warning Bell for Argentina's Lenders," *Latin America Weekly Report*, 3 July 1981, 1.

18. Honeywell and Pearce, *Falklands/Malvinas: Whose Crisis?*, 74.

19. "That Was the Week That Was," *Latin America Weekly Report*, 20 November 1981, 8.

20. "Viola and Parties Ready to Play Ball," *Latin America Weekly Report*, 17 July 1981, 3.

21. Honeywell and Pearce, *Falklands/Malvinas: Whose Crisis?*, 76.

22. Lewis, "The Right and Military Rule," 173.

23. Falcoff, *Tale of Two Policies*, 40–41.

24. "Viola and Parties Ready to Play Ball," 3.

25. Honeywell and Pearce, *Falklands/Malvinas: Whose Crisis?*, 76.

26. "Argentina's New President Faces Showdown With His Generals," *Latin America Weekly Report*, 1 May 1981, 1.

27. Ibid.

28. "Financial Panic and Political Rumors Shake Buenos Aires," *Latin America Weekly Report*, 5 June 1981, 1.

29. "Which Way Now For The Army?," *Latin America Weekly Report*, 3 July 1981, 9–10.

30. "Low Reserves and High Debts Sound Warning Bell For Argentina's Lenders," *Latin America Weekly Report*, 1.

31. "General Viola Wins a Breathing Space," *Latin America Weekly Report*, 10 July 1981, 2.

32. "U.S. Lauds Argentina For Improvements on Human Rights," *Baltimore Sun*, 19 March 1981, p.6.

33. Steven R. Weisman, "President May Repeal Argentine Military Embargo," *New York Times*, 18 March 1981, p.1.
34. Franks, *Falkland Islands Review*, para. 120.
35. Edward Walsh, "Reagan Seeking to Resume Aid to Argentine Forces," *Washington Post*, 15 March 1981, p.1.
36. U.S. Congress, House Committee on Foreign Affairs, *Review of United States Policy on Military Assistance to Argentina*, 97th Cong., 1st sess., April 12, 1981.
37. "Viola and Reagan Test the Water," *Latin America Weekly Report*, 20 March 1981, 3.
38. *FBIS-LAT*, 19 March 1981, p.B1.
39. Sunday Times Insight Team, *The Falklands War*, 60.
40. "General Meyer Leads U.S. Military on Pilgrimage to Buenos Aires," *Latin America Weekly Report*, 17 April 1981, 1.
41. "Foreign Minister Talks to Foreign Newsmen," *FBIS-LAT*, 24 April 1981, p.B2.
42. Falcoff, *Tale of Two Policies*, 44.
43. Franks, *Falkland Islands Review*, para. 88.
44. "Brazilian Government at Centre of Looming Nuclear Battle," *Latin America Weekly Report*, 26 June 1981, 1.
45. *The United Kingdom Defence Programme: The Way Forward* (London: HMSO, 1981) 13pp.
46. Ibid., 8.
47. Franks, *Falkland Islands Review*, para. 116.
48. Keith Speed, *Sea Change: The Battle for the Falklands and the Future of Britain's Navy* (Bath: Ashgrove Press, 1982), presents a critical analysis of the impact of the defense cuts on naval capabilities.
49. Charlton, *Little Platoon*, 109.
50. "Army Hawks Debate the Nuclear Balance With An Eye on Brazil," *Latin America Weekly Report*, 21 August 1981, 7. See also "Which Way Now For The Army?" Ibid., 3 July 1981, 9–10.
51. Edward Schumacher, "Latins Get Taste of Kirkpatrick Style," *New York Times*, 5 August 1981, p.3.
52. Cardoso, et al., *Falklands: Secret Plot*, 8–9.
53. For coverage of Galtieri's visit, see *Latin America Weekly Report*, 7 and 28 August 1981.
54. Cardoso, et al., *Falklands: Secret Plot*, 10.
55. "Military Diplomacy Tilts Argentine Foreign Policy Toward Washington," *Latin America Weekly Report*, 11 September 1981, 1.
56. "The Walters Friendship Formula," *Latin America Weekly Report*, 2 October 1981, 8.
57. Tom Dalyell, *One Man's Falklands* (London: Cecil Wolf, 1982), 133–34.
58. "Military Diplomacy Tilts Argentine Foreign Policy Toward Washington," 1.
59. "Galtieri Takes the Presidency and Retains Control of the Army," *Latin America Weekly Report*, 18 December 1981, 1.
60. Cardoso, et al., *Falklands: Secret Plot*, 11–12.
61. Burns, *Land That Lost Its Heroes*, 27.
62. "Army Commander Discusses Presidential Succession," *FBIS-LAT*, 6 November 1981, p.B2.
63. Sunday Times Insight Team, *The Falklands War*, 60.

64. Falcoff, *Tale of Two Policies*, 48.

65. Cardoso, et al., *Falklands: Secret Plot*, 14–15.

66. "Viola's Health Wanes and Galtieri Gets the U.S. Seal of Approval," *Latin America Weekly Report*, 13 November 1981, 1.

67. "President Roberto Viola Suffers Heart Attack," *FBIS-LAT*, 20 November 1981, p.B1.

68. Burns, *Land That Lost Its Heroes*, 29. See also "Viola's Health Wanes and Galtieri Gets the U.S. Seal of Approval," *Latin America Weekly Report*, 13 November 1981, 1 and "That Was the Week That Was," *Latin America Weekly Report*, 20 November 1981, 8.

69. "Argentine Army Debates Next Step as Liendo Becomes Interim President," *Latin America Weekly Report*, 27 November 1981, 1.

70. *Latin America Weekly Report*, 20 November 1981, 12.

71. "Chilean Radio Reports Date for Galtieri Takeover," *FBIS-LAT*, 30 November 1981, p.B1.

72. "Videla, Galtieri Consult as Speculation Abounds," *FBIS-LAT*, 4 December 1981, p.B1.

73. "Videla Denies Mediation Role in Argentine Crisis," *FBIS-LAT*, 8 December 1981, p.B1.

74. "General Galtieri Reshuffles Army High Command," *FBIS-LAT*, 4 December 1981, p.B2.

75. Cardoso, et al., *Falklands: Secret Plot*, 18.

76. "General Galtieri Reshuffles Army High Command," p.B2 and Cardoso, et al., *Falklands: Secret Plot*, 8 and 18.

77. "Argentine Generals Hammer the Last Nails Into Viola's Political Coffin," *Latin America Weekly Report*, 11 December 1981, 1.

78. Cardoso, et al., *Falklands: Secret Plot*, 18–19.

79. " 'By-Pass' Recommended for Viola," *FBIS-LAT*, 4 December 1981, p.B1. "Viola Refusal," Ibid., and "President Viola Leaves Hospital After Tests," Ibid., 7 December 1981, p.B1.

80. Cardoso, et al., *Falklands: Secret Plot*, 19–20 and "Galtieri Meets With Viola," *FBIS-LAT*, 10 December 1981, p.B1.

81. Cardoso, et al., *Falklands: Secret Plot*, 20 and Burns, *Land That Lost Its Heroes*, 29–30. Burns says that only Galtieri and Anaya met.

82. "Military Source Gives Account of Viola's Ouster," *FBIS-LAT*, 16 December 1981, p.B1.

83. "Junta Communiqué," *FBIS-LAT*, 14 December 1981, p.B1.

84. "Galtieri To Replace Viola," *FBIS-LAT*, 11 December 1981, pp.B1–2.

85. Cardoso, et al., *Falklands: Secret Plot*, 25.

86. "Galtieri Takes the Presidency and Retains Control of the Army," *Latin America Weekly Report*, 18 December 1981, 1.

87. Cardoso, et al., *Falklands: Secret Plot*, 3. Perkins, *Operation Paraquat*, 22, observes that: "It is most unlikely that the island of South Georgia came within the orbit of [Anaya's] scheme at that stage or, if it did, that it was of more than peripheral interest."

88. Cardoso, et al., *Falklands: Secret Plot*, 3.

89. Burns, *Land That Lost Its Heroes*, 30.

90. Cardoso, et al., *Falklands: Secret Plot*, 56–57, 32–34, give May 20 as the invasion date. Martin Middlebrook, *The Fight For The Malvinas: The Argentine Forces in the Falklands War* (New York: Viking, 1989), 4–5, gives mid-September as the invasion date. Freedman & Gamba-Stonehouse, *Signals*, 106, give July 9 as the "preferred date."

91. Burns, *Land That Lost Its Heroes*, 41–43 and Cardoso, et al., *Falklands: Secret Plot*, 66.

92. Adm. Harry Train, commander of the U.S. Atlantic Fleet and principal debriefer of Admiral Anaya after the war, insisted that Alpha had indeed been canceled, and that he had seen documents to that effect. Charlton, *Little Platoon*, 118–19.

93. For Viola's "bitterness," see Cardoso, et al., *Falklands: Secret Plot*, 19.

94. Burns, *Land That Lost Its Heroes*, 44.

95. Franks, *Falkland Islands Review*, para. 162.

96. Burns, *Land That Lost Its Heroes*, 44.

97. Perkins, *Operation Paraquat*, 32.

98. Burns, *Land That Lost Its Heroes*, 44.

99. Perkins, *Operation Paraquat*, 32–33.

100. Ibid., 34.

101. Cardoso, et al., *Falklands: Secret Plot*, 64.

102. Franks, *Falkland Islands Review*, para. 165.

CHAPTER 4

1. Perkins, *Operation Paraquat*, 39.

2. Ibid., 43.

3. Franks, *Falkland Islands Review*, para. 166.

4. Perkins, *Operation Paraquat*, 43.

5. Franks, *Falkland Islands Review*, para.166.

6. Burns, *Land That Lost Its Heroes*, 46.

7. Michael Bilton and Peter Kosminsky, *Speaking Out: Untold Stories From the Falklands War* (London: Andre Deutch, 1989), 9.

8. Franks, *Falkland Islands Review*, para.122–23.

9. Ibid., para. 123-24.

10. Ibid., appendix F, the remarks of Mr. Tom McNally.

11. Ibid., para. 129.

12. "CNEA Chairman Discusses Nuclear Capabilities," *FBIS-LAT*, 13 January 1982, p.B2.

13. Ibid., B3.

14. Franks, *Falkland Islands Review*, para. 126–27.

15. Ibid., para. 165 and 117.

16. Cardoso, et al., *Falklands: Secret Plot*, 34.

17. Lawrence Freedman, *Britain and the Falklands War* (Oxford: Basil Blackwell, 1988), 33–34.

18. See David Wood and Bryce Nelson, "Winter May Precipitate British Invasion," *Los Angeles Times*, 11 May 1982, p.1.

19. Adm. Sandy Woodward, *One Hundred Days* (Annapolis: Naval Institute Press, 1991), 92.

20. Sunday Times Insight Team, *The Falklands War*, 67–68.

21. Perkins, *Operation Paraquat*, 226.

22. Ibid., 35.

23. Sunday Times Insight Team, *The Falklands War*, 67. The *Times*' account is the only one to quote Davidoff directly and the only one to state that it was the British who asked him to take supplies for them, not the other way around. All other accounts state that Davidoff volunteered to take supplies. The source of this view is Franks, *Falkland Islands Review*, para. 168:

"[Davidoff] offered to transport supplies to the British Antarctic Survey and to make available to them the services of a doctor and nurse traveling with the party."

24. Perkins, *Operation Paraquat*, 35. There is confusion regarding the captain's identity. British sources refer to a "Captain Briatore," but Argentine naval records list the captain as Oswaldo Miello. "Briatore," who spoke English, may have posed as the captain in dealing with the British. I am grateful to Dr. Cristian Garcia-Godoy for providing this information.

25. Franks, *Falkland Islands Review*, para. 133.

26. Freedman and Gamba-Stonehouse, *Signals*, 26.

27. "Negotiations With UK Over Malvinas May End," *FBIS-LAT*, 3 March 1982, p.B1.

28. Franks, *Falkland Islands Review*, para. 152.

29. Ibid., para. 146, 142.

30. Ibid., para. 147.

31. Sunday Times Insight Team, *The Falklands War*, 76.

32. "Possibility of Nuclear Device Not Dismissed," *FBIS-LAT*, 9 March 1982, p.B1.

33. "No Comment On U.S. Government's Nuclear Warning," *FBIS-LAT*, 10 March 1982, p.B1.

34. Cardoso, et al., *Falklands: Secret Plot*, 50.

35. "Central America Dominates Enders' Meetings," *FBIS-LAT*, 9 March 1982, p.B3.

36. Franks, *Falkland Islands Review*, para.144 (emphasis supplied).

37. Ibid., para. 158. Enders vacillated. To one inquirer, he denied using the term "hands off." See Cardoso, et al., *Falklands: Secret Plot*, 49. To another, he acknowledged using the term, but said he used it only in reference to the "basic dispute," whatever that means. See Charlton, *Little Platoon*, 165.

38. Franks, *Falkland Islands Review*, para. 168.

39. Perkins, *Operation Paraquat*, 226 and 52.

40. Sunday Times Insight Team, *The Falklands War*, 64.

41. Only two accounts discuss the *Cing Gars Pour*, the Sunday Times Insight Team, *The Falklands War* and Roger Perkins, *Operation Paraquat*. Perkins, p.50, states flatly that the yacht arrived at South Georgia on March 14, while the *Times* account, p.64, implies that it was on the March 16. Even though Perkins dismisses the Frenchmen simply as "ocean wanderers in search of adventure" I use the date of March 14 because, had the yacht arrived on the 16th, HMS *Endurance* would have seen and noted its presence. The *Cing Gars Pour* thus must have arrived before HMS *Endurance*.

42. Sunday Times Insight Team, *The Falklands War*, 65.

43. Perkins, *Operation Paraquat*, 45–46.

44. Ibid., 46.

45. Freedman & Gamba-Stonehouse, *Signals*, 48.

46. Perkins, *Operation Paraquat*, 46–48.

47. Cardoso, et al., *Falklands: Secret Plot*, 67. Davidoff claimed later that his group had not raised the flag, asserting that it was already in place when they arrived. His assertion, suggestive as it is, can only be based on hearsay, since he did not accompany the work-party to South Georgia. See "Informe Final de la Comision Rattenbach (Part II), *Siete Dias*, Buenos Aires, Nov.-Dec. 1983, para. 192–214.

48. Perkins, *Operation Paraquat*, 46. Franks, *Falkland Islands Review*, para. 169, says "Briatore" claimed permission had been given by the British embassy in Buenos Aires. See fn. 24.

49. Ibid.

50. Perkins, *Operation Paraquat*, 47–48.

51. Franks, *Falkland Islands Review*, para. 169.

52. Charlton, *Little Platoon*, 185n5. According to Junior Foreign Office Minister Richard Luce, it was Thatcher's decision, not that of the Foreign Office, to "sail *Endurance* for South Georgia."

53. Franks, *Falkland Islands Review*, para. 174.

54. Sunday Times Insight Team, *The Falklands War*, 66.

55. Perkins, *Operation Paraquat*, 50.

56. Sunday Times Insight Team, *The Falklands War*, 66.

57. Other scholars have noted that the landing "seems to have been carried out without the connivance and perhaps even the prior knowledge of the Junta." See Richard Ned Lebow, "Miscalculation in the South Atlantic: The Origins of the Falkland War," *Journal of Strategic Studies* (March 1983):13.

58. Franks, *Falkland Islands Review*, para. 170.

59. Cardoso, et al., *Falklands: Secret Plot*, 68.

60. Burns, *Land That Lost Its Heroes*, 46, says that "the night before the *Bahía Buen Suceso* sailed for South Georgia, [Davidoff's] workforce had been joined by a small contingent of navy personnel, bearing crates filled with military equipment."

61. Franks, *Falkland Islands Review*, para. 171, 175.

62. Freedman and Gamba-Stonehouse, *Signals*, 55.

63. "Argentine Civilians Reportedly Occupy UK Islands," *FBIS-LAT*, 24 March 1982, p.B1.

64. Franks, *Falkland Islands Review*, para. 178.

65. Perkins, *Operation Paraquat*, 50.

66. Sunday Times Insight Team, *The Falklands War*, 69.

67. Perkins, *Operation Paraquat*, 50.

68. Freedman and Gamba-Stonehouse, *Signals*, 55.

69. Franks, *Falkland Islands Review*, para. 176.

70. "Communiqué Issued on S. Georgia Ship Incident," *FBIS-LAT*, 23 March 1982, p.B1.

71. Ibid.

72. Franks, *Falkland Islands Review*, para. 179–80.

73. Cardoso, et al., *Falklands: Secret Plot*, 71. Franks, *Falkland Islands Review*, para. 180 phrases it more gently. London informed Ambassador Williams that *Endurance* was proceeding to South Georgia "to remove the remaining Argentines." He was instructed to tell the Foreign Ministry that "the continued presence of the Argentines, contrary to previous assurances, left no option but to take this action, which was the regrettable result of Sr. Davidoff's own irresponsibility. The intention was to conduct the operation correctly, peacefully and in as low a key as possible."

74. Cardoso, et al., *Falklands: Secret Plot*, 71.

75. Charlton, *Little Platoon*, 118–19. U.S. Adm. Harry Train, who debriefed Admiral Anaya for a classified history of the Falklands War, insisted that Operation Alpha was never executed and that he had "seen the documentary evidence that it was canceled."

76. Ibid., 114.

77. Oriana Fallaci, "Galtieri: No Regrets, No Going Back," *London Times*, 12 June 1982, p.4.

78. Freedman and Gamba-Stonehouse, *Signals*, 64.
79. Ibid.
80. Franks, *Falkland Islands Review*, para. 182.
81. Ibid., para.184.
82. Freedman and Gamba-Stonehouse, *Signals*, 61.
83. Franks, *Falkland Islands Review*, para. 185.
84. Ibid., para. 186.
85. Cardoso, et al., *Falklands: Secret Plot*, 72.
86. Franks, *Falkland Islands Review*, para. 187.
87. Woodward, *One Hundred Days*, 70–71.
88. Burns, *Land That Lost Its Heroes*, 46.
89. Robert Headland, *The Island of South Georgia* (London: Cambridge University Press, 1984), 245. Headland believed that Trombetta had picked up thirty-two men on South Thule Island, as well. Captain Barker also noted that *Bahía Paraiso* "had arrived from Antarctica, not from Argentina." See Franks, *Falkland Islands Review*, para. 201.
90. "Informe Final de la Comision Rattenbach" (Part III), *Siete Dias*, para. 188–93 and Cardoso, et al., *Falklands: Secret Plot*, 64.
91. Freedman and Gamba-Stonehouse, *Signals*, 104.
92. Middlebrook, *Fight For The Malvinas*, 19–20, 24.
93. Oriana Fallaci, "Galtieri: No Regrets, No Going Back," *London Times*, 12 June 1982, 4.
94. Cardoso, et al., *Falklands: Secret Plot*, 56–57.
95. Ibid., 75.
96. Nora Kinzer Stewart, *Mates and Muchachos: Unit Cohesion in the Falklands/Malvinas War* (London: Brassey's, 1991), 45.
97. Drew Middleton, "Wanted: More Arms. Argentines Almost Frantically Search For the Weapons to Match Britain's," *New York Times*, 10 May 1982, p.A9.
98. Perkins, *Operation Paraquat*, 52.
99. Ibid., 53.
100. Ibid. Franks, *Falkland Islands Review*, para. 208, minimizes Mitchell's contribution to warning, while Freedman & Gamba-Stonehouse, *Signals*, 85, omit him entirely and argue unconvincingly that "there was little capacity for monitoring military movements within Argentina."
101. Franks, *Falkland Islands Review*, para.190–91.
102. Sunday Times Insight Team, *The Falklands War*, 68.
103. Ibid.
104. Franks, *Falkland Islands Review*, para. 193.
105. Sunday Times Insight Team, *The Falklands War*, 68.
106. Perkins, *Operation Paraquat*, 54.
107. Ibid., 55. Franks, *Falkland Islands Review*, para. 193, notes that on March 25 HMS *Endurance* "reported that a second Argentine ship, the *Bahía Paraiso*, had arrived at Leith and was working cargo."
108. Ibid., para. 197.
109. Ibid., para. 198. See, for example, John Miller, " 'Cut' Ship Sails to Oust Intruders," *The Daily*

Telegraph, 24 March 1982, p.1. The HMS *Endurance,* "sailing at full speed" to South Georgia, was "poised to eject a handful of Argentine scrap merchants who were refusing to leave."

110. Franks, *Falkland Islands Review,* para. 198.

111. Ibid.

112. Ibid., para. 203.

113. "Official" Argentine sources would note a few days later that the *Bahía Paraiso* had "200 marines aboard." See the *Buenos Aires Herald,* 29 March 1982, 1, in *FBIS-LAT,* 30 March 1982, p.B2.

114. Freedman and Gamba-Stonehouse, *Signals,* 72–73, assert British ignorance of the true situation at Leith in order to make the case for British surprise regarding the outbreak of the war. Thus, Britain had only "limited intelligence on what was actually going on at Leith." Then, "London's ignorance helps explain why there is no record in the Franks Report of ministers being apprised of the correct number of workers left by the *Bahía Buen Suceso,* and why the significance of the visit by the *Bahía Paraiso* was still not appreciated." Thus, "on 26 March it was still assumed that there was no Argentine military capability on the island."

115. See "Further Reportage on South Georgia Islands Conflict," 1411 GMT, 26 March, in *FBIS-LAT,* 29 March 1982, p.B1.

116. Perkins, *Operation Paraquat,* 53–54.

117. See Gerald W. Hopple, "Intelligence and Warning: Implications and Lessons of the Falkland Islands War," *World Politics* (April 1984), 352.

118. Derrick Mercer, Geoff Mungham, and Kevin Williams, *The Fog of War* (London: Heineman, 1987), 199.

119. Charlton, *Little Platoon,* 116. The reference to the broadcast contains an obvious misprint, saying March 17, but meaning March 25.

120. Ibid. See also Anaya's account in "La Crisis Argentino-Britanica en 1982," *La Nueva Provincia,* Bahia Blanca, 8 September 1988. Freedman & Gamba-Stonehouse, *Signals,* 74, argue that "when Argentine participants cite intelligence received on 25 March as critical to the decision to invade, it must be assumed that it was...two unarmed vessels [HMS *Bransfield* and HMS *John Brown* both en route to the Falklands] to which they refer." Thus, they conclude, the junta misperceived the nature of the British response.

121. Ibid., 75.

122. Charlton, *Little Platoon,* 116n.

123. Franks, *Falkland Islands Review,* para. 331.

124. Freedman and Gamba-Stonehouse, *Signals,* 77.

125. "Four Nuclear Subs Will Spearhead British flotilla," *New York Times,* 9 April 1982, p.8. R.W. Apple, "Britain Imposing A War Zone Around Falkland Islands," *New York Times,* 8 April 1982, p.1. Apple also cited the same "military sources" that HMS *Superb* had already "arrived off the Falklands, and several of her sister ships are believed to be on the way."

126. "America's Falklands War," *Economist,* 3 March 1984, p.30.

127. As Freedman & Gamba-Stonehouse, *Signals,* 78, observe: "Having persuaded itself that it was about to be pre-empted by Britain the Junta needed to act quickly."

128. Max Hastings and Simon Jenkins, *The Battle For The Falklands* (New York: Norton & Co., 1983), 61.

129. Franks, *Falkland Islands Review,* para. 230 (emphasis supplied).

130. Thatcher, *Downing Street Years*, 178.

131. Arthur Gavshon and Desmond Rice, *The Sinking of the Belgrano* (London: Secker and Warburg, 1984), 27.

CHAPTER 5

1. Two years after the conflict, the British side revealed the extent and timing of American support for Britain in the war. See "America's Falklands War," *Economist*, 3 March 1984, pp.29–32 (American edition).

2. For the forging of the compromise, as well as Kissinger's unsuccessful bid to create a Reagan-Ford "co-presidency," see Theodore H. White, *America In Search of Itself: The Making of the President, 1956–1980* (New York: Harper & Row, 1982), 320–26 and Joseph E. Persico, *Casey: From the OSS to the CIA,* (New York: Viking, 1990), 186ff.

3. "Excerpts From Haig's Speech on Relations Between U.S. and Soviet Union," *New York Times*, 12 August 1981, p.4.

4. Lawrence Barrett, *Gambling With History: Reagan in the White House* (London: Penguin Books, 1983), 236.

5. Haig, *Caveat: Realism, Reagan, and Foreign Policy* (New York: Macmillan, 1984), 271.

6. Ronald Reagan, *An American Life* (New York: Simon & Schuster, 1990), 358–59.

7. Cardoso, et al., *Falklands: Secret Plot*, 145.

8. Young, *Iron Lady*, 266.

9. Thatcher, *Downing Street Years*, 130–31.

10. Ibid., 187.

11. *The Falklands War*, 169.

12. Hastings and Jenkins, *Battle for the Falklands*, 138.

13. Reagan, *An American Life*, 358.

14. "America's Falklands War," *Economist*, 3 March 1984, p.29.

15. Ibid. Freedman and Gamba-Stonehouse, *Signals*, 190, assert that "the decision to support Britain was largely taken by Weinberger himself."

16. Haig, *Caveat*, p.261 and Franks, *Falkland Islands Review*, para. 203, 211.

17. Thatcher, *Downing Street Years*, 178–79. The phrase "out of the blue" was that of *Daily Express* columnist George Cale, who asked the prime minister the question regarding advance warning, on March 31. She maintained this position when asked again three months later in the House of Commons. See Gavshon & Rice, *Sinking of the Belgrano*, 26–27.

18. Franks, *Falkland Islands Review*, para. 187.

19. Cardoso, et al., *Falklands: Secret Plot*, 92. British Ambassador Anthony Parsons, "The Falklands Crisis in the United Nations, 31 March–14 June 1982," *International Affairs* (Spring 1983): 169, says that Roca "called on" Kirkpatrick. Freedman & Gamba-Stonehouse, *Signals*, 134, say simply that the two "met."

20. Cardoso, et al., *Falklands: Secret Plot*, 93.

21. Freedman and Gamba-Stonehouse, *Signals*, 135.

22. Cardoso, et al., *Falklands: Secret Plot*, 91, 107–9.

23. Ibid., p.93 and Parsons, "The Falklands Crisis in the United Nations," p.170.

24. Ibid.

25. Charlton, *Little Platoon*, 200.

26. Cardoso, et al., *Falklands: Secret Plot*, 89. On the morning of April 1, Kirkpatrick had called Argentine Ambassador Takacs to tell him that "no doubts remained about the imminence of an Argentine operation on the archipelago."

27. Parsons, "The Falklands Crisis in the United Nations," 170.

28. Thatcher, *Downing Street Years*, 182.

29. Parsons, "The Falklands Crisis in the United Nations," 170.

30. Freedman and Gamba-Stonehouse, *Signals*, 135.

31. Franks, *Falkland Islands Review*, para. 233, 235.

32. Thatcher, *Downing Street Years*, 179.

33. Haig, *Caveat*, 263.

34. Cardoso, et al., *Falklands: Secret Plot*, 81–82, Franks, *Falkland Islands Review*, para. 248, Freedman & Gamba-Stonehouse, *Signals*, 96.

35. Cardoso, et al., *Falklands: Secret Plot*, 82.

36. Haig, *Caveat*, 264.

37. Cardoso, et al., *Falklands: Secret Plot*, 81. Freedman & Gamba-Stonehouse, *Signals*, 97, explain Reagan's tardiness in placing the call to Galtieri by arguing that he was delayed because of a "medical checkup" and asserting, without evidence, that intelligence regarding the six o'clock deadline "had not reached Washington." Given the fact of extremely close intelligence cooperation between the United States and Great Britain, which includes the presence of a CIA representative at the meetings of the Joint Intelligence Committee, it is improbable that intelligence regarding Argentina failed to reach Washington in a timely manner. See Geoffrey Smith, *Reagan and* Thatcher, p.84.

38. For a reasonably comprehensive paraphrase of their conversation, see Bernard Gwertzman, "Reagan, in a Phone Call, Tried to Deter Invasion," *New York Times*, 3 April 1982, p.6.

39. Cardoso, et al., *Falklands: Secret Plot*, 82–86, contains a transcript of the conversation. Haig, *Caveat*, 264–65, offers a paraphrase of the conversation that differs in important respects. For example, Haig's claim that Reagan directly asked Galtieri whether or not he intended to use force is not found in the Cardoso account.

40. Haig, *Caveat*, 264, declares that Galtieri "declined both the good offices and the Vice-President."

41. Cardoso, et al., *Falklands: Secret Plot*, 85.

42. In view of the Iran hostage crisis, concluded just as Reagan was entering office, one wonders whether Great Britain would have responded with force had Argentina threatened to hold the islanders hostage.

43. Cardoso, et al., *Falklands: Secret Plot*, 86. Here, once again, and contrary to Haig, *Caveat*, 264, far from declining Washington's good offices, Galtieri expressly requested direct American involvement "as a friend."

44. For the actual battle plan, see Middlebrook, *Fight For The Malvinas*, 19–20, 24. For a contemporary report reflecting British military intelligence estimates, see Drew Middleton, "Falklands Conflict May Test the New Royal Navy," *New York Times*, 3 April 1982, p.6. Middleton says forty-five hundred. Freedman & Gamba-Stonehouse, *Signals*, 116, say twenty-eight hundred. Reagan, *An American Life*, p.358, comes closest, saying "about one thousand." Haig, *Caveat*, 265, in what may be a typographical error, says only 300.

45. Middlebrook, *Fight For The* Malvinas, 41. See also Freedman & Gamba-Stonehouse, *Signals*, 116–17.

46. Sunday Times Insight Team, *The Falklands War*, 119–22.

47. Cardoso, et al., *Falklands: Secret Plot*, 102.

48. Parsons, "The Falklands Crisis in the United Nations," p.170.

49. Hastings and Jenkins, *Battle for the Falklands*, 100.

50. Parsons, "The Falklands Crisis in the United Nations," p.170. The "pressure" Parsons referred to came from Panama. Cardoso, et al., *Falklands: Secret Plot*, 107, suggests that the postponement was rather more difficult to achieve than Parsons says, noting that it "required much effort" by the Argentine mission.

51. Cardoso, et al., *Falklands: Secret Plot*, 107.

52. Michael Bilton and Peter Kosminsky, *Speaking Out: Untold Stories From the Falklands War* (London: Andre Deutsch, 1989), 27–28.

53. The list included: Assistant Secretary of State Thomas Enders, number two at the Department of State, Walter Stoessel, Assistant Secretary of Defense, Frank Carlucci, army chief Gen. Edward Meyer, OAS Ambassador William Middendorf, and Vernon Walters.

54. Cardoso, et al., *Falklands: Secret Plot*, 100.

55. Ibid., 107.

56. Hastings and Jenkins, *Battle for the Falklands*, 100.

57. Thatcher, *Downing Street Years*, 183.

58. Cardoso, et al., *Falklands: Secret Plot*, 111.

59. Ibid., 113.

60. Hastings and Jenkins, *Battle for the Falklands*, 77 and Freedman & Gamba-Stonehouse, *Signals*, 124.

61. Hastings and Jenkins, *Battle for the Falklands*, 81–82.

62. Thatcher, *Downing Street Years*, 183.

63. Ibid., 183–84.

64. Haig, *Caveat*, 270–71.

65. "America's Falklands War," *Economist*, 3 March 1984, p.29. President Reagan, *An American Life*, 359, asserts for obvious diplomatic reasons that the United States "provided no…military assistance to the British" before May except for use of a military satellite under an arrangement made "long before" the crisis.

66. Howell Raines, "Reagan Order Tightens the Rules On Disclosing Secret Information," *New York Times*, 3 April 1982, p.1.

67. John Lehman, *Command of the Seas* (New York: Macmillan, 1988), 274–75.

68. "America's Falklands War," 29. Lehman, *Command of the Seas*, 274–75, makes the same point. The extent of secrecy was not only to deceive the junta, but also "because of the deep divisions within the administration…." According to Lehman, "it is highly unlikely that Jean Kirkpatrick or anyone at the State Department or the White House understood…the extent of the assistance we were providing."

69. "America's Falklands War," 29.

70. John Goshko, "Reagan Willing to Help Find 'Peaceful Resolution,'" *Washington Post*, 6 April 1982, p.1.

71. Haig, *Caveat*, 271.

72. As quoted in Freedman & Gamba-Stonehouse, *Signals*, 161.

73. Haig, *Caveat*, 271.

74. John Goshko, "Reagan Sending Haig To Britain, Argentina," *Washington Post*, 8 April 1982, p.1.

75. John Goshko, "Haig Takes Up Role Of Crisis Mediator," *Washington Post*, 7 April 1982, p.16.

76. Freedman and Gamba-Stonehouse, *Signals*, 160–61.

77. Sunday Times Insight Team, *The Falklands War*, 129.

78. Humphrey Atkins, Carrington's deputy, and Richard Luce, the junior foreign office minister for the Falkland Islands, also resigned.

79. R.W. Apple, "Carrington Quits In Falkland Crisis: British Ships Sail," *New York Times*, 6 April 1982, p.1.

80. Ibid.

81. Hastings and Jenkins, *Battle for the Falklands*, 80.

82. Thatcher, *Downing Street Years*, 208.

83. Casper Weinberger, *Fighting For Peace: Seven Critical Years in the Pentagon* (New York: Warner Books, 1990), 205.

84. John Goshko, "Reagan Willing to Help Find 'Peaceful Resolution,' " *Washington Post*, 6 April 1982, p.1.

85. "Transcript of Session on Foreign and U.S. Matters," *New York Times*, 6 April 1982, p.8.

86. Ibid.

87. John Goshko, "Reagan Willing to Help Find 'Peaceful Resolution,' " *Washington Post*, 6 April 1982, p.1.

88. Cardoso, et al., *Falklands: Secret Plot*, 128. Haig, *Caveat*, 271, omits specific mention of an interim administration.

89. Henderson, "America and the Falklands," 32.

90. Haig, *Caveat*, 272.

91. Leslie Gelb, "Britain Pressing U.S. On Falklands," *New York Times*, 8 April 1982, p.10.

92. R.W. Apple, "The Falklands Crisis," *New York Times*, 7 April 1982, p.1.

93. R.W. Apple, "Britain Imposing A War Zone Around Falkland Islands," *New York Times*, 8 April 1982, p.1. Hastings & Jenkins, *Battle for the Falklands*, 105, say that the HMS *Superb* did not arrive until the twelfth.

94. John Goshko, "Reagan Sending Haig To Britain, Argentina," *Washington Post*, 8 April 1982, p.1.

95. Ibid. Haig, *Caveat*, 272–73, omits his discussion with Pym, mentioning only his talks with Thatcher and the working dinner that followed.

96. Thatcher, *Downing Street Years*, 191–92.

97. Ibid., 192.

98. Haig, *Caveat*, 273.

99. Thatcher, *Downing Street Years*, 193.

100. Haig, *Caveat*, 273–74.

101. Cardoso, et al., *Falklands: Secret Plot*, 138.

102. Russel Warren Howe, "The Military Side of the Falklands Crisis," *Baltimore Sun*, 11 April 1982, p.K2. All early reports mentioned only three thousand troops.

103. R.W. Apple, "Britain Imposing A War Zone Around Falkland Islands," *New York Times*, 8 April 1982, p.1.

104. Edward Schumacher, "Argentine Asserts War Threat Fades," *New York Times*, 9 April 1982, p.1.

105. "Argentina to Keep Islands 'At Any Cost,' " *Baltimore Sun*, 7 April 1982, p.2.

106. Haig, *Caveat*, 276.

107. Cardoso, et al., *Falklands: Secret Plot*, 142.

108. Ibid., 143.

109. Haig, *Caveat*, 278.

110. Cardoso, et al., *Falklands: Secret Plot*, 148.

111. Ibid., 149.

112. Haig, *Caveat*, 280.

113. Charlton, *Little Platoon*, 173.

114. Haig, *Caveat*, 281.

115. Cardoso, et al., *Falklands: Secret Plot*, 154.

116. Ibid., 154–56.

117. Haig, *Caveat*, 282.

118. Gavshon and Rice, *Sinking of the* Belgrano, 61.

119. Freedman and Gamba-Stonehouse, *Signals*, 178.

120. Ibid., 180. The authors claim to the contrary that "none of the Argentines involved in the discussions knew of [a different] draft's existence or its contents." But they clearly suspected something was peculiar and attempted to constrain Haig with Costa Mendez's "paper."

121. Haig, *Caveat*, 282.

122. Ibid., 283.

123. Thatcher, *Downing Street Years*, 194–95.

124. Ibid., 195.

125. Ibid., 196.

126. Edward Schumacher, "Argentines Taking A Pessimistic View on Falkland Crisis," *New York Times*, 12 April 1982, p.1.

127. Haig, *Caveat*, 283.

128. Thatcher, *Downing Street Years*, 197.

129. Ibid.

130. Ibid., 197–98.

131. Haig, *Caveat*, 283.

132. Ibid.

CHAPTER 6

1. Thatcher, *Downing Street Years*, 218, states it plainly. A landing "would have to be done some time between 16 and 30 May. We could not leave it later because of the weather."

2. Ibid., 197–98.

3. Ibid.

4. Haig, *Caveat*, 284.

5. Ibid.

6. Cardoso, et al., *Falklands: Secret Plot*, 184.

7. Haig, *Caveat*, 285.

8. Cardoso, et al., *Falklands: Secret Plot*, 184.

9. Haig, *Caveat*, 285.

10. Thatcher, *Downing Street Years*, 198 (emphasis supplied).

11. Leonard Downie, "Haig Breaks Trip To Consult Reagan After Talks Falter," *Washington Post*, 14 April 1982, p.1.

12. Michael Getler, "U.S. Aiding British Fleet In Atlantic," *Washington Post*, 14 April 1982, p.1.

13. Haig, *Caveat*, 285.

14. Thatcher, *Downing Street Years*, 200.

15. Ibid. See also "Haig Statement on Falklands," *New York Times*, 15 April 1982, p.12.

16. John Goshko and Michael Getler, "Haig Is Returning To Buenos Aires With 'New Ideas,' " *Washington Post*, 15 April 1982, p.1.

17. Hedrick Smith, "A Fresh Storm Swirls Around Haig," *New York Times*, 15 April 1982, p. B14.

18. "Transcript of the News Conference Held by Reagan at the White House," *New York Times*, 15 April 1982, p. D20.

19. Goshko and Getler, "Haig Is Returning to Buenos Aires with 'New Ideas.' "

20. Richard Halloran, "U.S. Providing British a Wide Range of Intelligence," *New York Times*, 15 April 1982, p.11.

21. Cardoso, et al., *Falklands: Secret Plot*, 166, includes a transcript of their conversation.

22. Ibid. See also Hedrick Smith, "President Talks With Argentine; Urges Restraint," *New York Times*, 16 April 1982, p.1.

23. See "Jaw-jaw Continues as War-war Approaches," *Economist*, 24 April 1982, p.24.

24. Cardoso, et al., *Falklands: Secret Plot*, 168.

25. Haig, *Caveat*, 286. Haig presents only a truncated version of his proposal that omits all reference to decision by majority rule, an expansion of the Argentine role in the islands, or to decolonization.

26. Cardoso, et al., *Falklands: Secret Plot*, 169–70.

27. Ibid.

28. Ibid., 170.

29. Ibid., 171–72. The acronym MID stands for the "Integration and Development Movement."

30. Freedman and Gamba-Stonehouse, *Signals*, 198, also see Haig's proposal as "a trap."

31. Cardoso et al., *Falklands: Secret Plot*, 173.

32. Haig, *Caveat*, 286.

33. Henderson, "America and the Falklands," *Economist*, 13 November 1983, p.32, referring to Haig's second trip to Buenos Aires, makes the same point: "The Argentines may well have been spinning out negotiations to gain time in the belief that: (a) The longer the de facto occupation, the readier would international opinion become to accept a fait accompli: and (b) With the advance of winter, the problems attendant upon an 8,000-mile supply line, and the threats posed by Argentine submarines and air forces, the British would increasingly doubt the feasibility of a landing and prolonged military presence in the South Atlantic."

34. Haig, *Caveat*, 287.
35. Drew Middleton, "Britain Strengthens Its Naval Force With More Planes," *New York Times*, 15 April 1982, p.14.
36. Freedman and Gamba-Stonehouse, *Signals*, 201 and Charlton, *Little Platoon*, 166.
37. Haig, *Caveat*, 288.
38. Freedman and Gamba-Stonehouse, *Signals*, 202.
39. Haig, *Caveat*, 288.
40. Thatcher, *Downing Street Years*, 202.
41. Haig, *Caveat*, 289.
42. Gavshon and Rice, *Sinking of the* Belgrano, 187, citing the text of the April 19 proposal. Freedman & Gamba-Stonehouse, *Signals*, 210, say the councils would be "widened to include an equal number of Argentine representatives from among the local population." Cardoso, et al., *Falklands: Secret Plot*, 178, says the councils would be "broadened to include Argentines, but with a reduced participation…in respect to the original demand."
43. Freedman and Gamba-Stonehouse, *Signals*, 209.
44. Ibid., 210.
45. Haig, *Caveat*, 289.
46. Cardoso, et al., *Falklands: Secret Plot*, 178–79.
47. Freedman and Gamba-Stonehouse, *Signals*, 211.
48. Ibid.
49. Cardoso, et al., *Falklands: Secret Plot*, 179. See also Gavshon & Rice, *Sinking of the* Belgrano, appendix 2, 186–88, for the complete text of the Argentine proposal of April 19.
50. Freedman and Gamba-Stonehouse, *Signals*, 212.
51. Cardoso, et al., *Falklands: Secret Plot*, 179.
52. Ibid., 180.
53. Haig, *Caveat*, 289.
54. Freedman and Gamba-Stonehouse, *Signals*, 214.
55. Haig, *Caveat*, 289–90.
56. Ibid., 290.
57. Gavshon and Rice, *Sinking of the* Belgrano, 186–88.
58. Freedman and Gamba-Stonehouse, *Signals*, 214. See also, Sir Robin Renwick, *Fighting With Allies* (New York: Times Books, 1996), 335.
59. Edward Schumacher, "Haig Ends Talks With Argentines On A Somber Note," *New York Times*, 20 April 1982, p.1.
60. Jackson Diehl, "Argentina Announces Plan to Invoke Rio Pact Against Britain," *Washington Post*, 20 April 1982, p.1.
61. Thatcher, *Downing Street Years*, 203–4.
62. Hastings and Jenkins, *Battle for the Falklands*, 141, say that there is "no evidence" that the "war cabinet was deliberately orchestrating" military escalation at "key moments" in the negotiations, but it stretches the imagination to believe there was no connection. After all, the very purpose of the task force was to exert leverage on the negotiations.
63. R.W. Apple, "Britain Draws Up 3-Step Peace Plan On the Falklands," *New York Times*, 22 April 1982, p.1.

64. Thatcher, *Downing Street Years*, 204.

65. The R.W. Apple article of April 22 explicitly notes that restoration of the British administration to the islands "would inevitably result in the hauling down of the Argentine flag." Hastings & Jenkins, *Battle for the Falklands*, 138, however, say that one of the concessions Pym took with him to Washington was that "other flags might fly beside the British during the interim period."

66. Thatcher, *Downing Street Years*, 204.

67. Freedman and Gamba-Stonehouse, *Signals*, 220.

68. The *Santa Fe* was originally commissioned as the U.S.S. *Catfish* in 1945 and sold to Argentina in 1971. Thatcher said that the *Santa Fe* had dropped off "up to fifty military reinforcements." See "Transcript of Statement By Mrs. Thatcher," *New York Times*, 27 April 1982, p.12. Middlebrook, *Fight For The Malvinas*, 72, says about forty men disembarked.

69. Thatcher, *Downing Street Years*, 205.

70. Ibid., 205–6.

71. Ibid.

72. See Bernard Gwertzman, "Briton and Haig In 'Useful Start' To Negotiations," *New York Times*, 23 April 1982, p.1.

73. R.W. Apple, "Britain Draws Up 3-Step Peace Plan On The Falklands," *New York Times*, 22 April 1982, p.1. Thatcher herself, before Parliament on April 26 and during a television interview on the same date, set forth this position. See Leonard Downie, "Thatcher Hints at Possible New Military Move," *Washington Post*, 27 April 1982, p.1.

74. Thatcher, *Downing Street Years*, 207.

75. R.W. Apple, "Britain Draws Up 3-Step Peace Plan…"

76. Thatcher, *Downing Street Years*, 207.

77. Ibid., 208.

78. Ibid., 207–8.

79. "Transcript of Statement by Mrs. Thatcher," *New York Times*, 27 April 1982, p.12.

80. Haig, *Caveat*, 291.

81. John Goshko, "Haig, at OAS, Urges Calm," *Washington Post*, 27 April 1982, p.1.

82. Ibid.

83. Haig, *Caveat*, 291–92.

84. Cardoso, et al., *Falklands: Secret Plot*, 202.

85. John Goshko and Michael Getler, "U.S. Tries Again To Revive Talks," *Washington Post*, 29 April 1982, p.1. See also Bernard Gwertzman, "U.S. Calls on Both Sides to Accept Haig's Plan to Avert a Major War," *New York Times*, 29 April 1982, p.1.

86. Thatcher, *Downing Street Years*, 209.

87. Leonard Downie, "Thatcher Hints at Possible New Military Move," *Washington Post*, 27 April 1982, p.1.

88. Ibid.

89. Gavshon and Rice, *Sinking of the* Belgrano, 189–92, for the complete text of Haig's proposal.

90. Downie, "Thatcher Hints at Possible New Military Move…"

91. Hastings & Jenkins, *Battle for the Falklands*, 140. See also Freedman and Gamba-Stonehouse, *Signals*, 228.

92. Bernard Gwertzman, "U.S. Calls on Both Sides to Accept Haig's Plan to Avert a Major War," *New York Times*, 29 April 1982, p.1.

93. Cardoso, et al., *Falklands: Secret Plot*, 207–8. See also Freedman and Gamba-Stonehouse, *Signals*, 235–37.

94. Haig, *Caveat*, 292.

95. Ibid.

96. Gavshon and Rice, *Sinking of the* Belgrano, 69–70.

97. Thatcher, *Downing Street Years*, 211.

98. Cardoso, et al., *Falklands: Secret Plot*, 210.

99. Gavshon and Rice, *Sinking of the* Belgrano, 193.

100. Ibid., 71. The authors interpret the note as being "ingratiatingly mild," and an attempt "not to shut any doors decisively."

101. Jackson Diehl, Argentina Threatens British Ships, Planes Around Falklands," *Washington Post*, 30 April 1982, p.1.

102. John Goshko, "U.S. Concedes Optimism Fades," *Washington Post*, 30 April 1982, p.1.

103. Thatcher, *Downing Street Years*, 211.

104. Bernard Gwertzman, "U.S. Says Haig Effort Seems to Fail And Falklands Fighting Is Likely," *New York Times*, 30 April 1982, p.1.

105. "America's Falklands War," *Economist*, 3 March 1984, p.30.

106. "Transcript of Remarks By Haig on Falklands," *New York Times*, 1 May 1982, p.1.

107. Bernard Gwertzman, "President Offers London 'Materiel Support' and Bars Aid to Junta," *New York Times*, 1 May 1982, p.1.

108. Ibid.

109. Thatcher, *Downing Street Years*, 213.

CHAPTER 7

1. Hastings and Jenkins, *Battle For the Falklands*, 141.

2. Maj. Gen. Sir Jeremy Moore and Rear Adm. Sir John Woodward, "The Falklands Experience," *Journal of the Royal United Services Institute for Defence Studies* (March 1983), 28.

3. Cardoso, et al., *Falklands: Secret Plot*, 230.

4. Robert Scheina, "The Malvinas Campaign," *Proceedings of the U.S. Naval Institute* (March 1983): 105. (emphasis supplied)

5. Freedman & Gamba-Stonehouse, *Signals*, 252.

6. Ibid., 261.

7. Ibid., 253.

8. Thatcher, *Downing Street Years*, 212.

9. Peter Greig, "Revelations," *Granta* (Spring 1985): 257–58.

10. Hastings & Jenkins, *Battle for the Falklands*, 143–44.

11. Charles Corddry, "Raid Was Britain's First Major Step To Isolate Argentine Forces On Isles," *Baltimore Sun*, 2 May 1982, p.1.

12. Robert L. Scheina, "The Malvinas Campaign," *Proceedings of the U.S. Naval Institute* (March 1983): 105.

13. Charlton, *Little Platoon*, 211.

14. Henderson, "America and the Falklands," *Economist*, 12 November 1983, p.33.

15. Cardoso, et al., *Falklands: Secret Plot*, 231.

16. Freedman and Gamba-Stonehouse, *Signals*, 258.

17. Middlebrook, *Fight for the Malvinas*, 84–89.

18. Ibid. Middlebrook claims the attack was by three Daggers. Hastings & Jenkins, *Battle for the Falklands*, 145, claim it was by four Mirages.

19. Cardoso, et al., *Falklands: Secret Plot*, 232.

20. David Brown, *The Royal Navy and the Falklands War* (London: Leo Cooper, 1987), 130–31. See also Freedman & Gamba-Stonehouse, *Signals*, 264.

21. Cardoso, et al., *Falklands: Secret Plot*, 232.

22. Ibid., 233. Freedman & Gamba-Stonehouse, *Signals*, 259, offer a slightly different version. "There have been no further air attacks on the Malvinas after 011900. I do not know the position of the enemy aircraft carriers. The free-ranging enemy still constitutes a strong threat to task force 79."

23. Freedman and Gamba-Stonehouse, *Signals*, 260.

24. Cardoso, et al., *Falklands: Secret Plot*, 233.

25. Freedman and Gamba-Stonehouse, *Signals*, 260.

26. Henderson, "America and the Falklands," 36.

27. Cardoso, et al., *Falklands: Secret Plot*, 218.

28. Henderson, "America and the Falklands," 34.

29. Cardoso, et al., *Falklands: Secret Plot*, 247, 218.

30. Freedman and Gamba-Stonehouse, *Signals*, 273.

31. Gavshon and Rice, *Sinking of the* Belgrano, xiv.

32. Charlton, *Little Platoon*, 174.

33. Henderson, "America and the Falklands," 35, insisted that there was no proposal, only "ideas."

34. Thatcher, *Downing Street Years*, 213-14.

35. Charlton, *Little Platoon*, 175. Enders, following the lead of the interviewer, who said that May 1 was Sunday, refers to May 1 as Sunday, when it was actually Saturday.

36. Bernard Gwertzman, "Briton, in Washington Talks, Is Told What Kind of Aid U.S. Will Provide," *New York Times*, 3 May 1982, p. 12. Freedman & Gamba-Stonehouse, *Signals*, 272, contradict the press account and say that "Pym's first meeting was with Secretary of Defense Weinberger" that evening of May 1.

37. Haig, *Caveat*, 293.

38. See Freedman and Gamba-Stonehouse, *Signals*, 443n.6.

39. Gavshon & Rice, *Sinking of the* Belgrano, 82.

40. Ibid., 83.

41. Cardoso, et al., *Falklands: Secret Plot*, 220.

42. David Wood and Robert C. Toth, "British Get Edge From U.S. Electronics, Pentagon Says," *Los Angeles Times*, 4 May 1982, p.1.

43. Gavshon and Rice, *Sinking of the* Belgrano, 205n5.

44. Charles Corddry, "Sinking of Argentine Cruiser Part of British Readiness for Long War," *Baltimore Sun*, 4 May 1982, p.5.

45. Freedman and Gamba-Stonehouse, *Signals*, 131.

46. Maj. Gen. Sir Jeremy Moore and Rear Adm. Sir John Woodward, "The Falklands Experience," *Journal of the Royal United Services Institute for Defence Studies* (March 1983):28.

47. Freedman and Gamba-Stonehouse, *Signals*, 261.

48. Gavshon and Rice, *Sinking of the* Belgrano, 81, says the Harrier had "overflown" the carrier. Freedman and Gamba-Stonehouse, *Signals*, 259, 264., say the Harriers circled at a distance of sixty to seventy miles.

49. Gavshon and Rice, *Sinking of the* Belgrano, 99.

50. See Freedman and Gamba-Stonehouse, *Signals*, 268, who say that the course change "does not appear to have been assessed as significant at the time."

51. Gavshon and Rice, *Sinking of the* Belgrano, 112.

52. Freedman and Gamba-Stonehouse, *Signals*, 266.

53. Ibid., 267.

54. Thatcher, *Downing Street Years*, 215. See also Tam Dalyell, *Thatcher's Torpedo* (London: Cecil Wolf, 1983).

55. Henderson, "America and the Falklands," 35.

56. Ibid., 35.

57. Henderson was completely unaware of Pym's intentions, believing that he had come to Washington simply to "assuage parliamentarians who…were calling upon him to be more active diplomatically." See his *Mandarin: Diaries of an Ambassador, 1969–1982* (London: Weidenfeld & Nicolson, 1994), 456.

58. Gavshon and Rice, *Sinking of the* Belgrano, 90–92.

59. Ibid., 93–94.

60. Freedman and Gamba-Stonehouse, *Signals*, 268.

61. Cardoso, et al., *Falklands: Secret Plot*, 235.

62. Walter Mossberg and Frederick Kempe, "Argentina Says Cruiser Hit by British Sank in Icy Waters; 500 Are Feared Lost," *Wall Street Journal*, 4 May 1982, p.4.

63. Gavshon and Rice, *Sinking of the* Belgrano, 119.

64. Ibid., 115.

65. Henderson, "America and the Falklands," 35.

66. Gwertzman, "Briton, in Washington Talks, Is Told What Kind of Aid U.S. Will Provide," *New York Times*, 3 May 1982, p.12.

67. Henry Trewhitt, "Increased British Aid Promised By U.S.," *Baltimore Sun*, 3 May 1982, p.1.

68. See Charlton, *Little Platoon*, 207–8. Pym's explanation for not taking Haig's call was that the two men had already "talked over the whole thing."

69. Henderson, "America and the Falklands," 35.

70. Gavshon and Rice, *Sinking of the* Belgrano, 120.

71. Freedman and Gamba-Stonehouse, *Signals*, 284.

72. Cardoso, et al., *Falklands: Secret Plot*, 249.

73. Thatcher, *Downing Street Years*, 216.

74. Anthony Parsons, "The Falklands Crisis in the United Nations, 31 March–14 June 1982," *International Affairs* (Spring 1983): 173.

75. Cardoso, et al., *Falklands: Secret Plot*, 251–52.

76. Thatcher, *Downing Street Years*, 216. See also, Parsons, "The Falklands Crisis in the United Nations," 173.

77. Gavshon and Rice, *Sinking of the* Belgrano, 118.

78. Henderson, "America and the Falklands," 35.

79. Freedman and Gamba-Stonehouse, *Signals*, 288.

80. Henderson, "America and the Falklands," 36.

81. Thatcher, *Downing Street Years*, 217.

82. Charles Corddry, "Sinking of Argentine Cruiser Part of British Readiness for Long War," *Baltimore Sun*, 4 May 1982, p.5 and William Borders, "QE2 Is Taken As Troopship By the British," *New York Times*, 4 May 1982, p.20.

83. Michael Getler, "British Expected to Land Troops Soon," *Washington Post*, 4 May 1982, p.15.

84. Frank Greve, "Britain Capable of Long Fight," *Philadelphia Inquirer*, 4 May 1982, p.8.

85. Walter Mossberg and Frederick Kempe, "Argentina Says Cruiser Hit by British Sank in Icy Waters; 500 Are Feared Lost," *Wall Street Journal*, 4 May 1982, p.4.

86. Cardoso, et al., *Falklands: Secret Plot*, 283.

87. Hastings and Jenkins, *Battle for the Falklands*, 152 and Eric J. Grove, *Vanguard To Trident: British Naval Policy Since World War Two* (Annapolis: Naval Institute Press, 1987), 368.

88. Scheina, "The Malvinas Campaign," 107, 112.

89. Hastings and Jenkins, *Battle for the Falklands*, 153, says six miles. Freedman & Gamba-Stonehouse, *Signals*, 289, say twelve miles.

90. Middlebrook, *Fight for the Malvinas*, 123. The Sunday Times Insight Team account, *Falklands War*, 166, says that two targets were sighted and that each pilot fired at a different target. Gavshon & Rice, *Sinking of the* Belgrano, 121, however, note that there were three targets, "two medium- and one large-size vessels."

91. Hastings and Jenkins, *Battle for the Falklands*, 151.

92. Sunday Times Insight Team, *Falklands War*, 166–67.

93. Richard Halloran, "Argentines Said to Seek More French Missiles," *New York Times*, 7 May 1982, p.16.

CHAPTER 8

1. Bernard Gwertzman, "Haig Abruptly Summoned To Meet with British Envoy," *New York Times*, 5 May 1982, p.16.

2. Thatcher, *Downing Street Years*, 217.

3. Gavshon and Rice, *Sinking of the* Belgrano, 124.

4. Thatcher, *Downing Street Years*, 218.

5. Henderson, "America and the Falklands," 36.

6. John Goshko, "U.S., Peru Join in Seeking 72-Hour Falkland Cease-Fire," *Washington Post*, 6 May 1982, p.1.

7. Bernard Gwertzman, "Haig Abruptly Summoned To Meet With British Envoy," *New York Times*, 5 May 1982, p.16.

8. Bernard Gwertzman, "U.S. Expects Invasion of Falklands By British Unless Argentina Yields," *New York Times*, 8 May 1982, p.1.

9. Thatcher, *Downing Street Years*, 217.

10. Leonard Downie and Jay Ross, "London Says It Supports New Peace Efforts," *Washington Post*, 6 May 1982, p.1.

11. Hastings and Jenkins, *Battle for the Falklands*, 168.

12. Thatcher, *Downing Street Years*, 217.

13. Gavshon and Rice, *Sinking of the* Belgrano, 125.

14. Fallaci, "Galtieri: No Regrets, No Going Back," 4.

15. Gavshon and Rice, *Sinking of the* Belgrano, 125.

16. James Reston, "Beyond the Falklands," *New York Times*, 9 May 1982, p.29.

17. Glenn Frankel, "U.N. Reports 'Positive' Replies To Falklands Peace Proposal," *Washington Post*, 7 May 1982, p.1.

18. Bernard Gwertzman, "No Major Movement Seen in Washington Despite Diplomatic Efforts," *New York Times*, 7 May 1982, p.1.

19. Glenn Frankel, "U.N. Reports 'Positive' Replies To Falklands Peace Proposal," *Washington Post*, 7 May 1982, p.1.

20. Thatcher, *Downing Street Years*, 218.

21. Bernard Gwertzman, "No Major Movement Seen in Washington...."

22. Glenn Frankel, "U.N. Reports 'Positive' Replies To Falklands Peace Proposal," *Washington Post*, 7 May 1982, p.1.

23. Thatcher, *Downing Street Years*, 218.

24. "Text of Falkland Speech by Prime Minister Thatcher in House of Commons," *New York Times*, 21 May 1982, p.10.

25. Thatcher, *Downing Street Years*, 219.

26. Hastings and Jenkins, *Battle for the Falklands*, 167.

27. Thatcher, *Downing Street Years*, 219.

28. Hastings and Jenkins, *Battle for the Falklands*, 156.

29. Richard Halloran, "Britain Asks U.S. to Lend It an Air Force Tanker," *New York Times*, 11 May 1982, p.7 and Charles Corddry, "U.S. Considers Loan to Britain of Air Tankers," *Baltimore Sun*, 11 May 1982, p.2.

30. Frederick Kempe, "Britain Claims It Now Controls Falkland Sound," *Wall Street Journal*, 12 May 1982, p.2.

31. Hastings and Jenkins, *Battle for the Falklands*, 157.

32. Cardoso, et al., *Falklands: Secret Plot*, 255.

33. Leonard Downie, "British Ease Stand In Falklands Talks," *Washington Post*, 11 May 1982, p.1.

34. Edward Schumacher, "Argentina Eases Terms for Peace In the Falklands," *New York Times*, 11 May 1982, p.1.

35. R.W. Apple, "Argentine Vessel Is Reported Sunk Off The Falklands," *New York Times*, 12 May 1982, p.1.

36. Ibid.

37. R.W. Apple, "2 Argentine Jets Reported Downed off the Falklands," *New York Times*, 13 May 1982, p.1.

38. Leonard Downie, "British Plan No Halt in Hostilities," *Washington Post*, 14 May 1982, p.1. The junta members feared that Walters and also Ambassador Schlaudeman were involved in a

conspiracy against the regime. See Freedman & Gamba-Stonehouse, *Signals*, 401 and Edward Schumacher, "U.S. Embassy in Argentina Denies It Is Seeking to Undermine Junta," *New York Times*, 17 May 1982, p.1.

39. Hastings and Jenkins, *Battle for the Falklands*, 171, say May 12. Parsons, "The Falklands Crisis in the United Nations," 173, says the Argentine note came on May 11.

40. Downie, "British Plan No Halt in Hostilities."

41. Hastings and Jenkins, *Battle for the Falklands*, 171.

42. Freedman and Gamba-Stonehouse, *Signals*, 303.

43. Hastings and Jenkins, *Battle for the Falklands*, 171.

44. Downie, "British Plan No Halt in Hostilities."

45. Ibid.

46. Hastings and Jenkins, *Battle for the Falklands*, 171.

47. Thatcher, *Downing Street Years*, 220–21.

48. Henderson, "America and the Falklands," 36.

49. "Transcript of President's News Conference on Foreign and Domestic Matters," *New York Times*, 14 May 1982, p.16.

50. Freedman and Gamba-Stonehouse, *Signals*, 327–28 and Drew Middleton, "Argentina's Next Move: Its Military Options Against the British Task Force," *New York Times*, 16 May 1982, p.18.

51. Thatcher, *Downing Street Years*, 221–22.

52. Parsons, "The Falklands Crisis In The United Nations," 174. Henderson, *Mandarin*, 460–61, lists those who attended. Pym was excluded.

53. Hastings and Jenkins, *Battle for the Falklands*, 173.

54. Henderson, "America and the Falklands," 36–37.

55. Cardoso, et al., *Falklands: Secret Plot*, 261.

56. Henderson, "America and the Falklands," 37.

57. Parsons, "The Falklands Crisis In The United Nations," 175 and Cardoso, et al., *Falklands: Secret Plot*, 263.

58. Freedman and Gamba-Stonehouse, *Signals*, 309–10.

59. Thatcher, *Downing Street Years*, 224.

60. Attempting to strike a carrier with their remaining Exocet missiles, Argentine aircraft hit the container ship, *Atlantic Conveyor*, instead. Air strikes also sank the troop carriers, *Sir Tristam* and *Sir Galahad*.

61. "Transcript of President's News Conference on Foreign and Domestic Matters," *New York Times*, 14 May 1982, p.16 and "Interview with Western European Television Correspondents on the President's Trip to Europe," 1 June 1982, *Public Papers of the Presidents—Ronald Reagan, 1982* (Washington: GPO, 1982), 715.

62. Thatcher, *Downing Street Years*, 226.

63. See "America's Falklands War," *Economist*, 3 March 1984.

64. Thatcher, *Downing Street Years*, 227.

65. "America's Falklands War," *Economist*, 3 March 1984.

66. Don Oberdorfer, "Reagan, Brazil's Chief Focus on Falklands," *Washington Post*, 13 May 1982, p.21.

67. *Economic and Social Progress In Latin America*, 1983 Report (Inter-American Development Bank, Washington, D.C., 1983):172–75.

68. Oberdorfer, "Reagan, Brazil's Chief Focus on Falklands."

69. "Generals Demand Tougher Stand on South Atlantic," *Latin American Regional Reports—Brazil*, 23 April 1982, p.1.

70. Barrett, *Gambling With History*, 239. Haig told Clark that Kirkpatrick's efforts were part of a "conspiracy" to outflank him.

71. "Remarks and a Question and Answer Session at a Fundraising Reception for Senator John Heinz in Philadelphia, Pennsylvania," 14 May 1982, *Public Papers of the Presidents—Ronald Reagan* (1982): 642.

72. "Ripples From the South Atlantic," *Latin American Weekly Review*, 21 May 1982, p.10.

73. John Goshko, "Haig Urges OAS to Aid Peace Effort," *Washington Post*, 28 May 1982, p.1.

74. Cardoso, et al., *Falklands: Secret Plot*, 266.

75. "Weep Not for the Americas," *New York Times*, 3 June 1982, p.22.

76. Leonard Downie, "British Move to Seek A Definitive Victory Said to Unsettle U.S.," *Washington Post*, 26 May 1982, p.14.

77. "Statement by Deputy Press Secretary Speakes on the Dispute Between the United Kingdom and Argentina in the Falkland Islands," 21 May 1982, *Public Papers of the Presidents—Ronald Reagan*, 667.

78. Michael Getler, "White House Repeats Pledge to Keep 'Commitments' to London," *Washington Post*, 22 May 1982, p.12, Charles Corddry, "U.S. Restates Support of British; Request for Missiles Anticipated," *Baltimore Sun*, 22 May 1982, p.1, Bernard Gwertzman, "U.S. Ready to Seek Accord But Reports No Effort Now," *New York Times*, 22 May 1982, p.7 and "U.S. Sees Setback To Its Latin Ties," *New York Times*, 23 May 1982, p.1.

79. Gwertzman, "U.S. Sees Setback To Its Latin Ties."

80. Henderson, "America and the Falklands," 37.

81. Ibid., 38.

82. Robert J. McCartney, "Argentina Hits Ship in 'Mass' Air Strike," *Washington Post*, 26 May 1982, p.1.

83. Middlebrook, *Fight For The Malvinas*, 164-65.

84. Ibid., 174.

85. Drew Middleton, "British Given an Unexpected Bonus By Argentines' Inactivity on Ground," *New York Times*, 24 May 1982, p.6.

86. Henderson, "America and the Falklands," 37.

87. Leonard Downie, "British Move to Seek A Definitive Victory Said to Unsettle U.S.," *Washington Post*, 26 May 1982, p.14.

88. Henderson, "America and the Falklands," 37.

89. Richard Homan, "Heavy Fighting, Losses Reported in Falklands," *Washington Post*, 25 May 1982, p.1.

90. Freedman and Gamba-Stonehouse, *Signals*, 348.

91. Barrett, *Gambling With History*, 239.

92. Cardoso, et al., *Falklands: Secret Plot*, 265.

93. Hastings & Jenkins, *Battle for the Falklands*, 258. See also, John Goshko, "Latest Haig-Kirkpatrick Dispute Underscores Foreign Policy Rift," *Washington Post*, 2 June 1982, p.12.

94. Henderson, "America and the Falklands," 37.

95. Thatcher, *Downing Street Years*, 230–31.

96. Henderson, "America and the Falklands," pp.37–38.

97. Henderson, *Mandarin*, 467–68.

98. Henderson, "America and the Falklands," 38.

99. "Interview with Western European Television Correspondents on the President's Trip to Europe," 1 June 1982, *Public Papers of the Presidents—Ronald Reagan*, p.715.

100. "Reagan Defends British Actions, Saying Aggression Must Be Halted," *New York Times*, 2 June 1982, p.14.

101. Lou Cannon, "Reagan Restates Support for Britain," *Washington Post*, 2 June 1982, p.1.

102. Leonard Downie, "Thatcher Urges Argentina To Avoid Climactic Battle," *Washington Post*, 3 June 1982, p.1.

103. Thatcher, *Downing Street Years*, 231.

104. Freedman and Gamba-Stonehouse, *Signals*, 355.

105. "Haig Again," *Washington Times*, 7 June 1982, p.6.

106. Henderson, "America and the Falklands," 38.

107. Karen Elliott House and Alan Otten, "White House Hopes Summits Will Enhance the President's Stature," *Wall Street Journal*, 28 May 1982, p.33.

108. William Safire, "Dissareagan," *New York Times*, 7 June 1982, p.19.

109. Thatcher, *Downing Street Years*, 232.

110. Toasts of the President and British Prime Minister Margaret Thatcher at a Luncheon Honoring the President in London," 8 June 1982, *Public Papers of the Presidents—Ronald Reagan*, p.750.

111. R.W. Apple, "President Urges Britons to Fight For Democracy," *New York Times*, 9 June 1982, p.1.

CONCLUSION

1. *Washington Times*, 29 July 1996, p.A12.

2. See Tom Zamora Collina and Fernando de Souza Barros, "Transplanting Brazil and Argentina's Success," ISIS REPORT, Institute for Science and International Security, Washington, D.C., February 1995.

3. U.S. Arms Control and Disarmament Agency, *World Military Expenditures and Arms Transfers—1993–1994*, (Washington: GPO, 1994), 53, 95.

4. Thatcher, *Downing Street Years*, chap. 23–24 passim.

5. See Chistopher Johnson, *The Grand Experiment: Mrs. Thatcher's Economy and How It Spread* (Boulder: Westview, 1991).

6. John Nott, "The Falklands Campaign," *Proceedings/Naval Review* (March 1983), 137–39.

Selected
Bibliography

"Informe Final de la Comision Ratenbach (Part II)," *Siete Dias*. Buenos Aires, no. 859, November-December 1983.

Barrett, Lawrence. *Gambling With History: Reagan in the White House*. London: Penguin Books, 1983.

Bilton, Michael, and Peter Kosminsky. *Speaking Out: Untold Stories From the Falklands War*. London: Andre Deutch, 1989.

Brown, David. *The Royal Navy and the Falklands War*. London: Leo Cooper, 1987.

Burns, Jimmy. *The Land That Lost Its Heroes: The Falklands, The PostWar, and Alfonsín*. London: Bloomsbury, 1987.

Cardoso, Oscar, Ricardo Kirschbaum, and Eduardo Van Der Kooy. *Falklands—The Secret Plot*. Translated by Bernard Ethell. London: Preston Editions, 1983.

Cervenka, Zdenek, and Barbara Rogers. *The Nuclear Axis: Secret Collaboration Between West Germany and South Africa*. New York: Times Books, 1978.

Charlton, Michael. *The Little Platoon: Diplomacy and the Falklands Dispute*. Oxford: Basil Blackwell, 1989.

Collins, John. *U.S-Soviet Military Balance: Concepts and Capabilities, 1960–1980*. New York: McGraw-Hill, 1980.

Cosgrave, Patrick. *Carrington: A Life and a Policy*. London: J.M. Dent and Son, 1985.

Cosgrave, Patrick. *Thatcher: The First Term*. London: The Bodly Head, 1985.

Dalyell, Tam. *One Man's Falklands*. London: Cecil Wolf, 1982.

Dalyell, Tam. *Thatcher's Torpedo*. London: Cecil Wolf, 1983.

Deacon, Richard. *'C' A Biography of Sir Maurice Oldfield*. London: Macdonald, 1984.

Deutsch, Sandra McGee, and Ronald H. Dolkart, eds. *The Argentine Right: Its History and Intellectual Origins, 1910 to the Present*. Wilmington: Scholarly Resources, 1993.

Falcoff, Mark. *A Tale of Two Policies: U.S. Relations With The Argentine Junta, 1976–1983*. Philadelphia: Foreign Policy Research Institute, 1989.

Franks, R. Hon The Lord. *Falkland Islands Review: Report of a Committee of Privy Counsellors.* London: HMSO, 1983.

Freedman, Lawrence, and Virginia Gamba-Stonehouse. *Signals of War: The Falklands Conflict of 1982.* Princeton: Princeton University Press, 1991.

Freedman, Lawrence. *Britain and the Falklands War.* Oxford: Basil Blackwell, 1988.

Gavshon, Arthur, and Desmond Rice. *The Sinking of the* Belgrano. London: Secker & Warburg, 1984.

Grove, Eric J. *Vanguard To Trident: British Naval Policy Since World War Two.* Annapolis: Naval Institute Press, 1987.

Haig, Alexander M. Jr. *Caveat: Realism, Reagan, and Foreign Policy.* New York: Macmillan Publishing Co., 1984.

Hall, Marshall Van Sant. *Argentine Policy In The Falklands War: The Political Results.* Newport, R.I.: Naval War College, 1983.

Hastings, Max, and Simon Jenkins. *The Battle for the Falklands.* London: Michael Joseph, 1983.

Headland, Robert. *The Island of South Georgia.* London: Cambridge University Press, 1984.

Healey, Dennis. *The Time of My Life.* New York: W.W. Norton, 1989.

Henderson, Nicholas. *Mandarin: Diaries of an Ambassador, 1969–1982.* London: Weidenfeld & Nicolson, 1994.

Honeywell, Martin, and Jenny Pearce. *Falklands/Malvinas: Whose Crisis?* London: Latin American Bureau, 1982.

Johnson, Christopher. *The Grand Experiment: Mrs. Thatcher's Economy and How It Spread.* Boulder: Westview, 1991.

Lehman, John. *Command of the Seas.* New York: Macmillan Publishing Co., 1988.

Lewis, Russell. *Margaret Thatcher: A Person and Political Biography.* London: Routledge & Kegan, 1983.

Little, I.M.D., Richard N. Cooper, W. Max Corden, and Sarath Rajapatirana. *Boom, Crisis, and Adjustment: The Macroeconomic Experience of Developing Countries.* Washington, D.C.: IBRD, 1993.

Lowenthal, Abraham F. *Exporting Democracy: The United States and Latin America.* Baltimore: Johns Hopkins Press, 1991.

Maynard, Geoffrey. *The Economy Under Mrs. Thatcher.* London: Basil Blackwell, 1988.

Mercer, Derrick, Geoff Mungham, and Kevin Williams. *The Fog of War.* London: Heineman, 1987.

Middlebrook, Martin. *The Fight For The Malvinas: The Argentine Forces in the Falklands War.* New York: Viking, 1989.

Nitze, Paul H., and Leonard Sullivan. *Securing The Seas: The Soviet Naval Challenge and Western Alliance Options.* Boulder: Westview, 1990.

Nott, John. *The United Kingdom Defence Programme: The Way Forward.* London: HMSO, 1981.

Perkins, Roger. *Operation Paraquat: The Battle for South Georgia.* Chippenham: Picton Publishing, 1986.

Reagan, Ronald. *An American Life.* New York: Simon & Schuster, 1990.

Renwick, Sir Robin. *Fighting With Allies.* New York: Times Books, 1996.

Riddell, Peter. *The Thatcher Government.* London: Basil Blackwell, 1983.

Rock, David. *Argentina, 1516–1987: From Spanish Colonization to Alfonsin.* Berkeley: University of California Press, 1987.

Smith, Geoffrey. *Reagan and Thatcher.* New York: W.W. Norton and Co., 1991.

Snyder, William P., and James Brown, eds. *Defense Policy in the Reagan Administration.* Washington, D.C.: National Defense University Press, 1988.

Spector, Leonard S., and Jacqueline R. Smith. *Nuclear Ambitions: The Spread of Nuclear Weapons.* Boulder: Westview, 1990.

Speed, Keith. *Sea Change: The Battle for the Falklands and the Future of Britain's Navy.* Ashgrove: Bath, 1982.

Stewart, Nora Kinzer. *Mates and Muchachos: Unit Cohesion in the Falklands/Malvinas War.* London: Brassey's, 1991.

Thatcher, Margaret. *Downing Street Years.* New York: HarperCollins, 1993.

The *Sunday Times* Insight Team. *The Falklands War: The Full Story.* London: Sphere Books, 1982.

Tulchin, Joseph S. *Argentina and the United States: A Conflicted Relationship.* Boston: Twayne, 1990.

U.S. Arms Control and Disarmament Agency. *World Military Expenditures and Arms Transfers: 1986.* Washington, D.C.: GPO, 1987.

U.S. Bureau of Mines. *Metal Prices in the United States Through 1991.* Washington, D.C.: GPO, 1991.

U.S. Congress. House. Committee on Appropriations, Subcommittee on Defense. *Department of Defense Appropriations for 1982: Hearings.* 97th Cong., 1st sess. 1982. Part 9.

U.S. Congress. House: Committee on Foreign Affairs. *Review of United States Policy on Military Assistance to Argentina.* 97th Cong., 1st Sess. 1981.

U.S. Congress. Joint Economic Committee, *Monetary Policy, Selective Credit Policy, and Industrial Policy in France, Britain, West Germany, and Sweden.* 97th Cong. 1st Sess. June 26, 1981.

U.S. Department of State, *Conference on Antarctica.* 1960.

Weinberg, Alvin, Marcelo Alonso, and Jack Barkenbus. *The Nuclear Connection: A Reassessment of Nuclear Power and Nuclear Proliferation.* New York: Paragon, 1985.

Weinberger, Casper. *Fighting For Peace: Seven Critical Years in the Pentagon.* New York: Warner Books, 1990.

Woodward, Admiral Sandy. *One Hundred Days.* Annapolis: Naval Institute Press, 1991.

World Armaments and Disarmament, SIPRI-1982 Yearbook. London: Taylor & Francis Ltd., 1982.

Young, Hugo. *The Iron Lady: A Biography of Margaret Thatcher.* New York: Farrar, Straus, Giroux, 1989.

Index

··· About the Author

Richard C. Thornton is professor of history and international affairs at The George Washington University in Washington, D.C. He has written and lectured extensively on international affairs. His previous major works include: *The Carter Years: Toward a New World Order* (1991), *The Nixon-Kissinger Years: Reshaping America's Foreign Policy* (1989), and *China: A Political History, 1917–1980* (1982).